Research in Counseling

Research coursework has long been a recognized component of counselor preparation programs. Originally published in 1991, this groundbreaking book was designed to provide graduate students with an introduction to different types of counseling research (e.g., outcomes, processes, interventions), the variables and issues of relevance to know about in regard to research, and information about implementing research. Whenever possible, the text utilizes a real-world, practical approach showing the reader how to engage in various forms of counseling research inquiry. It is divided into three sections which cover the foundations of, approaches to, and issues and innovations in this realm of study. Other areas explored include philosophy of science, ethics, and the computer and counseling research. Written by experts in the field, the chapters offer a comprehensive, thorough analysis that can have implications for theory building, model building, and counseling practice.

Research in Counseling

Edited by
C. Edward Watkins, Jr.
Lawrence J. Schneider

Routledge
Taylor & Francis Group

LONDON AND NEW YORK

First published in 1991
by Lawrence Erlbaum Associates, Inc.

This edition first published in 2024 by Routledge
4 Park Square, Milton Park, Abingdon, Oxon, OX14 4RN

and by Routledge
605 Third Avenue, New York, NY 10017

Routledge is an imprint of the Taylor & Francis Group, an informa business

© 1991 by Lawrence Erlbaum Associates, Inc.

Publisher's Note
The publisher has gone to great lengths to ensure the quality of this reprint but points out that some imperfections in the original copies may be apparent.

Disclaimer
The publisher has made every effort to trace copyright holders and welcomes correspondence from those they have been unable to contact.

A Library of Congress record exists under ISBN: 080580689X

ISBN: 978-1-032-77394-0 (hbk)
ISBN: 978-1-003-48292-5 (ebk)
ISBN: 978-1-032-77407-7 (pbk)

Book DOI 10.4324/9781003482925

RESEARCH IN COUNSELING

C. Edward Watkins, Jr.
Lawrence J. Schneider
University of North Texas

LEA LAWRENCE ERLBAUM ASSOCIATES, PUBLISHERS
1991   Hillsdale, New Jersey   Hove and London

Lawrence Erlbaum Associates, Inc., Publishers
365 Broadway
Hillsdale, New Jersey 07642

Library of Congress Cataloging-in-Publication Data

Watkins, C. Edward.
Research in counseling / C. Edward Watkins, Jr., Lawrence J.
Schneider.
p.   cm.
Includes bibliographical references and indexes.
ISBN 0-8058-0689-X. — ISBN 0-8058-0690-3 (pbk.)
1. Counseling—Research. I. Schneider, Lawrence J. II. Title.
BF637.C6W38   1991
158'.3'072—dc20   91-9450
                                                    CIP

Printed in the United States of America
10 9 8 7 6 5 4 3 2 1

For Amelia and Grant
To my parents, Lawrence and Marie

CONTENTS

PREFACE

Research coursework has long been a recognized component of counselor preparation programs. Master's and doctoral programs generally require their students to receive some form of research training. Such training can be quite varied in its goals and scope, with some programs being primarily interested in making their graduates good research consumers and others primarily interested in making their graduates good research producers. Whatever the case, the development of knowledge about and understanding of research are important parts of counseling training; they serve to nicely round out and complement much of the practice-oriented side of the counseling curriculum.

Although the research process in general is valuable for us to know about, this book focuses specifically on a type of research of particular interest to counselors: counseling research. Counseling research studies the phenomenon of counseling—its processes, outcomes, interventions, and so on; it has the potential to provide us with insights into the counseling endeavor and ultimately can have implications for theory building, model building, and counseling practice. At a global level, the intent of this book is to provide counselors with a framework for conceptualizing counseling research. The book's more specific purposes are as follows: (a) to provide a relatively comprehensive introduction to the topic area of counseling research and its many facets; (b) to introduce the reader to some of the different forms of counseling research and provide ideas about how to engage in them; (c) to acquaint the reader with some of the various issues, concerns, and problems that attend these different forms of research: and (d) to consider other related issues (e.g., computer use, philosophy of science) that are more generally a part of the counseling research effort as a whole. This book is not designed to teach statistics; that type of information will have to be obtained elsewhere.

From our perspective, this book is highly suitable for graduate-level research in counseling courses or seminars and was developed with that purpose in mind. We hope that the book will prove useful to graduate students in counseling psychology, counselor education, and related counseling areas (e.g., mental health counseling, rehabilitation). Although the book is oriented toward graduate-level counseling students, it can prove to be of value to professionals as well. For individuals (whatever their level of training) wishing to get a solid, up-to-date introduction to counseling research or some aspect of it (e.g., outcome research), we believe this book will be quite informative.

The book is divided into four sections: (a) foundations of counseling research; (b) approaches to counseling research; (c) issues and innovations in counseling research; and (d) the conclusion. The first section considers two topics: a conceptual model about counseling research and philosophy of science. The second section takes a rather specific look at some different forms of counseling research—outcome, process, single-subject, qualitative, and career—and the issues that attend them. The third section, like the first, considers two topics: ethical issues in counseling research and the computer as a counseling research tool and topic. Last, we briefly provide a concluding statement, which presents some integrative summative postulates about counseling research as an area of study, inquiry, and practice.

In selecting chapter topics, we identified those areas that, in our opinion, were of salient interest and importance in contemporary counseling research training and practice. To identify these areas, we examined numerous counseling research journals and books for topics of concern, considered recent documents about research training in counseling,[1] made observations about the research efforts and struggles of students and professionals with whom we have come in contact, and reflected on our own counseling research training and practice. Although our biases may well have crept into the picture, we tried to make our final decisions about what to include in (what we hope was) a relatively objective, well-informed manner. In selecting chapter authors, we attempted to involve well-recognized counseling professionals who had an expertise in counseling research. Specifically, we attempted to involve individuals who had a particular counseling research expertise (e.g., process research) and then asked them to develop a chapter in their respective areas. As the list of authors shows, the people who contributed to this book clearly met that criterion.

---

[1]Gelso, C. G., Betz, N. E., Friedlander, M. L., Helms, J. E., Hill, C. E., Patton, M. J., Super, D. E., & Wampold, B. E. (1988). Research in counseling psychology: Prospects and recommendations. *The Counseling Psychologist, 16*, 385–406.

Like most books, this one has its limitations. First, although the book considers some of the most important issues in and forms of counseling research, other important counseling research issues and concerns have no doubt been overlooked or left out. All books have restrictions on their breadth, and ours is no exception. Second, even though each chapter provides a solid introduction to its topic area, the chapters can not and should not be seen as in-depth, exhaustive treatments in and of themselves. We do not consider it very likely that any of the topics in this book could receive such coverage in one chapter (and we suspect that the participating writers share our view). Rather, the purpose of these chapters is to give readers the best overview possible and, if more in-depth knowledge is desired, to point them to related sources where this can be obtained.

In closing, as we think back on our development of this book, we have several people that we would like to thank. Let us give special thanks to the chapter contributors. They all worked very hard, put in considerable effort, and produced high-quality work. Without them, none of what follows would have been possible, and we appreciate their helping us bring the *Research in Counseling* idea to realization. Let us also give very special thanks to our respective spouses, Wallene and Bette. They continue to support us in all of our professional endeavors and allow for our foibles as well. We owe much to their belief in and encouragement of us.

C. Edward Watkins, Jr.
Lawrence J. Schneider

I

FOUNDATIONS OF
COUNSELING RESEARCH

1

COUNSELING RESEARCH AS AN APPLIED SCIENCE

Terence J. Tracey
University of Illinois at Urbana-Champaign

Research in counseling is an example of applied research. As such, counseling research serves to link basic science to applications. This link covers how principles learned from theory and more basic scientific study apply in the "real" world, as well as how the possible contributions of principles gleaned from practice apply to theory and basic science. The purpose of this chapter is to review the role served by applied research in counseling in its very different relations to practice and to basic research.

The intermediate link of counseling research between more basic research and practice is very vivid when one considers the criticism commonly directed against counseling research. Researchers in the more basic areas of psychology (e.g., experimental and physiological) often look with disdain on research in the "softer" areas of social, clinical, community, industrial, and counseling; they believe that these applied disciplines tend to study very fuzzy, hard to operationalize concepts and do so in using very weak methodologies (i.e., with little experimental control). The utility of this research is questioned because it is difficult to determine what occurred and why. Ironically, practitioners also question the utility of applied (counseling) research. Many feel that the research gives them little to use in actually counseling clients. It is claimed that there is little that has direct applicability to clients. This utility dilemma of applied psychology, and specifically counseling research, is inherent to the role of applied research.

Counseling research fills the gap between basic knowledge and application and will always fall short in the view of each perspective. Briefly, utility in basic science is evaluated according to the extent to which research yields explicit, generalizable results regarding some variable or mechanism. Utility in practice is evaluated according to the extent something "works" with a specific client. The former looks to establish laws valid across people, and the latter looks to establish effects with one individual at a time. Counseling research looks to adequately serve both of these "masters." As is always the case with multiple masters, much less only one, it is not possible to adequately serve both to the extent that each would individually desire.

The obvious question arises: "Why bother with applied (counseling) research at all?" I have known colleagues who when faced with this question have opted for more basic research (i.e., less applied) and others who have abandoned research altogether and opted for practice entirely depending on which view (general laws or individual effects) they chose to emphasize. Prior to my justification of my position supporting the "why bother" question, I review applied research in general and counseling research specifically with respect to its usefulness to practice and as a science.

The purpose of applied research is to serve as the intermediary. Too typically, applied psychologists and counselors have focused on the applications of our research to practice. I think the profession has ignored its link to basic science in search for more direct applications to practice. This is a grievous error. A balanced view must always be kept. Those in counseling research as well as the American Psychological Association (APA) as a whole have managed to forget the need for emphasizing more basic research methods and constructs in the face of direct applicability. Many skilled researchers are leaving the APA because of its perceived lack of support for research, especially basic research.

There is some debate about exactly where counseling and psychotherapy research fit in the wider scope of psychology. Gelso (1979) viewed counseling as a very different activity, unique unto itself. Hence, researchers in this area have a specialized knowledge and need to focus specifically on issues that pertain directly to counseling and less on other situations (e.g., other relationships, attitude-change literature). Other areas may relate to counseling but this cannot be assumed and must be examined for veracity. Forsyth and Strong (1986), on the other hand, viewed research in counseling and psychotherapy as just another part of research on human behavior. Other areas of psychological research should have direct applicability to counseling and counseling research should have direct applicability to other areas of psychology. These conflicting views seem attributable to different authors focusing on opposite sides of the basic research–applied research–practice continuum. Forsyth and Strong focused on the link between basic research and applied research and wish to make it clear that each informs the other. Gelso focused on the applied research–practice link and is very interested in the generalizability of research results to practice. Both points of view are valid, but each is somewhat myopic. Both links, research to practice and practice to research, need to be in focus.

APPLIED RESEARCH–PRACTITIONER LINK

It has been repeatedly noted by both counseling practitioners and researchers that counseling and psychotherapy research has little impact on the practice of counseling and psychotherapy (Elliott, 1983; Hayes & Nelson, 1981; Rice & Greenberg, 1984). This conclusion seems based on the lack of direct applicability of research results to practice. It is generally acknowledged that no study will provide the practitioner with what should be done with any specific client at any one point in time. When practitioners are unsure of what to do or what would be the best approach, they would like to turn to the research and find unequivocal results that would determine their intervention. But they do not find this in the literature. As a consequence, the typical practitioner does not engage in research (Kelly, 1961; Kelly, Goldberg, Fiske, & Kilkowski, 1978; Prochaska & Norcross, 1983), or read research (Cohen, 1977, 1979; Cohen, Sargent, & Sechrest, 1986; Morrow-Bradley & Elliott, 1986; Weiss & Weiss, 1981), and generally holds negative attitudes about research (Kelly et al., 1978). It seems that two somewhat independent professions, counseling researchers and counseling practitioners, have evolved.

Application Problems of Counseling Research

Researchers have associated the lack of impact of counseling research on practice to the inability of practitioners to understand counseling research. But other observers lay the blame for this state of affairs at the feet of the researcher. The latter perspective holds that counseling research is of limited value to practice because it uses inappropriate methodology (e.g., Elliott, 1983; Goldman, 1976; Lambert, DeJulio, & Stein, 1978), addresses the wrong questions and focus (Elliott, 1983; Hill, 1982; Luborsky, 1972; Patton, 1989), and is too difficult to do well (Horowitz, 1982; Weissman, Rounsaville, & Chevron, 1982).

Inappropriate Methodology. The most frequently cited culprit for this lack of applicability of research to practice is inappropriate methodology. Specifically, issues of aggregation and verisimilitude are the focus of the criticism. Aggregation is necessary for most research as the goal of research is to generalize to a population or a situation. To do this, some form of aggregation is necessary. Although a variety of forms of aggregation exist, the two most common are aggregation over individuals (i.e., the study of group differences) and over time.

In aggregating across individuals, some researchers claim that issues of individual differences get lost and that results cannot be directly applied to any one individual case (Elliott, 1983; Kazdin, 1981). This claim rests on the recognition that there is a good amount of variability across individuals that a group mean does not accurately represent. This view is partially accurate, but the probabalistic nature of research results must be taken into account. By way of illustration, consider a hypothetical research finding that female clients respond best to affective questions, whereas male clients respond best to cognitive ones. Recognizing that there is a lot of variability in responding and that there is overlap in responding between the male and female client groups, it is true that this finding may not apply to every male and female client. Some male clients may respond best to affective questions, whereas some female clients may respond optimally to cognitive inquiries. If the research results were applied in a deterministic sense (e.g., I have a male client; therefore a cognitive question is always best), the criticism of no recognition of individual variation is quite accurate.

However, if the results were viewed probabalistically (e.g., in general it is better to use affective questions with female clients and cognitive questions with male clients), the research study provides accurate information that does take account of key individual differences. It is important for the practitioner to understand the amount of overlap in the groups to gauge the extent to which the results hold. If, in the research example just given, there was very little overlap in the distributions (i.e., almost all the men responded best to cognitive questions and almost all the women responded best to affective ones), the research results would have a much higher probability of applying for each and every client. However, if the distributions had extensive overlap (i.e., a good number of men responded best to affective questions and a good number of women responded best to cognitive ones), less confidence should be placed in the applicability of this result to all clients. The presence of differences between the groups demonstrates that there is some validity in differentially treating male and female clients, but the confidence placed in this differential treatment is a function of the extent of difference found. Some research yields results that have small effect sizes and are thus of limited utility in application to specific individuals, whereas other research yields results that have large effect sizes and are of great value in work with individuals. So the point of aggregated research being of limited value in application to individual cases is not entirely valid.

Another issue of aggregation that is frequently ignored is the aggregation over time. Any practitioner recognizes that what occurs in counseling varies greatly over the course of treatment. The process of the initial sessions is different from middle sessions that are both different from later sessions. Yet many researchers aggregate data over time (by combining sessions or ratings across sessions) so as to yield stable estimates of variable values, yet do so at the cost of yielding averages that are not representative of any specific point in time. This was demonstrated by Tracey and Ray (1984) who found the process of counseling looked very different when it was aggregated over the whole treatment than when it was examined as it varied over time. The aggregation over time yielded confounded results.

Given these differences between the practitioner's focus on one client at one point in time versus the researcher's focus on aggregate clients over time, many have advocated that counseling research should use methodologies that better reflect the focus of the practitioner, specifically the use of single-case designs (Barlow, Hayes, & Nelson, 1984; Kazdin, 1981). By doing so issues of aggregation are obviated. Indeed, it is becoming more common to see case studies (Hill, Carter, & O'Farrell, 1983) and repeated case studies (Tracey, 1985; Tracey & Ray, 1984) in the literature. But frequently these case studies are problematic in that they are not at all generalizable to other clients or other counselors. What is yielded are results of what occurred in one dyad only. For this reason the need for replication is crucial in single-case designs in order to be able to generalize to other cases or treatments and this is another form of aggregation.

The other main methodological issue is one of verisimilitude or the degree that the research study approximates actual practice. This issue is really one of internal versus external validity and has been termed the *rigor-relevance dimension* by Gelso (1979). Counseling research is considered by many, especially counseling practitioners, to not be applicable to service delivery because it is too far removed from how counseling is actually done. The particular criticism of practitioners is analogue research, where situations are designed to resemble counseling but care is taken to manipulate only key variables of interest. From a scientific view, analogue studies are desirable and important because they provide very strong tests of specific variables and relationships. By controlling the analogue conditions, the researcher can conclude whether or not the hypothesized effect occurred and what caused it. It is this ability to infer causation that makes this design valuable. An analogue study is rigorous in that it is internally valid; the specific variables being hypothesized to account for the differences actually do account for them because known alternate explanations have been eliminated. The drawback to analogue research is uncertainty about its external validity; it may not at all apply to actual counseling. The constraints placed on behavior in the experimental task may be so different from those in actual counseling that any results yielded in the experiment cannot be generalized in a straightforward fashion to counseling practice. The analogue may yield very conclusive information regarding a variable or relation but it may not at all hold in the real world as the situation is very different.

In response to this problem of verisimilitude, many have called for research that closely approximates actual practice, or preferably that focuses on actual counseling. This research would then obviously have more external validity or relevance. One of the most common means of increasing verisimilitude is to study actual individual cases and to abandon the aggregation and control or rigor of typical research designs. Researchers should attempt to study what actually transpires in treatment (Hill, 1982; Patton, 1989) and not attempt to artificially alter the course of treatment. Although increasing relevance, the internal validity is somewhat sacrificed. It is difficult for the researcher to conclude what the active mechanisms or variables were that caused any change.

Gelso noted this tension between rigor and relevance and coined the "Bubble hypothesis," which recognizes the inherent lack of perfection in any study. Designing a study is like trying to squeeze out a bubble under a windshield sticker: Any attempt to push it will result only in the bubble moving to a different spot; the flaw or bubble cannot be eliminated. One can attempt to enhance the external validity in a study by conducting it in an actual counseling setting but the internal validity or causal factors cannot be determined conclusively because there are too many uncontrolled alternative factors that could account for any results. Conversely, one could attempt to press out the flaw (bubble) by defining the variables and controlling the extraneous factors (increasing internal validity) but would sacrifice external validity as a result. The results might not apply to counseling because the extraneous variables are important. The bubble moves but is always present. This is not to deny that many studies are well designed and do excellent jobs of dealing with both internal and external validity, but it stresses that in some ways rigor and relevance are conflicting elements in research.

Although there is some validity for this dynamic tension between rigor and relevance, the tension between these two poles is not as mutually exclusive as presented. The work of Brunswick (1947) on ecological validity provides some interesting methods for actually dealing with both the internal and external validity issues. Briefly, Brunswick noted that we must sample from the populations to which we wish to generalize. If we wish to generalize to both populations of subjects as well as to populations of stimuli, we need to sample from both populations to be able to generalize adequately. For example, if we are interested in how clients respond to some stimuli (e.g., counselor warmth), we need first to make sure that we have sampled the population of clients well. This requires that we ensure that we are not dealing with atypical subjects. Thus, if we are interested in understanding how clients react to counselor warmth in the initial sessions, we need to sample representative clients, counselors, and sessions. It is obviously very questionable to generalize to clients based on students in introductory psychology classes who have not sought help. Nor is it appropriate to use intake interviews where there is no possibility of continued sessions. We need to take great pains to sample exactly and representatively from the population to which we wish to generalize. This sounds obvious but is rarely done in designing research because of difficulties in obtaining representative samples.

The other aspect of generalization (that of representative stimulus sampling) is rarely considered. In determining whether an effect exists, it is often necessary to sample extreme behaviors. In the previous example of counselor warmth, I could use extreme examples of counselor warmth (extreme backward lean, no eye contact, and minimal encouragement vs. a close, forward-leaning, earnest, caring gaze with many encouragers) to test the effects of counselor warmth on client behavior and perceptions. A test between these stimulus conditions will no doubt demonstrate that there may be differences in client responsiveness but it cannot be generalized anywhere because these extremes probably do not occur in actual counseling. These stimuli are not representative examples of counselor warmth. There is a fair amount of research in the field that uses extreme behavior such as this example to determine if the variables are important, yet the prevalence of these behaviors "in the wild" is neglected. Practitioners thus legitimately question the utility of this research to practice.

Another aspect of this stimulus representativeness deals with the controlling of other stimuli that are not of concern to the researcher. In the example of studying the effects of counselor warmth on client behavior and perceptions just discussed, the typical design would be to have two counselor interventions, both rated as exactly the same except with respect to the level of warmth demonstrated. Even if realistic and representative levels of counselor warmth had been used to define the high and low warmth conditions, it is still very possible for the results to have no external validity. Often the other variables that are controlled covary in the natural settings with the variables we wish to examine. Suppose our counselors both did an excellent job of following the client and capturing the client's content and affect. It would probably be rare that the low warmth counselor would do as good a job of these things as the high warmth counselor in actual counseling. So we may have created a counselor that does not exist in the real world. Hence, any results could not generalize outside of the artificial stimulus used in the study.

If we wish to have research that is generalizable, we need to pay very close attention to this stimulus and subject sampling issue as proposed by Brunswick (1947). Maher (1978) did an excellent job of summarizing many of these issues for the researcher. However, the practitioner must also assist the researcher in obtaining representative samples. If the practitioner wishes research results to apply to his or her clients, the practitioner must be willing to have representative samples of these examined. It is not surprising that research done on nonclient college students interacting with novice counselors does not generalize to experienced counselors dealing with middle-aged professionals who are clients. The researcher needs cooperation to study the exact population on which the practitioner needs information.

Wrong Questions and Focus.   Many researchers and practitioners think that there is a gap between those issues investigated by researchers and those issues of concern to practitioners (Elliott, 1983; Luborsky, 1972). This gap has been attributed to methodology driving the research rather than applied concerns (Elliott, 1983), many of which were discussed earlier in the issues of aggregation and verisimilitude. However, one difference is that some researchers are calling for a shift from the theory-testing model typically espoused by researchers to one that is more "discovery" oriented (Hill, 1982; Mahrer, 1988; Patton, 1989). These researchers claimed that we have learned little about what occurs in counseling and psychotherapy in part because we have been trying to study the counseling process from a theory-testing base. In a typical study, the researchers must use a theory to specify what they expect to occur (i.e., create testable hypotheses) and then establish a study to see if indeed this occurs, while controlling as many extraneous explanations as possible. These researchers claim that this model is far too limiting and not useful to the field. Hill (1982) argued that our knowledge and theory base are not sufficiently developed to allow adequate testing. The alternative of more discovery-oriented research (Mahrer, 1988) has been proposed where the researcher just studies the process of actual treatment and lets it inform him or her what the important elements and processes are. Patton (1989) has similarly called for more ethnographic research on the counseling process.

The argument for this more discovery-oriented research is based on the idea that a more descriptive and exploratory research program would have higher payoffs to the practitioner because the actual counseling process would inform the researcher of the crucial elements instead of the researcher viewing only isolated aspects. The issue is one of bias. Theory testing biases what we will examine and as a result we could be missing crucial information because we have not looked for it. A more exploratory or discovery-oriented focus would presumably allow other aspects to become apparent. I disagree with this call for decreased theory-testing studies and increased exploratory research because I think the blame for the research–practitioner gap is mislaid at the feet of the hypothesis-testing model. These authors have created a strawperson and have attempted to knock it down.

It goes without saying that we should study and describe what occurs in counseling and psychotherapy to determine what the key elements are and if indeed we are studying the relevant variables at all. However, this initial variable and process determination step (the goal of discovery research) is usually the first step in any well-conceived research study anyhow. Asking the researcher to only focus on this initial step, while ignoring later testing steps, does not seem much of a step forward. In most research, this exploratory step occurs before the study is conducted. The researcher uses existing research and his or her own clinical experience to describe and explore what is occurring in counseling and psychotherapy. Simple pilot examinations should be done to determine validity. A well done study should not forego the initial step of determining what variables are important. There are a variety of mechanisms for doing this, ranging from introspection to interviewing others (clients and practitioners) to reading prominent theorists and practitioners, but the key is to choose some significant events or variables worthy of focus. Assuming that traditional researchers that adopt a hypothesis-testing strategy do not engage in this initial exploratory, variable specification and operationalization step confuses the issues and does not give some very careful researchers credit.

Those advocating this discovery-oriented approach state that formal hypothesis testing introduces biases in what information is attended to. This is very true. Formalized hypothesis testing makes it very clear what variables are being examined and how. Other variables and conditions are intentionally being excluded such that only a small subset of possible variables are examined. If key variables are excluded, the research will be of limited value. However, it is very clear in formal hypothesis testing which variables are being examined and which are not. In more exploratory or discovery-oriented research, it is not at all clear which are the specific variables of focus.

Regardless of how open to experience we try to be, we are limited by our own view (as determined by any number of variables such as genetic makeup, cultural background, and early learning). We tend to focus on certain dimensions and to miss others. There is a wealth of literature on the limitations of humans as processors of information (Dawes, 1988; Tversky & Kahneman, 1974). We can only attend to limited amounts of information. Thus, we tend to use certain structures with which to view the world. These structures provide us with mechanisms to understand and interact with the world but simultaneously bias us. We will miss information that does not fit our perceptual structures (Anderson, 1983; Powers, 1973). In the softer exploratory research being advocated, there is still then a good amount of bias but it will be less obvious. It is still crucial to examine counseling using more exploratory and descriptive methods so that important information may be yielded but to presume that it will yield information that has more utility to practitioners is inaccurate and begging the issue.

Many of those advocating for more discovery-oriented research recognize that what they are proposing is not a new type of research, rather they are focusing on one end of a research continuum. Research can vary on the extent that it is controlled and operationalizes dimensions under examination (again the rigor-relevance continuum of Gelso, 1979). This call for more discovery-oriented research makes clear the initial phases of what is needed in a sound research program. This does not have to be written up in and of itself, but can and typically does serve as the unwritten first step in many research studies. My position is that the limited utility of current research is a function of applied research serving two masters: basic science (i.e., rigor) and practice (i.e., relevance). We tend to do a poor job of satisfying either. Practitioners operate in a more exploratory manner, whereas scientists operate in a more precise, explicit proposition-testing manner. Research in counseling has been in the middle of these two positions. It tends to use only a little theory to explore what is in the data; hence satisfying neither master.

Difficult to Conduct.   Several authors have noted the difficulties involved in conducting research (Horowitz, 1982; Weissman et al., 1982). These difficulties appear to be of both an ethical and a pragmatic nature. There does appear to be a fairly substantial burnout rate among researchers in counseling and psychotherapy (Elliott, 1983), which further attests to this difficulty.

Given that counselors are in the business to treat and aid clients, the first allegiance is to the client. The researcher must take all steps to ensure that all client rights are protected and that no harm will result as a function of the research. These issues of potential harm are crucial in all research involving human subjects, but it is even more important in research on counseling because of the confidential nature of the experience and the sensitivity of the issues involved. Researchers, practitioners, and clients all need to and do take these issues very seriously. But the added importance of these ethical concerns makes it even more difficult to conduct research. (It is beyond the scope of this chapter to review all the issues involved in the ethics of research in counseling, but the topic area is described in another chapter in this book.)

Given that counseling research often involves the study of actual counseling (as has been advocated by many), it is very difficult to obtain samples. As noted in the section on ecological validity, it is important to obtain representative samples. This requires that the researcher gather information in an agency that does counseling. Thus, the researcher has to be extremely skilled at entering organizations as well as at research design. Weissman et al. (1982) listed several potential areas of conflict with which the researcher must be able to cope prior to conducting any counseling research. The potential conflicts are: conflicting research goals between the therapists or agency and the researcher, conflicting clinical goals between the therapists and the researcher, therapists' concerns regarding restrictions placed on practice by the research design, and therapists' feelings of being evaluated. Loevinger (1963) noted the presence of several of these conflicts:

> The researcher and clinician may find themselves pitted against each other over numerous small and niggling issues. A common protest is that research interferes with the clinical process. The clinician indeed, has the duty to protect his patients against exploitation in the interest of research, an exploitation about which some researchers are cavalier. But the clinician must ask himself whether

he is protecting the patients or his own process-oriented frame of thought from the incursion of the research analysis. (p. 250)

This lack of practitioner cooperation was substantiated by Bednar and Shapiro (1970).

One suggestion aimed at aiding the researcher in gathering information from counseling agencies has been for the researcher to include practitioners on the research team (Lacrosse, 1986; Magoon & Holland, 1984; Sechrest, 1975). Staff members may, as a result, be more receptive to the research because they may feel that they have more input. Also, the inclusion of practitioners on the research team has the possible advantage of ensuring that the questions asked may have more relevance to the practitioner. Indeed some have gone so far as to state that practitioners should be included on the research teams of all counseling research projects (Lacrosse, 1986). The value of sweeping recommendations such as this is dubious, but the intent is a clear one and potentially valuable. What recommendations of this sort neglect is the inherent differences between researchers and practitioners that I have tried to highlight. Each speaks a different language at times and mandating collaboration may not always be the best recommendation.

One wonders whether we as a profession may be asking too much from our researchers. Counseling research is found lacking by practitioners because it does not result in direct applications, and it is found lacking by those in more basic areas of psychology and science as being too applied and not tied to sound methodology. Counseling researchers are expected to be skilled clinicians so that they know what occurs in counseling; they are expected to be skilled negotiators to enter organizations and establish research programs; they are expected to be well read and conversant in all relevant areas of psychology to be able to tie concepts to theory; they are expected to be skilled and knowledgeable in research design and data analysis; they are expected to be skilled writers and presenters to disseminate the findings; and they are expected to translate the findings in theoretical terms to the basic scientists and in practical terms to the practitioners. Where are these superfolk?

Art Versus Science

Many have likened counseling and psychotherapy to art, with the practitioner as the artist (Storr, 1979). It is viewed as a creative and intuitive endeavor. The skilled practitioner, for example, learns over time how to phrase things, when to make an interpretation, how to approach certain clients, and what the key underlying issues are. Much of this process defies explanation as it is covert or intuitive. When asked why a practitioner knows something is true with respect to a client, many practitioners respond simply "Because

I know it is and my experience tells me so." Attempting to define and operationalize components of the process is difficult at best given their subtle and covert nature. Any attempts to study the process of counseling would thus not yield anything that could conceivably be of value to the practitioner-artist.

This extreme position of the practitioner as artist is endorsed by some practitioners, but it appears that many more see the utility of defining and being much more specific in their thinking about and approach to clients. This is true if only because the predominant training model for psychologists is the scientist-practitioner, wherein each practitioner is taught to use the scientific principle of hypothesis testing to determine what the most appropriate approaches to use with certain clients are. (The scientist-practitioner model is discussed in a subsequent section.)

Another distinction that has been made between researchers and practitioners is that practitioners are technologists, whereas researchers are scientists (Forsyth & Strong, 1986). In some ways this distinction may more appropriately capture the differences between practitioners and researchers than the artist-scientist distinction because it does not require as much emphasis on covert, intuitive processes. In Forsyth and Strong's view, the main point of differentiation between technology and science is the goal. Technology is concerned with problem solving, whereas science is concerned with increasing knowledge. Problem solving centers on the determination of the best method of dealing with specific situations or problems. Direct application is the goal and focus. Technology is thus defined very broadly as any application of resources, which could be past learning, current skills, as well as tools. A technological question would be "How can I use the resources I have to best deal with this problem or situation?" There arises no need for consensus across situations or people because a technologist is concerned most with specific situations and immediate effects. A scientist is focused on the generation of knowledge. Knowledge consists of generalizable principles that apply across specific situations. So there is more of a focus in science on consensus across people and situations, which is aimed at theory testing and theory construction, general questions, and principles. A scientist asks why and how something works, whereas a technologist asks does something work here?

Given their direct applicability focus, practitioners seem to embody the technologist side of this technology–science distinction. Practitioners are forced to deal with completely unique situations and individuals each hour, hence the focus on problem solving and technology (or the application of resources). Interventions are evaluated with respect to effects, not the information they provide regarding knowledge or principles. What a technologist expects from research is thus a demonstration of what is effective. Science does not, will not, and cannot provide information of this sort given its focus on more general principles of why and how things work. Given sound principles or theories, any number of interventions can be designed depending on the specifics of the situation. So if one endorses either the art versus science or the technology versus science distinction as a valid representation of the differences between practitioners and researchers, then it is understandable why the complaints regarding the lack of impact of counseling research on counseling practice are so common. Scientific research will not yield information that will be immediately useable to individual cases. But the need for research and its utility is demonstrated in the literature on the accuracy of clinical judgment.

Problems in Clinical Judgment

The apparent lack of impact of research on practice is very apparent in the area of behavioral decision research. Research in this area demonstrates the clear utility and necessity of counseling research to the practitioner. Starting with Meehl's (1954) seminal book on clinical versus statistical prediction, there has been a wealth of research on the relative inaccuracy of clinical judgment when compared with simple statistical (typically regression) models. In a wealth of research studies, there is unequivocal evidence that clinicians do a poor job of making accurate decisions regarding client diagnosis and prediction (Dawes, 1976, 1979, 1986; Dawes, Faust, & Meehl, 1989; Goldberg, 1959, 1968, 1970; Sawyer, 1966). Without exception, the research has demonstrated that simple regression models are far more accurate than clinical judgment. This has led Meehl (1986) to comment: "There is no controversy in social sciences which shows such a large body of qualitatively diverse studies coming out so uniformly in the same direction as this one" (p. 370). And Dawes (1988) concluded that these results have had "almost zilch" by way of an effect on practice. These authors question the practitioners' incessant insistence that clinical decision making is the best source of diagnosis and determining how the client will act in the future.

   This lack of support of practitioner decision accuracy is not specific to counselors and psychotherapists. Similar results have been obtained in a wide variety of contexts with a wide variety of experts, for example, predicting Hodgkin's disease (Einhorn, 1979); predicting which banks will fail (Libby, 1976); predicting graduate school success (Dawes, 1979); predicting stock market fluctuations (Johnson, 1988); medical internship matching (Johnson, 1988). The lack of accuracy appears attributable to the heuristics and biases used by humans. Tversky and Kahneman (1974) have documented a variety of these heuristics and biases that result in inaccurate decisions. They propose three heuristics used by humans to assess probabilities and predict values in conditions of uncertainty (i.e., similar to most decisions required of counselors and psychotherapists): representativeness, availability, and adjustment and anchoring.

Representativeness. In determining the probability that a person is a certain diagnostic type, the decision maker judges the representativeness of the person to the diagnosis. If the person is similar (i.e., representative) to the diagnosis, then the decision maker concludes that the probability of this client belonging in this diagnostic type is high; otherwise it is low. This is a very effective heuristic in aiding decision making, but as used, other elements that affect representativeness are not taken into account. Decision makers tend to be insensitive to prior probability of outcomes, to sample size, and to predictability, to have misconceptions of regression, and have illusions of validity. *Insensitivity to prior probabilities* refers to ignoring base rates of issues (e.g., some diagnostic types are much more probable than others). I have seen many novice counselors diagnose their clients as having multiple personalities. Besides obviously exaggerating client symptoms, these counselors ignore the fact that this diagnosis is extremely rare. A similar issue pertains to the *insensitivity to sample size.* Decision makers typically attach the same probability to samples drawn from small and large samples. No account is taken of the fact that having biased information is much more likely in a small sample. *Insensitivity to predictability* refers to lack of account taken with respect to the relative predictability of certain events. Decision makers often place equal confidence in their judgments of events that are highly predictable (e.g., how well a client will function in the next week) and those that are less predictable (e.g., how well the client will function next year).

The *misconception of regression* refers to the lack of account taken for regression to the mean. For example, a supervisee of mine had a client who had a terrible day and was very down and listless. I predicted that the client would demonstrate much elevated affect the following week, and my supervisee thought I was an extremely astute clinician because, lo and behold, the client returned the following week feeling much better. This prediction was due only to regression to the mean; extreme values are followed by more moderate levels. The student could have associated the increase in affect as attributable to a particularly "astute" interpretation about the client made the previous week (e.g., "Your mood seems associated with your anger at your father"). Given that this interpretation was followed by increased affect, the student could incorrectly conclude that Oedipal interpretations provided when the client is very depressed are effective in elevating the mood. Finally, the *illusion of validity* refers to the amount of confidence placed in the judgments. Decision makers frequently use the degree of representativeness (i.e., similarity of object to category) as the determinant of the degree of confidence in the decision; ignoring issues of the reliability or quality of information used in predicting. Information of poor and high quality are often used interchangably resulting in overconfident judgments.

Availability. The heuristic of availability refers to likelihood of seeing an object belonging to a class or category related to the ease with which instances of the class can be brought to mind. For example, if I am to predict how a young woman client complaining of low self-esteem will act and I have recently seen a lot of women clients with eating disorders, it is highly likely that I will use my knowledge of eating disorder clients, as this is frequently used and very available, in making judgments about this client. However, like the representativeness heuristic, there are several biases that go along with this availability heuristic: biases due to the retrievability of instances, biases due to the effectiveness of a search set, biases of imaginability, and illusory correlation. The more salient and familiar (i.e., *retrievable*) a certain class is, the more likely that it will be accessed. In the example of using eating disorders, it is not known whether or not the client has an eating disorder, but the recent familiarity with this sort of problem will necessitate that the client will be viewed as if she did, even though the base-rate probability of her having an eating disorder is lower than her not having one.

The second bias attributable to the availability heuristic is differences in the *effectiveness of searches for relevant categories or classes.* Some cues or information elicit more information than others. For example, decision makers are better able to remember abstract terms and concepts than concrete ones. Applying this to counseling, it would be easier to pull up relevant diagnostic cues to someone who we are able to describe in more abstract terms (e.g., difficulty getting along with others) than concrete terms (e.g., had a fight with his roommate). *Biases of imaginability* refers to how many judgments require the decision maker to imagine certain events and then plan for them. Often the decision maker does not take account of the probability of these imagined events. With a client, the counselor may need to decide what to do if the client becomes suicidal (imagine events and these are imagined based on past events or availability). The imagined events may be so difficult that the counselor may then chart an extremely conservative course, neglecting to determine the likelihood of these events. *Illusionary correlation* occurs when two events are associationally relevant (e.g., happen contiguously in time) but logically irrelevant (Dawes, 1988). An example of this was found by Chapman and Chapman (1969), who demonstrated that clinicians had an illusionary correlation between the way eyes were drawn on the draw-a-person test and paranoia.

Adjustment and Anchoring. The adjustment-and-anchoring heuristic refers to the decision maker starting with an initial value or starting point and then adjusting this to fit. This starting point can be determined any number of ways, for example, by availability or initial problem formulation, but biases can result due to insufficient adjustment. Inaccurate initial starting points frequently are not adjusted enough to attain accuracy. In the case of diagnosis, it is more likely to reach a correct diagnosis of avoidant personality if one starts by looking for personality disorders than if one started from the initial point that the client may be alcoholic.

A particularly common bias in clinical judgment is the confusion of *directionality in conditional probabilities*. Much of the information we obtain as practitioners is conditional. A common example is to associate certain current problems with past difficulties. Using the previous example of eating disorders, many practitioners have noticed their eating disorder clients tend to be overachievers (i.e., given an eating disorder client, the probability of her being an overachiever is high). However, this in no way implies that given an overachiever, the probability of her having an eating disorder is high. The probability of being an overachiever without an eating disorder is much higher than the probability of being one with an eating disorder. Many clinicians note the first conditional probability and then assume the second. I have heard several practitioners suggest that one should look for eating disorders because the client is an overachiever.

Many of these biases are understandable if one examines the typical caseload of the practitioner. Several surveys have demonstrated that the great bulk of therapy sessions are accounted for by a very small number of clients (Cohen & Cohen, 1984; Howard, Davidson, O'Mahony, Orlinsky, & Brown, 1989; Taube, Kessler, & Feuerberg, 1984). For example, Howard et al. (1989) found that 32% of outpatients accounted for 77% of the sessions in one clinic. Given the heuristics of representativeness, availability, and adjustment and anchoring, it is easy to see how inaccurate judgments are made. The clients seen most frequently (thus more available and representative as well as serving as initial anchors) tend to be much more disturbed than the typical clients seen at any center (as most clients are presumably less disturbed and stay for a relatively short duration) and much more disturbed than the normal population. Thus, the sample used as a basis in all clinical judgments is skewed and unrepresentative. Cohen and Cohen (1984) demonstrated how any caseload will over time consist almost exclusively of very disturbed clients supporting the skewed basis of the comparison population and referred to this as the "clinician's illusion." So, given the information source that practitioners have to use in their judgments and the literature on decision making, it is apparent why practitioners are less accurate in their predictions than statistical methods.

However, the lack of accuracy of practitioners in making clinical judgments does not appear related to the confidence that practitioners place in their judgments. Oskamp (1982) examined the accuracy and confidence of clinicians in predicting client behavior as a function of the amount of information presented to the clinician. He found that the accuracy of prediction did not improve at all with increasing amounts of information beyond the initial minimal amount of information. However, the clinicians grew progressively more confident of their accuracy with more information. This disturbing picture of judgment indicated that clinicians' confidence was not related to accuracy and that the increasing confidence was unfounded, and indeed given the heuristic biases listed earlier, this overconfidence could hinder the adjustment heuristic.

Another problem with practitioner judgment is summarized in the literature that has compared the prediction accuracy of expert, experienced practitioners with that of novices. Expert, experienced practitioners are generally no better, and sometimes worse, in diagnosing and predicting client behavior than are novices (Goldberg, 1959, 1965; Johnson, 1988; Kelly & Fiske, 1951; Kremers, 1960; Oskamp, 1962, 1982; Taft, 1955). There is a wealth of research, however, that supports the differences between experts and novices, but much of this literature has focused on determining the differences in information processing between experts and novices and not differences in accuracy of judgments. The research on expertise has demonstrated that experts have more complete representations of the task domain (Chi, Feltovich, & Glaser, 1981), attend to different information (Johnson, 1988), are quicker in their processing (Chase & Simon, 1973; Johnson & Russo, 1984), have a more extensive set of strategies for applying judgments (Larkin, McDermott, Simon, & Simon, 1980), and are more flexible in applying their advanced knowledge (Spiro, Coulson, Feltovich, & Anderson, 1988). Presumably, graduate and internship training, supervision, and counseling experience contribute to these differences in processing between experts and novices.

Johnson (1988) examined expert, novice, and regression accuracy in several different contexts. He found that experts and novices tended to use case-specific data in their judgments at the expense of base-rate data. The superiority of regression models was attributed to their inclusion of base-rate data (i.e., regression models require large samples of data—certainly larger than a few cases of a certain type), and these are typically not available to the individual practitioner. Practitioners focus on the information at hand (perhaps too much so) relating to single cases. Johnson demonstrated that experts' strength was in the selection of and interpretation of cues. The experts were most able to pick out the specific variables to examine in making judgments. However, the experts and novices were equally unable to adequately integrate the information in a manner that would result in accurate judgments.

There are several ways to improve practitioner accuracy, but most involve explicit examination of base-rate issues. Kahneman and Tversky (1982) focused on training decision makers to use both singular (case) and distributional (base-rate) information in judgments. They propose a five-step judgment process wherein the decision maker makes an intuitive judgment using typical heuristics, but then checks against biases are incorporated and the initial intuitive judgment corrected. Perhaps the biggest factors involved in the correction are base-rate and predictability assessments.

The provision of information regarding base rates, information reliability and validity, predictability, and various other biases are obtained through formal research. This is a function that research can serve for the practitioner. Research provides exactly the type of information lacking from the practitioner's experience: reliable, valid information obtained over a large, more representative sample. The practitioner needs to combine these pieces of information with his or her own judgments to yield more accurate judgments. Given the limitations of ability of human information processors to integrate information, it may also be advisable for the practitioner to use some straightforward, mathematical means of combining the information to yield judgments. Dawes (1979) found that almost any method of combining information (ranging from optimal regressions, to using random weights, to simple summing of variables) is more accurate than clinicians' judgments. Practitioners could be used to determine what variables are important and to rate these variables (again the practitioners' strength), but other methods of data integration would be used in the final judgment. Whether or not one decides to turn the judgment process over to simple mathematical models does not affect the point that clinical judgments are extremely biased and that research is the only source of information that can serve to provide the practitioner with the correct information (e.g., base rates) that would correct these biases. So the skilled practitioner should be one who uses the scientific method and research to guide clinical judgments.

Scientist-Practitioner Model

The scientist-practitioner model has been the predominant training model for applied psychologists. Most training programs in counseling psychology espouse the scientist-practitioner training model at least to some extent. However, the meaning of the term *scientist-practitioner* is far from clear. Some of the more common definitions focus on: (a) the need for each practitioner to use the scientific method in his or her practice (Barlow et al., 1984; Pepinsky & Pepinsky, 1954), (b) the desirability for each psychologist to engage in both research and practice (Gelso, 1979), and (c) the need for practitioners to see the value of research and apply it to their practice (Magoon & Holland, 1984).

As originally conceived by Pepinsky and Pepinsky (1954) the scientist-practitioner was viewed as the ideal for the practicing psychologist. It was not originally proposed that each psychologist would do both research and practice, but that each psychologist would be a personal scientist in a manner similar to Kelly's (1970) personality theory. The skilled practitioner would apply scientific principles to his or her practice. It is believed that only through the skillful application of scientific principles, even on a very limited basis in one's practice, can the practitioner improve and better treat clients. Those who do not apply these scientific principles were believed to not be skilled practitioners. The skilled practitioner engages in the exact same processes as the researcher: problem definition, using appropriate theory in hypothesis generation, operationalization of constructs, application of intervention, and assessment of effects. The main difference between the researcher and practitioner is the generalization sought.

One advantage of approaching practice in this scientific manner is that it is easier to correct misperceptions and biases, which occur frequently as noted earlier. If it is clear on what the practitioner is basing decisions and the decisions do not fit the data, it is relatively easy to change the underlying assumptions because they are explicit and operationalized. Without explicit assumptions and hypotheses, it is difficult to correct mistakes in judgment. What is being advocated is limited single-case research on the part of the practitioner, much as proposed by Barlow et al. (1984) and by Tracey (1983). Freud's work is perhaps one of the best examples of a practitioner who clearly applied the scientific method to his practice. Although he did not quantitatively examine what occurred in therapy, he was a master at specifying assumptions, operationalizing them, generating hypotheses, and testing their validity. So the extent to which practitioners apply the scientific method is assumed to be related to the quality of treatment and the growth in skill over time. Also, having practitioners be skilled at operationalizing and hypothesis generation may make it easier for them to point researchers in profitable directions.

Gelso (1979) noted that some view the scientist-practitioner model as representing someone who is 50% scientist and 50% practitioner, where the scientist engages in formal empirical research (presumably of the generalizable and publishable type) and the practitioner sees clients and applies interventions. Somewhere this definition of the concept arose, but I, like Gelso, doubt the viability of it if only for the reason that being 50–50 on anything strikes me as difficult at best, much less with something as different as practice and research. If I see clients, my research in counseling may be better informed. Also, staying abreast of innovations in theory and basic psychological research, as well as new design issues, may affect the quality of any research I conduct. It is hard to conceive someone who is able to do both of these well. I can think of no one who fits this 50–50 model. Several colleagues have started out aspiring to this split, but over time they found that they had to declare proclivities. This is not to imply that they have any less respect for the side in which they had to decrease their commitment; it seemed to be more an issue of pragmatics. There is, however, a clear appreciation for the struggles faced by both the researcher and the practitioner.

One advantage of having all students engage in formal research is they may become more sensitive to the issues involved and perhaps become more supportive of the value of research. This is similar to Magoon and Holland's

(1984) argument for the value of research advocates. The scientist-practitioner does not have to actively engage in research him or herself. It cannot be expected that all applied psychologists would engage in formal research; however, it is possible to expect that practitioners see the value of research to themselves, their practice, and society. Thus, these practitioners could work with applied researchers in aiding their investigations as well as in helping these investigators ask questions important to them. So minimally, what Magoon and Holland are advocating is that all students should have a good appreciation of research and be supportive of it.

The training and experience in formal research is necessary in each of these three definitions of the scientist-practitioner. Also all three definitions of the scientist-practitioner focus on educating students in research and practice; not training them. There is a crucial distinction between education and training. Education involves giving the student the tools and experience to independently make decisions and view the world in a complete and thorough manner. Training involves imparting skills that the student can then use. By educating students in research, it is expected that they will independently evaluate the research and consider how the results affect them and their practice. If, on the other hand, we trained the students in research, we would expect that the students would see the value of research and directly apply the results to their practice. Obviously, what I and many others are proposing is that we wish the scientist-practitioner to view research from an educated position, as something to be pondered and evaluated; not as something that will have direct applicability (a training position). Indeed, some research (Rich, 1977; Weiss & Bucuvalas, 1980) has demonstrated that many clinicians use research in this conceptual way, as different from direct applications (instrumental use).

BASIC RESEARCH–APPLIED RESEARCH LINK

Certainly one of the predominant goals of applied research as opposed to more basic research is to examine theoretical propositions or research findings with respect to their validity in natural settings or more pragmatic contexts. The latest developments in the areas of cognitive, social, personality, physiological, and experimental psychology are excellent for application to counseling. All of these specializations can provide possible insights into why and how people experience difficulties in life and some appropriate ways in which we can intervene to ameliorate these difficulties. However, the extent to which basic psychological concepts are applied to counseling is nowhere near as prevalent as it should be. It is much more common for researchers in counseling psychology to borrow constructs from the practitioner literature. As stated earlier, counseling practice is a crucial and important source of research topics; however, the possibility of more basic research areas being fruitful with respect to appropriate topics is neglected.

The impact of proposing simple extrapolation of social psychological findings and theory to the counseling situation has had widespread impact on the research in counseling. One example of an application of constructs from another area of psychology is Strong's (1968) extrapolation of social influence theory and power bases (French & Raven, 1959) from social psychology. Wampold and White (1985) have found that research following this line of inquiry has been the most popular in the field. Social psychology has moved on from social influence theory and so have we as a field. New developments in social psychology are being applied in counseling (e.g., elaboration likelihood model of attitude change). Another area that is only now being applied to counseling is information-processing models from cognitive psychology. It appears obvious that if we could understand how people process information, we could design interventions with maximal probability of being attended to and having an effect. Yet only initial applications are being proposed (e.g., Heppner & Krauskopf, 1987; Rounds & Tracey, 1990). This is an expanding area of which most counselors and counseling psychologists are ignorant. We can learn much about client personality and client change from these other specialties, but it appears that the application is too infrequent.

Counseling research can thus benefit greatly, and indeed has benefited greatly, from the application of concepts from other, more basic psychological specialties. However, it does not appear as if applied research areas such as counseling have as much impact on more basic areas. I could find no examples of where there has been a reverse effect. This lack of reverse effect of this area of applied research on more basic research could be just a function of applied research. It serves as the link between basic research and practice and the directional flow of information could be one way: from basic research to applied research to practice. In general, counseling research lags behind more basic research in terms of application of new concepts. Other specialties develop theories, test them and only after being widely accepted are they then applied to counseling, if at all. As with most theories in psychology, they tend to decay with time (Cronbach, 1975). All generalizations decay as research finds that they are valid in increasingly restrictive conditions and that the results are not stable. So many of these new theories are modified, changed, or abandoned altogether. Counseling researchers are often just applying these theories as they are being pared down in the parent area.

An area where this does not appear to be true is in the person–environment fit area in vocational psychology. Theorists and researchers in vocational psychology (Dawis & Lofquist, 1978, 1984; Dawis, Lofquist, & Weiss, 1968; Holland, 1973) were actively involved in these issues simultaneous with their introduction into personality psychology (Magnusson & Endler, 1977). However, much of the excellent work had little impact on these other fields.

Certainly it would be desirable for counseling researchers as applied research-ers to be able to apply our research results to basic research; but it does not appear to work in this manner. For this reverse influence to work, we as an area of research may have to be viewed as more than applied research. This may be too much to ask from an area of research that distinctly aims to serve as the link between two very different views—basic researchers and practitioners.

Perhaps one problem with the lack of effect of counseling research on other areas is the focus of the research. Meehl (1978) pointed out that soft psychol-ogy (certainly including counseling) does not really move forward as a science. He attributed this to many causes, with the two major ones being the lack of focus on theory disconfirmation (a la Popper, 1959) and the examination of statistical differences between groups. Meehl noted (like Cronbach, 1975) that in soft psychology theories are rarely, if ever disproved; they are simply discarded with time as they fall out of favor. Rarely do investigators attempt to explicitly disprove any theory or at least test the validity of alternate the-ories. In general, we continually attempt to prove what we hold to be true. Research is not designed to be a strong disconfirmation. Without research of this disconfirmation sort, we can learn little.

Further, we tend to focus on statistical tests of differences between groups or simple covariation among variables and have yielded a wealth of results that have limited utility and do not hold over time. He explained that null hypotheses are generally false; it is almost inconceivable that two groups would be different on all dimensions except the one being examined (as is tested in group difference studies on such things as gender differences; it is impossible to conclude that the only difference between the two groups is gender). Given an adequate design, reliable measurement, and enough statisti-cal power (largely a function of sample size in this case), significant results will most likely be obtained. The probability of either a positive (confirming the hypothesis) or a negative (disconfirming the hypothesis) result will ap-proach 50–50. Obviously the utility of conducting these tests of statistical differ-ences between groups is very limited.

Instead of an overfocus on tests of differences, Meehl advocated examina-tions of form function (overall shape of the data distribution) or, better yet, an assessment of how well data conform to specific numerical point values generated from explicit hypotheses. According to Meehl (1978), "It is always more valuable to show approximate agreement with a theoretically predict-ed numerical point value, rank order, or function form, than it is to compute a precise probability that something merely differs from something else" (p. 825). This sort of research is rarely conducted in counseling. Research of this sort requires exact specification of what should occur if the theory is true. The data are collected, and then examined to see if they conform to the ex-pected values. If not, the theory is invalid. I could find no study in counseling that clearly specified the theory and the theoretically derived numerical values for the variables that would support or disconfirm the theory. One of the few that sought to examine a form function (i.e., graph of the shape or form of the distribution) was conducted by Tracey (Tracey, 1985; Tracey & Ray, 1984). Typically vague hypotheses are provided (if at all) and then very weak tests of differences, once conducted, yield little. For counseling research to have an effect on other areas of psychology, much less in other disciplines, it is imperative that counseling researchers adopt this examination of explicit theoretically derived values or form function as advocated by Meehl.

A MODEL OF RESEARCH AND PRACTICE

I have presented counseling research as representative of applied research and as an intervening step between more basic research and practice. I chose this characterization, besides the obvious reason that I think it is the most accurate representation, because it highlighted the differences that exist between applied and more basic research. The focus of counseling research is much more on the application to practice and on our success or failure to fulfill this application to practice than on integration with more basic research and science. A prominent example of this focus only on the applied research-practice link is the model of psychotherapeutic research designed by Bergin and Strupp (1972). They devoted great detail to how practice informs applied research and vice versa but they devote relatively little detail to the basic science–applied research link. In their model, practice affects case experiments that affect field trials that yield new methods that affect practice. Basic science enters this model only as a precursor to analogue studies that affect case experiments. Although this is an excellent model of the applied research-practice link, what is notable is the remoteness of basic research in this model.

Counseling researchers tend not to direct their gaze toward the harder, more basic areas of psychology for information and theories. It should be obvious that this is a regrettable state of affairs. The relative lack of reference to more basic research could be attributable to the relative absence of counseling researchers in departments of psychology. Most all accredited counseling psychology programs are housed in colleges of education. This is valuable for a variety of reasons (it is beyond the scope of this paper to review these issues here), but colleges of education tend to be much more applied in focus out of choice and necessity. The focus is on applied research; how techniques apply to practice. This is the focus of counseling research. Contact and familiarity with more basic research areas is less extensive than for the fewer counseling researchers in psychology departments with a strong basic science orientation. Counseling researchers need to be more aware of advancements in basic psychological research as it can have great impact on the development of our knowledge base. I am not advocating the abandonment of the focus on practice; however, it is far from sufficient in and of itself.

The only way in which more basic science affects current counseling research is in the areas of research design and evaluation. Counseling researchers strive to design better studies and apply more appropriate statistical examinations of their questions. These are very appropriate; however, counseling researchers do not tend to pay as much attention, if any, to the substantive material that can be learned from these more basic areas.

I have also argued that the position of the counseling researcher as an applied researcher is inherently a difficult one as the researcher must serve two masters: more basic science (with its standards of research evaluation) and practical application (with its focus on individual effectiveness). I have tried to make it clear that the counseling researcher has a difficult task doing an adequate job of satisfying either master, much less two conflicting ones. Counseling research, due to its focus on application and the "fuzzy" variables examined, will never "bootstrap" itself up to be a more basic scientific branch of psychology. Further, given the needs of formal research (i.e., generalization), practitioners will never be wholly satisfied with the direct application utility of counseling research.

Neither basic research nor practice have a direct impact on counseling research. The impact of each is mediated by theories or constructs. Basic research is concerned with establishing the validity of theories and theoretical constructs. These constructs are then applied to counseling research. Basic research focuses on operationalizing and testing theoretical propositions. As these propositions are supported or refuted, the theory is validated or altered. As these theories or theoretical propositions gain support and acceptance, they are available for application. Counseling research is one such application. These theoretical propositions can be examined with respect to their validity in application. The results of this research on the theoretical application then should have some effect on the initial theory, providing information on the limits of generalizability. Applied research serves the important function of determining the limits of validity of any theoretical propositions substantiated in basic research. The theory thus serves as the bridging link between basic research and applied research. In this conception, it is impossible for basic research to directly affect applied research or vice versa. Only after a wealth of basic research supports a theory do applied researchers set out to examine a theory. And as I have argued, this application and testing of theory from basic research does not occur frequently enough.

The other aspect of applied research is the tie to practice. Here too we see theory as the mediating link. Although the theory here is less precise and more practice focused than those that are obtained from basic research, these practice-oriented theories are much more general and global than those above (differing in the areas of precision, explicitness, and operationalization). Indeed using most common definitions of a theory (e.g., simplicity, interpretability, usefulness, generalizability, testability, disconfirmability, and logical consistency as listed in Forsyth & Strong, 1986), these more practice-oriented theories are not technically theories. More frequently, they are sets of propositions that may be loosely organized into a larger framework. We refer to these propositions and the embedded loose framework as *models*, which are less precise than theories. These models serve as the intervening step between applied research and practice. Applied research can get testable propositions from these models and then reveal information about their validity, thus enabling confirmation, refinement, or abandonment of the propositions. These propositions derive from or affect actual counseling practice. This simple conception of counseling research is presented in Fig. 1.1.

One implication of this model is that counseling research cannot have any direct, instrumental impact on counseling practice. Counseling research should affect many of the propositions that counselors use in deciding how to interact with their clients (i.e., conceptual impact), but the research cannot directly apply, nor should it. As argued, skilled practitioners are viewed as utilizing the scientific method in how they develop and test these practice models in their own practice. Applied research can have bearing on the validity of these practice models. The practitioner can thus use counseling research results as information to confirm, modify, or abandon these practice-guiding models as well as extra information to improve decision making (e.g., base-rate information). The literature demonstrates how biased practitioners are with respect to key clinical decisions (even expert practitioners), so it is important that practitioners be able to use counseling research to augment their clinical model building and decision making. To do this the practitioner needs to have enough research evaluation skill to be able to evaluate formal counseling research. I argued for the education view of professional development over the training view. Skilled practitioners should be able to use research results in their thinking and theorizing, not in direct application. The evaluation of counseling research with respect to direct application is an undesirable criterion.

One implication of this counseling research conception is that applied research fulfills an important role in theory development. Besides being a key step in terms of determining the limits of generalizability of theory, it can serve as the vehicle through which principles and models derived from prac-

FIG. 1.1. Conception of relation of basic research, applied research, and practice.

tice can have an impact on the theories that guide the science of psychology. However, this link from applied research, especially counseling research,
to basic psychological theory is rather weak and is infrequently traversed.
The recommendations proposed by Meehl are perhaps the best way to ensure that the results of our research have an effect on the rest of psychology.

ACKNOWLEDGMENT

Appreciation is expressed to James B. Rounds for his helpful comments regarding this chapter.

REFERENCES

Anderson, J. R. (1983). *The architecture of cognition.* Cambridge, MA: Harvard.
Barlow, D., Hayes, S., & Nelson, R. (1984). *The scientist-practitioner.* New York: Pergamon.
Bednar, R. L., & Shapiro, J. G. (1970). Professional research commitment: A symptom or a syn-
    drome. *Journal of Consulting and Clinical Psychology, 34,* 323–326.
Bergin, A. E., & Strupp, H. H. (1972). *Changing frontiers in the science of psychotherapy.* Chica-
    go: Aldine.
Brunswick, E. (1947). *Systematic and representative design of psychological experiments.* Berke-
    ley, CA: University of California Press.
Chapman, L. J., & Chapman, J. P. (1969). Illusory correlation as an obstacle to the use of valid
    diagnostic signs. *Journal of Abnormal Psychology, 73,* 193–204.
Chase, W. G., & Simon, H. A. (1973). Perception in chess. *Cognitive Psychology, 4,* 55–81.
Chi, M., Feltovich, P., & Glaser, R. (1981). Categorization and representation of physics problems
    by experts and novices. *Cognitive Science, 5,* 121–152.
Cohen, L. H. (1977). Factors affecting the utilization of mental health evaluation research find-
    ings. *Professional Psychology, 8,* 526–534.
Cohen, L. H. (1979). The research readership and information reliance of clinical psychologists.
    Professional Psychology, 10, 780–785.
Cohen, L. H., Sargent, M. M., & Sechrest, L. B. (1986). Use of psychotherapy research by profes-
    sional psychologists. *American Psychologist, 41,* 198–206.
Cohen, P., & Cohen, J. (1984). The clinician's illusion. *Archives of General Psychiatry, 41,*
    1178–1182.
Cronbach, L. J. (1975). Beyond the two disciplines of scientific psychology. *American Psycholo-
    gist, 30,* 116–127.
Dawes, R. M. (1976). Shallow psychology. In J. S. Carroll & J. W. Payne (Eds.), *Cognition and
    social behavior* (pp. 3–11). Hillsdale, NJ: Lawrence Erlbaum Associates.
Dawes, R. M. (1979). The robust beauty of improper linear models in decision making. *Ameri-
    can Psychologist, 34,* 571–582.
Dawes, R. M. (1986). Representative thinking in clinical judgment. *Clinical Psychology Review,
    6,* 425–441.
Dawes, R. M. (1988). *Rational choice in an uncertain world.* San Diego: Harcourt, Brace,
    Jovanovich.

Dawes, R. M., Faust, D., & Meehl, P. E. (1989). Clinical and actuarial judgment. *Science, 243,* 1668–1674.

Dawis, R. V., & Lofquist, L. H. (1978). A note on the dynamics of work adjustment. *Journal of Vocational Behavior, 12,* 76–79.

Dawis, R. V., & Lofquist, L. H. (1984). *A psychological theory of work adjustment: An individual differences model and its applications.* Minneapolis: University of Minnesota Press.

Dawis, R. V., Lofquist, L. H., Weiss, D. J. (1968). *A theory of work adjustment (a revision).* Minnesota Studies in Vocational Rehabilitation (XXIII). Minneapolis: Work Adjustment Project, Department of Psychology, University of Minnesota.

Elliott, R. (1983). Fitting process research to the practicing psychotherapist. *Psychotherapy: Theory, Research, and Practice, 20,* 47–55.

Einhorn, H. (1979). Expert measurement and mechanical combination. *Organizational Behavior and Human Performance, 13,* 171–192.

Forsyth, D. R., & Strong, S. R. (1986). The scientific study of counseling and psychotherapy: A unificationist view. *American Psychologist, 41,* 113–119.

French, J., & Raven, B. (1959). The bases of social power. In D. Cartwright (Ed.), *Studies in social power* (pp. 150–167). Ann Arbor, MI: Institute for Social Research.

Gelso, C. J. (1979). Research in counseling: Methodological and professional issues. *The Counseling Psychologist, 8*(3), 7–35.

Goldberg, L. R. (1959). The effectiveness of clinicians' judgments: The diagnosis of organic brain damage from the Bender-Gestalt. *Journal of Consulting Psychology, 23,* 25–33.

Goldberg, L. R. (1965). Diagnostician versus diagnostic signs: The diagnosis of psychosis versus neurosis from the MMPI. *Psychological Monograph, 79.*

Goldberg, L. R. (1968). Simple models or simple processes? Some research on clinical judgement. *American Psychologist, 23,* 483–496.

Goldberg, L. R. (1970). Man versus model of man: A rationale plus some evidence for a method of improving on clinical inferences. *Psychological Bulletin, 73,* 422–432.

Goldman, L. (1976). A revolution in counseling research. *Journal of Counseling Psychology, 23,* 543–552.

Hayes, S. C., & Nelson, R. O. (1981). Clinically relevant research: Requirements, problems, and solutions. *Behavioral Assessment, 3,* 209–215.

Heppner, P. P., & Krauskopf, C. J. (1987). An information-processing approach to personal problem solving. *The Counseling Psychologist, 15,* 371–447.

Hill, C. E. (1982). Counseling process research: Philosophical and methodological dilemmas. *The Counseling Psychologist, 10*(4), 7–20.

Hill, C. E., Carter, J. A., & O'Farrell, M. K. (1983). A case study of the process and outcome of time-limited counseling. *Journal of Counseling Psychology, 30,* 3–18.

Holland, J. L. (1973). *Making vocational choices: A theory of careers.* Englewood Cliffs, NJ: Prentice-Hall.

Horowitz, M. J. (1982). Strategic dilemmas and the socialization of psychotherapy researchers. *British Journal of Clinical Psychology, 21,* 119–127.

Howard, K. I., Davidson, C. V., O'Mahoney, M. T., Orlinsky, D. E., & Brown, K. P. (1989). Patterns of psychotherapy utilization. *American Journal of Psychiatry, 146,* 775–778.

Johnson, E. J. (1988). Expertise and decision under uncertainty: Performance and process. In M. T. H. Chi, R. Glaser, & M. J. Farr (Eds.), *The nature of expertise* (pp. 209–228). Hillsdale, NJ: Lawrence Erlbaum Associates.

Johnson, E. J., & Russo, J. E. (1984). Product familiarity and learning new information. *Journal of Consumer Research, 11,* 542–550.

Kahneman, D., & Tversky, A. (1982). Intuitive prediction: Biases and corrective procedures. In D. Kahneman, P. Slovic, & A. Tversky (Eds.), *Judgement under uncertainty: Heuristics and biases* (pp. 414–421). New York: Cambridge.

Kazdin, A. E. (1981). Drawing valid inferences from case studies. *Journal of Consulting and Clinical Psychology, 49,* 183–192.

Kelly, E. L. (1961). Clinical psychology-1960. Report of survey findings. *Newsletter: Division of Clinical Psychology of APA, 14*(1), 1–11.

Kelly, E. L., & Fiske, D. W. (1951). *The prediction of performance in clinical psychology.* Ann Arbor, MI: University of Michigan Press.

Kelly, E. L., Goldberg, L. R., Fiske, D. W., & Kilkowski, V. M. (1978). Twenty-five years later: A follow-up study of the graduate students in clinical psychology assessed in the VA student research project. *American Psychologist, 33,* 746–755.

Kelly, G. A. (1970). A brief introduction to personal construct theory. In D. Bannister (Ed.), *Perspectives in personal construct theory* (pp. 1–29). London: Academic Press.

Kremers, J. (1960). *Scientific psychology and naive psychology.* Nijmegen, Netherlands: Drukkerij Gebr. Janssen.

Lacrosse, M. J. (1986). Research training: In search of a human science. *The Counseling Psychologist, 14,* 147–151.

Lambert, M. J., DeJulio, S. S., & Stein, D. M. (1978). Therapist interpersonal skills: Process, outcome, methodological considerations, and recommendations for future research. *Psychological Bulletin, 85,* 467–489.

Larkin, J., McDermott, J., Simon, D. P., & Simon, H. A. (1980). Expert and novice performance in solving physics problems. *Science, 208,* 1335–1342.

Libby, R. (1976). Man versus model of man: Some conflicting evidence. *Organizational Behavior and Human Performance, 16,* 1–12.

Loevinger, J. (1963). Conflict of commitment in clinical research. *American Psychologist, 18,* 241–251.

Luborsky, L. (1972). Research cannot yet influence clinical practice. In A. E. Bergin & H. H. Strupp (Eds.), *Changing frontiers in the science of psychotherapy* (pp. 120–127). Chicago: Aldine.

Magnusson, D., & Endler, N. S. (1977). Interactional psychology: Present status and future prospects. In D. Magnusson & N. S. Endler (Eds.), *Personality at the crossroads* (pp. 3–29). New York: Wiley.

Magoon, T. M., & Holland, J. L. (1984). Research training and supervision. In S. Brown & R. Lent (Eds.), *Handbook of counseling psychology* (pp. 682–715). New York: Wiley.

Maher, B. A. (1978). Stimulus sampling in clinical research: Representative design reviewed. *Journal of Consulting and Clinical Psychology, 46,* 643–647.

Mahrer, A. R. (1988). Discovery-oriented psychotherapy research: Rationale, aims, and methods. *American Psychologist, 43,* 694–702.

Meehl, P. E. (1954). *Clinical versus statistical prediction: A theoretical analysis and a review of the evidence.* Minneapolis: University of Minnesota.

Meehl, P. E. (1978). Theoretical risks and tabular asterisks: Sir Karl, Sir Ronald, and the slow progress of soft psychology. *Journal of Consulting and Clinical Psychology, 46,* 806–834.

Meehl, P. E. (1986). Causes and effects of my disturbing little book. *Journal of Personality Assessment, 50,* 370–375.

Morrow-Bradley, C., & Elliott, R. (1986). Utilization of psychotherapy research by practicing psychotherapists. *American Psychologist, 41,* 188–197.

Oskamp, S. (1962). The relationship of clinical experience and training methods to several criteria of clinical prediction. *Psychological Monographs, 76* (*28,* Whole No. 547).

Oskamp, S. (1982). Overconfidence in case-study judgements. In D. Kahneman, P. Slovic, & A. Tversky (Eds.), *Judgement under uncertainty: Heuristics and biases* (pp. 287–293). New York: Cambridge.

Patton, M. J. (1989). Problems with and alternatives to the use of coding schemes in research in counseling. *The Counseling Psychologist, 17,* 490–506.

Pepinsky, H. B., & Pepinsky, P. N. (1954). *Counseling: Theory and practice.* New York: Ronald.

Popper, K. R. (1959). *The logic of scientific discovery.* New York: Basic Books.

Powers, W. T. (1973). *Behavior: The control of perception.* Chicago: Aldine.

Prochaska, J. O., & Norcross, J. C. (1983). Contemporary psychotherapists: A national survey of characteristics, practices, orientations, and attitudes. *Psychotherapy: Theory, Research, and Practice, 20,* 161–173.

Rice, L. N., & Greenberg, L. (1984). *Patterns of change.* New York: Guilford.

Rich, R. (1977). Use of social science information by federal bureaucrats: Knowledge for action versus knowledge for understanding. In C. Weiss (Ed.), *Using social science research in public policy making* (pp. 199–233). Lexington, MA: Lexington-Heath.

Rounds, J. B., & Tracey, T. J. (1990). From trait-and-factor to person-environment fit counseling: Theory and process. In W. B. Walsh & S. H. Osipow (Eds.), *Contemporary topics in vocational psychology* (pp. 1–44). Hillsdale, NJ: Lawrence Erlbaum Associates.

Sawyer, J. (1966). Measurement and prediction, clinical and statistical. *Psychological Bulletin, 66,* 178–200.

Sechrest, L. (1975). Research considerations of practicing clinical psychologists. *Professional Psychology, 6,* 413–419.

Spiro, R. J., Coulson, R. L., Feltovich, P. J., & Anderson, D. K. (1988). Cognitive flexibility theory: Advanced knowledge acquisition in ill-structured domains. In *Tenth annual conference of the Cognitive Science Society* (pp. 312–328). Hillsdale, NJ: Lawrence Erlbaum Associates.

Storr, A. (1979). *The art of psychotherapy.* New York: Methuen.

Strong, S. R. (1968). Counseling: An interpersonal influence process. *Journal of Counseling Psychology, 15,* 215–224.

Taft, R. (1955). The ability to judge people. *Psychological Bulletin, 52,* 1–23.

Taube, C. A., Kessler, L., & Feuerberg, M. (1984). Utilization and expenditures for ambulatory mental health care during 1980. In *National Medical Care Utilization and Expenditure Survey: Data Report 5.* Washington, DC: Department of Health and Human Services.

Tracey, T. J. (1983). Single case research: An added tool for the counselor and supervisor. *Counselor Education and Supervision, 22,* 197–206.

Tracey, T. J. (1985). Dominance and outcome: A sequential examination. *Journal of Counseling Psychology, 32,* 119–122.

Tracey, T. J., & Ray, P. B. (1984). Stages of successful time-limited counseling: An interactional examination. *Journal of Counseling Psychology, 31,* 13–27.

Tversky, A., & Kahneman, D. (1974). Judgement under uncertainty: Heuristics and biases. *Science, 185,* 1124–1131.

Wampold, B. E., & White, T. B. (1985). Research themes in counseling psychology: A cluster analysis of citations in the Process and Outcomes section of the *Journal of Counseling Psychology. Journal of Counseling Psychology, 32,* 123–126.

Weiss, C., & Bucuvalas, M. (1980). *Social sciences research and decision making.* New York: Columbia.

Weiss, J. A., & Weiss, C. H. (1981). Social scientists and decision makers look at the usefulness of mental health research. *American Psychologist, 36,* 837–847.

Weissman, M. M., Rounsaville, B. J., & Chevron, E. (1982). Training psychotherapists to participate in psychotherapy outcome studies. *American Journal of Psychiatry, 139,* 1442–1446.

2

PHILOSOPHY OF SCIENCE AND COUNSELING RESEARCH

George S. Howard
Paul R. Myers
University of Notre Dame

Who says that philosophy of science is irrelevant to counseling research? Well, sad to say, many of our faculty, practitioner, and graduate student colleagues make that claim quite frequently. This chapter attempts to persuade the reader that counseling research can profit greatly from a consideration of the insights of philosophy of science. But persuading the reader will not be easy. It is not that the insights of philosophy of science are unworthy, but because there are enormous translation problems in transforming abstract philosophical arguments into nourishing nuggets fit for consumption by counseling researchers. Consider the following quote from MacIntyre (1977) on "psychological crises":

> What is a "psychological crisis?" Consider first, the situation of "clients" who are thrown into such crises. Someone who has believed that he *[sic]* was highly valued by his employer and colleagues is suddenly fired; someone proposed for membership of a club whose members were all, so he believed, close friends, is blackballed. Or someone falls in love and needs to know what the loved one *really* feels; someone falls out of love and needs to know how he or she can possibly have been so mistaken in the other. For all such persons the relationship of *seems* to *is* becomes crucial. (p. 453)

We (and our clients) have all experienced those terrifying moments when we realize that the wind has been taken out of the sails of our realities. It is quite disturbing when one confronts the possibility that his or her construction of reality might represent an enormous self-deception. If the assault on one's picture of life is massive, counseling is typically recommended to help the client see him or herself clear of the psychological crisis.

But we must confess that we played a bit fast-and-loose with Alasdair MacIntyre's quote—which is why we inserted a few scare quotes. MacIntyre was talking about *epistemological crises,* which we changed to "psychological crises." Epistemological crises usually involve impasses, conflicts, or contradictions pertaining to what people think they know or had thought to be true. MacIntyre also did not speak of "clients," but rather referred to ordinary agents—people like us. But the quote seems to work well in describing problems that we as counselors often encounter, and feel we understand.

What we attempt to probe further here is the possibility that scientists sometimes encounter epistemological crises in their work that (in some respects) resemble the psychological crises that clients experience from time to time in their own lives. Also, a healthy dose of philosophy of science might prove as therapeutic for a disoriented scientist as counseling can be for the victim of a psychological crisis. But as Bergin (1963) and Truax (1963) pointed out long ago, counseling can be for better or for worse. The possibility of deterioration within therapy must be acknowledged. Similarly, if philosophy of science represented some magical exilir that unfailingly remedied scientists' epistemological crises-of-confidence, there would be no need to argue for its value. Its satisfied customers would convince one and all of its value through their tales of wondrous, magical cures. But the obvious absence of a chorus of hosannas to philosophy of science suggests that it is not a cure-all. Rather, consulting the wrong philosopher of science (or reading the wrong book) could well be hazardous to one's scientific health.

Just as counseling is frequently misunderstood by potential clients, the place of philosophy of science is often misunderstood by researchers. We next explore a few beliefs about the proper relationship between philosophy of science and science, in order to suggest some ways that counseling researchers might profit from philosophy of science. That is, we explore whether researchers might from time to time profit from an examination of their beliefs about human behavior, causality, nature, the proper form of scientific explanations, proper methodology, and so forth.

WHEN PHILOSOPHY OF SCIENCE IS AND IS NOT A STAPLE OF SCIENTIFIC LIFE

First, a distinction must be made between the academic discipline called the history and philosophy of science and each scientist's personal, implicit (and explicit) philosophy of science. The former is typically explored by historians and philosophers (and occasionally by scientists) who are intrigued by the historical development of science and the study of epistemology. That is, they seek to understand the social, political, and intellectual contexts that fueled or inspired the maturation of various scientific disciplines. These scholars have developed their own system of language (e.g., realism, constructivism, scientism, logical positivism, idealism, etc.) They have constructed elegant theories and elaborate stories to help shed light on how and when various disciplines have made advances, or experienced revolutions. We argue here that the progress of science itself is not dependent on the insights of these scholars. There may be advantages to understanding these arguments, but strict adherence to teachings in philosophy of science can be detrimental to the advancement of science. How? This question is examined later, but first we consider the role that each scientist's own philosophy of science plays in his or her work.

We suggest that each scientist/researcher has a personal philosophy of science. By this, we mean a set of assumptions, not about scientists of the past, but about how proper science is to be conducted today. In fact, even the contemporary skeptic who claims to have no philosophy of science, has paradoxically professed what he or she denies (recall the Cretan Liar). Further, such an individual demonstrates in his or her scientific theories and methods the nature of his or her implicit philosophy of science. For example, he or she may demonstrate beliefs in, or assumptions about causality, laws of nature, hypothesis testing, the role of quantification, and so forth. The scientist who claims to have no personal philosophy of science is like the client who claims to have no personality or no philosophy of life. Just as a client sometimes is unclear about his or her purpose in life (or obstacles appear that prevent him or her from reaching his or her full potential), a scientist can also lose his or her focus in science. And it is when the client/scientist is stuck, that some reflection and self-examination can provide insight into new ways of being.

Although one can argue that the progress of science is not dependent on the thorough understanding of the history and philosophy of science as it is practiced by historians and philosophers, we suggest that the step from technician to scientist is made when one frees his or her practice of research from blind obedience to convention, and develops an explicit understanding of the complex interaction between the methods of a discipline and the assumptions of scientists. It is believed that such an understanding can decrease the likelihood that an individual researcher would allow the methodological tail of science to wag his or her theoretical dog, or some other equally awkward and frustrating scenario. Given this distinction we examine the contribution of philosophy of science as a discipline.

Kuhn (1962, 1977) has sketched a straightforward view of the progress of science that can serve as a useful orienting mechanism for our discussion. Science proceeds in his model through a series of stages of *normal* and *revolutionary* science. In terms of "normal" science, a particular paradigm dominates, and the majority of the scientific advances take place within that paradigm's frame (or view of the world, science, etc.). An oft-cited example is that of Newtonian physics. Revolutionary science is exemplified by the radical paradigm shift born of Einstein's theory of relativity and Heisenberg's uncertainty principle in atomic (and subatomic) physics. The shift to a relativistic physics was revolutionary because basic concepts of time, space, matter, and causality were drastically altered. One might claim that similar changes have occurred in psychology. New paradigms, for example, Freudian psychoanalysis during the first half of this century, offered researchers a complete package of ontological and epistemological commitments (e.g., id, ego, superego, unconscious motives, transference), favored methodologies (e.g., dream analysis, hypnosis, projective techniques, free association), along with an established research literature (e.g., established empirical relationships, clinical demonstrations, case studies). Together these assumptions, techniques, and empirical findings meld together to form a more or less coherent picture of the world of human action—from a psychodynamic perspective. Now if one is inclined to see psychodynamic construals of human motivation as a paradigmatic step in the science of human action, then Freud was clearly involved in creating a scientific revolution. (Many are disinclined to see psychodynamic approaches as scientific endeavors, but we opt for a broad construal of what activities might be seen as scientific in this chapter.) Freud's correspondence and published works reveal that he was convinced that he was bringing about a scientific revolution in our thinking about human action. Similarly, Watson promoted a behavioral revolution; Carl Rogers (or Gordon Allport, or perhaps Henry Murray) engineered a humanistic revolution; Ludwig von Bertalanfy (or perhaps Gregory Bateson) fathered a cybernetic or systemic revolution; George Kelly produced a constructivist revolution; and so forth.

Although it is open to argument as to exactly which conceptual breakthroughs are to be accorded "revolutionary" status (and sometimes even unclear who should be credited with the conceptual creation), it is clear that each perspective on human action affords us a radically different conception of human nature. For these revolutionary thinkers, the issues of philosophy of science are critically important, as their critics frequently pressed them to justify their conceptual systems in light of the prevailing philosophy of science. But by their own admission, many of these conceptual giants knew very little about philosophy of science. Rather, they knew something important about their subject matter—(typically) human nature. (Later we explain why it is unimportant even for revolutionary thinkers in science to possess expert knowledge in philosophy of science.)

Strictly speaking, revolutionary, scientific thinkers need not care what philosophers of science think about their proposed reconceptualizations of their subject matter. This is because the relevant jury for such ideas is the community of *scientists* in their own field. The success of scientific revolutions is determined by the acceptance of the new paradigm by scientists in that domain—not by philosophers of science! "Good science is what good science does," might serve as an appropriate rule of thumb in this regard. If (over the long haul) we research psychologists find it scientifically productive (vis-á-vis the epistemic values involved in theory choice, cf. Howard, 1985; Kuhn, 1977; McMullin, 1983) to think of human beings as reinforcement maximizers, or as active construers, or as self-determining active agents, or unconsciously motivated, then we should push forward with our newer paradigms, in spite of the fact that such construals might not square well with the prevailing philosophies of science.

Although it is proper to raise questions of revolutionary thinkers regarding their paradigmatic innovations from the perspective of philosophy of science, such questions may not help the progress of science. Thus, conceptual innovators might be expected to try to clarify the implications of their conceptual moves. However, an innovator's inability to offer cogent answers to objections raised from the regnant perspective in philosophy of science should not be viewed as cause for undue alarm.

But chances are that the reader (and these authors) are not now engaged in engineering an important scientific revolution in counseling psychology. More likely, we are engaged in unscrambling scientific puzzles bequeathed by the paradigm out of which we work. We are engaged in *normal* science. What is the role of philosophy of science for the day-to-day activities of scientists engaged in normal science?

The answer is—it depends. It depends on whether or not your research program is currently successful (a "progressive"—rather than "regressive"—research program, in Lakatos', 1978, terms). If your work seems to be moving forward, the rule of thumb is to not second guess what looks like a productive program. Similarly, should one's personal life be proceeding nicely, there seems to be no need to seek therapy. But what if one's life gets a bit out of control in some domain (e.g., substance abuse, relationship difficulties, thought disorders)? After self-change efforts prove ineffectual, one might consider professional help. Similarly, if one's research program continues to disappoint over time, is that the time to thumb through the Yellow Pages under "Epistemologist?" Hardly!

WHEN PRESCRIPTIVE PHILOSOPHY OF SCIENCE MIGHT BE HELPFUL

When one's research program is stuck or even floundering, the type of person who might be most likely to give solid, helpful hints, is another scientist who shares your research paradigm. Thus, if our research program floundered badly, we would first seek wisdom from people like Donald Polkinghorne (1984, 1989), Michael Patton (1984), Naomi Meara (1989), Miller Mair (1989a, 1989b), Joseph Rychlak (1989), Albert Bandura (1986), Leo Goldman (1976), and Paul Secord (1982, 1984). Most of these people believe in the importance of agency and self-determination in human action; the role of personal meaning in the genesis of human action; and the narrative approach to understanding development in human lives. All happen to be skilled theoreticians and deft researchers. If there is a solution to our problems within our scientific paradigm, these kindred spirits are the ones most likely to help us find that solution.

Returning to our counseling analogy, seeking aid from a like-minded researcher might be analogous to seeking a good counselor–client match on such potentially important dimensions such as gender, race, and religion. Although any counselor may be of help to a client, the odds of a successful therapeutic experience appear to increase when client and counselor are similar on important dimensions. Researchers who share your paradigmatic allegiances know the ground rules of your conceptual terrain, and thus are familiar with theoretical and methodological moves that might circumvent your research problems. But suppose like-minded scientists are unable to help you—in part because they share the same theoretical preconceptions. What then?

Perhaps we should now turn to an individual with extensive background in the history and philosophy of science. But just as a counselor must have good helping skills in order to facilitate therapeutic change, many philosophers of science lack the raw consulting skills that would enable you to profit from their insights. But suppose you are fortunate enough to get a good consultant, how might that person be helpful to you?

In our experience, philosophy of science can serve the liberating function of giving scientists a greater perspective on their scientific tasks. Howard (1986) drew a helpful analogy between a scientist tackling theoretical problems and a lumberjack felling trees in a forest. If a lumberjack/scientist thinks the goal of science is to cut down as many trees as possible (analogously, to publish a large number of articles), then he or she is lost—he or she simply fails to understand the aims and goals of science. The ultimate goal of science is to satisfy human understanding—pure and simple. And, as it turns out, human understanding can be satisfied in a variety of ways—such as uncontrolled but ecologically valid observations, controlled experiments, impossibility arguments, thought experiments, plausible explanation sketches, and many more. So the task of our lumberjack/scientist is not the crude ambition (of knocking down as many trees as possible), but the more precise and refined goal of satisfying human understanding in a particular domain. Analogously, the lumberjack's task might be to clear the way for a road through the forest in order to connect two towns. And as everyone knows, unless there are severe geological constraints, there are many different paths that a road might take to join two towns. Philosophy of science can sometimes function like a map of the forest.

If one thinks of a map as telling the scientist when to turn left and when to turn right, then the analogy is misleading. Philosophy of science is like a map insofar as it gives the scientist an overview of his or her task. If one thinks of the perspective that might be achieved by flying the scientist over the forest in a helicopter, that is the more correct sense in which philosophy of science acts like a map to enhance a scientist's perspective on his or her work. We have found that philosophy of science has had a liberating effect upon our thinking as scientists. But many psychologists tell us that they find philosophy of science too confusing to be of help in their research efforts. Perhaps many early philosophers of science were poor map makers indeed.

Finally, to complete the analogy we have traced thus far, it should be noted that philosophers of science do not explore the forest and make new discoveries. It is the scientist who plumbs the depths of the woods. The philosopher of science studies the history of science and then reconstructs the lessons to be learned from the experiences of scientists. Philosophy of science should never be proscriptive (i.e., to tell the scientist what he or she must not do) to mature and skilled researchers, because good science is what good science does. No one (not even a philosopher of science) can foresee the form that the next scientific breakthrough will take, or the manner in which scientists will achieve it. This is precisely why we suggested earlier that too thorough a knowledge of current philosophy of science might actually be detrimental to the revolutionary scientist. For in his or her search for a richer understanding of a particular subject matter, the revolutionary scientist actually abandons accepted paradigmatic commitments in order to reach toward a richer, fuller appreciation of the phenomenon of interest. In the process, the scientist might violate one or more of the fundamental canons of science itself (consider Einstein on relativity and Bohr on complementarity as obvious cases). Thus, too strong a commitment to the regnant views in philosophy of science might actually serve to inhibit the creative speculations of the revolutionary scientific thinker.

Philosophy of science might be helpful when it is prescriptive. That is, it might point out numerous ways scientific insights have been achieved, demonstrated, and expressed throughout the history of science. In doing so it might afford the scientist alternative routes to a solution to a problem of which he or she might not have been aware. The philosopher of science can suggest alternative routes that this road might take through the forest. But issues of geography and logging practicalities will ultimately decide the optimal path for the road. Analogously, characteristics of the scientist's subject matter, theoretical insights, and methodological aids are the issues the scientist will weigh in selecting which among the alternate routes looks most promising. In such matters, it is the scientist (not the philosopher of science) who is the appropriate expert. And just as the gifted therapist senses that the client has his or her life back in control and thus begins the process of termination, so too the philosopher of science should now also ride off into the sunset with a hearty "Hiyo Silver." This, leaving the townfolk to wonder, "Say, who was that masked man?".

PHILOSOPHY OF SCIENCE IS DEPENDENT ON SCIENCE: OR, THE RETURN OF THE LONE RANGER

You know, at no point in the history of science did the clouds part, and God announce,

> Listen up dummies! The ultimate goal of science is improved human understanding—pure and simple. Now it is important to identify some of the ways that we will know when our understanding of some phenomenon is getting better. By that I mean, we should have some criteria for knowing when our scientific theories are getting closer and closer to the "Truth"—which is, after all, the best possible understanding—pure and simple. So, the working scientist should keep his or her eyes firmly fixed on the *epistemic criteria*—you know, things like the predictive accuracy, coherence, fertility, and so forth of a theory— in order to be able to judge the likely validity of his or her theory. The epistemic criteria are the best criteria (or guideposts) that anyone can find to guide one's pursuit of "Truth" in science. (Howard, 1989, pp. 9–10)

It is a pity that the Deity never saw fit to make such a speech! But because God never told us exactly how we were to play the game of science, it fell to the men and women of science to evolve not only the ultimate purpose of science, but also the rules by which it is played. Scientists had to first conduct science (some of which was later determined to have been "good" science and other efforts deemed "bad") before philosophers of science could reflect on which characteristics of the "good" science had made it good. The major task of philosophers of science is to rationally reconstruct progress within science. That is, given the absence of divine revelation regarding the nature of science, philosophers of science can only construct a temporary theory of what constitutes good science. The next successful scientific revolution might well furnish the evidence that clarifies the exact way in which that temporary theory of science was incorrect. The hope is that (in the long run) such amendments will lead to a better understanding of the nature of good science. Just as current theories in science do not tell "the Truth" about the world, current construals of science within philosophy of science also do not speak "the Truth." But there is ample justification for believing that our current theories of human nature are more likely to be closer to the truth about human nature than were the theories of most psychologists of a century ago. Similarly, current beliefs about the nature of science within philosophy of science are likely to be closer to "the Truth" about science than were, for example, their 16th-century predecessors.

We are now ready to explain why philosophy of science might be ill-advised to channel scientific practice into the accepted modes of inquiry within the current view of science (i.e., to be proscriptive, to tell scientists what they must not do). In being proscriptive, the philosopher of science might serve to cut off the stream of revolutionary scientific innovations—innovations that later could have been the source of successful scientific revolutions. Because it is this evolving corpus of successful scientific paradigms that serves as the raw data necessary to improve our evolving notions of what constitutes good science (within philosophy of science), it is an essential component for future development. To constrain scientific rationality to only one approach (by considering all other forms as unscientific) would be to move toward a self-fulfilling prophecy where scientific rationality is decreed to be what a certain view of science says it should be. Such a constrained view would produce science consistent with the regnant philosophy of science—which might, in turn, appear to verify the validity of the model. And such confirmation-by-fiat would be deceptive, because all philosophies of science are time bound and history bound. One would be ill-advised, therefore, to assert that any particular construal represents "the True" or the best approach to conducting scientific inquiry.

This last point is important when addressing psychologists, because it helps to clarify why many research psychologists have found their experiences with philosophy of science unsatisfactory. Logical positivism was a philosophy of science that exerted some degree of importance in the first half of the 20th century. Logical positivism involved (among other things) the employment of operational definitions. That is, a concept could be defined by the presence of a "point-at-able" (observable). Operational definitions allow for a kind of objectivity that did not rely on strategies such as syllogism, metaphysical argumentation, and other rationalistic strategies (Hilgard, 1987). Although it represented a reasonable position within philosophy of science for a while, logical positivism has not left a particularly deep or distinctive mark on current philosophy of science. But for reasons of historical accident, logical positivism had a great influence upon the development of scientific psychology—especially in the United States. This is, in part, due to the fact that positivism reached its ascendancy at a critical juncture in the formation of psychology's identity as a scientific discipline.

The advocates of positivism all-too-ofen exhibited autocratic styles and authoritarian positions regarding what constituted good science. Committed to operationalism and championing the deductive-nomological view of hypothesis testing, positivists frequently disparaged alternative views of scientific rationality. Thus, for many research psychologists, their experience with philosophy of science consisted of a brush with positivist orthodoxy. Such experiences frequently left researchers with the feeling that they were being force fed a rather rigid bill of goods. Thus, counseling psychologists' feelings about the larger enterprise—namely, philosophy of science—are often rather negative. Although guilt by association might be regrettable, it remains a fact of human nature that our own experiences with particular members of a group do serve to color our feelings about that group as a whole.

But suppose your experiences with philosophers of science had been positive. Imagine your research program reached an impasse, and a friendly philosopher of science gave you 8 or 10 suggestions: different ways in which you might reconceptualize your problem; different types of demonstration that might be compelling; or different ways of viewing the empirical findings in the field thus far. Upon reflection, you ruled out 5 or 6 possibilities as unlikely to pan out, but several others seemed to hold some promise, so you tried them out. Wouldn't it be lovely if one or more of the suggestions worked out, and your entire research program was radically altered?

If this were a perfect world (or the movies), the point at which your revivified research program achieved success, would be precisely the moment that your Lone Ranger philosopher of science rode back into your research life. Of course the Long Ranger would be pleased that some of the advice helped, but his or her dominant interest would be driven by the desire to know what makes science tick. What was it about that particular advice that dissolved the epistemological crisis? Did a genuine revolution occur in the way research is conducted in this domain? Why didn't the other suggestions pan out? Remember, philosophy of science is symbiotic with science. The resolution of your epistemological crisis becomes the latest empirical datum in the Lone Ranger's domain of professional interest.

"Much obliged, masked man."
"Don't mention it, pardner."

To complete our intersecting analogies, consider the "ordinary agent" (or client) who experienced a "psychological crisis" and then received therapeutic help. In an ideal world, the counselor would ride back into the client's world to make a long-term assessment of the value of the therapy. By examining therapeutic successes, and contrasting these cases with failures, the counseling practitioner might learn something about what he or she does in therapy that leads to success, and what might produce failure. Such knowledge might serve to improve his or her future ministrations. But does not the sketch just presented represent the ideal of the scientist-practitioner model? Isn't the model's ambition to employ systematic techniques of inquiry to glean valid insights that can, in turn, be used to improve practice? Then why would any-one be surprised to find that philosophers of science are energized by a simi-lar ambition in their professional activities?

CHANGES IN SCIENCE ARE MORE LIKE EVOLUTION THAN REVOLUTION

Earlier, we talked of Kuhn's notions of how change occurs in science because most of us possess some knowledge of Kuhn's perspective. We then tried to connect Kuhn's notion of crises in science (which call for revolutionary shifts in paradigms) with psychological crises (which often require massive shifts in clients' thinking, actions, etc.). But neo-Kuhnian thought visualizes change in science as an evolutionary (i.e., gradual change by small increments) process, rather than progress through radical, revolutionary paradigm shifts, as suggested by Kuhn.

In his Reticulational Model of scientific change, Lauden (1984) proposed that changes in any of the three levels of scientific activity (the axiological, or the aims and goals of science; the methodological; or the factual, which includes both theories and evidence) are possible at any point in time. Such changes are usually not accompanied by suggested modifications at other levels, as Kuhn's revolutionary analysis would suggest. Kuhn spoke of quick, radical reconceptualizations (using terms like, *conversion experience, gestalt shifts, incommensurable worldviews,* and the like) when paradigm shifts oc-cur at moments of revolutionary science. For Lauden, several scientists, work-ing over an extended period of time, make piecemeal amendments to the regnant paradigm. These minor changes coalesce over time and result in a substantial shift in paradigmatic characteristics. On Lauden's view, small changes on one level, if they prove successful, might actually produce changes at other levels also, which could in time lead to the massive conceptual changes associated (in retrospect) with paradigm shifts. However, we hasten to add that although many such minor changes are suggested, few are suc-cessful, and fewer still lead to changes at other levels. But it is precisely this trial and error, piecemeal approach that constitutes the fuel for scientific change and the backbone of scientific rationality. Stephen Toulmin viewed the rationality of science as being embedded in the manner in which sciences change and evolve, rather than remaining stagnant, "A man [sic] demonstrates his rationality, not by a commitment to fixed ideas, stereotyped procedures, or immutable concepts, but by the manner in which and the occasions on which he changes those ideas, procedures, and concepts" (Toulmin, 1972, p. X).

Seeing paradigmatic changes in science as part of an evolutionary process, allows for a slightly revised conception of our role in the process of change.

Rather than seeing ourselves as something like worker bees conducting the simple puzzle-solving tasks of normal science (as Kuhn's revolutionary view implies), many of us are instead contributing small theoretical and methodological innovations that will cumulatively represent the seeds for scientific revolutions. The increasing evidence of multiple, simultaneous discoveries in science suggests that an army of scientists prepares the conceptual ground so that a great new insight is possible (perhaps even inevitable). This vision is quite different from the position that a few great geniuses are responsible for great ideas—and (conveniently) the fact that a genius produced the seminal idea represents the proof of his or her enormous intellectual capacities.

There is a role that philosophy of science might play in the generation of change and progress in any domain of science, but we argue that it is a carefully defined role. However, once a major shift in scientific rationality occurs in a domain, then it is important that philosophers of science study the change intensively so as to determine if that change has implications for their understanding of scientific rationality in general. It is this latter domain that is appropriately their central field of interest.

Summary

Science generally proceeds quite well without interference from philosophy of science. In fact, one can easily imagine that it would be counterproductive, at moments of rapid scientific change in a domain, for scientists to worry too much about the accepted rules of science that their innovations appear to be breaking. Creative and productive scientists might be well-advised to focus on their science—especially when important developments appear to be taking place.

But if a scientist's research program meets with what seem to be intractable obstacles, then an historian and philosopher of science can be a helpful source of new ideas (and alternative perspectives on the project's goals, the nature of the problem, and the variety of forms that a putative solution might take) that could get the scientist un-stuck. As a counselor might be an important resource when an "ordinary agent" encounters a psychological crisis, so might a philosopher of science be an invaluable resource when a scientist encounters an epistemological crisis.

AFTER WORDS

Student: Excuse me, but I'm a bit confused about the role of philosophy of science for counseling researchers. I get a sense that philosophers of science have a good deal of insight to share with us, yet there seems to be great emphasis in this chapter on the idea that philosophy of science is only to be explored as a last resort, or when all self-help efforts have failed.

Authors: Sorry, we didn't mean to imply that philosophy of science should be considered only in moments of dire necessity. Our point in noting instances when philosophy of science was *not* likely to be a researcher's optimal resource, was to undo a good deal of propaganda that has been fed to psychological researchers over the last 40 years or so. Critics have often reviewed the "deplorable" state of research in the "soft" sciences, and then implied that research in psychology would be improved greatly if only we would study how "good" research is conducted (presumably by looking at a "mature" science such as physics, or by studying philosophy of science). We believe that our discipline's efforts to turn psychological research into a "people physics" has borne all the fruit it has to offer. Therefore, we should push ahead trusting *our own intuitions* as to when to zig and when to zag. The philosopher of science Stephen Toulmin (1981) expressed a similar sentiment in the following way,

> I think what one can do, as a philosopher of science or as an historian of science, is (so to say) to give psychologists the courage of all their different convictions; to show them that by seeking to be one and only one kind of science, they are placing needless restrictions on themselves; and that if they will just take the first necessary step . . . that of thinking out clearly what the problems are from which they start, and using the methods that are appropriate to those different kinds of problems . . . then they will be able to be more self-confident. They won't spend so much time . . . looking over their methodological shoulders to see if they are being quite "respectable." (pp. 245–246)

Student: It sounds as if you are not the kind of counseling psychologists who believe that the discipline's problems result from fuzzy theorizing and imperfect methodologies—that if we would only develop tight theories, and test them with rigorous methodologies, then the discipline would make progress.

Authors: Indeed we are not! In our opinion, psychology's problems resulted from a premature hardening of the categories. What we need is more radical theorizing and unusual methodologies that might represent our subject matter with less distortion and more vitality. Toulmin (1981) also thinks psychology has too firmly set its sights on being rigorous—much to its detriment:

> I don't believe that there is anything called "the scientific method," and the "rigor" of the scientific method seems to be *rigor mortis*. My own view is that, historically speaking, the idea of scientific method was fathered onto the actual procedure of scientists by formal logicians, and that the relationship between logic and scientific thought . . . is like the relationship between accountancy

and business planning. The accountant can always tell you how well you did last year; he can't tell you what to do in order to do well next year. (Least of all can he tell you what criteria you should adopt for deciding what counts as doing well.) And in science what we need to do is clarify our ideas about our aims—which really means understanding the basic character of our problems— and then see what strategies are open to us, in working toward the intellectual realization of those aims. (pp. 247–248)

And these tasks are best thought-through by counseling psychologists— not by philosophers and historians of science.

Student: I see. Then it's up to us. But surely there must be some good readings in philosophy of science that will help us in our journey toward an understanding of human beings.

Authors: There are some good books and articles in philosophy of science, but they are not all equally easy to read. Our readable favorites are T. S. Kuhn's (1962) *The Structure of Scientific Revolutions*, W. V. O. Quine and J. S. Ullian's (1970) *The Web of Belief*, and S. Toulmin's (1961) *Foresight and Understanding*. J. Kourany's (1987) excellent book of readings entitled *Scientific Knowledge* and R. Rorty's (1979) *Philosophy and the Mirror of Nature* are a bit more complex, but worth the extra effort. Finally, several psychologists have recently written wonderful books on philosophy for psychologists. D. N. Robinson's (1985) *Philosophy of Psychology* and D. Polkinghorne's (1983) *Methodology for the Human Sciences* stand out as particularly good works.

REFERENCES

Bandura, A. (1986). *Social foundations of thought and action: A social cognitive theory.* Englewood Cliffs, NJ: Prentice-Hall.

Bergin, A. E. (1963). The effects of psychotherapy: Negative results revisited. *Journal of Counseling Psychology, 10,* 244–250.

Goldman, L. (1976). A revolution in counseling research. *Journal of Counseling Psychology, 23,* 543–552.

Hilgard, E. R. (1987). *Psychology in America: A historical survey.* New York: Harcourt, Brace, Jovanovich.

Howard, G. S. (1985). The role of values in the science of psychology. *American Psychologist, 40,* 255–265.

Howard, G. S. (1986). *Dare we develop a human science?* Notre Dame, IN: Academic Publications.

Howard, G. S. (1989). *A tale of two stories: Excursions into a narrative approach to psychology.* Notre Dame, IN: Academic Publications.

Kourany, J. (Ed.). (1987). *Scientific knowledge: Basic issues in the philosophy of science.* Belmont, CA: Wadsworth.

Kuhn, T. (1962). *The structure of scientific revolutions.* Chicago: University of Chicago Press.

Kuhn, T. (1977). *The essential tension.* Chicago: University of Chicago Press.

Lakatos, I. (1978). The methodology of scientific research programs. In J. Worrall & G. Currie (Eds.), *Philosophical papers* (Vol. 1, pp. 102–138). Cambridge, England: Cambridge University Press.

Lauden, L. (1984). *Science and values: The aims of science and their role in scientific debate.* Berkeley: University of California Press.

MacIntyre, A. (1977). Epistemological crises, dramatic narrative, and the philosophy of science. *The Monist, 60,* 453–472.

Mair, M. (1989a). *Between psychology and psychotherapy: A poetics of experience.* London: Routledge.

Mair, M. (1989b). Kelly, Bannister and a storytelling psychology. *International Journal of Personal Construct Psychology, 2,* 1–14.

McMullin, E. (1983). Values in science. In P. D. Asquith & T. Nickles (Eds.), *Proceedings of the 1982 Philosophy of Science Association* (Vol. 2, pp. 3–23). East Lansing, MI: Philosophy of Science Association.

Meara, N. M. (1989). Selected theoretical and philosophical aspects of counseling psychology: A personal view. *Theoretical and Philosophical Psychology, 9,* 48–52.

Patton, M. J. (1984). Managing social interaction in counseling: A contribution from the philosophy of science. *Journal of Counseling Psychology, 31,* 442–456.

Polkinghorne, D. (1983). *Methodology for the human sciences.* Albany: SUNY Press.

Polkinghorne, D. (1984). Further extensions of methodological diversity for counseling psychology. *Journal of Counseling Psychology, 31,* 416–429.

Polkinghorne, D. (1989). *Narrative knowing and the human sciences.* Albany: SUNY Press.

Quine, W. V. O., & Ullian, J. S. (1970). *The web of belief.* New York: Random House.

Robinson, D. N. (1985). *Philosophy of psychology.* New York: Columbia University Press.

Rorty, R. (1979). *Philosophy and the mirror of nature.* Princeton, NJ: Princeton University Press.

Rychlak, J. R. (1989). *The psychology of rigorous humanism.* New York: NYU Press.

Secord, P. F. (1982). *Explaining human behavior: Consciousness, human action and social structure.* Beverly Hills: Sage.

Secord, P. F. (1984). Determinism, free will and self-interaction: A psychological perspective. *New Ideas in Psychology, 2,* 25–33.

Toulmin, S. (1961). *Foresight and understanding: An inquiry into the aims of science.* New York: Harper & Row.

Toulmin, S. (1972). *Human understanding.* Princeton, NJ: Princeton University Press.

Toulmin, S. (1981). Concluding comments. In R. A. Kasschan & C. N. Cofer (Eds.), *Houston symposium II: Enduring issues in psychology's second century* (pp. 211–298). New York: Praeger.

Truax, C. B. (1963). Effective ingredients in psychotherapy. *Journal of Counseling Psychology, 10,* 256–263.

PART

II

APPROACHES TO COUNSELING RESEARCH

3

OUTCOME RESEARCH
IN COUNSELING

Michael J. Lambert
Brigham Young University

Kevin S. Masters
Ball State University

Benjamin M. Ogles
Ohio University

A fundamental commitment of counseling, counseling psychology, and other health-related fields is the well-being of the client seeking services in applied settings. The ethics of our profession inspire practitioners to make "every effort to protect the welfare of those who seek their services" (American Psychological Association [APA], 1981, p. 637). When clients turn to a professional for help they expect a professional service, one that is based not only on our best thinking and theories of facilitating human growth, but one that is based on our best scientific efforts. The purpose of empirical research is to satisfy the highest aims of ethical practice by exploring and verifying the relationships that exist between variables that affect the well being of clients. Specifically, outcome research in counseling and psychotherapy is largely aimed at illuminating the effects of treatment variables (such as counseling techniques, counselor attitudes, etc.) on client functioning. Although many treatment approaches are based on naturalistic observations and intuition, the complexity of the natural situation and the limited perspective of examining the single case suggest the need for an experimental approach that provides an additional perspective from which to view clinical phenomena. Without such a perspective, it is doubtful that the client's welfare will be best served. Thus, counseling-outcome research is a necessary component of the highest ethical practice and a fundamental aspect of counseling services.

In this chapter, we describe outcome research, its goals, methods, issues that are of contemporary importance, and topics that are especially important in the study of client change. First, we consider the most important goals of outcome research including some of the achievements of past research. Next, we examine the methods that are commonly employed to study the goals set forth in the first section. We then examine several of the most important issues that confront the practitioner and outcome researcher. Finally, we make some recommendations for the eager graduate student who may have an interest in contributing to this growing body of essential information.

GOALS AND ACHIEVEMENTS OF OUTCOME RESEARCH

Outcome research is the experimental investigation of the impact of counseling on the client. The goals of outcome research have evolved over time. The questions that were of great significance in the 1930s are not the same as those that were of interest in the 1960s or that are of interest in the 1990s. Outcome research has evolved toward questions that are more sophisticated and reflect greater diversity and differentiation. Table 3.1 lists some of the questions that have been asked in outcome research. The three major categories of questions organize the goals of outcome research into groups that reflect their differing focus. By studying these questions, the reader can begin to understand the breadth of the purposes of counseling research and the type of questions that hold and have held center stage in our quest for knowledge. Later in this chapter we link certain methods and procedures to these questions so that the reader becomes familiar with the empirical analysis of counseling outcomes.

Class I: Effectiveness Questions

The earliest studies of counseling and psychotherapy outcome (between 1930 and the mid-1960s) have been reviewed by Bergin (1971), and Meltzoff and Kornreich (1970). This research was largely aimed at answering the general question (Major Class I): Is psychotherapy effective? Unfortunately these studies were not sophisticated in their research design (a subject we address later) and left many questions unanswered.

Fenichel (1930) is a case in point. He was interested in evaluating the effect of psychoanalysis on patients at the Berlin Psychoanalytic Institute. This unpublished study was written with Sando Rado and Carl Muller-Braunschweig while Sigmund Freud wrote the foreword. The report covered the first 10 years of the Institute, which had 1,955 client consultations that resulted in the commencement of therapy for 721 cases. At the time of the report, 363 of these had concluded treatment, with an additional 241 terminating treatment prematurely, whereas 117 were still in treatment. Of those who had

TABLE 3.1
The Goals of Outcome Research as Reflected in Historically Important
and Contemporary Questions

Major Class I: Is Counseling/Psychotherapy Effective?

Representative Questions:
- Is psychoanalysis effective?
- Is client-centered therapy effective?
- Do people who articipate in therapy change more than people who do not?
- Are the effects of therapy short-term or long-lasting?
- Are improvements in therapy limited to symptomatic changes?

Major Class II: What Aspects of Counseling/Therapy are Helpful?

Representative Questions:
- Are the positive outcomes in therapy due to patient expectancies or therapy techniques?
- Are the positive outcomes in therapy due to therapist expectancies? Attitudes? Personality? Verbal style? Gender? Race? Socioeconomic Status?
- Are the techniques of psychodynamic therapy more helpful than the techniques of behavior therapy?
- Is client-centered therapy more effective than rational-emotive therapy?
- Is cognitive therapy more effective than behavioral therapy?
- Are the specific techniques of therapy more important than the specific therapist offering the treatment?
- Do high levels of accurate empathy, unconditional positive regard, genuineness and warmth facilitate positive personality change?
- Are professionally trained therapists more helpful than paraprofessionals?
- Is group therapy more effective than individual, marital or family therapy?

Major Class III: How Can the Effects of Counseling/Therapy be Enhanced?

Representative Questions:
- Will matching therapy and patient increase efficacy?
- Will ideal matching of therapist and client improve outcome?
- Does offering therapy for longer periods, more often, improve outcome?
- Does phasing out treatment improve the durability of treatment effects?
- Does adding a "gains maintenance" component reduce relapse?
- Will adding a cognitive rehearsal element enhance the effects of behavior therapy?

---

completed treatment, 47 were considered uncured, 116 improved, 89 very much improved, and 11 cured. There are various ways of calculating the percentage of cases that improved, depending on whether dropouts are included (they could be excluded because one is interested in the effects of treatment, and dropouts were not fully treated) but a reasonable estimate is 59% to 91% (cf. Bergin & Lambert, 1978, for an extensive discussion). This may be an impressive showing for psychoanalysis depending on how the data are interpreted.

This study employed a simple research design that involved assessing patient status before treatment on dimensions considered highly important in their life functioning and reassessing those same traits and symptoms following treatment. In most cases the length and intensity of treatment was extensive, lasting years with several contacts per week.

A serious problem in this (and similar studies) is that although it allowed evaluation of the outcome of counseling as assessed by counselors and independent clinicians, it did not provide an estimate of change that might have occurred in clients simply due to the passage of time. That is, perhaps these same clients would have changed an equivalent amount if left untreated. Many studies conducted in the ensuing years had the same problem and those who were skeptical about the value of therapy were quick to point out that people who are disturbed and who do not undergo counseling also improve. In fact, Hans Eysenck (1952) wrote a very challenging paper in which he purported to show that the "spontaneous remission rate" in untreated patients was identical (67%, if not higher) to the rates quoted by Fenichel and others who had published reports on psychotherapy at the time. Eysenck's critical view did not go unchallenged; but it was difficult to demonstrate the effects of counseling because the usual research design did not include random assignment of clients to treatment and a no-treatment comparison group.

Following Eysenck's article, the number of outcome studies that assigned patients to either the counseling group or to a wait-list or no-treatment control group increased substantially, thus allowing for a reasonable comparison of treated with untreated clients over time. This research is typified by a study of client-centered therapy reported by Rogers and Dymond (1954). These authors conducted one of the more important early studies of therapy that incorporated outcome for a group of clients with which the treatment group could be compared. Unfortunately this study (and many others) had a critical flaw. They divided clients into two groups, one receiving treatment (client-centered therapy), the other remaining on a wait-list. Clients in the treatment group were assessed on outcome measures at the beginning of therapy and after its completion. The wait-list group was assessed at the start of the waiting period (that lasted 60 days), after the wait, and again when they finished their (delayed) counseling experience. However, clients were *not* assigned to groups randomly (or through some other method that assured their equivalence) but were assigned to the wait-list only if it was felt that they could wait for counseling without serious harm or discomfort.

Researchers of the day were very concerned about the ethical problems associated with withholding counseling from clients in need. The wait-list control group seemed to be a solution to this problem because clients may well be delayed in entering treatment anyhow because of limited clinic resources. Early studies of therapy that employed a comparison group to answer the Class I question often draw their comparison group from clients who needed counseling, but refused it, or who dropped out of counseling early in the process but would agree to undergo posttesting. Unfortunately these groups of clients were often not equivalent to those who actually underwent treatment. Often they were less motivated, less insightful, and more disturbed (and sometimes less disturbed) than the treated clients. These differences were frequently not assessed or reported.

Therefore, a problem with this procedure was that it did not establish the initial equivalence of the treatment and comparison groups. If the two groups differ from the start, how can we conclude following treatment that client status is due to counseling and not to processes within the client? The usual method for overcoming this problem is to randomly assign clients to counseling and control groups or to match clients on important dimensions (like psychopathology) to ensure equivalence.

A study that matched clients was published by Arbuckle and Boy (1961). They evaluated the effectiveness of client-centered therapy for counseling students classified by two junior high schools in Massachusetts as having behavior problems. The students were displaying overt forms of misbehavior in the school setting and were undergoing daily after-school detention. The 36 subjects included in the study were divided into three numerically equal groups that were matched in terms of means and standard deviations on seven important variables. The variables were age, grade, IQ, Stanford Achievement Test average, teachers' behavior ratings, proportion of peer groups accepting them, and proportion of peer groups rejecting them. Prior to the study the three groups were also compared on nine other variables: gender, health, siblings in attendance, socioeconomic status, extent of part-time work, participation in co-curricular activities, participation in out-of-school activities, Q-sort correlations between the actual-self and ideal-self, and definiteness of education and/or vocational objectives. No pretest differences between groups were found on any of these variables. Thus, the matching technique and statistical analyses conducted prior to the study established the equivalence of the groups. The experimental group received weekly individual client-centered counseling and was released from after-school detention. The traditional control continued with after-school detention but received no counseling. The "laissez-faire control" was released from after-school detention but received no counseling. The experimental group showed substantial changes relative to the controls in terms of actual-ideal-self correlations, teachers' behavior ratings, being less rejected by peers, and improved status of their education–vocational objectives. This study nicely demonstrated the effectiveness of client-centered therapy by using well-conceived and matched control groups.

Class I questions have now been addressed in hundreds of studies, both well and poorly designed. The essential element of these studies is that they allow the researcher to observe changes in equivalent subjects, some of whom are exposed to the independent variable (counseling) and some of whom are not. Changes in all subjects are measured before and after therapy on the relevant dependent variables. This and similar research was reviewed by Bergin and Lambert (1978), Lambert, Shapiro, and Bergin (1986) as well as Smith, Glass, and Miller (1980), among others, with the general conclusion that counseling and psychotherapy are, in general, effective with clients, achieving outcomes that are superior to those that result from the client's natural healing processes and the passage of time. This conclusion is limited by the fact that new "therapies" are being developed with staggering rapidly and clinicians appear to be amazingly eager to advocate and apply them without any formal evaluation!

Class II: Therapeutic Ingredients Questions

The critics of outcome research (and researchers themselves) were quick to point out that although the outcome of treated groups was superior to the outcome of untreated groups, it did not mean the difference was due to the procedures or factors that the researcher believed were effective. So the focus of research shifted to Class II questions dealing with a clearer specification of "what causes improvement?" We discuss four approaches to resolving the therapeutic ingredients question: placebo controls, comparison trials, process/outcome studies, and dismantling strategies.

Placebo Controls. The first method of determining what causes improvement was based on the observation that many clients may be improving just because they are being attended to (Halo effect) and believe they are being treated and therefore expect to change (placebo effect). As a result counseling investigators borrowed from psychopharmacological research and began applying the concept of placebo controls, contrasting the outcome of treated groups with placebo groups. In medicine, where the effects of an active chemical are contrasted with the effects of pharmacologically inert substances (i.e., the placebo), this contrast allows researchers to rule out the effects of attention. In addition, this contrast can help to understand the effects of belief by the patient that they are being treated and will get better (because the patients do not know if they are receiving the active drug or the placebo drug) as well as belief in the treatment by the physician (who is also "blind" to which patients actually get the experimental drug). In counseling, the placebo construct has been variously conceptualized (e.g., expectations for change, attention, nonspecific support, etc.). Thus, placebo research calls for a control group that attempts to control variables other than the passage of time as with the no-treatment or wait-list controls). This group is designed to control for nonspecific aspects of the treatment that may be causing improvements. Through the use of a placebo control the likelihood that improvement in the treatment group can be attributed to such theory-based mechanisms as insight, systematic desensitization, transference interpretations, and similar specific theory-based interventions, is increased.

The study by Wojciechowski (1984) is a good example of research that attempts to investigate therapy outcome and measure the impact of client and therapist placebo factors. This study investigated the outcome of 68 adult females who suffered from headaches. Clients, who were recruited through newspaper ads, were randomly assigned to one of four treatment conditions. A "double-blind" design was used in which both counselors and clients were misled about the positive effects of a placebo control treatment for which there was actually no existing rationale. This "therapy" (concentration therapy) contained all the theoretically noncritical elements of relaxation therapy (same duration, daily home practice, etc.) but not the theoretically critical element (deep muscle) relaxation instructions.

Counselors were trained and then asked to provide either the relaxation treatment or the concentration therapy. Therapists were also misled about the matching of treatment with client type. They treated clients for whom they thought they had a correct match as well as clients for whom they thought they had an incorrect match. With this design the researchers were able to evaluate not only the effects of a bona fide treatment (relaxation) but a placebo thought to be a bona fide treatment by both clients and therapists. In addition they were able to study differential outcomes when counselors thought clients were ill suited to either the bona fide treatment or the placebo control. The results were complicated by the use of a variety of outcome measures but generally there was limited evidence of superiority for the bona fide treatment, although the placebo subjects did surprisingly well.

Currently there is considerable controversy over the meaning of the placebo concept in outcome research (Bloch & Lambert, 1985; Lambert et al., 1986; Prioleau, Murdock, & Brody, 1983; Shepherd, 1984). Clients in so-called placebo control groups typically show greater improvement than patients in waitlist or no-treatment control groups (Shapiro & Shapiro, 1982; Smith et al., 1980). But patients in these groups show less improvement than those who are receiving psychological interventions (e.g., Blanchard, Andrasik, Ahler, Teders, & O'Keefe, 1980).

In addition to the effects of placebo variables on counseling outcome, researchers are also interested in finding out what else it is in counseling interventions that facilitates change in clients. These questions have been asked in a wide variety of ways that deal directly with those variables that therapists and researchers hypothesize to be the "active ingredients of psychotherapy." The earliest studies of these questions compared competing theories of counseling.

Comparison Questions. Is dynamic psychotherapy more effective than client-centered psychotherapy? Is rational–emotive counseling more effective than Gestalt therapy? Is short-term counseling as effective as long-term counseling? Is group counseling as effective as individual counseling?, and so on. Gottman and Markman (1978) labeled this the Grand Prix question. In a competitive race, which therapy will win and prove itself to be superior? So a subset of Class II questions involved comparative outcome studies. Studies by Sloane, Staples, Cristol, Yorkston, and Whipple (1975) as well as Paul (1966) are prototypical of this research, and are described elsewhere in this chapter.

A more recent study illustrating this approach was published by Pilkonis, Imber, Lewis, and Rubinsky (1984), who compared the effects of *mode* of treatment rather than treatment orientation on clients. Sixty-four outpatients were randomly assigned to either individual, group, or conjoint marital psychotherapy offered by experienced private clinicians for an average of 27 sessions. This study is probably the first to simultaneously compare these three popular treatment modalities. The therapists were nine (three for each modality) medical- or doctoral-level practitioners with at least 7 years of postdoctoral experience who were committed to either dynamic or humanistic orientations. The patients were diagnosed as neurotic or personality disordered, and were willing to participate in conjoint counseling if required. They also had to be living with another adult who would agree to act as an informant in the study.

Outcome was assessed by a variety of measures of global and symptomatic improvement, including measures that might be expected to be most responsive to the effects of each specific treatment modality. Despite the anticipation of differential impact on specific areas of client functioning, no difference in treatment groups was found. Patients did improve and maintained gains at the 8-month follow-up. But differential effects seemed more a function of client variables (e.g., degree of initial disturbance) or the impact of specific therapists.

Comparative outcome studies have been reviewed by numerous authors (Bergin & Lambert, 1978; Lambert et al., 1986; Miller & Berman, 1983; Shapiro & Shapiro, 1982; Smith et al., 1980). Most reviews are consistent with the conclusion of Luborsky, Singer, and Luborsky (1975), who suggested the results were like the verdict proclaimed by Alice in Wonderland's DoDo Bird: "Everyone has won and so all must have prizes."

The apparent practical comparability of different treatment approaches, as well as clinical experience and psychological theory itself, has led to several other questions that are also of contemporary interest to outcome researchers (and perhaps of more interest because the vast majority of practitioners today are eclectic in practice, using a variety of techniques integrated from various theories of counseling). These questions are a subset of Class II questions that may be categorized as either process/outcome questions or dismantling questions.

Process/Outcome Questions. One way of answering questions about what causes positive counseling outcome is to operationalize those aspects of the counseling thought to cause change and study them within the context of the interaction between client and counselor. In contrast to comparative questions that are addressed by operationalizing the counseling as a whole, process studies operationalize specific in-therapy events. These events, once operationalized, are categorized, coded, and counted and then correlated with outcomes. Research strategies in this domain are reviewed by Hill (chapter 4, this volume).

The following study by Kirtner and Cartwright (1958) is typical of early attempts to use the process-outcome strategy. These authors attempted to demonstrate that client's initial manner of problem presentation and mode of approaching problem resolution would affect the length and outcome of counseling. They had judges rate the initial interviews of 42 clients presenting at the University of Chicago Counseling Center. Each client was then matched with one of five problem presentation descriptions. These descriptions ranged from "immediately deals with a feeling problem" and "has already localized a specific problem area of difficulty" to "deals with problems as though they are almost entirely external." Outcome was rated by the counselor on a 1–9 scale, 6–9 representing good outcome and 1–3 representing poor outcome.

After matching each interview with the best description, a table was developed displaying the length and success of treatment by the five initial session descriptions. Although no statistics were calculated, clients described as having "feeling immediacy" and "specific problem areas" were more frequently rated by the counselor as having a positive outcome. They were also more likely to continue in counseling. At the same time, clients who were described as having an external focus were more frequently classified as having a poor outcome and were more likely to drop out of therapy.

A great deal of process research has explored the correlation between therapist-offered conditions of accurate empathy, warmth, unconditional positive regard, and genuineness (the client-centered facilitative conditions) and changes in clients. This research has been summarized by various reviewers (Lambert, DeJulio, & Stein, 1978; Truax & Mitchell, 1971) and suggests that there is a relationship between these variables and counseling outcome. Additionally, these variables loom large as *predictors of outcome,* although it is not always clear if it is the counselor or client who is responsible for high and low empathy; or some other variables that are responsible for both empathy levels and client change (e.g., the motivation level/active participation of the client in counseling). If we were to assume that a process variable, like empathy, actually causes positive changes in clients (not just correlates with or predicts change) then this causal relation would lead us to emphasize empathy development in clinical training, the selection of counseling trainees on the basis of their empathic ability, and the evaluation of this skill in the comprehensive examination of students. That is a great advantage of some process research (i.e., it can have clear implications for both training and practice).

Empirical studies examining the relationship between many process variables (cf. Greenberg & Pinsoff, 1986; Kiesler, 1973) and outcome have been undertaken. Unfortunately, the correlational nature of most of these data is just a "first step" in the scientific task of establishing cause–effect relationships. But it can and does lead to experimental studies of the process variables and their contribution to the ultimate outcome of counseling.

Dismantling Questions.   A final strategy discussed here in relation to Class II questions is the dismantling strategy. This is a method that deemphasizes the counselor and focuses on the techniques of treatment. The dismantling strategy, typically associated with behavioral and cognitive therapies, attempts to answer the general question: What causes positive outcomes? Researchers using this strategy think of treatment as a "package" with component parts. After initial research has shown the treatment to be more effective than no-treatment, placebo treatment, or the best alternate treatment, the researchers begin to break the counseling down (dismantle it) into its basic components to see which are necessary and sufficient for positive effects. The research design and methods are often identical to those used in comparative outcome studies but the question becomes—what aspect of this effective treatment is critical to positive change?

Typical of this approach is the study reported by Rehm et al. (1981). These researchers dismantled Rehm's (1977) self-control therapy for depression. In this treatment, depressed persons are viewed as manifesting maladaptive self-monitoring, self-evaluation (self-attribution), and self-reinforcement behavior to which the therapy is directed. The authors randomly assigned patients to the full treatment (including self-monitoring, self-reinforcement, and self-evaluation components); or to self-monitoring plus self-evaluation; or self-monitoring plus self-reinforcement; or to self-monitoring alone. Thus they hoped to find a more efficient (or necessary and sufficient) treatment for depression. Surprisingly, the self-evaluation and self-reinforcement conditions were found to add little to the impact of self-monitoring alone.

Class III: Enhancement Questions

The final set of questions are often studied in a context in which the researcher is attempting to enhance the effects of a treatment of proven value. We discuss matching, constructive, and other strategies of outcome enhancement.

Matching Strategies.   Matching research is based on the idea that even if counseling is generally effective, and one counseling approach is not more effective than another, not all clients benefit to the same degree in a given treatment or equally well in every treatment. It is also plausible that clients may respond better to counseling offered by one counselor rather than another counselor (Lambert, 1989). Can counseling effects be enhanced by ideal matching of client and therapy or client and counselor?

An early example of a study that attempted to examine the interaction of therapy schools with client types was published by DiLoreto (1971) who compared group treatments that employed systematic desensitization, rational emotive counseling, or client-centered counseling. The study involved 100 college student volunteers who reported high interpersonal anxiety and a desire for treatment. Twenty were randomly assigned to each treatment group, 20 were assigned to a placebo control, and 20 remained in a no-contact control group. One half of the clients were extroverts and the other half were introverts.

All groups (except the no-contact group) were seen for 11 hours of counseling in group sessions with five persons in each group. The counselors were "advanced graduate students" who had experience in and a commitment to each of the three main orientations. Evaluations of the clients were based on a battery of tests and behavioral observation. All clients in the active therapies were found to improve more than the clients in either of the control groups.

In terms of interaction effects, systematic desensitization was found to be equally effective with introverts and extroverts. In contrast client-centered and rational–emotive interventions tended to be most effective with introverts. As can be seen the addition of a client variable to the usual treatment (school) comparison adds an important, potentially clinically useful dimension—matching client with therapy type. Unfortunately, in the 20 years since this study was published, the results have not been replicated (with regard to school by client personality interactions), although some interactional effects in the Sloane et al. (1975) study are similar.

We have not yet found a *robust* client dimension that interacts with counseling orientation. Clinical lore aside, there is no empirical basis for differential treatment (therapy) assignment based on a client personality variable or any other client variable for that matter. Past research on this topic remains merely suggestive and there is a need for further research of this type.

Another research strategy related to matching client characteristics to theoretical orientation is that of matching clients with *counselors* on the basis of personality. Seminal work on this topic was conducted by Whitehorn and Betz (1960). These authors differentiated counselors first on the basis of relative differences in the outcome of schizophrenics with whom they worked. Those who were especially effective with schizophrenics were labeled A-types based on items from the Strong Vocational Interest Inventory (SVII). Further research (McNair, Callahan, & Lorr, 1962) suggested that B-type therapists could also be identified on the basis of SVII items and were more effective than A-types with neurotic clients. Although the AB research never resulted in consistent findings it was a precursor to similar studies that are being conducted at present.

A study that used more rigorous experimental methods was reported by Abramowitz, Abramowitz, Roback, and Jackson (1974). These authors divided clients who were high versus low on a measure of locus of control into two groups. The low-internal locus of control clients were further divided into two groups, one of which participated in an encounter group that was high in structure, whereas the other half of the low-internal clients participated in low-structure groups. The same procedure was followed with the high-internal locus of control clients. Results showed that there was indeed an interaction between client personality and treatment structure. Specifically, clients who were high in locus of control fared best in the unstructured group, whereas lows were best served in the structured group.

Constructive Strategy. Another way of enhancing therapy has been operationalized through the use of so-called construction strategies. These research designs ask: "Does adding a new component to an existing package enhance the effect of the existing treatment?" Notice that this is the opposite of the dismantling strategy and a rigorous test of the added component, because the existing treatment is known to already have positive effects. For example, Greenberg, Scott, Pisa, and Friesen (1975) compared the effects of a reinforcement program alone versus the effects of this program plus milieu therapy on the adjustment of institutionalized inpatients. Both groups received the reinforcement counseling aimed at the in-hospital adaptive behaviors of the patients. One of the groups also received small group discussion and decision-making tasks related to the patients' own treatment. The results favored the combined treatment on a number of out-of-hospital measures such as days out of the hospital, and number of days at work in the community.

This strategy is also well illustrated in research on modeling conducted by Bandura (Rosenthal & Bandura, 1978) and his associates. They have reported that modeling is enhanced when the client not only observes the model but also engages in the behavior to be modeled during treatment. The careful application of the construction approach can lead to an empirically based therapy and could provide a useful design in future outcome research. If every counselor who invented a new therapy only advocated it after it was shown *in research* to add to client outcome beyond those gains already achieved by an existing approach, the current trend for new therapies to be widely (wildly) advocated would be greatly reduced.

Other Strategies. The remaining issues addressed by Class III questions involve modifying the basic treatment parameters. In contrast to the constructive approach, which adds a *qualitatively* different component to treatment, these questions fine tune a treatment by adjusting *quantity.* Through experiments that test the effects of increasing the number of sessions, their spacing, frequency or duration, the counseling can be made more cost effective, efficient or generally applicable.

Counseling outcome research has addressed and is addressing a myriad of other questions that bear directly on the quality of services offered clients and on theory development. Both practical applications and questions of theoretical importance are fundamental in counseling outcome research. We have touched on important questions and some of the more important conclusions that can be drawn from the hundreds of studies that have been undertaken.

Great strides have been made in the research methods employed in outcome research. The astute reader will notice the trend toward greater sophistication in not only the design of studies but in the complexity of the questions that are appropriate to ask and answer.

The unique contribution of outcome research to the psychotherapeutic endeavor is that well-controlled experiments help to rule out competing variables that might explain a particular phenomenon. Although an experiment cannot rule out all possible explanations it can rule out some. Causality cannot be absolutely attained but the more alternative explanations (variables) that are ruled out the more plausible it is the results are due to the theoretically hypothesized variable. One can see in the literature already reviewed that counseling research has been aimed at reducing the probability that outcomes are due to certain variables such as spontaneous remission and placebo effects.

In the following section we discuss outcome research methodology and design. This would enable the student to grasp the advantages and limitations of different methods and designs as applied to current research. As we pursue this discussion it becomes clear that there are as many paradoxes in outcome research as there are paradoxes in counseling. Although it is easy to design elegant studies on paper, the execution of such studies is always difficult. Practical considerations rather than scientific needs often require alterations in the best designs, and even the best design for a specific question, coupled with millions of dollars, may not result in satisfactory findings. All outcome research is highly imperfect. But the accumulation of evidence provided by hundreds of outcome studies is slowly providing both needed information and new questions. What then are the methods and designs that are used to provide an empirical base for our professional helping endeavors?

METHODS, DESIGNS, AND ISSUES

The most popular and meaningful conceptual scheme for understanding outcome was developed in educational research investigating the effects of teaching interventions on student knowledge. Campbell and Stanley (1963) suggested two broad categories that were of great importance in outcome research—the *internal* and *external validity* of studies. They suggested that the internal validity of a study was the degree to which it eliminated competing, plausible hypotheses to account for the causal relations between treatment and outcome. Thus, a study with high-internal validity had few competing hypotheses, whereas those with low-internal validity had many. External validity on the other hand has to do with the generalizability of a study's findings. Threats to external validity reduce the reasonableness with which we can generalize the results of a study to other (external) situations, settings, clients, and counselors. These distinct categories can be used to analyze the strengths and weaknesses of a study—the boundaries within which the results of a study may be understood.

These authors suggested several common threats to both the external and internal validity of the most common research designs employed in educational research but they apply equally well to outcome research in counseling. The threats (factors other than the independent variable that could explain results) to internal validity are as follows: history, maturation, testing, instrumentation, statistical regression, attrition, and selection. The threats to external validity are as follows: reactivity of outcome measurement, pretest sensitization, posttest sensitization, generalization across outcome measures, reactivity to experimental arrangements, multiple-treatment interference, novelty effects, combination of selection and treatment, combination of experimental setting and treatment, combination of history and treatment, and time of measurement and treatment effects. Understanding these threats is critical to understanding and conducting experiments.

In order to increase understanding, without replicating the work of Campbell and Stanley (1963) and Cook and Campbell (1976), we have placed the threats to validity in table form. Tables 3.2 and 3.3 provide definitions for these terms, and concrete examples that hopefully make clear the way in which these factors, when not controlled, can weaken confidence in the research findings.

As Table 3.1 suggests the questions, and therefore designs, employed in outcome research have varied over time, in response to weaknesses in the earlier designs as well as to the findings of that research. Before providing a more formal presentation of the important components of research designs, it is enlightening to label and discuss the commonly used designs in counseling research and discuss their strengths and limitations. Within the history of outcome research two research designs have been most commonly used: the one-group pretest–posttest design and the pretest–posttest control group design.

The earliest studies employed in counseling research in Table 3.1 utilized pre-experimental designs such as the one-group pretest–posttest design. In this type of study, one group of subjects is administered a test before and

TABLE 3.2
Threats to Internal Invalidity as Related to Counseling/Therapy
Outcome Research

Source	Definition	Example
History	Events other than therapy (i.e., the independent variable) that are common to clients during the same time period.	Clients start therapy in an inpatient setting where they receive "therapy" from a nurse as well as the counseling intervention.
Imitation of treatment (a special case of history)	The treatment given to one group may be inadvertently provided to some subjects in the control group.	Unknown to the investigator, the treatment to be tested was routinely provided to clients at a different institution who were serving as the control group.
Maturation	Changes over time due to processes within the subjects.	As children mature they become more able to understand another's perspective and therefore are more capable of problem solving in social situations. Thus treatment to improve social skills may be affected by maturation factors.
Testing	Taking a test one time (e.g., pretest) may affect performance on the test at a later time (e.g., posttest).	Clients improve on the Beck Depression Inventory from pre- to posttest because they have become sensitized to the fact that depression is being measured and therefore respond in a way depicting more healthy functioning.
Instrumentation	Change in the measuring instrument or measuring procedure.	Raters judging indicators of speech anxiety gradually "drift" in their ratings (i.e., their criteria for rating anxiety gradually change over time).
Statistical regression	Tendency for extreme scores (high or low) to revert toward the mean when the measure is readministered.	A client who scores extremely high on the MMPI is more likely to score lower on a second administration since, with an extremely high score, further increases are difficult to obtain.
Selection biases	Different methods of selecting subjects for the therapy and control or comparison groups.	Subjects are assigned to a wait-list control because it appears that they can wait for treatment (and therefore their case is not as severe as those who enter therapy/treatment).
Mortality/Attrition	Differential loss of subjects from the comparison groups over time.	Patients assigned to a drug therapy comparison group drop out more quickly than those assigned to a cognitive treatment group.
Combination of selection and history (or maturation)	When groups are not formed through random assignment it is possible that selection will lead to combinations of threats. This is particularly a problem in studies using groups already formed prior to the onset of the study.	In a study of relaxation interventions, local members of a meditation club are compared with persons trained in progressive muscle relaxation who are not meditators.

TABLE 3.3

Threats to External Validity as Related to Counseling/Therapy
Outcome Research

Source	Definition	Example
Pretest sensitization	The pretest may sensitize clients so that they are affected differently by treatment than would be clients who do not take a pretest.	Clients taking the Irrational Beliefs Test prior to receiving rational–emotive therapy may respond better to the therapy because of the pretest.
Reactivity of outcome assessment	Clients who are aware that their behavior is being assessed may respond differently as a result. This is a particular problem when "reactive" (e.g., relatively obvious paper–pencil) measures are used.	Clients aware that depression is being assessed may respond on the depression inventory with decreased sypmtomatology whereas their behavior and affect remain unchanged.
Reactivity of experimental arrangements	Clients may change due to a reaction to the knowledge that they are participating in an experiment.	In an evaluation of the effectiveness of an outpatient clinic, results are found to differ depending on whether the clients know that they are in an experiment.
Multiple-treatment interference	When several types of intervention are used for the treatment of a client, any one given intervention cannot be evaluated.	In an intervention of muscle relaxation treatment for Type A behavior, clients are first taught various cognitive strategies to reduce tension and are then taught relaxation. The effects of relaxation may be influenced by the prior exposure to cognitive strategies.
Interaction of selection and treatment	If clients selected are differentially responsive (or unresponsive) to treatment, as compared to those unselected, then results based on these subjects cannot be generalized to the rest of the population.	College students who are well-functioning but score high on a test of social anxiety are used as subjects in a trial of counseling to treat social phobia. The student results may not relevant to actual phobic patients.
Interaction of setting and treatment	Findings may be restricted to a particular setting or situation.	A counseling outcome study conducted in a university clinic may not be generalizable to other outpatient clinics due to differences in the settings.
Interaction of history and treatment	Findings obtained at one particular point in time may not be generalizable to another point in time.	If a new treatment has received widespread acclaim in the popular media then patients who are treated with it at that particular time may respond more favorably than those treated at a later date when the publicity has subsided.
Time of measurement and treatment effects	The results of a treatment may depend on when the assessment is conducted.	Results of an intervention designed to increase compliance with cardiac rehabilitation programs show no differences at 3 months; however, at 1 year substantial differences between treated and nontreated groups are evident.

after being treated. Although this type of study was popular in the 1930s, 1940s, and 1950s it had a serious flaw, namely it could rule out few threats to internal validity. In fact Eysenck's (1952) major criticism of this research design took exactly this tack—he gave very plausible reasons for patient change other than the effect of therapy—namely, that maturation and history factors (spontaneous remission) could easily, and probably did, account for the results that had been attributed to counseling. The response of later researchers to these threats to internal validity was to add control groups to experiments so that these factors could be ruled out.

Many of the Class II and III questions (e.g., therapeutic ingredients, comparison, process/outcome, dismantling, and enhancement) were addressed, therefore, with designs such as the pretest–posttest control group that included a no-treatment control group in which "spontaneous changes" (history and maturation effects) could be studied and contrasted with the experimental group. In this design subjects are randomly assigned to groups. Both groups receive a pretest and a posttest, but only the experimental group is treated. Counseling outcome studies utilizing this design represent truly experimental research methods. Numerous other experimental (e.g., Solomon Four Group, Posttest-Only Control Group) and quasi-experimental (e.g., Time Series, Separate-Sample Pretest–Posttest) designs are available but are used much less often. (For examples and additional information please refer to Campbell & Stanley, 1963.)

Selection bias and differential attrition are serious sources of threat to counseling outcome research. Obviously, the effect of an independent variable cannot be unambiguously assessed if some systematic difference exists between the clients based on their selection or assignment to treatment. Researchers are, of course, well aware of this problem, but practical and ethical demands occasionally require that clients not be randomly assigned to treatment. When this is the case either the research remains seriously flawed or alternative designs have to be considered. In the case of Rogers and Dymond (1954) the researchers were able to examine changes in the wait-list group after the wait-list period as well as after their counseling experience. In this way clients served as their own control. The researchers, by virtue of their design, were able to overcome some of the problems of the initial group assignment.

Subject selection is emphasized here because it is one of the more difficult problems facing outcome researchers working in applied settings. Ensuring the initial similarity of subjects for between-group comparisons is crucial if the researcher is interested in attributing later differences between groups to the experimental intervention. The attrition (or loss of subjects) from a group is another way in which the conclusions of a study are often confounded. This can be a problem in wait-list designs, where clients often leave studies and seek treatment in another setting. It is also a problem in some treatment groups (especially drug studies) where the treatments have side effects that the client does not wish to tolerate. This is an obvious problem in long-term follow-up of clients and in counseling approaches that are long term. The clients who remain to take the final assessment may be a highly select portion of those who began the study.

MEANING VERSUS RIGOR:
A PARADOX IN (OUTCOME) RESEARCH

Outcome research must be concerned with both internal and external validity if it is to have an impact on clinical practice. Internal validity is a logical precursor to concerns with external validity. If the results of an experiment cannot be unambiguously interpreted there is no reason to worry about the extent to which they can be generalized across situations, clients, and counselors. A well-designed study that exercises considerable control over important variables maximizes internal validity and reduces the tentativeness with which conclusions can be stated. Such an experiment requires rigor. To the extent possible it calls for uniformity in outcome research. The most rigorous studies are those that might be most sensitive to the relationship between the independent and dependent variables. The more a study holds all conditions constant except for the independent variable the more likely a treatment effect will be detected. This requires that the client sample be as homogeneous as possible—if the study is of depression, then only carefully diagnosed cases are included and many people who are depressed but have other disorders may not be studied. Those who are studied would also be similar in age, social class, intelligence, and so forth.

Likewise, the therapists would also be as homogeneous as possible, similar in age, orientation, training, commitment, experience, and other demographic variables. The treatment would be well defined and possibly offered in just the same manner by all therapists who might use a treatment manual with ongoing supervision that acts to make sure the skill level and conformance to the manual is maintained. The more variability in how or what is offered the more difficult to find an effect.

In such a rigorous experiment, which maximizes the likelihood of discovering the relationship between treatment and outcome, there may be little resemblance to the realities of the clinical world. The clients with whom we work are not a specialized, highly selected subset of depressed persons. We, the counselors may or may not be experienced, committed, supervised, well trained, or indoctrinated into the school-based therapy to be applied. The treatment offered may not be as "pure" as it was in the experiment. Who can afford a supervisor to view every case and provide immediate feedback regarding competence and conformance? So the question naturally arises:

Can these rather certain findings that come from the most rigorous studies apply in the real world of clinical practice?

This contrast is even clearer when one tries to generalize the findings of "analogue" research that often has considerable internal validity. This research sets up an analogy to applied research by studying nonclients, in brief therapy-like situations. For example, Cash, Begley, McCown, and Weise (1975) wanted to understand the impact of therapist "attractiveness" on clients' evaluations of the helpfulness of counselors. They asked college students (not clients) to watch a videotape of a counselor describing himself (education, beliefs, etc). For half the students, the counselor was cosmetically altered to be physically attractive, for the other half, the counselor was presented as unattractive. Two control groups of students heard the same descriptions on audiotape but did not see the counselor. When he was physically attractive, the counselor was rated as significantly more intelligent, friendly, assertive, trustworthy, competent, and more likely to produce a positive outcome than when he was less attractive. No difference was found in those who listened to audiotape presentations. This study may have theoretical implications for factors affecting client evaluations of counselors and, potentially, counseling outcome. However, this study has unknown applications to the actual counseling process since neither clients nor counseling were actually studied (Strong, 1971).

Kazdin (1980) illustrated the same paradox between experimental precision and generalizability (meaning) by contrasting two "classic" comparative outcome studies that analyzed counseling and behavior therapy. Paul (1966) was contrasted with Sloane et al. (1975). They gave different priorities to experimental control and generality. A comparison of these studies could be made on numerous dimensions but to simplify only the procedures related to clients, therapies, and counselors are considered here.

Briefly, Sloane et al. (1975) compared behavior therapy and psychotherapy on self-referred patients at an outpatient clinic. Clients (age 18 to 45) were carefully screened but represented persons who had a range of neurotic or personality disorders. These patients were assigned randomly to either of the two therapies or to a wait-list control group. They received counseling from either a (one of five) highly experienced and committed behavior therapist or a dynamically oriented psychotherapist (one of five). Treatment lasted for 4 months on a 1-hour per week basis. The treatments were defined by general definitions agreed to by the counselors, but no attempt was made to standardize either treatment.

In contrast, Paul (1966) was interested in comparing the effects of systematic desensitization and counseling on anxiety. He used college student subjects (age 18 to 24) who were recruited from public speaking courses and who were screened and found to have public speaking anxiety. Those who agreed to participate were randomly assigned to a systematic desensitization group or to group psychotherapy, or to one of several different control groups. Treatments were offered by experienced professionals who administered *each* of the treatments. The treatments were offered for five sessions to each subject. For desensitization a manual and training were provided, detailing the steps to be followed. Counselors did not have a manual for psychotherapy, but had considerable experience with "insight" oriented treatment. In this case "insight-oriented therapy" focused on helping the subjects understand their public speaking anxiety.

As Kazdin (1980) pointed out, a number of features of the Sloane et al. study contribute to error variance: Patients who have heterogeneous problems won't change as uniformly as those with a homogeneous problem; counselors delivering relatively loosely defined treatments will not have as uniform an effect as those delivering a more clearly defined and limited treatment; and having different counselors offering different treatments adds more variability than Paul's use of the same therapists to offer both treatments. Considering these three factors, the Paul study was more rigorous and a more powerful test of treatment outcome differences than the Sloane et al. study. In gaining this greater control, however, many of the conditions in Paul's study limit its meaning for clinical practice. Gelso (1979) accurately captured the essence of the internal versus external validity issue by coining the term "bubble hypothesis." Designing a counseling-outcome study is like trying to eliminate the evasive bubble that appears under a sticker placed on the windshield of a car. When you push in one direction, the bubble consistently reappears in another. Similarly, when emphasizing internal validity, external validity is compromised and vice versa. "The *bubble hypothesis* underscores the fact that all experiments are highly imperfect" (Gelso, 1979, p. 12).

The solution to this paradox is to pursue research that emphasizes both meaning and rigor. In other words, research aimed at establishing a causal relationship between a treatment and outcome must give priority to studies that exercise considerable control over as many variables as possible (internal validity). Whereas research aimed at having generalizations to applied counseling settings must give priority to studies in which experimental conditions closely resemble those of actual counseling practice (external validity).

ISSUES IN MEASURING CHANGE–OUTCOME MEASUREMENT: A HARDY PERENNIAL

Advancements in our knowledge of how to facilitate behavior changes in those seeking treatment are dependent on our ability to assess the effects of treatment. Luborsky (1971) affectionately referred to problems in this area of outcome research as "hardy perennials" in the field. Historically, researchers have repeatedly turned their attention to problems and issues in selecting and employing measures of counseling outcome. We deal here mainly with three important issues that impinge on methodology in counseling outcome: the nature of change, selection of outcome measures, and statistical versus clinical significance.

The Nature of Change

Although measurement and quantification are central properties of empirical science, the earliest attempts at quantifying treatment gains lacked scientific rigor. The field has gradually moved from complete reliance on therapist ratings of improvement to the use of data from a variety of sources including therapist, patient, outside observers, objective rating, relatives, work mates, physiological measures, and environmental data such as employment and educational records. Attempts at measuring change frequently reflect current, fashionable theoretical positions. Early studies relied on devices developed out of Freudian dynamic psychology. Such devices (e.g., Rorschach, TAT, etc.) have been largely discarded because of their poor psychometric qualities, reliance on inference, and the fact that they mainly reflect the interest of orientations that emphasize unconscious processes. The use of these measures was followed by the use of devices consistent with client-centered theory (e.g., Q-Sort technique), behaviorism, and more recently cognitive theories. But, by and large, theoretically based devices are less prevalent than atheoretical measures of symptomatic states, or the direct observation of behavior in relevant and important areas of personal and social functioning.

Despite improvements in measuring outcome there is clearly a lack of organization and direction in current practices and procedures. Like counseling itself, counseling-outcome measurement sometimes appears to be in a state of chaos. In a recent review of contemporary research studies, current instruments and procedures for measuring counseling outcome were surveyed (Froyd & Lambert, 1989; Ogles & Lambert, 1989). We were startled to discover the seemingly endless number of measures used. In our first review, 348 studies published in 20 selected journals between 1983 and 1989 were examined. We found 1,430 outcome measures. Of this rather large number, 840 different measures were used! This review considered a wide variety of patient diagnoses, treatment modalities, and therapy types (Froyd & Lambert, 1989). In our second review we examined studies of agoraphobia outcome published during the 1980s (Ogles, Lambert, Weight, & Payne, 1990). We located 106 studies that used no less than 98 unique outcome measures. This occurred in a well-defined, limited disorder, treated with an equally narrow range of interventions, mainly behavioral and cognitive/behavioral therapies. The proliferation of outcome measures (a sizable portion of which were unstandardized scales) is overwhelming.

This seeming disarray of instruments is partly a function of the complex and multifaceted nature of counseling outcome as reflected in the divergence in clients and their problems, treatments and their underlying assumptions and techniques, as well as the multidimensionality of the change process itself. It has proved far too simplistic to expect clients to show consistent and integrated improvement as a result of therapy. As Lambert et al. (1986) suggested "divergent processes are occurring in therapeutic change; that people themselves embody divergent dimensions or phenomena, and that divergent methods of criterion measurement must be used to match the divergency in human beings and in the change process that occurs within them" (p. 188). Nevertheless, the lack of consistency in measuring even the most common problems is disheartening.

Several researchers have tried to bring some order into the complexity and chaos now rampant in the matter of conceptualizing outcome assessment. Strupp and Hadley (1977) have noted that there are different perspectives that are relevant to evaluating treatment outcome based on their impression of what constitutes mental health: the patient, society, and mental health professionals. The patient is primarily concerned with subjective discomfort and relief. Society is primarily concerned with the client's role in the community (employment, socialization, criminal behavior, and the like). Mental health professionals on the other hand have idealized theoretical notions about health and adjustment (e.g., autonomy, negative cognition, Oedipal complex, etc.). Each perspective reflects different standards and values and ultimately, of course, is assessed through different measures of outcome. Conclusions about the effects of counseling may depend heavily on the perspective that is assessed.

Past research has suggested that the picture we get of the effects of counseling not only depends on the efficacy of treatments but also on the way in which treatments are measured. Figure 3.1 presents a conceptual scheme that emphasizes three broad ways in which we can classify outcome measures. This scheme was developed because outcome seems to depend on the targets of treatment, the way in which data are collected, and the source that provides the data. This scheme could be used to evaluate past research practices or to direct future research. The student can use the scheme to conceptualize the limitations of a proposed or existing study by listing measures according to the *content* they assess, the methods or *technology* of the measuring instrument, and the *source* of ratings. Each category suggests a hierarchy of interests.

Content. This category refers to differences among instruments in terms of the domain or topical area they attempt to assess. Some instruments are developed to assess outcome that is primarily personal (intrapersonal) such as psychopathology, mood, self-concept, self-control, negative cognitions, behavioral deficits, and so forth. Next in the hierarchy are measures of inter-

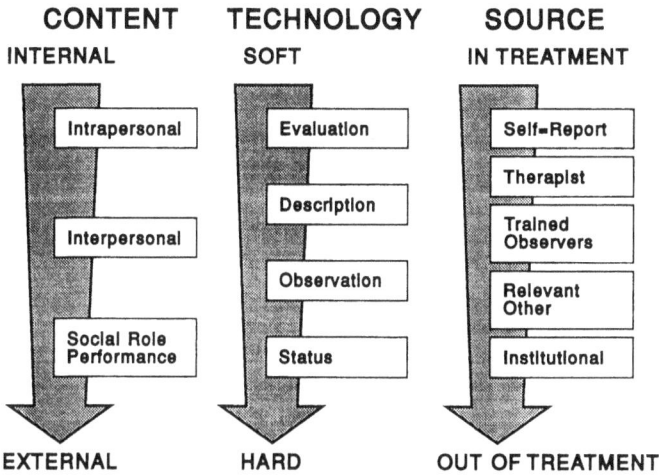

FIG. 3.1. Critical dimensions of assessment tools.

personal functioning that reflect the client's adjustment to intimacy and friendship. Measures in this area would include marital adjustment scales, sexual performance, and aspects of social adjustment rating scales. Completing the hierarchy are measures that tap clients' adjustment to their social role performance with society at large. Measures in this area might include adjustment at work, in school, delinquency, and the like.

Technology. The technology hierarchy varies along a dimension of rigor and reactivity, roughly speaking it is a "soft"–"hard" dimension. Evaluation is the least rigorous and usually consists of asking the client or therapist to give a gross rating of improvement after treatment. Satisfaction (with treatment) is the simple dimension usually tapped. Descriptive data involve actual specification of changes. Typical of this technology would be the Symptom Checklist 90-R or the Beck Depression Inventory in which the client must rate the presence, absence, or intensity/frequency of specific symptoms during a specified time period. Changes are then assessed by comparing pre- and posttreatment levels of symptomatology. Observational data require a technology that usually involves outside ratings obtained through actual observation of specific behaviors. Several types of observational data can be obtained. For example, clients can be observed before and after treatment attempting to approach a feared stimulus. Status data, the bottom of this hierarchy, include measures such as weight, biofeedback, blood levels of drugs, and serve perhaps as the most "disinterested" form of inquiry.

Source. The source of outcome ratings has been ordered along a hierarchy of participation in treatment, beginning with self-reports by the client, followed by counselor ratings. Both these people were at the center of the treatment process. Ratings made by these sources are followed by trained observers who are either part of the process or who have been given specific targets to rate that are highly relevant to the treatment process. Trained observer ratings are followed by ratings made by relevant others (such as spouse, friend, work mate, fellow group member) who enter the rating task usually with an agenda that is quite different from the client, therapist, or trained observers. Finally, institutional data are obtained by sources completely extraneous to the treatment process, such as the use of public records in studies of alcohol and drug addiction.

It is hoped that the use of this scheme by the reader may help in organizing the measurement of change in counseling research. It is important to note that great care should be exercised in assuming which measurement sources, technologies, and content areas are best for reflecting client change. All have their strengths, weaknesses, and limitations (Lambert, Christensen, & DeJulio, 1983). But studies can be examined to see if the conclusions drawn are based solely on self-reports, the use of evaluative technology, and only intrapersonal content or whether conclusions are based on a broader sampling of contents, technologies, and sources. Froyd and Lambert's (1989) review of measurement practices suggests that the typical study published in major journals over the past 5 years included 3.5 measures that most often focused on intrapersonal content, descriptive technology, and self-report ratings.

Selection of Outcome Measures

Beyond the conceptual scheme and its implications for selecting outcome measures for a specific study there are a number of other important issues to be considered in selecting measures.

Individualized Measures Versus Standardized Measures. In assessing changes in groups of clients, it is common for researchers to use a standardized scale (such as the MMPI) or a single criterion with all patients in treatment regardless of their unique characteristics and problems. The possibility of tailoring change criteria to each individual in counseling was mentioned frequently in the 1970s and the idea offers intriguing alternatives for resolving several recalcitrant dilemmas in measuring change. An example of such a method for individualizing goals that has received widespread attention and increased use is Goal Attainment Scaling (Kiresuk & Sherman, 1968).

Goal Attainment Scaling requires that a number of mental health goals be set up prior to treatment. These goals are formulated by an individual or a combination of clinician, client, and staff assigned to the task. For each goal specified, a scale with a graded series of likely outcomes, ranging from least to most favorable, is devised. These goals are (presumably) formulated and specified with sufficient precision that an independent observer can determine the point at which the patient is functioning at any given time. The procedure also allows for transformation of the overall attainment of specific goals into a standardized score.

In using this procedure with clients in a weight loss treatment, for example, one goal could be the specification of amount of weight loss desired. A second goal could be a reduction of depressive symptoms as measured by a standardized scale such as the MMPI. The particular scale examined could vary from client to client, as another group member may not be depressed but show very high levels of anxiety. Additional goals are included as they are identified as important to each unique client. Thus, Goal Attainment Scaling and other individualized methods such as the Battle Target Complaints (Battle et al., 1966) may make outcome measurement more precise and test the effects on the actual goals of clients rather than ignoring individual differences (as is often done when change in all clients is assessed on the same scale).

Unfortunately there are many problems with individualization of goals. Questions have been raised about their reliability and validity (Calsyn & Davidson, 1978) and the influence of clients and counselors on setting too easy or too difficult goals. To a large degree they are subjective and rely heavily on the expectations of the participants rather than the symptoms themselves. The units of change derived from individually tailored goals are unequal (within and across studies) and are therefore difficult to compare. Finally, goals often change during the process of counseling, especially in early sessions, which makes their assessment difficult. Thus, the advantages of individualizing treatment goals remain more of an ideal than a reality. Depending on the research question, and especially the heterogeneity of the clients studied, individualized outcome measures could be recommended for further study, especially when used in conjunction with other outcome measures.

The Need for Integration.   With seemingly limitless options for measuring outcome the researcher should give careful consideration to the need for integration of the results of a study with the existing literature. There is a fine line between the need for creativity and freedom to create new measures and the need to use already existing and commonly employed measures. The possibility is that the new measure will fail to make a contribution to the field. So without discouraging diversity it is important to the field (and the welfare of clients) to take precautions to insure that a study builds on past research by using measures that have a history within the discipline. For example, although Ogles et al. (1990) found 98 measures used to measure change in agoraphobia, there was also some consensus across the 106 studies published in the 1980s. The Fear Questionnaire (Marks & Matthews, 1979) was used in 39% of the studies. Future outcome studies of agoraphobia treatment that fail to use this device as one of their outcome measures will fail to some degree to contribute to the growing knowledge in this area. By using the Fear Questionnaire researchers allow important comparisons to be made across treatments, treatment settings, and cultures.

Many such examples could be given and the point is worth making: The single study of counseling outcome will *never*, by itself, make a substantial contribution to knowledge on treatment effects (remember the bubble hypothesis?). It is the integration of results from many studies that produces sound, robust, conclusions for practice. Students who contemplate outcome research are encouraged to become familiar with past research on their topic, and to consider frequently used outcome measures for their own study, not to the exclusion of other measures, but as the core of their measurement efforts.

This suggestion raises the question of the advantages of a *core battery* for use in outcome assessment. In fact, the development of such a battery was sponsored by the National Institute of Mental Health and published by Waskow and Parloff (1975). The core battery that was recommended included many of the perspectives and criteria already mentioned. Nevertheless, the core battery was not adopted by the field and has seldom been employed in outcome studies. A major problem with the concept of a core battery is the great diversity in clients and the nature of their problems. With the growing emphasis on studying specific interventions with specific disorders a broad spectrum battery hardly seems appropriate. Lambert (1979) called for the development of several core batteries that would be specific to client problem areas or treatment goals. Such batteries could be limited to broad areas such as anxiety disorders, depression, and the like. These core batteries could also be limited enough so that individual researchers could add experimental devices without over taxing the client's goodwill. Undoubtedly there will be disagreement about the best instruments to include in each battery, but if some minimal consensus could be reached, the advancement of knowledge could be markedly accelerated.

Statistical Versus Clinical Significance

The data acquired in counseling outcome studies are submitted to statistical tests of significance. Group means are compared, the within-group and between-group variability are considered, and the resulting numerical figure is compared with a pre-set critical value. When the magnitude of the distance between groups is sufficiently large it is agreed that the results are not likely to be the result of chance fluctuations in sampling, thus statistical significance has been demonstrated. This is the standard for most research and is a necessary part of the scientific process. A common criticism of counseling research, however, is that the results of studies, as they are typically reported in terms of statistical significance, obscure both the clinical relevance of the findings and the impact of the treatment on specific individuals. Unfortunately, statistically significant improvements do not necessarily equal practically important improvements for the individual client.

Clinical significance refers to the meaningfulness of the magnitude of change. It is conceivable that in a well-designed study small differences between groups after treatment could produce findings that reach statistical significance, whereas the real-life difference between clients is trivial in terms of the reduction of painful symptoms. For example, a behavioral method of treatment for obesity may create a statistically significant difference between treated and untreated groups if all treated subjects lost 10 pounds and all untreated subjects lost 5 pounds. However, the clinical utility of an extra 5-pound weight loss is debatable, especially in the clinically obese client. It is this phenomenon that clinical significance addresses—to what extent does an intervention produce changes that truly affect the quality of life the person is living? In the earliest studies of counseling outcome, clients were categorized with gross ratings of "improved," "cured," and the like, implying meaningful change. The lack of precision in such ratings resulted in their waning use (Lambert, 1983).

The most promising alternative presently in use (although only beginning to be used) is *normative comparison.* This method has the advantage of precise operationalization of clinical significance and promises to be both replicable and well defined. With some disorders, this type of criterion is commonly used in the form of well-defined conventions for improvement. Examples include the use of abstinence rates in alcohol and drug abuse studies; the use of definitions of adequate sexual performance (e.g., ratio of orgasms to attempts at sex, or as time to orgasm following penetration, Sabalis, 1983). These criteria are based on data about the normative functioning of individuals and can be easily and meaningfully applied with a number of disorders where normal or ideal functioning is readily apparent and measured (e.g., obesity).

In the same way conventions defining improvement can be developed for almost all the disorders that are commonly treated. Such conventions can be based on the psychological tests that are commonly used to measure outcome, if they are standardized measures or have a database with which to compare treated subjects. Normative comparison requires the presentation of normative data long with data for clients in the treatment and control groups. Standards of clinical improvement can be based on normative data and posttreatment status instead of (or in addition to) the magnitude of change as reflected in statistical tests.

For example, Jacobson, Follette, and Revenstorf (1984) in their studies of behavioral marital counseling, developed cutoff scores based on normative data of functional and dysfunctional couples who had taken the Locke–Wallace Marital Adjustment Inventory. They have also proposed a "reliable change index" as a standard method for determining whether an individual's treatment gains reliably exceed measurement error.

These same procedures were applied to the Symptom Check List 90-R (Derogotis, 1983) by Tingey, Burlingame, and Lambert (in press). The Symptom Check List was chosen because it is a frequently applied psychotherapy outcome measure that taps a variety of frequently encountered complaints including depression and anxiety. Figure 3.2 presents a graph of the General Symptom Index (GSI; total symptom score) for the purpose of demonstrating how cutoff scores on the SCL-90R can be used to define clinically significant change.

Plotted points (A and B) would indicate subject A's and subject B's pre- and posttreatment GSI score; pretreatment along the horizontal axis and posttreatment along the vertical. The continuous diagonal line signifies no change between pre- and posttreatment scores; a subject receiving identical pre- and posttreatment scores would fall on this line. The area above this line denotes an increase in the GSI score from pretreatment indicating greater symptomology (Subject A); whereas the area below denotes a decrease and less symptomology (Subject B).

The three horizontal lines signify the cutoff point between two adjacent samples' distributions, and are used in determining the clinical significance

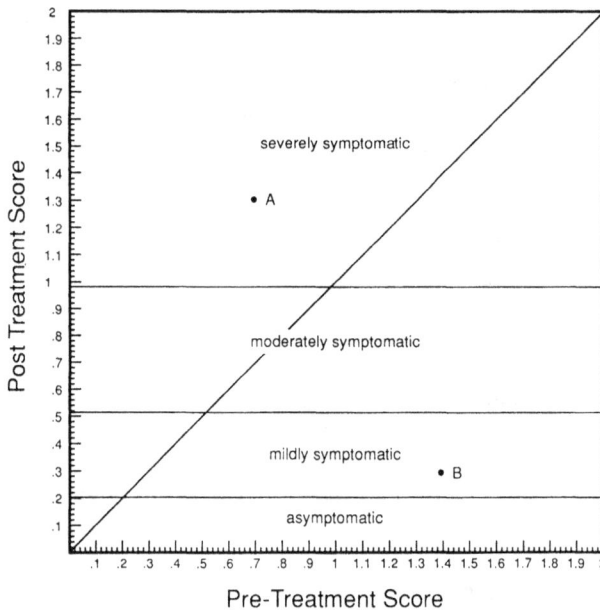

FIG. 3.2. Sample figure illustrating cutoffs (horizontal lines) between the normative samples (continuous diagonal line indicates points of no change between pre- and posttreatment scores).

of pre- to posttreatment change. The areas they separate indicate the four normative samples: asymptomatic, mildly, moderately, and severely symptomatic. A plotted point on the graph indicates a subject's placement (in reference to the normative samples) at posttreatment. Unless there is no change pre- to posttreatment, this point will fall some place other than on the diagonal line. By drawing an imaginary vertical line from this point to the no-change diagonal line, the subject's placement at pretreatment can be determined. For example, Subject A's posttreatment plotted point places him or her in the severely symptomatic sample and the vertical line drawn down from this point places him or her at pretreatment in the moderately symptomatic sample (it intersects the no-change line within this sample's area). This indicates, according to GSI scores, that during the course of counseling this subject deteriorated and moved from the moderately symptomatic to the severely symptomatic sample. Subject B, however, improved and moved from the severely symptomatic sample to the mildly symptomatic sample.

In order to produce Fig. 3.2, it was necessary to find normative data. These normative data for the severely symptomatic sample were found in existing literature on the SCL-90R as applied to inpatients (Derogotis, 1983), outpatients (Burlingame & Barlow, in press) and the original normative standardization sample collected by Derogotis (1983). The asymptomatic sample was collected for the purpose of identifying a group of subjects who were nominated and carefully screened to exclude persons who were not well adjusted (in contrast to the typical normative sample that is based on a random sample of persons, some of whom may evidence psychopathology).

Through these procedures the patient's status in relation to patients and nonpatients was carefully defined and could be observed along the dimension of mental health with severe pathology at one end and ideal mental health (being asymptomatic) at the other end.

Efforts such as this have not been carried out on many standardized measures, so that we are not yet able to use this procedure for defining clinical significance to any great degree. Also there are numerous questions about the procedures and their limitations (cf. Jacobson, 1988; Lambert et al., 1986). The focus on clinical significance promises to be an important aspect of psychotherapy outcome research—one that emphasizes the researchers' interest in producing results that are useful to the clinician, and the evolution of research questions beyond those of the last decade.

SUMMARY AND CONCLUSIONS

In this chapter, we have attempted to "tell the story" of counseling-outcome research. We noted that the assessment of therapeutic effectiveness is not simply of interest to "ivory-towered" researchers but rather is a necessary component to insure ethical practice.

The earliest investigations addressed the question: Is counseling effective? These studies were not sophisticated and due to their generally inadequate pre-experimental designs, left many questions unanswered. Soon researchers began correcting for these deficiencies by using pretest–posttest experimental designs in which subjects were randomly assigned to control and experimental groups. Correspondingly the principal question shifted to: What causes improvement? Studies using placebo controls, other therapy comparison groups, process/outcome measures, and dismantling strategies are characteristic of the attempts to respond to this question. As evidence began to accrue regarding the effectiveness of counseling and the effective ingredients in therapeutic techniques, researchers began to investigate a third question: How can counseling be made more effective? By using matching and constructive strategies efforts have been made to address this issue.

In telling this story the paradox of internal and external validity became evident. That is, the more precise and well-controlled is the study, the more likely it is that the conditions utilized do not resemble those found in the typical "real-world" counseling situation. Therefore, the findings of some of the most rigorous studies may not be generalizable to actual clinical practice. On the other hand, naturalistic procedures that more closely resemble the actual clinical situation often do not control conditions well enough to allow for valid inferences regarding the effects of the independent variables (usually treatment). Because no individual study can adequately address both of these concerns it is obvious that systematic investigations utilizing a variety of research designs are needed to allow for the development of a coherent and meaningful body of knowledge.

Fundamental to any science is accurate measurement. Although counseling-outcome studies have made improvements in this area, there is clearly a lack of direction and organization in current practices and procedures. The complex nature of the phenomenon (counseling) is partly to blame for this confusion. Several investigators have tried to bring order to the chaos and we have suggested three broad categories that may help to direct decisions regarding measurement issues. Additionally, the issue of individual versus standardized measurement was raised and it seems that while creativity and freedom must not be stifled, there is clearly a need for integration in this area. Finally, clinical versus statistical significance was discussed along with the promise of normative comparison procedures.

So what then can we conclude? First, counseling has been subjected to empirical study and has been found to have positive, lasting, and clinically meaningful effects on a variety of clients. Second, these effects surpass those of placebo treatments or pseudotherapies. Third, the effectiveness of different types of counseling appears to be more similar than might be expected. Fourth, more research needs to be conducted that uses valid and sensitive measures and that builds on existing findings in an integrative manner. Obviously this, in many cases, will necessitate the development of solid measurement instruments. Finally, more research needs to be conducted that will clarify the complex nature of the therapeutic endeavor and its impact on those it is intended to help.

REFERENCES

Abramowitz, C. V., Abramowitz, S. I., Roback, H. B., & Jackson, C. (1974). Differential effectiveness of directive and non-directive therapies as a function of client internal-external control. *Journal of Consulting and Clinical Psychology, 42,* 849–853.

American Psychological Association. (1981). Ethical principles of psychologists. *American Psychologist, 36,* 637–638.

Arbuckle, D. S., & Boy, A. V. (1961). Client-centered therapy in counseling students with behavior problems. *Journal of Counseling Psychology, 8,* 136–139.

Battle, C. C., Imber, S. D., Hoehn-Saric, R., Stone, A. R., Nash, E. H., & Frank, J. D. (1966). Target complaints as a criteria of improvement. *American Journal of Psychotherapy, 20,* 184–192.

Bergin, A. E. (1971). The evaluation of therapeutic outcomes. In A. E. Bergin & S. L. Garfield (Eds.), *Handbook of psychotherapy and behavior change* (pp. 217–270). New York: Wiley.

Bergin, A. E., & Lambert, M. J. (1978). The evaluation of therapeutic outcomes. In S. L. Garfield & A. E. Bergin (Eds.), *Handbook of psychotherapy and behavior change* (pp. 139–189). New York: Wiley.

Blanchard, E. G., Andrasik, F., Ahler, T. A., Teders, S. J., & O'Keefe, D. O. (1980). Migraine and tension headache: A meta-analytic review. *Behavior Therapy, 11,* 613–631.

Bloch, S., & Lambert, M. J. (1985). What price psychotherapy? A rejoinder. *British Journal of Psychiatry, 146,* 96–98.

Burlingame, G. M., & Barlow, S. H. (in press). Specific and non-specific factors in time-limited psychotherapy. *Journal of Counseling Psychology.*

Calsyn, R. J., & Davidson, W. S. (1978). Do we really want a program evaluation strategy based on individualized goals? A critique of goal attainment scaling. *Evaluation Studies: Review Annual, 1,* 700–713.

Campbell, D. T., & Stanley, J. C. (1963). *Experimental and quasi-experimental designs for research.* Chicago: Rand McNally.

Cash, T. F., Begley, P. J., McCown, D. A., & Weise, B. C. (1975). When counselors are heard but not seen: Initial impact of physical attractiveness. *Journal of Counseling Psychology, 22,* 273–279.

Cook, T. D., & Campbell, D. T. (1976). The design and conduct of quasi-experimental and true experiments in field settings. In M. D. Dunnette (Ed.), *Handbook of industrial and organizational psychology* (pp. 223–326). Chicago: Rand McNally.

Derogotis, L. R. (1983). SCL-90: *Administration, scoring & procedures manual for the revised version.* Baltimore: Clinical Psychometric Research.

DiLoreto, A. O. (1971). *Comparative psychotherapy: An experimental analysis.* Chicago: Aldine-Atherton.

Eysenck, H. J. (1952). The effects of psychotherapy: An evaluation. *Journal of Consulting Psychology, 16,* 319–324.

Fenichel, O. (1930). *Ten years of the Berlin Psychoanalytic Institute, 1920–1930.* Berlin: Berlin Psychoanalytic Institute.

Froyd, J., & Lambert, M. J. (1989, May). *A 5-year survey of outcome measures in psychotherapy research.* Poster presented to the Western Psychological Association, Reno, NE.

Gelso, C. J. (1979). Research in counseling: Methodological and professional issues. *Counseling Psychologist, 8,* 7–35.

Gottman, J., & Markman, H. J. (1978). Experimental designs in psychotherapy research. In S. L. Garfield & A. E. Bergin (Eds.), *Handbook of psychotherapy and behavior change* (pp. 23–62). New York: Wiley.

Greenberg, D. J., Scott, S. B., Pisa, A., & Friesen, D. D. (1975). Beyond the token economy: A comparison of two contingency programs. *Journal of Consulting and Clinical Psychology, 43,* 498–503.

Greenberg, L. S., & Pinsoff, W. M. (Eds.). (1986). *The Psychotherapeutic process: A research handbook.* New York: Guilford.

Jacobson, J. S., Follette, W. C., & Revenstorf, D. (1984). Psychotherapy outcome research: Methods for reporting variability and evaluating clinical significance. *Behavior Therapy, 15,* 336–352.

Jacobson, N. S. (Ed.). (1988). Special issue on clinical significance. *Behavioral Assessment, 10,* 120–230.

Kazdin, A. E. (1980). *Research design in clinical psychology.* New York: Harper & Row.

Kiesler, D. J. (1973). *The process of psychotherapy.* Chicago: Aldine.

Kiresuk, T. J., & Sherman, R. E. (1968). Goal attainment scaling: A general method for evaluating comprehensive community mental health programs. *Community Mental Health Journal, 4,* 443–452.

Kirtner, W. L., & Cartwright, D. S. (1958). Success and failure in client-centered therapy as a function of initial interview behavior. *Journal of Consulting Psychology, 22,* 329–333.

Lambert, M. J. (1979). *The effects of psychotherapy* (Vol. 1). Montreal, Quebec: Eden Press.

Lambert, M. J. (1983). Introduction to assessment of psychotherapy outcome: Historical perspective and current issues. In M. J. Lambert, E. R. Christensen, & S. S. DeJulio (Eds.), *The assessment of psychotherapy outcome* (pp. 3–32). New York: Wiley.

Lambert, M. J. (1989). The therapist's contribution to psychotherapy process and outcome. *Clinical Psychology Review, 9,* 469–485.

Lambert, M. J., Christensen, E. R., & DeJulio, S. S. (Eds.). (1983). *The assessment of psychotherapy outcome.* New York: Wiley.

Lambert, M. J., DeJulio, S. S., & Stein, D. M. (1978). Therapist interpersonal skills: Process, outcome, methodological considerations and recommendations for future research. *Psychological Bulletin, 85,* 467–489.

Lambert, M. J., Shapiro, D. A., & Bergin, A. E. (1986). The effectiveness of psychotherapy. In S. L. Garfield & A. E. Bergin (Eds.), *Handbook of psychotherapy and behavior change* (3rd ed., pp. 157–211). New York: Wiley.

Luborsky, L. (1971). Perennial mystery of poor agreement among criteria for psychotherapy outcome. *Journal of Consulting and Clinical Psychology, 37,* 316–319.

Luborsky, L., Singer, B., & Luborsky, L. (1975). Comparative outcome studies of psychotherapies. *Archives of General Psychiatry, 32,* 995–1008.

Marks, I. M., & Matthews, A. M. (1979). Brief standard self-rating for phobic patients. *Behavior Research and Therapy, 17,* 263–267.

McNair, D. M., Callahan, D. M., & Lorr, M. (1962). Therapist "type" and patient response to psychotherapy. *Journal of Consulting Psychology, 26,* 425–429.

Meltzoff, J., & Kornreich, M. (1970). *Research in psychotherapy.* New York: Atherton Press.

Miller, R. C., & Berman, J. S. (1983). The efficacy of cognitive behavior therapies: A quantitative review of the research evidence. *Psychological Bulletin, 94,* 39–53.

Ogles, B. M., & Lambert, M. J. (1989). A meta-analytic comparison of twelve agoraphobia outcome instruments. *Phobia Practice and Research Journal, 2,* 115–125.

Ogles, B. M., Lambert, M. J., Weight, D. G., & Payne, I. R. (1990). Agoraphobia Outcome Measurement: A review and meta-analysis. *Journal of Consulting & Clinical Psychology, 2,* 317–325.

Paul, G. L. (1966). *Insight versus desensitization in psychotherapy: An experiment in anxiety reduction.* Stanford, CA: University of Stanford Press.

Pilkonis, P. A., Imber, S. D., Lewis, P., & Rubinsky, P. (1984). A comparative outcome study of individual, group, and conjoint psychotherapy. *Archives of General Psychiatry, 44,* 431–437.

Prioleau, L., Murdock, M., & Brody, N. (1983). An analysis of psychotherapy versus placebo studies. *The Behavioral and Brain Sciences, 6,* 275–310.

Rehm, L. P. (1977). A self-control model of depression. *Behavior Therapy, 8,* 787–804.

Rehm, L. P., Kornblith, S. J., O'Hara, M. W., Lamparski, K. M., Roman, J. M., & Volkin, J. (1981). An evaluation of major components in a self-control behavior therapy program for depression. *Behavior Modification, 5,* 459–489.

Rogers, C. R., & Dymond, R. (1954). *Psychotherapy and personality change.* Chicago: University of Chicago Press.

Rosenthal, T. L., & Bandura, A. (1978). Psychological modeling: Theory and practice. In S. L. Garfield & A. E. Bergin (Eds.), *Handbook of psychotherapy and behavior change* (2nd ed., pp. 621–658). New York: Wiley.

Sabalis, R. F. (1983). Assessing outcome in patients with sexual dysfunctions and sexual deviations. In M. J. Lambert, E. R. Christensen, & S. S. DeJulio (Eds.), *The assessment of psychotherapy outcome* (pp. 205–262). New York: Wiley.

Shapiro, D. A., & Shapiro, K. (1982). Meta-analysis of comparative outcome studies: A replication and refinement. *Psychological Bulletin, 92,* 581–604.

Shepherd, M. (1984). What price psychotherapy? *British Medical Journal, 288,* 809–810.

Sloane, R. B., Staples, F. R., Cristol, A. H., Yorkston, N. J., & Whipple, K. (1975). *Psychotherapy versus behavior therapy.* Cambridge, MA: Harvard University Press.

Smith, M. L., Glass, G. V., & Miller, T. I. (1980). *The benefits of Psychotherapy.* Baltimore: Johns Hopkins University Press.

Strong, S. R. (1971). Experimental laboratory research in counseling. *Journal of Counseling Psychology, 18,* 106–110.

Strupp, H. H., & Hadley, S. W. (1977). A tripartite model of mental health and therapeutic outcome: With special reference to negative effects in psychotherapy. *American Psychologist, 32,* 187–196.

Tingey, R., Burlingame, G., & Lambert, M. J. (in press). Assessing clinical significance: Extensions and applications. *Psychotherapy Research.*

Truax, C. B., & Mitchell, K. M. (1971). Research on certain therapist interpersonal skills in relationship to process and outcome. In A. E. Bergin & S. L. Garfield (Eds.), *Handbook of psychotherapy and behavior change* (pp. 299–344). New York: Wiley.

Waskow, I. E., & Parloff, M. B. (1975). *Psychotherapy change measures* (DHEW Publication No. (ADM) 74-120). Washington, DC: U.S. Government Printing Office.

Whitehorn, J. C., & Betz, B. J. (1960). Further studies of the doctor as a crucial variable in the outcome of treatment with schizophrenic patients. *American Journal of Psychiatry, 117,* 215–223.

Wojciechowski, F. L. (1984). *Double-blind research in psychotherapy.* Netherlands: Swets & Zeitlinger.

4

ALMOST EVERYTHING YOU EVER WANTED TO KNOW ABOUT HOW TO DO PROCESS RESEARCH ON COUNSELING AND PSYCHOTHERAPY BUT DIDN'T KNOW WHO TO ASK

Clara E. Hill
University of Maryland

The purpose of this chapter is to define *process research* and discuss the steps involved in doing a process study. My emphasis is on how to develop process measures and how to select, train, and use judges to code data. This chapter is based on my experience in doing process research and in reviewing manuscripts on process research for publication.

The findings of process studies, per se, are not reviewed here, because they have been reviewed extensively elsewhere (Highlen & Hill, 1984; Hill, 1990; Luborsky, 1990; Marsden, 1965, 1971; Orlinsky & Howard, 1978, 1986; Pope, 1977). Methodological issues (e.g., use of coached clients, units, analogue vs. naturalistic designs, data-analytic strategies) that are covered in other reviews (Bordin et al., 1954; Gormally & Hill, 1974; Gottman & Markman, 1978; Greenberg & Pinsof, 1986; Hill, 1982; Kiesler, 1966, 1971, 1973) are covered only briefly. Although many of the guidelines apply to group and family research, most of the emphasis in the chapter is on individual counseling. Readers should check other sources for more specific information on other modalities (e.g., Fuhriman & Burlingame, 1990; Gurman, Kniskern, & Pinsof, 1986). The terms *counseling* and *psychotherapy*, as well as *counselor* and *therapist* are used interchangeably in this chapter.

WHAT IS PROCESS RESEARCH?

Definition of Process

Process research focuses on what happens in counseling and therapy sessions. Each of you undoubtedly tries to understand the counseling process.

When you are in a counseling session, you probably find yourself intrigued by many questions. What would happen if I touched the client? Have I harmed the client by my confrontation? How can I establish the therapeutic alliance? Why do different clients respond so differently to interpretations? What is the best timing of an interpretation? In process research, these are exactly the kinds of questions we seek to answer. We want to know what makes counseling work. We want to know how to help clients change and how we can be better counselors and therapists.

Hill (1982) and Highlen and Hill (1984) have listed several different types of behaviors within the process area. These behaviors, slightly revised, are listed here in the order of ascending levels of complexity. The initial types are observable, discrete, relatively easily operationalized behaviors, whereas the latter types involve abstract behaviors that occur over longer periods of time and require more inference of judgment. The seven types of behaviors are:

1. ancillary behaviors, such as speech disfluency (Mahl, 1963) and non-verbal behaviors (Hill, Siegelman, Gronsky, Sturniolo, & Fretz, 1981);

2. verbal behaviors, such as therapist response modes (e.g., Friedlander, 1982; Hill, 1986; Stiles, 1979) and client experiencing (Klein, Mathieu-Coughlan, & Kiesler, 1986);

3. covert behaviors, such as therapist intentions (e.g., to clarify, to promote change; Hill & O'Grady, 1985) and client reactions (e.g., feel educated, feel misunderstood; Elliott, 1985; Hill, Helms, Spiegel, & Tichenor, 1988);

4. content, such as Hall and Van de Castle's (1966) content analysis of dreams;

5. strategies, such as counselor use of the empty chair technique (Greenberg & Dompierre, 1981) or analysis of transference (Greenson, 1967) or client attempts to disconfirm pathogenic beliefs (Weiss & Sampson, 1986);

6. interpersonal manner, such as therapist empathy (Carkhuff, 1969) and client involvement (Gomes-Schwartz, 1978); and

7. the therapeutic relationship (which includes the working alliance, transference and countertransference, and the real relationship; Gelso & Carter, 1985), interpersonal transactions (Kiesler, 1988), and relational control (Friedlander, 1984).

Most of the existing process research has focused on the verbal behaviors of counselors and therapists. As an example, therapist-response modes refer to the grammatical structure of the therapist's verbal interventions, independent of the topic or content of the speech (Hill, 1982). Thus, in the latest version of my category system (Hill, 1985, 1986), there are 10 response modes: approval, information, direct guidance, closed question, open question, paraphrase, interpretation, confrontation, self-disclosure, and other. Less emphasis has been given to other behaviors within the list just outlined (Hill, 1990). Further, most research has been done on types of behaviors, with less emphasis on the quality of these behaviors (Schaffer, 1982).

Distinguishing Process From Other Variables

Process variables can be distinguished from input variables, extratherapy events, and outcome. These four sets of variables are intertwined and influence each other, but it is important to separate them for the purposes of research so that we can be clear about the impact of separate variables.

Input Variables. These are present before counseling or therapy starts and are independent of the process, although they certainly moderate or influence the process. Input can be divided into three categories:

1. *client variables,* such as presenting problem, severity and chronicity of disturbance, diagnosis, personality characteristics, history, gender, age, racial and ethnic background, physical characteristics, educational background, intellectual abilities, expectations for counseling or therapy, motivation, and appropriateness for a given type of treatment;
2. *counselor/therapist variables,* such as type of training, theoretical orientation, personality characteristics, history, gender, age, racial and ethnic background, physical characteristics, intellectual abilities, expectations for therapy, and motivation; and
3. *setting variables,* such as the physical arrangement of the room, whether treatment is conducted in an agency or in private practice, and amount of fees.

Extratherapy Events. These are events that transpire outside of counseling while the treatment is ongoing. Such events can be either helpful or hindering to the process. In an earlier work (Hill, 1989), I reported on one case in which the client's mother was dying during the course of therapy. Because the client was preoccupied with the mother's illness, she did not really want to be in therapy. In contrast, another client had a very supportive group of friends whom she asked for feedback. Because their feedback matched the therapist's feedback, she had more faith in the therapist's perceptions, enhancing the therapy. Yalom (1975) used the term *adaptive spiral* to refer to the process whereby one change in the client instigates other changes in the client's interpersonal environment, which, in turn, augments further personal change. Thus, extratherapy events can be either positive or negative, but do affect the therapy process.

Outcome. Outcome refers to changes that occur as a result of counseling or therapy. Outcome can occur at several different levels:

1. *immediate outcome,* or client change that occurs immediately following therapist interventions (e.g., Hill, Helms, Tichenor et al., 1988, found that therapist self-disclosure led to higher levels of client experiencing than did other therapist response modes);
2. *outcome of a counseling event,* or client change that occurs as a result of a series of therapeutic transactions (e.g., Greenberg, 1980) found that clients who resolved an internal conflict event within counseling moved from being externally focused and harsh critics of themselves to becoming more internally focused);
3. *session outcome,* or change that occurs as a result of a specific session. Measures at this level typically evaluate the quality of the session or satisfaction with the session, using measures such as the Session Evaluation Questionnaire (Stiles & Snow, 1984);
4. *treatment outcome,* change that occurs as a result of the entire treatment.

The first two levels can be conceptualized as measuring the "process of change" (Greenberg & Pinsof, 1986), whereas the latter two levels measure change as a result of treatment. Ideally, outcome should be measured from the perspective of the client, counselor, and significant other (Strupp & Hadley, 1977). A standard battery of tests has been recommended for assessing outcome (Waskow & Parloff, 1975).

Process and outcome *both* need to be examined within studies. Without process, outcome tells us little about how change comes about. Without outcome, we have no context for giving meaning to process events. Additionally, input and extratherapy variables should be included in future process studies. Although not all variables can be included in a single study, researchers need to begin examining the relative roles and importance of, plus the possible interactions between input, process, extratherapy experiences, and outcome.

DESIGNING THE STUDY

Many of the guidelines for designing studies are also relevant for areas other than process research. In my examples, however, I focus only on the process area.

Appropriate Expectations for Doing Process Research

Earlier (Hill, 1982), I noted that process research can often be overwhelming and frustrating. Not only does process research involve many complex steps, but the data are inherently messy. As in any type of research, but especially for the process area, researchers need to avoid the trap of unrealistic expectations. It is helpful to realize that no one study will answer any question definitively. In fact, it is not until there are a number of studies conducted by different researchers at different sites that we can have confidence in our findings. Through a *series* of studies, we can identify useful methodologies and new ways to approach issues.

A way to make the research process less frustrating is to enjoy the *process* at each stage of the research. One of the gratifying things about process research is the opportunity to watch counseling sessions. If you allow yourself to sit back and learn from the counseling session rather than focusing on finishing the project, you can learn much about process. Many of my new research ideas have come while I was monitoring counseling sessions. Another way of not losing heart in the middle of a project is to stay focused on what excited you about the project in the beginning. Additionally, team research can make the process of research more enjoyable, especially for social types who do not like the isolation of doing research alone.

I would advise the beginning researcher to become an apprentice to an experienced process researcher who knows the literature and the pitfalls to avoid in doing process research. Further, if you can carve your study out of that person's existing data set, it is easier than collecting new data. The experienced researcher also benefits from such collaboration, by having people to work with who have new and stimulating ideas.

Developing Questions

Many argue that questions should be theory-based to be meaningful (cf. Kiesler, 1973). Others argue that more can be gained from observing and discovering what is present in counseling sessions (Elliott, 1984; Greenberg, 1986; Hill, 1990; Mahrer, 1988). One charge made against exploratory research is that all research is theory-based at some level and that when the theory is unacknowledged, it will affect the research. Although our world views influence everything, we can still approach phenomena with an attitude of eagerness to discover and an openness to disconfirming evidence. Being aware of your biases (cf. Berman, 1989) and anticipating how they might intrude on the data is helpful in this regard. As suggested for qualitative research, you can record your predictions prior to conducting your study. If you find yourself changing your opinions based on the data, you can be more sure that you are discovering from your data rather than operating on preconceived ideas. The bottom line is that both theory-based and exploratory research are useful. The type of research should fit your style and help in answering your research questions.

As you are becoming more clear on the research question, you should also search the literature on the topic. It is important to go back to all the old literature on process, as well as searching through recent years. When I first developed my therapist response modes measure (Hill, 1978), Sam Osipow, then editor of the *Journal of Counseling Psychology* pointed out several measures that had been developed in the 1940s that I had neglected to consider in developing my instrument. I, like many others, had been biased toward examining just the recent literature. In examining the literature, it is useful to look at what methodologies have been used, although it is important not to feel obliged to use the same methodologies as the previous literature. New methodologies are often useful to approach the same questions.

I suggest writing a complete proposal of the research project including the data analyses, even if it is not a thesis or dissertation. Writing forces you to consider each step thoroughly and allows you to get feedback from colleagues. Making changes at this stage is easier than when the study is completed.

Choice of Design

In a previous article (Hill, 1982), I have discussed at length the relative merits of analogue versus naturalistic designs. Analogues (or simulations) are useful for answering questions about first impressions of clients or therapists, for example, how potential clients react to various levels of attractiveness (Carter, 1978). They are less adequate, however, for answering questions about events that occur within the context of ongoing counseling. For example, therapist interpretation is difficult to study in an analogue design (Spiegel & Hill, 1989) because success of interpretation appears to depend on a complex interplay of factors such as the relationship and the timing and accuracy of the interpretation.

The major complaint against analogue studies is that the results are difficult to generalize to actual counseling. Strong (1971) has listed several boundary conditions of counseling that an analogue study should meet to make it more generalizable to counseling: (a) counseling is a conversation between or among people, (b) status or power differences between or among interactants constrain the conversation, (c) the duration of contact between interactants varies and is at times extended, (d) clients are often motivated to change and actively seek counseling, and (e) clients are often psychologically distressed and heavily invested in changing their behaviors.

In our research, we usually use a quasi-naturalistic design. We recruit therapists and clients and have them meet in a clinic setting with videotaping and monitoring capabilities. In this manner, we have some degree of control over the participants. The therapists and clients have agreed from the start to participate in a research project. Cooperation is thus more assured than in an agency-based design where participants are asked to participate when they begin treatment (unless the agency is set up as a research agency). The design is naturalistic in the sense that we allow the therapy process to unfold with minimal restrictions. We instruct therapists to be as helpful as possible, without restraints on their actions within the session itself. Participants often forget the monitoring equipment once they become involved in the therapy session. Following the session, we sometimes have participants review the tapes to get more information about covert experiences.

Questions remain about how similar quasi-naturalistic research sessions are to non-research sessions. Recording does seem to have an impact on the process of counseling (Gelso, 1973, 1974), but we have no empirical data at this point about the effects of reviewing sessions on the process of counseling. Anecdotal evidence (Hill, 1989) indicates that some clients dislike the repetitiveness of the reviews and some feel embarrassed, whereas other clients have reported that the review was as or more helpful than the actual counseling session. The value in obtaining the data seems to outweigh the fact that the research process intrudes on and alters the process somewhat. Data from empirical studies, however, would enable us to make more informed decisions about these issues.

CHOOSING A MEASURE

Most of the widely used process measures are reviewed in three excellent volumes (Greenberg & Pinsof, 1986; Kiesler, 1973; Russell, 1987). I would encourage beginning researchers to use existing instruments, especially if they plan on doing only one study in the area. Otherwise, data from a study using an esoteric instrument are quickly forgotten because no one knows what the variables mean or how to compare the results to other studies. Further, we need to build on each other's work to accumulate knowledge in the process area.

No instrument developed by someone else will fit your own approach perfectly. My response mode system looks different from other researchers' systems (e.g., Friedlander, 1982; Stiles, 1979), partly because we all see the world differently and focus on different things. When therapists use my intentions system (Hill & O'Grady, 1985) and clients use my reactions system (Hill, Helms,

Spiegel, & Tichenor, 1988), they often complain that the categories do not fit exactly the way they think. I agree with them. Anytime you partition real-world behaviors or events into categories, you create problems. Because of this, you should look through several measures and select one that does the least violence to your way of perceiving the world.

If you plan to do more than one study in the area, I would recommend using someone else's measure first and then revising that measure to fit your study. For example, when we (Hill, Mahalik, & Thompson, 1989) first studied therapist self-disclosures, we used dimensions modified only slightly from the existing literature. After completing one study, we devised dimensions that seemed more relevant to our data (Hill, 1989).

In choosing any instrument, good validity and reliability are basic requirements. Without adequate validity and reliability, you cannot be confident of your results. Beyond the psychometric properties, however, you should choose a measure that holds the possibility of answering your question.

DEVELOPING A MEASURE

If you do not find a measure that is useful for your exact question, you may decide to develop your own. In this section, I provide guidelines about how to develop a process measure. I emphasize that these are merely guidelines based on my experience in developing measures. Not all development of measures, including my own, follows all the steps. If you are planning to develop a measure, I suggest that you read this section over carefully before you start and then reread each section as you come to that stage.

Initial Variable Selection

In this step, the researcher needs to develop a preliminary version of the measure. There are several potential sources for gaining information about the measure: the participants, archival data, the literature, experts, and your own experience.

The first and most important source of data is the counselor or client. For example, in developing the Therapist Intentions List (Hill & O'Grady, 1985), we were most interested in therapists' perspectives. We reviewed tapes with therapists and asked them to tell us their aims and intentions. It took several tries before we cleared up methodological problems such as when to stop the tape and how to ask the right questions. We realized that rather than asking about the therapist's goals for the entire session, we needed to focus on intentions for specific interventions. A useful method for collecting descriptive data from counselors and clients has been described by Elliott (1986).

In this method, you ask standardized open-ended questions (e.g., "What were you feeling then?") to draw the person out without interpreting or imposing your frame of reference on the person.

Archival materials, such as videotapes or transcripts, are a second source of data. Examining archival therapy sessions of target behavior can provide ideas about possible categories. For example, when we studied metaphors (Hill & Regan, in press), we studied instances that occurred within sessions and then formed categories based on our observations.

A third source of data is the literature. If other studies in the area have been done, they can serve as excellent sources of categories. For example, in developing the response-modes system (Hill, 1978), I collated categories from 11 existing systems. When we (Falk & Hill, 1990) developed a system for examining therapist humor, we collated categories from three existing measures. When systems use different labels and terms to describe similar behaviors, these can be combined into a single category.

A fourth source of data is experts. When Hollon et al. (1988) developed the Collaborative Study Psychotherapy Rating Scale, they asked experts in their target treatment modalities to specify the important components of treatment.

The final source of data is the researcher's experience in therapy as both a therapist and a client. For example, in developing the Client Reactions System (Hill, Helms, Spiegel, & Tichenor, 1988), we relied not only on client reports of their experiences, but also on our own experiences as clients. We went through our own sessions and tried to understand what our reactions had been to different therapist interventions.

Once the material is collected from the various sources, you can develop a preliminary measure. This should be done by sticking closely to the data. Using the words of counselors and clients is helpful here. The measure should cover a wide range of behaviors, with as much discrimination as possible between behaviors. Two or three persons should be used to develop the preliminary measure because each person will have different perspectives, which can lead to a more comprehensive measure.

Good definitions need to be written for each item. These definitions should be as operational as possible, requiring minimal inference. This is more difficult with abstract constructs like transference or empathy, but without clear definitions raters will interpret constructs in idiosyncratic ways. I remember how surprised I was to hear researchers from other disciplines talk about empathy. Even though we all used the same word, we meant something different (see Gladstein, 1983). Because many of our constructs are fuzzy, we have to be even more careful to write clear definitions. Only if we have clear definitions can we begin to separate out error due to the measures from error due to the judgment process. Additionally, you need to provide many examples, preferably taken from actual data, to make the definitions concrete and clarify the meanings of items.

Decisions About the Form of the Measure

You will need to decide about the form of your measure: whether items are
nominal or interval, level of abstraction of the items, perspective, unit of measurement, whether categories are mutually exclusive or not, perspective,
whether ratings are to be made using transcripts or tapes, and whether context is needed for ratings.

Nominal Versus Interval. Rating scales usually use 5-, 7-, or 9-point Likert-
type scales, although you can use even-numbered scales if you wish to force
a decision on one side of the scale or the other. Rating scales are advanta-
geous from a data-analytic point of view because one can pretend that the
data are interval and combine data. For example, an average score of depth
could be calculated across all interpretations. Unfortunately, many of our variables do not fit the assumptions necessary for interval data, in that there is
not equal distance between points nor is there often even a hierarchical difference between items. For example, when measuring therapist behavior, all
response modes may be equally valuable. To place therapist behaviors on
a continuum, as in Carkhuff's (1969) empathy scale, creates validity problems
(see Gormally & Hill, 1974; Hill, 1978).

Many counseling behaviors can be depicted more accurately through categorical data, which are nominal in nature. Nominal data are harder to work
with because categories cannot readily be summed. Nominal categories place
data into a category, such that a judgment is made about the presence or
absence of that behavior without regard to manner and quality of the behavior.

If rating scales are used, you need to be careful to measure only one construct per scale. The client Experiencing Scale (Klein et al., 1986) is an example of a rating scale that contains a number of different behaviors all on one
continuum. At the lower levels of the scale, clients behave in an impersonal
manner; at middle levels, clients are aware of their feelings; at upper levels,
clients exhibit insight. When all of these constructs are present in one scale,
there is no way of separating out which construct is present when ratings
differ.

One measure cannot be used to capture all of the important behaviors.
One solution to this is to have separate measures for each behavior. For example, separate measures could be used to investigate therapist-response
modes, therapist empathy, and the quality of the therapist intervention. An
example of the concurrent use of several different measures is Elliott's (1989)
Comprehensive Process Analysis.

Level of Abstraction. All categories within a system should be on the same
level of abstraction. If highly operationalized categories (e.g., head nods) are
mixed with abstract categories (e.g., empathy), problems with reliability and

interpretation can result. It is preferable to use separate measures to assess different levels of abstraction than to try to combine the levels in a single measure.

Unit of Measurement. Units range from words or phrases to sentences, thought units, speaking turns, events, specific time intervals such as 5-minute segments, whole sessions, or whole treatments. Thus, nonverbal behaviors are often measured in 5-second units (e.g., Hill & Stephany, 1990), therapist-response modes are measured in grammatical sentences (e.g., Hill, 1986), whereas the Working Alliance Inventory is rated on the basis of entire sessions (e.g., Horvath & Greenberg, 1986).

The unit will influence what data are collected and how they are interpreted. For example, in judging therapist intentions, we have had researchers stop the tape after each therapist speaking turn (all therapist speech between two client speeches), which averages approximately once a minute. Horvath, Marx, and Kamann (1990), on the other hand, allowed therapists to stop the tape whenever they thought that their intentions changed, which averaged about 5–6 minutes. If therapists stop the tape every 5–6 minutes, they combine a lot more information into their judgments than they do for each individual speaking turn. Neither method is necessarily "right," but different data will result based on the unit chosen.

Although we discuss units as though they were inherent in data, most units are arbitrary divisions of data. For example, people generally do not speak in grammatical sentences. To divide speech into units, rules are necessary, such as have been devised for grammatical sentences by Auld and White (1954) and revised by Hill (1985). Although words, phrases, and sentences are relatively easy to determine, longer units such as thought units and events are more difficult to determine reliably. These longer units, however, are often more clinically meaningful.

Mutual Exclusivity. If categories are being developed, you need to decide if only one category can be used for each piece of data (unit) or whether more than one category can be applied. For example, in our response-modes system, each therapist-response unit (sentence) can be assigned to only one response mode because each unit usually fits only one grammatical structure of speech. In our Intentions List, in contrast, up to three intentions can be assigned to each therapist speaking turn because therapists often have more than one intention in delivering interventions. You have to fit the measure to the reality of the data.

If you use nonmutually exclusive categories, you should be careful to make your definitions as distinct as possible, so that truly separate behaviors are occurring rather than simply having two categories that cannot be distinguished. You would be able to tell this if judges always assign the same categories together. If you opt for nonmutual exclusivity, you should limit the number of categories raters can assign at one time; otherwise some raters might assign two or three categories, whereas others assign one category to each unit, leading to low interrater reliability.

Perspective. Measures can be used directly by counselors and clients or they can be applied to archival data by nonparticipant judges. Examples of participant application of measures are my therapist intentions (Hill & O'Grady, 1985) and client reactions (Hill, Helms, Spiegel, & Tichenor, 1988) measures, in which therapists and clients categorize their own behaviors while viewing a videotape of the session. The advantage of this approach is that participants categorize their experiences themselves rather than having judges place the material into categories with potential loss of accuracy. Further, data can be collected about covert experiences that are not available from observation by nonparticipant judges. The disadvantages are in terms of obtaining indices of reliability. Because no one else can really know what the person is experiencing, interrater reliability does not make sense. Intrarater reliability is not possible because memory fades rapidly for such experiences, which are difficult to capture even immediately after sessions.

Use of nonparticipant judges is by far the most typical perspective relied on in process research. In my therapist-response modes system (Hill, 1985), for example, three trained judges are used to rate all the data from transcripts. In the past, judges were thought to be objective about the process, because they were not involved personally. We are more aware now that judges are not more objective, rather they just have different perspectives than therapists and clients (Hill, 1974; Hill, Helms, Tichenor et al., 1988). Each of the three perspectives is biased in some ways, but all provide valuable information as long as one is aware of the biases.

In an interesting combination of the participant and nonparticipant perspectives, Elliott (1986) questioned participants about their experiences and then trains judges to rate the resulting open-ended data. An advantage of this approach is that the richness of the clinical material is retained from the participant perspective and yet reliability can still be obtained.

Transcript Versus Tape. If using archival data, researchers need to decide whether they should use transcripts or whether they can use audiotapes or videotapes. Using only audio or videotapes is quite appropriate for measures in which there are clearly defined units (e.g., 5-minute time spans or speaking turns). When data need to be broken into more arbitrary units such as thought units, using tapes without transcripts is difficult for raters. Raters essentially have to unitize at the same time as they categorize data. Thus, you are in some jeopardy because raters often hear different things and rate different units, leading to lowered reliability. Transcripts are expensive to obtain, but they are invaluable for increasing reliability.

Obtaining an accurate transcript of a 1-hour session can take up to 40 hours. Transcribers often have to listen several times to ensure that they have heard properly. A second person then needs to correct the transcript to avoid biases in the listening process. With the advent of voice-operated computers, we will probably be a step ahead in obtaining transcripts, but there will still be problems because people talk over one another and are inarticulate. Imagine a computer trying to figure out the voices in a group or family session!

Context. Heatherington (1989) has noted that some measures need context for raters to make accurate judgments. In her measure of relational control, for example, context is necessary to judge whether a question is "one-up" or "one-down." Similarly, raters need to know what has transpired up until that point in the counseling to judge the depth of an interpretation.

In contrast, if context is present for some types of data, raters are prone to bias. For example, when we had raters coding nonverbal behaviors (Hill et al., 1981; Hill & Stephany, 1990), we deleted the sound so that raters would not be influenced by the content of the session. Similarly, in judging therapist empathy, raters need to hear what the client has said prior to the therapist intervention, but they might be unduly influenced if they hear how the client responds afterward.

Using the Preliminary System

After developing the preliminary list of variables, you will want to try the system out on some real data. The results will undoubtedly be abysmal. Judges probably will not understand the definitions and/or will not agree on how a given piece of data should be rated. Rather than getting discouraged, view your preliminary group of raters as colleagues who can help you refine your system. By being included in the process, your raters will be much more invested in helping you develop a good measure. Ask them for lots of feedback. As you try to describe to a rater what you really mean by a category, you will reveal your implicit definitions. Write down every bit of clarification or else you might forget the details once your raters understand the definitions. In communicating the definitions to new raters, you need to have these clarifications to help them understand your measure. Although you need to listen carefully to your raters, you may also need to take a definitive stand at times, reminding yourself and the raters about the questions and purpose of the study so that you do not get side-tracked.

At this stage, you will rewrite definitions to make items more meaningful, add items to account for data that none of your initial items addressed, delete items that do not apply to your data, and collapse items that measure the same things. During this stage, your team of raters will apply the evolving measure to several samples of data. This stage can be frustrating because you may feel that you will never finish developing the measure, but it can also be exciting and fruitful because you are so close to the data and new ideas are constantly emerging.

The raters who are used for developing the measure should be similar to raters who will eventually be rating the real data. If you plan on having undergraduate students rate the actual data, then having expert judges develop the measure might result in an instrument that undergraduate students cannot understand or use.

Testing the Reliability of the Revised Measure

At this time, the team of judges should go through a new set of data. All judgments should be made independently, that is, made separately by the judges without discussion. We are interested in the independent judgments because we want to see if different people agree before the social influence process takes effect. It is helpful to place judges in separate rooms when they watch the videotapes and make their judgments. When they are in the same room, comments and even nonverbal movements may give away their thinking about the behavior being rated.

I only touch briefly on reliability issues and refer the reader to Tinsley and Weiss (1975). Nominal categories typically use a kappa statistic, which is percent agreement corrected for chance. A weighted kappa can be used if some disagreements are worse than others, for example, a mistake of categorizing a restatement as information is a more serious problem than categorizing a restatement as a reflection. You should be aware that if you have only a couple of categories and the proportions of data in some of the categories are extremely low, kappas can be artificially low. In this case, you can report percentage agreement in addition to the kappa. Additionally, in some cases when kappa is low because of the nature of the system, you can calculate the significance of the kappa, which provides evidence that the ratings are reliable.

For interval categories, reliability is determined through some form of intraclass correlation (Shrout & Fleiss, 1979). In general, kappas are lower than intraclass correlations, so the two figures are not completely comparable.

You should assess both interrater reliability (similarity between raters), as well as intrarater reliability (similarity within raters over time). Most studies report only interrater reliability, but both types of reliability are important estimates of the stability of the rating process. Numbers of raters and problems with rater bias are discussed later under the section dealing with judges.

If you get high reliability (i.e., > .70 for intraclass correlation, .60 or significant for kappas) at this point, you can proceed to the next stage. If you do not gain high reliability, you need to determine the cause of the low reliability. Better definitions or examples may be needed. Perhaps the constructs are too fuzzy and need to be operationalized more clearly. Maybe a new format is needed for the measure. On many of our measures, we have tried several different formats and have gone through several trials before we hit upon what eventually worked.

Testing the Measure With a New Sample of Judges

Once initial reliability is established, the measure should be tested with a new set of judges. The new raters should be able to obtain high interrater and intrarater reliability. The new raters should also have judgments that are similar to the original raters on a common set of data (referred to as a *calibration set*). Because new raters tend to see the process with fresh eyes, they will be able to point out problems with the measure. This process thus ensures that the measure is "transportable" or can be used with another set of raters. This process was used in the development of the Collaborative Study Psychotherapy Rating Scale (CSPRS). The CSPRS was developed by Hollon et al. (1988) with one team of raters and then applied by Hill, O'Grady, and Elkin (in press) with another team. When equally high reliability and equivalent data on the calibration set were obtained, we felt confident that the measure was psychometrically sound.

If you use rating scales to measure a particular area, you also need to be concerned with the internal consistency of your measure. In addition, you may need to do factor analyses (Tinsley & Tinsley, 1987) on interval rating scales to determine the underlying structure of the measure (i.e., whether it has several subscales). With nominal data, you may want to do cluster analyses (Borgen & Barnett, 1987) or multidimensional scaling (Fitzgerald & Hubert, 1987) to determine the underlying structure.

Testing the Validity of the Measure

Face and Content Validity. This type of validity can be obtained by asking several experts from a range of orientations to give you feedback about your instrument. Experts can give you advice from their theoretical perspectives and/or past research experience. By asking experts from several orientations, you are more likely to get a variety of feedback to augment your blindspots. Alternatively, experts can act as "self-surrogates" by taking your perspective and criticizing the instrument if you tell them about its purpose and rationale.

Because it is sometimes difficult for experts to just look at an instrument and give feedback, it helps to think of ways to get them involved in using your instrument. One way is to ask experts to match the labels of items with the definitions and/or the examples. Additionally, you might ask experts to use the measure to describe a recent session.

Based on the feedback, you will again need to revise your measure. If many changes are made, you should ask another set of experts to examine the system again. You may begin to wonder at this point if you will ever be done revising this measure and whether perhaps you should change your field of interest.

Construct Validity.   One way to establish construct validity is to demonstrate that your measure is sensitive to predictable differences between groups. For example, we found that Rogers, Perls, and Ellis used different response modes (Hill, Thames, & Rardin, 1979). Similarly, we found that therapists from different theoretical orientations used intentions differently (Hill & O'Grady, 1985). In both cases, the response modes and intentions used were consistent with stated theoretical orientations.

Concurrent Validity. The new measure should be administered along with other measures of the same construct to determine whether similar results will be obtained. Although this step is rarely done, it aids tremendously in the comparison of measures. For example, Elliott et al. (1987) compared six measures of therapist-response modes and found relatively good congruence between measures for six response modes. Tichenor and Hill (1989) compared four measures of working alliance from three different perspectives (therapist, client, and raters). We found that three of four rater-completed measures were highly related, indicating that they were measuring similar constructs. When one measure (the Working Alliance Inventory; Horvath & Greenberg, 1986) was rated from the perspective of therapist, client, and outside judges, no congruence between perspectives was found. Thus, perception of the working alliance depended on perspective (i.e., validity was limited to data collected from the same perspective). Client views on working alliance tell us different things than therapist or outside judges' views on working alliance.

If there are not other measures of the construct, you can compare the new measure to measures of related constructs. For example, a measure of client behavior could be related to client experiencing (Klein et al., 1986) or client vocal quality (Rice & Kerr, 1986). If you find consistent results between measures, your confidence in the new measure will increase. If your measures are highly correlated ($>.70$ if using a Pearson correlation), you will know that you have not developed a measure of a different construct. The choice of which instrument to use would then rely on other factors such as the clarity of definitions or the ease of use.

Developing a Manual

All the information about a measure needs to be compiled in a manual so that other researchers can use the instrument. The manual should include all the information discussed in this section: labels of items, definitions, examples, format of measure, perspective, unit of measurement, contextual issues, use of transcript versus tape, and indications of validity and reliability. Additionally, including expert judgments on several calibration segments can enable future researchers to compare their ratings to the original ratings.

DATA COLLECTION

You need to have control over data collection. If you are in an agency, you should have some control over the staff who will participate in your study. To attempt to conduct a study when you do not have such control often leads to disaster. Counselors "forget" to turn on tape recorders. Clients do not want to participate in research because that was not what they bargained for in coming for services. In general, I would not recommend relying on other people to collect data without close supervision.

When running sessions, you should turn on tape recorders, monitor sessions to ensure that counselors adhere to your instructions, and distribute and collect measures. When you collect any data, check it carefully for missing data or inaccuracy in completion. We repeat directions many times so that participants can remember what is entailed, particularly in detailed assignments. In a current study we are doing, clients review the videotape of the session and indicate up to three reactions they have to each therapist intervention and also tell us which reactions are hidden. They also indicate the most and least helpful events by bracketing those turns on the review sheet. We train them for this task prior to therapy and also repeat the directions at the beginning of the review and then check their rating sheet after 5–10 minutes of the review. A side point here is that using good quality equipment and videotapes is essential to guarantee quality data.

You should not burden participants with having to complete too many measures and procedures. When the research takes more time than the intervention, you run the risk of not gaining cooperation. Although participants do learn something from testing procedures, they also may quit if it requires too much time. Further, the more research time required, the less generalizable to naturally occurring therapy your study becomes.

Collecting process data from counselors and clients needs to be done carefully to minimize the intrusiveness of the research on the treatment. In the past, some studies had participants push buttons under their seats to indicate their feelings at particular moments in the session, which is quite intrusive.

Beyond the videotaping equipment, we allow the process to unfold natural-ly. Participants usually then focus more on what is going on between them than on the research. Additionally, you will gain more cooperation if you treat your counselors and clients as collaborators. If you believe and com-municate to them that they are the only ones who can inform you about their experiences of the process, you can form a research alliance with them that will enable you to get richer, more complete information. Such collabo-ration also increases the probability that participants will become more in-vested in the research.

One major way for collecting data has been through having participants do postsession reviews of the videotape (e.g., Hill, Helms, Spiegel, & Ticheron, 1988). Although research has not been done on the limits of using videotape reviews, my experience suggests that it is best to review the tape immedi-ately after the session and certainly no later than 24 hours after the ses-sion. Watching the videotape seems to put the person back into the ex-perience of the session. But if the distance from the session is too long, the freshness of the person's emotions dissipates. They react more than to what they might have felt, how they feel after reflection, or how they think you want them to feel, than according to how they actually did feel at the moment.

A final point is to make sure to obtain permanent addresses and phone numbers from participants to use for follow-ups. At least with college popu-lations, mobility makes it difficult to contact people again without this infor-mation.

USE OF TRAINED JUDGES

Judges are often used for doing ratings that therapists and clients are not able to make or that would be too intrusive on the counseling/psychothera-py process. Additionally, judges are used to rate archival data when ther-apists and clients are no longer available. In using judges, you must remem-ber that they are people and not static measuring tools. You need to address several methodological issues to ensure valid ratings by judges.

Rater Selection

As reviewed by Moras and Hill (in press), adequate attention typically has not been given to rater selection. Most research reports provide minimal data about raters, typically reporting only on how many were used, their level of training (e.g., undergraduate or graduate student), and the reliability achieved.

Level of Training of Raters.   Moras and Hill (in press) noted that the level of expertise of raters used tends to be directly related to the amount of inference required by the measure. Highly operationalized variables can be rated by trained undergraduate judges, whereas abstract constructs such as transference require experienced clinicians who have some grasp of the construct. However, Mahrer, Paterson, Theriault, Roessler, and Quenneville (1986) have noted that when clinicians know a lot about constructs from their own experience, they sometimes have difficulty accepting someone else's definitions. Because of the lower reliability that results with clinicians, Mahrer et al. recommended using a greater number of raters.

Screening Raters.   Giving potential raters a chance to rate a sample task is a useful selection device. Ability to do this trial task will provide you with an approximation of how adequately raters will perform the actual task. The trial will also provide raters with an example of the task they will be expected to do. Because the level of detail required for some rating tasks is difficult for some raters, a trial task is a realistic job preview. Self-selection may be the most effective means of screening out inappropriate raters.

Most process researchers value raters who are attentive to detail, yet not so compulsive that they cannot make decisions about gray areas. Raters who ask questions are also valued because questions help to clarify the concepts involved. The raters must be able, however, to "buy" into the system that is being used even though it may not match their thinking style. Thus, someone who can point out the imperfections thoughtfully, but who can still work within the system is a desirable rater. Other desired rater characteristics are dependability, trustworthiness, and a sense of ethics (discussed in more detail later). These characteristics are difficult to assess without extensive knowledge of the person. My recommendation is to hire more raters than will be needed, with the expectation that some will drop out and others will need to be dropped.

It is invaluable for the trainer to be a rater as well as "the expert." The data must be coded, of course, so that the trainer is unaware of the identity of the participants or the condition of treatment. By getting close to the data, the trainer will be more aware of the problems with the task and can make modifications based on that experience. Especially when a new instrument is being developed, the trainer will learn far more about how the instrument operates by being intimately involved with the rating process. It also serves to heighten your empathy with the raters when you realize that you are not any better as a rater than others. This helps you to see more clearly the problems with the instrument rather than to blame the raters for not trying hard enough or for messing up.

Rater Bias.   Recently, we have examined how characteristics of raters influence their ratings. Hill, O'Grady, and Price (1988) did not find evidence of rater bias on scales that were highly operationalized, such as therapist adherence to their assigned treatment condition. With ratings of therapist facilitative conditions, however, we did find evidence of bias. The more the raters liked and thought they were similar to the therapists and clients (called *perceived similarity*), the higher they rated the therapists on facilitative conditions. In another study (Mahalik, Hill, Thompson, & O'Grady, 1989), we found that perceived similarity as well as rater personality characteristics influenced ratings of affiliation. Thus, raters seem to have difficulty rating items about global therapeutic conditions such as facilitative conditions or affiliation, perhaps because their personal feelings interfere with the judgment process. Such bias can compromise the validity of ratings.

In a study examining rater bias on a categorical measure, Mahrer et al. (1986) counted the number of times each rater endorsed each category when others did not, as well as the number of times each rater did not endorse each category when others did. They did not relate this resulting response bias to personality characteristics, but that could be done.

One possible solution to the problem of bias is to choose raters who are homogeneous on the problematic personality dimensions. There are two problems with this solution. First, we do not know what the relevant personality dimensions are for each measure since this is such a new research area and minimal information exists for the different measures. More importantly, if homogeneous groups of raters were selected, the data would be even more seriously compromised in terms of validity even though it would yield high interrater reliability. There would be consistent bias within the data that would reflect the raters rather than the target being rated. Thus, for example, if all the raters were dominant, they might consistently misperceive ratees' behavior as aggressive (this is hypothetical of course), which would be a reflection of the raters rather than the ratees.

A reasonable solution to the bias problem is to choose a group of raters who represent a wide range on the problematic personality characteristics. This, however, will lead to lower interrater reliability, even though the validity of the ratings is higher. A solution to the problem of lower reliability is to use a larger number of raters and also to control statistically for rater characteristics (cf. Mahalik et al., 1989). I would also encourage more researchers to administer personality tests to raters to determine whether personality variables interact with ratings on their measures.

Rater Training

From the section on rater selection, it may appear that selection is everything in the process of obtaining ratings. This is not true. Several researchers, for example Elliott (1988) and Benjamin (1988), have noted that training can often be used to overcome negative traits of raters. Training can often reduce or eliminate the influence of some rater characteristics on the rating process. For example, when raters make idiosyncratic interpretations of items, these can be corrected through discussion. A side benefit is that training can sometimes be beneficial for raters. Through the process of discussion, raters may come to understand how their world view is discrepant from other raters. Further, by watching tapes of sessions, raters often learn about treatment. If they identify with clients, raters sometimes resolve issues by heeding the therapist's advice.

For most measures, rater training is essential. In general, the more abstract the ratings, the longer the training will probably be. Prior to training, trainers should become familiar with the system and, if possible, be trained by an expert who has used the system to ensure that they are interpreting items correctly. Similarly, it is important to use a manual for training so that one can train according to the original system.

When people are first learning the system, they need to be given the clearest examples. Once they get a preliminary grasp of the definitions, examples from gray areas can be introduced. Having ratings on a calibration set of tapes is also extremely useful, so that you can train your raters to achieve high reliability with the original team of raters. If you are using a new instrument, you can run into problems because many issues fall between the cracks. The original team may have developed conventions that they did not record. You may have to communicate with the developer to find out how to handle specific issues, which will help the developer clarify these issues.

The social influence process is important to be aware of during training. Essentially, this means that one rater might dominate the process and persuade the other raters to adopt his or her opinion. One way to handle this is to have everyone spend time first thinking of their judgments. You can then rotate who talks first, so that everyone has to take a turn defending his or her ideas first. Thorough discussion of each item helps raters sort through their thinking process, clarify their rationales, and incorporate the measure. You should not set yourself up as the expert who cannot be questioned. Otherwise, raters will simply mimic you without thinking through the issues and internalizing their conceptualization of the variable.

Relatedly, you will encounter raters who always rate in the middle of an interval scale or who choose the safest alternative on a category system. They seem afraid to take a stand for fear of making a mistake. Gentle encouragement that their opinions are important can be helpful. Forcing them to take a stand for the sake of practice can also help.

For all raters, it can be helpful to provide them with individualized feedback about categories with which they are having trouble. If you are calculating reliability of the separate categories for each rater (as you should be) during training, this can be a valuable form of feedback.

On the other hand, you have to careful not to brainwash your raters (e.g., get raters to agree by using conventions, such as, "Every time you hear a why question, it's an open question"). If they use such conventions, the raters will then not look further at the data but will automatically judge the behavior to be an open question. This will provide great reliability, but the validity is questionable. The reason for having raters is to have them examine the materials and make judgments. Thus, you must let the raters use their judgment.

There is often a period shortly after training begins in which raters get worse at making judgments before they get better. This is because they are confused between old definitions and ways of thinking and the requirements of the new system. If the trainer and raters are prepared ahead of time that the raters may get worse before getting better, they may be innoculated against the discouragement that can occur. At the point of discouragement may be a key time to reinforce the raters about how hard they are working, if such is the case. Of course, those raters who cannot get beyond the confusion within a short time and "buy" into the system should probably be dropped.

Training should be on data that are not part of the actual study. If no other data are available for ratings, then the ratings done for training should be redone at the end. This is because ratings during training vary radically until the rater gets an understanding for the system. Further it takes awhile for the rater to get a sense of what the universe of responses is and to anchor which responses are deviant. You would expect very low intrarater reliability between ratings made during training and those made after rating a lot of data.

The ultimate criterion to indicate that training is completed is the reliability check. Generally, both intrarater and interrater reliability need to be above .70 for intraclass correlations and above .60 or significant for kappas. Too many researchers plunge right from training into the actual ratings without making a detailed assessment of the reliability. Unfortunately, they then find at the end of their ratings that the data are not publishable because of the lack of reliability.

Doing the Actual Ratings

Independence of Ratings. All data should be judged independently by judges prior to discussion. The reliability should be calculated on these independent judgments, but the data analysis will rely on master judgments (discussed later).

Units. Judgments of units should be done separately from judgments of behaviors. One set of raters should judge how the raw data breaks down into units. Another set of raters should make the judgments on the measure of choice. For example, we have one set of judges determine response units and another set of judges rate response modes. Reliability will be much lower if judges determine units at the same time as they judge behaviors.

Number of Raters. Many researchers consider a reliability of .70 as an adequate demonstration of reliability and proceed with having one rater rate the remainder of the data. This procedure is problematic from a methodological standpoint because a reliability of .70 leaves a lot of room for error. At .70, raters are disagreeing with each other quite often. Unless researchers reach incredibly high reliability (e.g., above .95, which is possible only for highly operationalized constructs such as nonverbal behavior), more than one rater (at least two for rating scales and three for nominal categories) should be used for all ratings. For measures with low reliability, more raters should be used. In general, it is better to err on the side of too many raters rather than too few raters. Using more raters and pooling the data can result in more reliable data.

You should use the same raters throughout your study. If you must add or change raters in the middle of a rating task, you should demonstrate that your new raters are rating in the same manner as your original raters on calibration sets of data.

Choosing What Data to Rate and When. My general preference is to rate all of the data that I can because then I have represented everything that occurs within the treatment. Rating everything is not always feasible, however, due to the amount of data. So then the question becomes, How much needs to be rated to be representative of the treatment?

Friedlander, Ellis, Siegel, Raymond, and Haase (1988) tested whether different lengths of excerpts and different starting points within sessions affected the ratings of judges. Results indicated that starting points made no difference, but that generalizing from any size segment to a whole session could not be done when interviews were examined individually. When interviews were aggregated across several cases, however, even small segments were representative of whole sessions. My guess is that there was so much variability across cases in particular segments that it erased differences between segment sizes. In other words, there is a tremendous amount of variability across therapists and clients in their behavior. The point to remember, however, is that if you are interested in characterizing a single case, you must rate whole sessions to obtain an accurate picture.

Another issue here regards whether data should be presented to raters in a random sequence or in the naturally occurring sequence. In general, it is probably ideal for the data to be presented in a random sequence, interspersed for cases and sessions, to avoid response biases. Some studies, however, require that the data be presented in a sequence because the ratings depend on an awareness of what has transpired previously.

Assigning Raters to Data. If not all raters will be rating every piece of data, raters should be paired with different partners constantly so that the error associated with each rater gets spread around. A randomized incomplete block design (Fleiss, 1981) is a useful way to organize rotating teams so that each judge rates an equivalent number of tapes of each type (e.g., each counselor/therapist, client, agency, etc.).

Care and Feeding of Raters

Elliott (1988) has spoken about "the care and feeding of raters." Raters need to feel that what they are doing is important and that their contribution is valued. They need to be listened to. After all, because the raters are close to the phenomena being studied, they have more firsthand knowledge of the construct than you do if you are not a rater.

To get rater cooperation, it is helpful to make the task as meaningful as possible. Rating repetitive things can be boring, so you need to do something to offset the boredom. Assigning readings, as long as they do not reveal the hypothesis of the study, can be a useful way to involve the raters in the scientific endeavor. Talking about therapy can also be beneficial to raters.

You should spend time with the raters talking about their reactions to the task, so that you know if they are bored or unhappy. You might also be aware that working conditions, such as time pressures or administrative problems with paychecks, may influence rater motivation and performance.

Rater Drift

At the beginning of ratings, raters typically are very conscientious. They listen very carefully to everything, take notes, and carefully evaluate all the evidence. After a while, some raters become bored with the task. They may rate too many sessions at one sitting or quit listening as attentively as they did at the beginning. You need to find something to keep them engaged in performing the task. This issue is more important when raters do the ratings after listening to the entire session. If raters keep some running tally or commentary about the session, they are more likely to stay engaged.

Our experience in examining rater drift (Hill, O'Grady, & Price, 1988) indicated no consistent patterns for rater drift across raters. Raters did, however, indicate that they approached the task quite differently over time. Part of this is to be expected as raters grow more familiar with the task and become less vigilant about making careful ratings. For example, they may make more assumptions about the data as they grow familiar with the task and listen less adeptly to nuances in the data or they may make snap judgments about data after listening to just a small segment. Once a judgment is made, they may listen only for confirming evidence rather than for disconfirming evidence.

One way to maintain group morale and to reduce rater drift is to have continued meetings even after training. This helps the raters feel that they are part of a team. When they have responsibility to the team, they are more likely to get their work done. Having raters meet as a team on a regular basis and discuss their ratings prevents raters from developing idiosyncratic ways of interpreting items. Standard calibration tapes should be used occasionally, so that raters can be compared not only to their earlier rating, but also to other calibrated sets of raters. Making raters aware of the problem of rater drift and remotivating them for the task is also helpful.

Reliability on the Actual Data

Reliability for the independent ratings of actual data needs to be reported in addition to the reliability obtained during training. The sample on which reliability is determined should be drawn randomly from across all the data that has been rated and should include at least one third to one half of the data.

Debriefing of Raters

While being trained and doing their ratings, raters should be kept blind to the hypotheses being studied. Raters will be very aware of what variable they are attending to, but they should not be aware of the hypotheses regarding how that variable relates to other variables. For example, in Hill and Stephany (1990), judges coded client nonverbal behavior. They spent a great deal of time discussing nonverbal behavior, but they were not informed that we were relating nonverbal behavior to client reactions. After a study is completed, however, raters should be informed about the hypotheses of the study. I like to ask raters about their predictions for the hypotheses of the study. This is also a good opportunity to discuss problems with the measure and explore different ways to conduct the rating process.

Data Aggregation

For interval data, ratings can be averaged across raters to yield a master rating. For nominal data, you need to determine a master judgment. When we use three judges, we consider the master judgment to be the one in which two of three agree in their independent judgments. If all three judges disagree, we have them discuss the judgment until they come to a consensus.

Mahrer, Markow, Gervaize, and Boulet (1987) used a procedure in which 8 out of 11 judges had to agree. If this level of agreement is not reached, the piece of data is thrown back and rerated at a later time. If consensus is still not reached, the data is not used in the study. My problem with this method, although methodologically very sound, is that it requires a lot of judges and also results in potentially valuable data being thrown out.

In aggregating nominal data across sessions, Marsden, Kalter, and Ericson (1974) suggested that the proportion of each behavior to the total number of behaviors is more appropriate than the raw frequencies. Proportions correct for the amount of activity in the session. For example, two counselors who use the same number of questions but differ in their overall amount of talking will have very different proportions of questions to total utterances.

Data Analysis

Traditionally, most researchers have used a correlational strategy, in which they relate the frequency of occurrence of the specific variable to some outcome measure. Several reviewers have written about the inadequacies of correlational designs (Gottman & Markman, 1978; Hill, 1982; Hill, Helms, Tichenor et al., 1988; Russell & Trull, 1986; Stiles, 1988) because they do not take into account the timing, appropriateness, quality, or context of the behavior. For example, one moderately deep interpretation given to an introspective client who is pondering why she or he behaves in a particular way is undoubtedly more helpful than 10 poorly timed interpretations (see Spiegel & Hill, 1989). To illustrate, Hill, Helms, Tichenor et al. (1988) found that the frequency of occurrence of response modes was not correlated with session and treatment outcome, nor were the findings consistent with analyses linking response modes to immediate outcome. Thus, relating frequency of process behaviors to distal outcome was not useful. I recommend using more immediate measures of outcome because it is easier to establish the temporal contiguity of the effect. However, we also need to develop new methods of relating process to distal outcome. Such methods would probably include the quality of the responses along with the frequency of occurrence of the different responses.

Another analytic issue regards the most appropriate analyses for nominal data. Although nominal data do not meet the assumptions necessary for analysis of variance models, researchers (including myself, e.g., Hill, Helms, Tichenor et al., 1988), have often analyzed data with analysis of variance models because other methods were not well known. Use of loglinear analyses may be more appropriate for nominal data (Marascuilo & Busk, 1987).

Additionally, researchers need to consider using some form of sequential analysis (e.g., Hill, Carter, & O'Farrell, 1983; Wampold & Kim, 1989) for examining interactive data, for example, to determine which therapist intentions lead to which client reactions. One special issue arises in sequential analyses when more than one type of a behavior can lead to more than one type of another behavior. Using the last example, if a therapist lists more than one intention and the client lists more than one reaction, each combination of these behaviors needs to be counted, which leads to an inflation in the number of behaviors reported. This inflation is necessary for the data analysis, but you need to keep aware that it is a distortion of the data.

ETHICAL CONSIDERATIONS IN DOING PROCESS RESEARCH

Ethics in Collecting Data From Cases

Participants need to be informed of what they will be expected to do in the research project. Clients need to be told whether they will be assigned to different types of treatment groups. For example, in a study Mary Cogar and I are conducting on the effects of dream interpretation, potential clients are informed that they will be randomly assigned to individual dream interpretation, to a condition in which they will keep a journal of their dreams, or to a no-treatment control condition, with the latter two groups receiving a workshop at the end of the study. Potential subjects must indicate a willingness to participate in any one of the three groups should they be assigned to it.

Prior to their participation, counselors and clients should sign consent forms detailing what will be expected of them in the project. Because the consent forms provide a good overview of the study, we have found it useful to give copies to participants. As a part of this pretreatment informed consent, participants should be informed as to whether other participants will see the data. Unless otherwise informed, clients may view research measures as a way of communicating with their therapists and may assume that the therapist knows everything they are reporting. If participants drop out of treatment, they have the right to request that all of the data, especially the videotapes, be destroyed. This right should be specified on the consent form.

We also ask participants to sign an informed consent at the end of treatment. In this form, we ask the person to indicate the ways in which they will allow us to use the data, particularly the videotapes: our own research, other team's research, use for viewing by professional audiences, and use for viewing by undergraduate classes. Even though you may not plan to use the data for all of these purposes, having such release allows you to plan further studies without having to contact the participants again for further permission. We also allow clients to indicate whether they would allow their therapists to see their data. Participants may be willing to share information with the researchers that they would not share with other participants. In one of my cases (Hill, 1989), a client reported negative reactions about the therapist to the researchers that she did not want revealed directly to the therapist. It can be very valuable for therapists to get this feedback from clients.

Sometimes participants want the data. We have maintained a policy that they can have access to the data if it does not interfere with our purposes for using the data. For example, one therapist who wanted to write a case study using the data was turned down because that was what we were planning on doing with the data. More frequently, clients have asked for transcripts of sessions, which we have provided. Although we have told clients that they could come into the lab and view the videotapes, none have done so. We would not give test data or interpretations directly to clients because that is against APA ethical policy, but we would release it to a qualified professional if the client signed a consent form.

On all data, code numbers should be used rather than names. We use a system whereby we indicate case, session number, and date. All materials, especially videotapes, should be kept in a locked area, with access only by the research team. In any write-up of case material, pseudonyms should always be used. Allowing therapists and clients to review and comment on any extensive case write-ups of individual cases is also important. When I did this in my case studies (Hill, 1989), it allowed me to correct factual data and often provided me with new insights about the data. At times, participants asked to delete information that they were not comfortable revealing to the general public.

Ethics With Raters

Raters also need to sign informed consent forms specifying what their tasks will be in the project. In addition, they need to sign confidentiality forms, in which they promise not to discuss the counseling material with anyone outside the research team. The trainer and researcher need to stress the importance of confidentiality. Raters should consider how they would want their data treated if they had participated in the research.

Prior to rating the actual data, we devise a list that includes the names of all the clients interspersed with random names. We ask the raters to indicate if they know any of the people on the list. We make clear to the raters that just because a name is on the list does not mean that that person is a client in our study; this protects clients who may not want others to know that they are in any kind of treatment. If raters know a client on the list, they should not rate any of the data for that person. If raters discover upon listening to the videotape that they know a client, they should stop listening immediately. These guidelines are particularly important when raters are chosen from the same institution or city as the clients because it reduces the problems associated with failures of confidentiality.

We have not been as careful in disguising therapist identity as we have been for client identity. Therapists typically do not reveal as much personal information about themselves, so the confidentiality issues are not as great. Further, we have found that it is hard to find raters who are not as familiar with therapists. However, if questions were directly related to therapist competence, for example, it would be important to disguise the therapist identity.

I have heard mixed suggestions as to whether raters should take data home with them. On the hard line, researchers insist that no data should ever leave the locked room. On the more lenient side, when raters are allowed to take data home, they may do better work. In addition to confidentiality, a problem is the possibility of loss of valuable, unreplaceable data. Data have been stolen from cars, with the result that no one knows who now has access to the data. I sometimes let raters take data home, especially when I trust them thoroughly, if we have copies of the data, and if *all the identifying information is removed.*

A final point is that when your project is completed, videotapes need to be erased. Although it is hard to see all that data destroyed, confidentiality can only be protected by destroying the tapes because the identifying characteristics cannot be altered on videotapes. Participants of course need to be reassured that the tapes will be erased at some point. Because I usually do several projects on a set of data, I keep the tapes until I am sure that I will not be doing any further projects. They should not, however, be kept beyond 1–2 years after the last project is completed.

FINAL STATEMENT

If you are a graduate student, you might be wondering after reading all of this whether it is feasible to do process research for your thesis or dissertation. Such a project is certainly time consuming, involves innumerable details, and requires time, energy, and financial resources. You do need to have patience and enjoy the process. On the other hand, the opportunity of getting close to the process of counseling and therapy in a meaningful way can be very exciting. The opportunity to translate what you learn in research into practice helps make the research process less of an isolated process. For example, our finding that therapists are often unable to identify negative client reactions (Thompson & Hill, 1991) has led me to question clients more about their reactions within sessions. Keeping a narrow focus helps to prevent you from becoming overwhelmed.

My suggestion to students designing a project is to pick a narrow focus and ask very specific questions, so that the project is manageable. For example, in a case study without a very specific focus, you can easily be overwhelmed with the plethora of details, all of which are important to understand the case from a clinical perspective.

ACKNOWLEDGMENTS

I would like to express my appreciation to Mary Cogar, Maureen Corbett, Roberta Diemer, Lee Edwards, Bruce Fretz, Jim Mahalik, Kevin O'Grady, Anne Regan, and Barbara Thompson for helpful comments on drafts of this chapter.

REFERENCES

Auld, F., & White, A. M. (1954). Rules for dividing interviews into sentences. *Journal of Psychology, 42,* 273–281.

Benjamin, L. S. (1988, June). Selecting and training SASB coders. In K. Moras & C. E. Hill (Co-Chairs), *Selecting raters for psychotherapy process research.* Workshop conducted at the Society for Psychotherapy Research, Santa Fe, NM.

Berman, J. S. (1989, June). *Investigator allegiance and the findings from comparative outcome studies.* Paper presented at the Society for Psychotherapy Research, Toronto, Canada.

Bordin, E. S., Cutler, R. I., Dittmann, A. T., Harway, N. I., Rausch, H. L., & Rigler, D. (1954). Measurement problems in process research on psychotherapy. *Journal of Consulting Psychology, 18,* 79–82.

Borgen, F. H., & Barnett, D. C. (1987). Applying cluster analysis in counseling psychology research. *Journal of Counseling Psychology, 34,* 456–468.

Carkhuff, R. R. (1969). *Human and helping relations* (Vols. 1 & 2). New York: Holt, Rinehart, & Winston.

Carter, J. (1978). Impressions of counselors as a function of counselor physical attractiveness. *Journal of Counseling Psychology, 25,* 28–34.

Elliott, R. (1984). A discovery-oriented approach to significant events in psychotherapy: Interpersonal process recall and comprehensive process analysis. In L. Rice & L. Greenberg (Eds.), *Patterns of change* (pp. 249–286). New York: Guilford.

Elliott, R. (1985). Helpful and unhelpful events in brief counseling interviews: An empirical taxonomy. *Journal of Counseling Psychology, 32,* 307–322.

Elliott, R. (1986). Interpersonal Process Recall (IPR) as a psychotherapy process research method. In L. S. Greenberg & W. M. Pinsof (Eds.), *The psychotherapeutic process: A research handbook* (pp. 503–527). New York: Guilford.

Elliott, R. (1988, June). Issues in the selection, training, and management of raters. In K. Moras & C. E. Hill (Co-Chairs), *Selecting raters for psychotherapy process research.* Workshop conducted at the Society for Psychotherapy Research, Santa Fe, NM.

Elliott, R. (1989). Comprehensive process analysis: Understanding the change process in significant therapy events. In M. J. Packer & R. B. Addison (Eds.), *Entering the circle: Hermaneutic investigation in psychology.* Albany, NY: SUNY Press.

Elliott, R., Hill, C. E., Stiles, W. B., Friedlander, M. L., Mahrer, A. R., & Margison, F. R. (1987). Primary therapist response modes: Comparison of six rating systems. *Journal of Consulting and Clinical Psychology, 55,* 218–223.

Falk, D., & Hill, C. E. (1990, June). *Therapist behavior preceding client laughter.* Paper presented at the Society for Psychotherapy Research, Wintergreen, VA.

Fitzgerald, L. F., & Hubert, L. J. (1987). Multidimensional scaling: Some possibilities for counseling psychology. *Journal of Counseling Psychology, 34,* 469–480.

Fleiss, J. L. (1981). Balanced incomplete block designs for interrater reliability studies. *Applied Psychological Measurement, 5,* 105–112.

Friedlander, M. L. (1982). Counseling discourse as a speech event: Revision and extension of the Hill Counselor Verbal Response Category System. *Journal of Counseling Psychology, 29,* 425–429.

Friedlander, M. L. (1984). Psychotherapy talk as social control. *Psychotherapy, 21,* 335–341.

Friedlander, M. L., Ellis, M. V., Siegel, S. M., Raymond, L., & Haase, R. F. (1988). Generalizing from segments to sessions: Should it be done? *Journal of Counseling Psychology, 35,* 243–250.

Fuhriman, A., & Burlingame, G. M. (1990). Consistency of matter: A comparative analysis of individual and group process variables. *Counseling Psychologist, 18*(1), 6–63.

Gelso, C. J. (1973). The effects of audiorecording and videorecording on client satisfaction and self-exploration. *Journal of Consulting and Clinical Psychology, 40,* 455–461.

Gelso, C. J. (1974). Effects of recording on counselors and clients. *Counselor Education and Supervision, 14,* 5–12.

Gelso, C. J., & Carter, J. A. (1985). The relationship in counseling and psychotherapy. *The Counseling Psychologist, 13,* 155–244.

Gladstein, G. A. (1983). Understanding empathy: Integrating counseling, developmental, and social psychology perspectives. *Journal of Counseling Psychology, 30,* 467–482.

Gomes-Schwartz, B. (1978). Effective ingredients in psychotherapy: Prediction of outcome from process variables. *Journal of Consulting and Clinical Psychology, 46,* 1023–1035.

Gormally, J., & Hill, C. E. (1974). Guidelines for research on Carkhuff's training model. *Journal of Counseling Psychology, 21,* 539–547.

Gottman, J. M., & Markman, H. J. (1978). Experimental designs in psychotherapy research. In S. L. Garfield & A. E. Bergin (Eds.), *Handbook of psychotherapy and behavior change* (2nd ed., pp. 23–62). New York: Wiley.

Greenberg, L. S. (1980). The intensive analysis of recurring events from the practice of Gestalt therapy. *Psychotherapy: Theory, Research, and Practice, 17,* 143–152.

Greenberg, L. S. (1986). Change process research. *Journal of Consulting and Clinical Psychology, 54,* 4–9.

Greenberg, L. S., & Dompierre, L. (1981). The specific effects of Gestalt two-chair dialogue on intrapsychic conflict in counseling. *Journal of Counseling Psychology, 28,* 288–294.

Greenberg, L., & Pinsof, W. (Eds.). (1986). *The psychotherapeutic process: A research handbook.* New York: Guilford.

Greenson, R. R. (1967). *The technique and practice of psychoanalysis* (Vol. 1). New York: International Universities Press.

Gurman, A. S., Kniskern, D. P., & Pinsof, W. M. (1986). Research on marital and family therapies. In S. Garfield & A. Bergin (Eds.), *Handbook of psychotherapy and behavior change: An empirical analysis* (3rd ed., pp. 311–384). New York: Wiley.

Hall, C. S., & Van de Castle, R. L. (1966). *The content analysis of dreams.* New York: Appleton-Century-Crofts.

Heatherington, L. (1989). Toward more meaningful clinical research: Taking context into account in coding psychotherapy interaction. *Psychotherapy, 26,* 436–447.

Highlen, P. S., & Hill, C. E. (1984). Factors affecting client change in individual counseling: Current status and theoretical speculations. In S. D. Brown & R. W. Lent (Eds.), *Handbook of counseling psychology* (pp. 334–398). New York: Wiley.

Hill, C. E. (1974). A comparison of the perceptions of a therapy session by clients, therapists, and objective judges. *Journal Supplements Abstract Service, 4,* No. 564.

Hill, C. E. (1978). Development of a counselor verbal response category system. *Journal of Counseling Psychology, 25,* 461–468.

Hill, C. E. (1982). Counseling process research: Philosophical and methodological dilemmas. *Counseling Psychologist, 10*(4), 7–19.

Hill, C. E. (1985). *Manual for the Hill Counselor Verbal Response Modes Category System* (rev. ed.). Unpublished manuscript, University of Maryland, College Park, MD.

Hill, C. E. (1986). An overview of the Hill counselor and client verbal response modes category systems. In L. S. Greenberg & W. M. Pinsof (Eds.), *The psychotherapeutic process: A research handbook* (pp. 131–160). New York: Guilford.

Hill, C. E. (1989). *Therapist techniques and client outcomes: Eight cases of brief psychotherapy.* Newbury Park, CA: Sage.

Hill, C. E. (1990). A review of exploratory in-session process research. *Journal of Consulting and Clinical Psychology, 58,* 288–294.

Hill, C. E., Carter, J. A., & O'Farrell, M. K. (1983). A case study of the process and outcome of time-limited counseling. *Journal of Counseling Psychology, 30,* 3–18.

Hill, C. E., Helms, J. E., Spiegel, S. B., & Tichenor, V. (1988). Development of a system for assessing client reactions to therapist interventions. *Journal of Counseling Psychology, 34,* 27–36.

Hill, C. E., Helms, J. E., Tichenor, V., Spiegel, S. B., O'Grady, K. E., & Perry, E. (1988). The effects of therapist response modes in brief psychotherapy. *Journal of Counseling Psychology, 35,* 222–233.

Hill, C. E., Mahalik, J., & Thompson, B. (1989). Therapist self-disclosure. *Psychotherapy, 26,* 290–295.

Hill, C. E., & O'Grady, K. E. (1985). List of therapist intentions illustrated in a case study and with therapists of varying theoretical orientations. *Journal of Counseling Psychology, 32,* 3–22.

Hill, C. E., O'Grady, K. E., & Elkin, I. E. (in press). Applying the Collaborative Study Psychotherapy Rating Scale to rate therapist adherence in cognitive behavioral therapy, interpersonal therapy, and clinical management. *Journal of Consulting and Clinical Psychology.*

Hill, C. E., O'Grady, K. E., & Price, P. (1988). A method for investigating sources of rater bias. *Journal of Counseling Psychology, 35,* 346–350.

Hill, C. E., & Regan, A. (in press). The use of metaphors within a case of brief psychotherapy. *Journal of Integrative and Eclectic Psychotherapy.*

Hill, C. E., Siegelman, L., Gronsky, B., Sturniolo, F., & Fretz, B. R. (1981). Nonverbal communication and counseling outcome. *Journal of Counseling Psychology, 28,* 203–212.

Hill, C. E., & Stephany, A. (1990). The relationship of nonverbal behaviors to client reactions. *Journal of Counseling Psychology, 37,* 22–26.

Hill, C. E., Thames, T. B., & Rardin, D. (1979). A comparison of Rogers, Perls, and Ellis on the Hill Counselor Verbal Response Category System. *Journal of Counseling Psychology, 26,* 198–203.

Hollon, S. D., Evans, M. D., Auerbach, A., DeRubeis, R. J., Elkin, I., Lowery, A., Kriss, M., Grove, W., Tuason, V. B., & Piasecki, J. (1988, June). *Development of a system for rating therapies for depression: Differentiating cognitive therapy, interpersonal psychotherapy, and clinical management pharmacotherapy.* Paper presented at the Society for Psychotherapy Research, Santa Fe, NM.

Horvath, A. O., Marx, R. W., & Kamann, A. M. (1990). Thinking about thinking in therapy: An examination of clients' understanding of their therapists' intentions. *Journal of Consulting and Clinical Psychology, 58,* 614–621.

Horvath, A. O., & Greenberg, L. S. (1986). The development of the Working Alliance Inventory. In L. S. Greenberg & W. M. Pinsof (Eds.), *The psychotherapeutic process: A research handbook* (pp. 529–556). New York: Guilford.

Kiesler, D. J. (1966). Basic methodological issues implicit in psychotherapy research. *American Journal of Psychotherapy, 20,* 135–155.

Kiesler, D. J. (1971). Experimental designs in psychotherapy research. In A. E. Bergin & S. L. Garfield (Eds.), *Handbook of psychotherapy and behavior change* (pp. 36–74). New York: Wiley.

Kiesler, D. J. (1973). *The process of psychotherapy.* Chicago: Aldine.

Kiesler, D. J. (1988). *Revised versions of Checklist of Psychotherapy Transactions (CLOPT) and Checklist of Interpersonal Transactions (CLOIT).* Richmond, VA: Virginia Commonwealth University.

Klein, M. H., Mathieu-Coughlan, P., & Kiesler, D. J. (1986). The Experiencing Scales. In L. Greenberg & W. Pinsof (Eds.), *The psychotherapeutic process: A research handbook* (pp. 21–71). New York: Guilford.

Luborsky, L. (1990). A review of theory-based process research. *Journal of Consulting and Clinical Psychology, 58,* 281–287.

Mahalik, J., Hill, C. E., Thompson, B., & O'Grady, K. E. (1989, June). *Rater bias in the Checklist of Psychotherapy Transactions Measure.* Paper presented at the Society for Psychotherapy Research, Toronto, Canada.

Mahl, G. F. (1963). The lexical and linguistic levels in the expression of the emotions. In P. H. Knapp (Ed.), *Expression of the emotion in man* (pp. 77–105). New York: International University Press.

Mahrer, A. R. (1988). Discovery-oriented psychotherapy research. *American Psychologist, 43,* 694–702.

Mahrer, A. R., Markow, R., Gervaize, P. A., & Boulet, D. B. (1987). Strong laughter in psychotherapy: Concomitant patient verbal behavior and implications for therapeutic use. *Voices, 23,* 80–88.

Mahrer, A. R., Paterson, W. E., Theriault, A. T., Roessler, C., & Quenneville, A. (1986). How and why to use a large number of clinically sophisticated judges in psychotherapy research. *Voices, 22,* 57–66.

Marascuilo, L. A., & Busk, P. L. (1987). Loglinear models: A way to study main effects and interactions for multidimensional contingency tables with categorical data. *Journal of Counseling Psychology, 34,* 443–456.

Marsden, G. (1965). Content analysis studies of therapeutic interviews: 1954–1964. *Psychological Bulletin, 63,* 298–321.

Marsden, G. (1971). Content analysis studies of psychotherapy: 1954 to 1968. In A. E. Bergin & S. L. Garfield (Eds.), *Handbook of psychotherapy and behavior change* (pp. 345–407). New York: Wiley.

Marsden, G., Kalter, N., & Ericson, W. A. (1974). Response productivity: A methodological problem in content analysis studies in psychotherapy. *Journal of Consulting and Clinical Psychology, 42,* 224–230.

Moras, K., & Hill, C. E. (in press). Rater selection in psychotherapy process research: Observations on the state-of-the-art. *Psychotherapy Research.*

Orlinsky, D., & Howard, K. (1978). The relation of process to outcome in psychotherapy. In S. Garfield & A. Bergin (Eds.), *Handbook of psychotherapy and behavior change: An empirical analysis* (2nd ed., pp. 283–329). New York: Wiley.

Pope, B. (1977). Research on therapeutic style. In A. S. Gurman & A. M. Razin (Eds.), *Effective psychotherapy: A handbook of research* (pp. 356–394). New York: Pergamon.

Rice, L. N., & Kerr, G. P. (1986). Measures of client and therapist vocal quality. In L. Greenberg & W. Pinsof (Eds.), *The psychotherapeutic process: A research handbook* (pp. 73–105). New York: Guilford.

Russell, R. L. (1987). *Language in psychotherapy: Strategies of discovery.* New York: Plenum.

Russell, R. L., & Trull, T. J. (1986). Sequential analyses of language variables in psychotherapy process research. *Journal of Consulting and Clinical Psychology, 54,* 16–21.

Schaffer, N. D. (1982). Multidimensional measures of therapist behaviors as predictors of outcome. *Psychological Bulletin, 92,* 670–681.

Shrout, P. E., & Fleiss, J. L. (1979). Intraclass correlations: Uses in assessing rater reliability. *Psychological Bulletin, 86,* 420–428.

Spiegel, S. B., & Hill, C. E. (1989). Guidelines for research on therapist interpretation: Toward greater methodological rigor and relevance to practice. *Journal of Counseling Psychology, 36,* 121–129.

Stiles, W. B. (1979). Verbal response modes and psychotherapeutic technique. *Psychiatry, 42,* 49–62.

Stiles, W. B. (1988). Psychotherapy process-outcome correlations may be misleading. *Psychotherapy, 25,* 27–35.

Stiles, W. B., & Snow, J. S. (1984). Counseling session impact as viewed by novice counselors and their clients. *Journal of Counseling Psychology, 31,* 3–12.

Strong, S. R. (1971). Experimental laboratory research in counseling. *Journal of Counseling Psychology, 18,* 106–110.

Strupp, H. H., & Hadley, S. W. (1977). A tripartite model of mental health and therapeutic outcomes: With special reference to negative effects in psychotherapy. *American Psychologist, 32,* 187–196.

Thompson, B. J., & Hill, C. E. (1991). Therapist perceptions of client reactions. *Journal of Counseling and Development, 69,* 261–265.

Tichenor, V., & Hill, C. E. (1989). A comparison of six measures of working alliance. *Psychotherapy, 26,* 195–199.

Tinsley, H. E. A., & Tinsley, D. J. (1987). Uses of factor analysis in counseling psychology research. *Journal of Counseling Psychology, 34,* 414–424.

Tinsley, H. E. A., & Weiss, D. J. (1975). Interrater reliability and agreement of subjective judgments. *Journal of Counseling Psychology, 22,* 358–376.

Wampold, B. E., & Kim, K. (1989). Sequential analysis applied to counseling process and outcome: A case study revisited. *Journal of Counseling Psychology, 36,* 357–364.

Waskow, I. E., & Parloff, M. B. (1975). *Psychotherapy Change Measures.* DHEW Publication No. (ADM) 74-120.

Weiss, J., Sampson, H., & the Mount Zion Psychotherapy Research Group. (1986). *The psychoanalytic process: Theory, observation, and empirical research.* New York: Guilford.

Yalom, I. D. (1975). *The theory and practice of group psychotherapy* (2nd ed.). New York: Basic.

5

SINGLE-CASE RESEARCH IN COUNSELING

John P. Galassi
Tracey L. Gersh
University of North Carolina at Chapel Hill

A TALE OF TWO JOURNALS: JABA AND JCP

First published in 1968 by the Society for the Experimental Analysis of Behavior as an off-shoot of the *Journal of the Experimental Analysis of Behavior,* the *Journal of Applied Behavior Analysis* (JABA) is undoubtedly the principal and most prestigious outlet for single-case[1] research. Its focus is on experimental studies in which treatment variables are applied to subjects in a scientifically controlled fashion (Baer, Wolf, & Risley, 1968). A review of the 1989[2] issues of JABA reveals 43 articles, of which 35 were data-based studies. Of these, 31 (89%) were single-case experiments with the multiple baseline design as the most frequently used design.

The *Journal of Counseling Psychology* (JCP), which first appeared in 1954, is published by the American Psychological Association (APA) and is the most prestigious counseling research journal. As is seen here, however, the methodology employed in that journal differs markedly from the studies in JABA. Until recently, single-case research appears to have been unknown and/or

---

[1]A variety of terms including $N = 1$, *single case, time-series research, time-series design, intensive design, single subject, intrasubject replication,* and *own-control designs,* among others have been used to refer to the subject matter in this chapter. Each of these terms has its unique definitional problems (see Hayes, 1981; Kratochwill, 1978). We have chosen the term, *single-case.* However, the reader should recognize that this type of research typically involves more than one subject and, more importantly, a set of assumptions that are somewhat different from those of between-groups research.

[2]The authors thank Eric Swift for his assistance in compiling the data for JABA and JCP and Merna Galassi, Eric Swift, and Barbara Wasik for their helpful suggestions.

unappreciated either by the individuals who published in the JCP or the editors and editorial board members who screened articles for it.

Over a 10-year period (1980–1989) 783 articles, including 668 data-based studies, were published in the JCP. Of the data-based studies, only 21 (3%) could be classified as being conducted, at least in part, from a single-case rather than a between-groups perspective (see the next section). Interestingly, 8 of these 21 were studies of the verbal interaction of well-known therapists with an individual client, family, or supervisee as depicted on a commercially available film (e.g., the *Gloria* films; Shostrom, 1966) or audiotape. Another four involved conventional case studies (agoraphobia, identity problem, career change, and religious lifestyle), and two involved extensive qualitative and quantitative analyses of the same single case (the Hill, Carter, & O'Farrell, 1983 study). In only one study (Mueser, Foy, & Carter, 1986) was a single-case (multiple baseline) experimental design employed.

Undoubtedly, there are a number of reasons why counseling researchers have shunned single-case designs in favor of more conventional between-groups designs. One factor may have to do with journal editorial philosophy and policy. Interestingly, however, recent JCP editors have called for greater methodological diversity in counseling research, including the use of case studies and single-case research (Gelso, 1979, 1982, 1985; Harmon, 1988). This call has been echoed by reviewers of JCP research article patterns (Scherman & Doan, 1985) and other JCP authors (Howard, 1984; Patton, 1984; Polkinghorne; 1984). Second, although a number of investigators (e.g., Barlow, Hayes, & Nelson, 1984; Kazdin, 1982; Leitenberg, 1973) have suggested that single-case research designs are widely applicable in counseling and psychotherapy, these designs are still linked in many researchers' minds to behavioral approaches (see McCullough & Carr, 1987). Finally, most counselors and counseling psychologists have probably received little training in single-case methodology, and therefore rarely consider it as a viable design alternative.

However, single-case designs have considerable potential with regard to research, accountability, and evaluation procedures in counseling and psychotherapy. Moreover, they often seem more compatible with clinical practice than do traditional between-groups designs. As such, they deserve to be better known and understood by counseling professionals. The objective of this chapter therefore is to provide an introduction to single-case research methods. We begin by comparing them with between-groups methods.

CHARACTERISTICS OF SINGLE-CASE AND BETWEEN-GROUPS RESEARCH

Table 5.1 summarizes a number of assumptions and characteristics that are typical of single-case research and distinguish it from between-group, "large *N*" research. It should be recognized, however, that global distinctions are

TABLE 5.1
Characteristics of Between-Groups and Single-Case Research

	Between Groups	*Single Case*
Focus	The group mean or the "average" client	The individual client
Variability	Between groups	Intrasubject
Assessment	Usually pre–post	Repeated, "continuous"
Measures	Observational, physiological, self-report	Observational, physiological, self-report
Design structure	Predetermined	Flexible
Control	Comparison with control groups	Comparison with subjects as own control and replication
Evaluation criteria	Statistical significance	Clinical or statistical significance
Generalizability	Via random sampling, logical generalization, and replication	Via logical generalization and replication
Sample size	Typically > 10 per group	Typically < 5 total, although far larger N possible

being drawn between the two general research strategies. These distinctions might not be completely applicable for a given design, and the two strategies should not be viewed as diametrically opposed or separate.

In comparing single-subject (intrasubject-replication) and between-group designs, Kazdin (1980) portrayed single-subject designs as being related to a particular subset of within-subject designs.

> The *intrasubject-replication design strategy* is a special category of within subject designs. . . . In *within-subject designs,* subjects receive each of the different treatments or interventions. In the most common example, separate groups of subjects receive all of the treatments but in a different order. . . . The various designs warrant special treatment because they uniquely allow experimental evaluation of interventions with individual subjects. (pp. 104–106)

In many instances, both design strategies may be appropriate for answering the same question. Whether treatment is better than no treatment or whether one treatment is more effective than another are examples of counseling research questions equally amenable to between-group and single-case research experimentation.

A major distinction between the strategies is whether the emphasis is placed on the "average" (the group mean) or on the individual client as the focus of analysis. In the typical between-groups study, clients displaying a common clinical problem (e.g., depression) are randomly assigned to a counseling treatment and to one or more comparison (e.g. a control group and/or alternative treatment) groups. After treatment, the groups are compared statistically to determine whether the average (mean) level of depression for the counseling group is significantly lower than that of the other group(s). Statistically, the issue is whether the variability in depression between the groups significantly exceeds the amount of variability in depression within the groups. If it does, then we conclude that our treatment was more effective than the control group (in the two group case). In other words, after treatment, the level of depression for the average client in the treatment group is significantly lower than that of the average client in the control group. Therefore, counseling was effective (for the average client). Hidden in our analysis, however, is the fact that all clients are not equally responsive to the counseling treatment. There is variability of responding within the counseling group with clients[3] showing different amounts and possibly different directions of change. However, that variability is treated as unexplained variance or as random error. In other words, the possible reasons for differential treatment responsiveness by individual clients within a group are typically not explored in a between-groups design. What is important is that the mean level of depression of clients in the counseling group is lower than that of the control group and that this is demonstrated statistically.

In single-case designs, the focus is on the individual client. Individual client variability in depression over time and in response to one or more conditions (e.g., treatment and comparison) that are systematically manipulated and often replicated is of primary importance. If the client demonstrates differential responding to the conditions in the desired direction and at an appropriate significance level (frequently a clinical rather than statistical criterion), then the treatment is judged to be effective with respect to the comparison condition for that client. Thus, the analysis might be regarded as a more intensive and fine-grained one with single-case as opposed to between-groups designs.

Another important distinguishing factor is the frequency with which dependent variables are measured. The between-groups study is characterized by assessment at a limited number of planned assessment points. Assessment typically occurs once prior to treatment and once after treatment (i.e., pretest–posttest). At times, follow-up assessment is also included. In contrast, a *sine qua non* of single-case research is repeated, "continuous" (frequent) assessment throughout the entire period of study. The purpose is for tracking and analyzing intrasubject variability over time and in response to the various conditions employed. The type of dependent variables used in between-groups and single-case research, however, is not a distinguishing factor as observational, physiological, and self-report measures are relevant in both cases (Barlow et al., 1984).

A major strength of single-case designs is their flexibility and adaptive-

---

[3]Variability occurs in the responses of the control group subjects as well.

ness. Unlike between-groups designs in which the researcher determines the research design and length of treatment ahead of time in a rather static fashion, single-case designs are intended to be used in a more dynamic, interactive manner (Hayes, 1981). The counselor/researcher makes tentative decisions about issues such as design and treatment length. Client data are then closely monitored throughout the study, and design alterations are made in response to those data as needed. This notion of tentativeness and making alterations to fit client needs tends to fit more closely with actual counseling practice than does the more fixed design requirements of between-groups research. As with between-groups research, however, single-case designs require clear specification of all procedures and replication of results if one is to have confidence in the findings.

The manner in which the two strategies control for threats to internal validity (see Campbell & Stanley, 1963; Cook & Campbell, 1979) represents an additional important distinguishing factor. Threats to internal validity are variables other than the one of interest (the independent variable or counseling treatment) that could plausibly account for the obtained results. Some of the most common of these include:

1. history (extraneous events occurring at the time of the study),
2. maturation (developmental or other processes occurring within clients at the time of the study),
3. testing (the effects of repeated assessment),
4. instrumentation (changes in measures or scoring procedures over time),
5. statistical regression (the tendency of extreme scores to revert toward the mean on a subsequent assessment),
6. selection (differential composition of groups of subjects), and
7. diffusion of treatment (receiving treatment at times when treatment should not be in effect or providing treatment to groups for which it is not intended).

In between-groups research, many threats are controlled by using large samples, random assignment, and control (e.g., no-treatment or waiting-list) groups. Control is achieved in the sense that, if these variables are present, there is no reason to assume that they will differentially affect the treatment and control groups. Therefore, any group differences should reflect the effects of treatment over and above these nuisance variables.

In single-case research, many of these threats are reduced by using the client as his or her own control coupled with replication. Thus, a client is assessed repeatedly across two or more conditions (e.g., treatment and a control or baseline condition, or treatment one and treatment two) which are systematically manipulated (e.g., first one condition or treatment is applied and then another) by the counselor. If the client's data change in the expected directions across the conditions, then suggestive evidence exists that treatment rather than the threats to internal validity account for the results. Confidence in the effects of the treatment are further strengthened if the client's data demonstrate a similar pattern of change if the same conditions (e.g., treatment and control or treatment one and two) are systematically manipulated in the same way again (replicated). The logic is that it would be an unlikely coincidence for one or more of these threats to internal validity to produce a pattern of change in the dependent variables identical to that expected from the systematic alternation of treatment and control (baseline) conditions or of two specific treatment conditions. Of course, it is still possible that the obtained variation is due to some complex, idiosyncratic or cyclical pattern. Confidence in the effects of the independent variable is further strengthened by replications either simultaneously or subsequently with a few (typically four or less) additional clients demonstrating similar problems and characteristics. If similar results are obtained, then it is highly probable that the results can be attributable to counseling rather than to the threats to internal validity.

In addition to whether the results of an investigation are internally valid and attributable to counseling for a particular client or group of clients, investigators are typically interested in the generalizability (external validity) of their findings. Would the findings be obtained by other investigators working in different settings with clients who manifested similar or related problems? For our purposes, it is sufficient to concentrate on how the problem of generalizability to other clients is addressed by the two research strategies. For the sake of argument, we assume that transfer occurs across investigators and settings.

In between-groups research, the ability to generalize beyond the original sample (Barlow & Hersen, 1984) is governed by the principles of random sampling, logical generalization (Edgington, 1966), and replication. If a given sample is randomly selected from a population and large enough to be representative of that population, then it may be reasonably assumed that results also apply to that population. Although random sampling may be possible in survey research, it is rarely practical in counseling treatment as researchers are simply unable to randomly select from all clients who display a particular concern. Rather, they must be content to draw their samples from those clients who demonstrate the concern at a given moment in time and ordinarily at a particular treatment site. As such, generalization of results based on random sampling is not viable. Moreover, even if random sampling were possible, a problem would still exist in generalizing the results from a between-groups research study to a particular client being seen by a particular counselor. Recall that the important results from such a study are whether the "average" client improved compared to the "average" subject in a comparison group. To the extent that the client being seen by the counselor does not display characteristics identical to those of the "average" client (which is quite likely), then generalizability to that client may not be warranted.

An alternative to random sampling is provided by logical generalization. One can generalize results to similar clients based on logical rather than statistical considerations. To the extent that a client demonstrates characteristics highly similar or identical to those used in a given study, generalization to that client is warranted. The implication of logical generalization is that between-groups research must employ samples that are homogeneous on the clinical problem as well as on other client characteristics (e.g., age, problem duration, etc.) presumed or previously shown to affect treatment. External validity is extended by demonstrating replication with other homogeneous samples that differ in well-defined ways from the original sample.

In single-case research, logical generalization and replication are crucial principles by which external validity is demonstrated. Careful specification of the exact treatment procedures and a detailed accounting of the characteristics of a given client with whom they are used are fundamental. These procedures are then replicated with several additional clients who display similar characteristics to the original client. To the extent that a given client being treated by a counselor is similar to the original client or his or her replications, then generalizability is warranted. External validity is then extended by demonstrating replication with several additional clients who differ from the original client in well-defined ways. Barlow and Hersen (1984) contended that "in terms of external validity or generality of findings, a series of single-case designs in similar clients in which the original experiment is directly replicated three or four times can far surpass the experimental group/no-treatment control group" (p. 57). The reason for their assertion is that the repeated assessment and treatment design flexibility of single-case research provides a great deal more information about client responsiveness to treatment than is provided in between-groups research.

Sample size is a final typical but not invariable distinguishing factor of the two research strategies. Between-groups research ordinarily involves 10 or more subjects per group, whereas single-case studies usually involve fewer than 5 subjects totally. However, single-case methodology has been used in investigations involving thousands or even a million subjects (see McSweeney, 1978; Schnelle et al., 1978; cited in Kazdin, 1982).

PHASES IN SINGLE-CASE RESEARCH

With few exceptions, most single-case designs have at least the following two phases: baseline (generally termed the *A phase*) and an intervention (usually denoted as the *B phase*) or other alternative conditions. In addition, there are different variations in single-case designs in which the baseline (A) may be taken more than once along with the implementation of more than one treatment (B) phase. For example, in ABAB designs (commonly referred to as *withdrawal* or *reversal* designs), a second baseline is collected after the initial treatment. The purpose of this second baseline is to see if the client's behavior reverts back toward the original level, given that treatment is no longer in effect. If so, the data would suggest a causal relationship. Following the second baseline, the treatment is then reintroduced to produce the desired change in behavior. A more detailed description of ABAB designs is provided later in the chapter. This section focuses on the characteristics of data, considerations in implementing the first (e.g., baseline) and subsequent (e.g., intervention) phases, and guidelines for changing phases.

Baseline

Barlow and Hersen (1984) defined the *baseline* as "the initial period of observation involving the repeated measurement of the natural frequency of occurrence of the target behaviors under study" (p. 71). This initial observation period serves two functions that will subsequently influence implementation of the intervention(s) (Kazdin, 1982). First, a baseline provides information regarding current level of performance (descriptive function). Second, the paseline serves a predictive function, providing information regarding the client's anticipated future level of performance assuming no changes in the conditions under which that performance is assessed.

There are basically four different baseline patterns: stable, improving, deteriorating, and variable. Space restrictions permit the illustration of only the first type (stable) of pattern. The stable baseline (see first A phase of Fig. 5.3) is represented by only minor variations or fluctuations in the data (i.e., representing a constant rate in behavior) and is the most desirable type of paseline for determining subsequent efficacy of the intervention phase. The second type of baseline is represented by a trend in the data such that the client's behavior appears to be deteriorating (Barlow & Hersen, 1984). Ideally, this trend would be reversed as a result of treatment. If the treatment were not effective, then no change in the client's data pattern would be apparent. If the intervention were detrimental, however, it might be difficult to assess whether the continued decline was due to the detrimental treatment or was simply a continuation of the baseline pattern.

A third type of baseline is represented by a steady improvement in the data. This type of baseline can be particularly problematic because it can pe difficult to separate treatment effects from the increasing trend that is already present. Barlow and Hersen (1984) pointed out that one possible strategy is to continue the baseline phase until a more stable pattern hopefully emerges, thus allowing treatment effects to be evaluated more easily. In other words, if the client is already showing improvement during the baseline phase, then it will be difficult to adequately assess the subsequent effects of the treatment.

Another problematic baseline is one in which the data are variable (i.e., there is not a clear trend in the data in one direction or the other and the data points fluctuate substantially). Barlow and Hersen (1984) suggested four possible strategies for combating this type of baseline. The first requires extending the baseline until a more stable pattern in the data emerges. The second involves the use of inferential statistics. The third strategy involves the systematic assessment of the sources of variability in an attempt to isolate them, and the fourth strategy consists of blocking (averaging) the data across longer intervals (e.g., every 2 or 3 days rather than on a daily basis). Of course, the last procedure must be continued throughout the study and does result in some loss of data points.

There are three additional types of baselines that are problematic. The first is characterized by an initial deterioration in the client's behavior and is followed by a trend toward improvement and thus is called an *increasing–decreasing baseline*. The second is the reciprocal of the first and is the *decreasing–increasing baseline*. This data pattern "often reflects the placebo effects of initially being part of an experiment or being monitored" (Barlow & Hersen, 1984, p. 78). The last type, referred to as the *unstable baseline*, has both variability and no particular pattern in the data, although particular segments of it might suggest trends (see Barlow & Hersen, 1984).

There are four basic factors involved in inspecting baseline data (or data for any phase for that matter). Ideally, these factors should be considered before moving onto the next phase, although there are instances in which this may not be possible as when the client's presenting problem requires immediate treatment and a delay in instituting treatment would result in deterioration.

The first consideration involves the length of the baseline. At least three data points, although more are preferable, must be collected in any phase, in order to be able to distinguish between stability, level, and trend in the data (Barlow et al., 1984). In general, a phase should be continued until patterns in the data are relatively clear (Kazdin, 1982). Thus, if an extreme score(s) occurs toward the end of the phase, additional data may need to be collected in order to clarify the pattern.

A second consideration is stability of the data. Stability refers to the amount of variability or fluctuation in the client's behavior over time (Kazdin, 1982). This characteristic is of primary importance especially during the first phase because one of the functions of baseline is to predict future behavior. Stability in the baseline and other phases is necessary in order for inferences to be made regarding the effects of treatment. "As a general rule, the greater the variability in the data, the more difficult it is to draw conclusions about the effects of the intervention" (Kazdin, 1982, p. 109). Ideally, the investigator wants little variability in baseline data (Kazdin, 1982). Of course, given that most treatment is time-limited, one cannot wait indefinitely for baseline data to stabilize. Thus, in some instances, it might be necessary to proceed to the next phase without first having achieved a stable baseline.

A third consideration is the level of the data, where level refers to elevation. During the baseline phase, the level of data should be such that a phase change is warranted. It would not make sense to implement treatment if the client's behavior during the baseline phase did not show a need for improvement. Conversely, if the initial baseline indicates an immediate need for treatment (e.g., frequent panic attacks of high intensity in a variety of situations), then it may be unethical to continue to withhold treatment from some of the situations in order to meet the requirements of a particular single-subject (e.g., multiple baseline across situations) design.

The fourth consideration is trend, "the tendency for performance to decrease or increase systematically or consistently over time" (Kazdin, 1982, p. 263). Trend refers to the slope or the direction of the data. This characteristic of the data also serves to justify a change from the baseline phase to the intervention phase. The investigator will want the data during the baseline phase either to show no trend or a trend in the opposite direction to what is expected from treatment. An increasing trend in the data makes it more difficult to document the effects of the intervention as the data are already moving in the desired direction. Nevertheless, it still may be possible under certain circumstances to demonstrate via statistical procedures that the existing trend was further accelerated by treatment.

Intervention

The second phase of most single-case designs is usually an intervention phase, although there are exceptions (e.g., BAB design). This phase involves the implementation of the treatment(s) or other experimental condition(s). A major consideration in experimental single-case research is for treatment to begin at full force whenever possible (Barlow & Hersen, 1984). By implementing treatment in this way, the desired differences between two phases will be maximized. When treatment is implemented gradually, behavior changes will tend to be less apparent, and replication will be especially important to validate the delayed effects resulting from gradual implementation.

As we have already implied, there are several guidelines for determining when to shift phases. Ideally, shifts are desirable after stability in the data has been demonstrated. Although stability is a relative notion, some numerical rules of thumb have been suggested (see Kazdin, 1982; Tawney & Gast, 1984). Second, data trends also need to be considered. An absence of a trend or, at least, a trend that runs counter to the anticipated effects of treatment is desirable. Third, when possible, specific criteria should be determined in advance so that condition alterations will less likely be a function of data fluctuation (Kazdin, 1982). Specifying criteria in advance reduces the subjectivity of decision making. Finally, the individual needs and treatment-related considerations for particular clients must also be taken into account.

EVALUATING SINGLE-CASE DATA

In contrast to between-groups research, much of the evaluation in experimental single-case research is of the formative rather than summative variety. Formative evaluation involves inspecting data and making changes in the intervention and/or the design as the study proceeds. By making adjustments along the way, the counselor/researcher has greater opportunity to alter conditions to meet client needs. In contrast, summative evaluation involves waiting until the end of treatment to evaluate effectiveness and tends to be concerned primarily with statistical changes from pre- to posttest.

In addition to being concerned with ongoing evaluation, experimental single-case proponents have focused on producing changes of applied or clinical significance for clients. These are changes that are readily observable rather than changes that are detectable primarily by statistical means. Because of these dual emphases, single-case data have tended to be presented and evaluated through visual means. The most common of these has been graphic displays with line graphs (to display serial or sequential data) and bar graphs (to display discrete data) predominating (see Parsonson & Baer, 1978; Tawney & Gast, 1984, for details). Of course, these graphs separate data according to their respective phase—baseline, and so forth.

In evaluating such data, we are concerned with changes in a variety of factors including stability/variability, level, and trend as we move from one phase to another. The following general guidelines are useful in evaluating changes from one phase to an adjacent phase: (a) large changes in level, or level and trend, (relative to variability) are more believable; (b) immediate effects are more believable; and (c) consistent effects are more believable (Barlow et al., 1984; Barlow & Hersen, 1984). Figure 5.1 presents some examples of different types of changes from one phase to an adjacent one. In evaluating changes across several phases, the following guidelines are useful: (a) replicated effects are more believable; (b) the more applications the more believable; and (c) due to potential multiple treatment interactions, comparisons of data from phases early in the sequence and closely related in time are more believable (drawn in part from Barlow et al., 1984). For an in-depth discussion of this topic, the reader is referred to Tawney and Gast (1984) who provide a systematic approach to "visual" analysis of data within conditions, between conditions, and across similar conditions for a variety of designs.

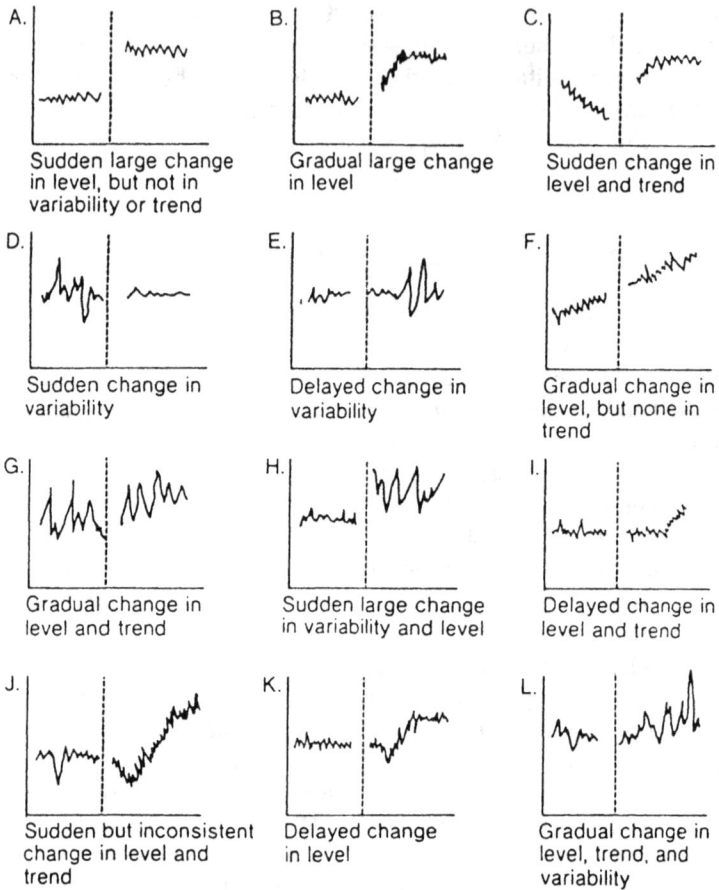

FIG. 5.1. Some examples of changes in variability, level, and trend in a simple phase change. (*Source*: Figure 8.1, p. 183 from Barlow, Hayes, & Nelson, 1984. Reproduced by permission.)

Inferential statistical analysis is an alternative to visual inspection for evaluating single-case data, although it should be noted that these designs have been associated with a tradition in which statistical analysis was viewed as unnecessary and even undesirable. What was important to the early proponents of these designs was clearly visible, practically important, and clinically significant changes. If a technique produced only statistically significant results, it was considered to have little practical value.

Although visual analysis is still the more common method, there are a number of arguments for using statistical analysis with single-case data. These include the following: (a) individual researchers often have difficulty arriving at similar conclusions using visual inspection of data; (b) a newly developed technique may, prior to refinement, produce only weak effects which may be overlooked by visual inspection procedures; (c) statistical procedures are better suited when there is initial trend; and (d) statistical analysis is useful when there is a great deal of variability in the data (Kazdin, 1984).

An extended discussion of single-case statistical methods is beyond the scope of this chapter. However, several good introductions are available (e.g., Edgington 1984, 1987; Kazdin 1982, 1984). In addition, Lichtenberg and Heck (1986) provided a useful introduction to Markov chain models, lag-sequential analysis, and information theory, which are methods for analyzing sequential data such as the verbal interactions of a counselor–client dyad during a counseling interview. Wampold (1984) and Wampold and Margolin (1982) provided additional statistical procedures for that purpose.

COMMON SINGLE-CASE RESEARCH DESIGNS

Case Studies and A–B Designs

Case studies have played an important role in a variety of forms of counseling and psychotherapy, from psychoanalysis (e.g., Little Hans; Freud, 1933) to behavior therapy (e.g., Little Albert; Watson & Rayner, 1920). Case studies range from anecdotal reports of treatment to well-designed simple phase-change (A–B) designs (Barlow et al., 1984; Kazdin, 1981). In general, the case study tends to connote a description of *anecdotal* information about an individual or small group of clients. The case study is typically viewed as *distinct* from an experimental investigation because it fails to control for threats to internal validity and ordinarily is not regarded as a source of scientifically valid inferences. For example, Frey (1978) distinguished three major types of N of 1 research: psychohistory (studies of the life patterns of historical figures), case study, and intensive design. In contrast, contemporary views (Barlow et al., 1984; Kazdin, 1981) place case studies and other single-case designs on a continuum reflecting the degree to which scientifically valid inferences can be drawn from the results. Under some circumstances, as is seen here, case studies may be arranged in such a way as to rule out major threats to internal validity and yield information which approximates that from more experimentally oriented, single-case designs. However, prior to considering these circumstances, it is necessary to discuss some different types of single-case investigations and the inferences that can be drawn from them.

Shapiro (1966) described four types of single-case investigations. *Simple covariation* involves *descriptive* investigation of covarying phenomena produced by the individual. Phenomena are simply described as they are observed in nature. Consider the findings of Hill et al. (1983) who published what was described by McCullough (1984a) as the "first" case study in JCP. Hill et al. (1983) reported that client insight and experiencing increased, and client description of problems decreased both within and across counseling sessions.

Complex covariation consists of descriptive investigation of changes in the client in conjunction with changes in phenomena outside the individual (e.g., changes in the counselor). In the Hill et al. study, client experiencing was most likely to occur after counselor silence and least likely to occur after closed questions. On the other hand, client description of problems was most likely to occur after closed questions and least likely to occur after counselor-direct guidance and interpretation. Client insight was most likely to occur in the first unit after counselor silence or in the second unit after open question or confrontation.

Both types of covariation descriptive studies can serve as rich sources of hypotheses for the counselor/investigator. However, it is difficult to draw causal conclusions from them because a variety of credible explanations for the covariation might be offered. Any number of uncontrolled variables (internal validity threats) might account for the results.

In contrast, a *simple experimental* single-case investigation involves observing changes in dependent variables in relation to controlled manipulation of an independent variable. The simple experiment provides a more solid basis for causal inference than descriptive investigations. If change in the dependent variable(s) is regularly associated with variations in the independent variable (as in the A–B–A–B design where following the initial A stage, the independent variable is successively applied and withdrawn and then applied again), it is unlikely that an internal threat to validity would produce an identical cyclical pattern of results.

Predictive experimental is Shapiro's fourth type of single-case investigation. It involves observing changes in dependent variables in response to new and hitherto unobserved manipulations of the independent variable. Predictions about how the client will behave in the new situation are made based on previous results (e.g., with the client in different situations). To the extent that these specific predictions are confirmed, the predictive experiment provides a very strong basis for causal inferences.

Tracey (1983) distinguished experimental from associational designs. Tracey's view of experimental single-case designs is similar to Shapiro's in that they involve manipulating independent variables and permit causal inferences. However, Tracey stated that they are primarily applicable to behavioral counseling as it is difficult to "undo" or withdraw many nonbehavioral interventions (see McCullough, 1984a, 1984b).

Although associational designs (including Shapiro's descriptive covariation investigations) do not permit causal inferences, Tracey views them as more flexible because they are applicable to most types of counseling and can be used to study both process and outcome. In Fig. 5.2, Tracey illustrates how a simple associational (A–B) design might be used to investigate process and outcome. In Graph a, an increase in study time is associated with (not necessarily caused by) the counseling intervention. If the counselor had reason to believe that client introspection during counseling was related to client study time, the data might look like those in Graph b. Further, if counselor behavior is assumed to influence client behavior, then the data might look like Graph c. These data suggest that client introspection is positively related to study time and counselor interpretations and inversely related to counselor questions. Increasing counselor interpretations and decreasing counselor questions may lead to more client introspection and understanding that, in turn, may increase study time. Once again, however, the observed relation-

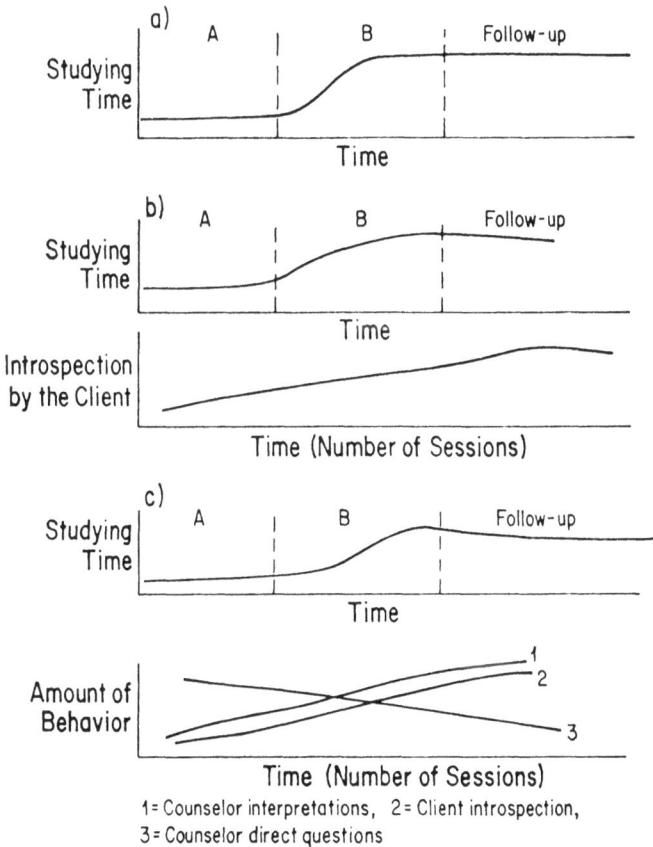

FIG. 5.2. Graphic examples of some applications of the AB *N* of 1 design. (*Source*: Figure 2 from Tracey, 1983. American Association for Counseling and Development copyright holder and publisher. Reproduced by permission.)

ships are associational and not necessarily causal. Replication would be needed to add confidence that the relationships are reliable, and experimental manipulation would be needed to isolate the causal variables.

Inability to manipulate the independent variable is not the only factor affecting our ability to draw causal inferences. Kazdin (1981) identified five additional factors, which if controlled, markedly reduce threats to the internal validity and permit a level of causal inference from case studies approaching what is possible from single-case experimental designs. These factors include reliable, objective measures (e.g., self-reports, ratings by others, overt behaviors, etc.) that are administered on a repeated, continuous systematic basis rather than intermittent, unsystematic anecdotal reports. Credibility of inference is also increased if the problem is stable as shown by an extended past baseline or whose future course is known from previous research. Finally, if immediate and marked effects are obtained when treatment is implemented, and if the results are replicated with multiple, heterogeneous clients, confidence in the causal effects of treatment is similarly elevated. Under these conditions, Kazdin asserted that the five major threats—history, maturation, testing, instrumentation, and statistical regression—to the internal validity of the case study most likely have been controlled. Thus, if the problem has been stable in the past, then several different cases treated at different times are not likely to display identical history and maturational effects that manifest themselves in a dramatic way precisely when treatment is administered. Moreover, any effects due to repeated testing, instrumentation changes, and statistical regression probably would have appeared earlier in the sequence.

Even if only three of these factors are present (objective data, continuous assessment, and immediate and marked treatment effects), testing, instrumentation, and statistical regression are highly unlikely threats and history and maturation explanations are probably unlikely as well. The point is that a variety of factors affect our ability to draw inferences from single-case investigations. Knowing what needs to be controlled and whether it has been may be more important than whether a case study (e.g., an A–B design) or some more elaborate design structure was employed.

Withdrawal Designs

This category includes a seemingly endless number of designs (e.g., A–B–A, B–A–B, B–C–B–C, etc.) to answer questions such as the following: Is treatment better than no treatment? Is one treatment better than another? Does the combination (interaction) of two treatment components produce better effects than either of the components alone? However, the logic of interpreting results is similar across withdrawal designs. It involves comparing the

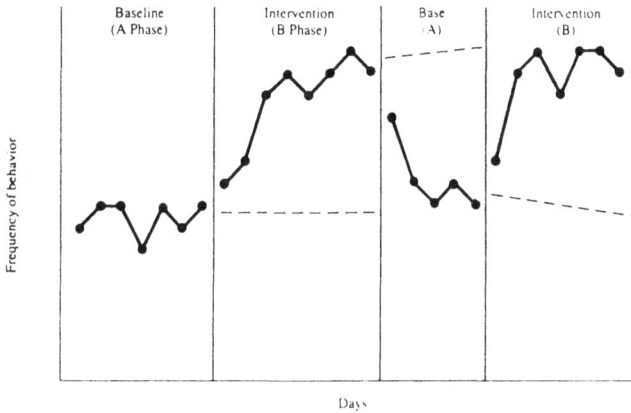

FIG. 5.3. Hypothetical data for an A-B-AB design. The solid lines in each phase present the actual data. The dashed lines indicate the projection or predicted level of performance from the previous phase. (*Source:* Figure 5-4, p. 111 from Kazdin, 1982. Reproduced by permission.)

stability, level, and trend of data in adjacent phases to determine whether reliable differences exist as a function of presenting and withdrawing treatment across successive time periods (phases). Except in the case of evaluating a complex treatment package (e.g., A–BCD–A–BCD), only one variable is generally changed per phase in order to avoid confounding the results across phases. Moreover, because extraneous variables (e.g., maturational variables) are more likely to occur over a long time period than a short one, comparisons of data that are contiguous are stronger than comparisons that are further apart (Barlow et al., 1984). As is recalled, our "rules of thumb" for interpreting data include the following: (a) large changes (relative to the previous level of variability) in level and trend occurring in close proximity to phase shifts are more easily interpreted than smaller, delayed, or more gradual changes; and (b) confidence is increased to the extent that effects are replicated across repeated phase shifts.

With these considerations in mind, it can be seen from the hypothetical data (Fig. 5.3) presented by Kazdin (1982) that the initial baseline (A) data are stable and show relatively little variability. As is recalled, the purpose of the baseline is to describe current behavior and to predict (assuming baseline stability) future behavior if conditions are unchanged. That prediction is represented by the dashed line that has been projected into the first B phase. As is seen, the data (solid line) obtained during the first intervention depart from baseline and its associated prediction. These data demonstrate a stable increase in trend and a gradual and ultimately stable increase in level. In turn, the graphic representation of the B_1 phase not only describes the data but also is used to predict (the dashed line in the second baseline period) how the data should appear if conditions are unchanged. Withdrawing the intervention (reintroducing the baseline condition), however, produces data in the second A phase that depart from that prediction. This increases our confidence in the likely causal effect of the intervention because the data in the absence of the intervention revert toward the initial baseline in both level and trend. These data, in turn, can be used to predict future behavior if conditions are unchanged (the dashed line in the second B phase). In addition, the second A phase tests the prediction of the first A phase (dashed line in first B phase vs. solid line in second A phase). As can be seen, the data in the second B phase depart in both level and trend from the second baseline and its associated prediction, thus replicating the results of the first A–B phase shift. This pattern further strengthens our confidence in the causal effects of the intervention. In addition, the data of the second baseline, confirm the prediction from the first baseline (dashed line in the first B phase). It should be noted, however, that the logic of the withdrawal design does not require that the original baseline level of performance be recovered for causal inferences to be warranted. In fact, treatment carry-over effects may prevent total recovery of initial baseline performance. All that is required is that performance revert toward baseline and that improvement be shown when treatment is reintroduced (Barlow et al., 1984; Hayes, 1981). Of course, recovery of the initial baseline level would permit clearer inferences.

In order to better understand withdrawal designs, a few examples are presented. The first (Truax & Carkhuff, 1965) illustrates a single-case design in process research with three schizophrenic female inpatients. The study involved the systematic alteration of high and low "therapeutic conditions" in what has been described (Barlow & Hersen, 1984) as a B–A–B design, although it might be more appropriate to refer to it as a B–C–B design because the low therapeutic condition seems more like an alternative treatment than a baseline condition. High therapeutic conditions consisted of highly rated therapist responses on the Truax Accurate Empathy and Unconditional Positive Regard scales. The single dependent variable in the study was a process measure: ratings on Truax's Depth of Intrapersonal Exploration scale. Therapist and patient data were recorded for a 1-hour initial interview. A 45-minute period was subdivided into three phases that included five, 3-minute time blocks. During the first and last phase, the therapist was instructed to offer high levels of empathy and unconditional regard. The middle period involved lowered conditions. It was punctuated by two interruptions by an outsider, one at the beginning and one at the end of the period. These interruptions were intended to suggest that the therapist was preoccupied during this period. Therapist and patient behavior for the 5-minute segments were presented in random order and reliably rated by different sets of independent judges. With the possible exception of empathy with Patient C, therapist empathy and unconditional regard were manipulated as intended across the phases.

Figure 5.4 displays the effects of these manipulations on client self-exploration. At least for Patients A and B, there would appear to be a systematic relationship between level of therapist offered conditions and depth of client self-exploration even though there is some overlap of data points in the different phases. The relationship is not as apparent for Patient C and may reflect a failure to manipulate the therapeutic conditions although other explanations are possible.

The most well-known withdrawal design is the A–B–A–B design. It is sometimes referred to as a *reversal* design. However, the reversal terminology is appropriate only when reinforcement is applied to one behavior in the intervention phase and then either to an incompatible behavior or noncontingently in the second baseline. Experimentally, the A–B–A–B design is probably the most powerful single-case design because it requires the repeated introduction and withdrawal of the intervention. In essence, it requires a direct replication of a treatment effect in order to demonstrate internal validity.

Building on our Rogerian counseling example, Fig. 5.5 presents hypothetical data concerning the effects of counselor reflections of feeling on depth of client self-exploration in an initial interview. In this example, the 50-minute interview was divided into four 10-minute phases excluding the first and last 5 minutes. Each 10-minute phase was subdivided into five 2-minute segments in which judges' ratings of client depth of self-exploration were averaged. During baseline, the counselor was told to stress the following counseling leads: paraphrase, questions, suggestions, and minimal encouragers such as "yes," "OK," and brief repetitions of portions of the client's response and to use these at least 90% of the time. In the intervention phase, the counselor was told to use reflection of feeling responses at least 50% of the time and to intersperse the other leads as needed. If the study were actually carried out, it would be important to verify with tape recordings that the therapist behaved as instructed in each phase.

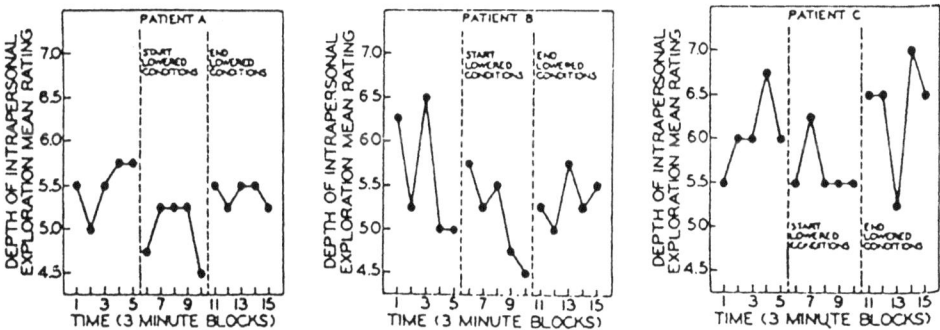

FIG. 5.4. Depth of intrapersonal exploration. (*Source*: Figure 4 from Truax & Carkhuff, 1965. Copyright © 1965 by the American Psychological Association. Reprinted by permission.)

PHASE

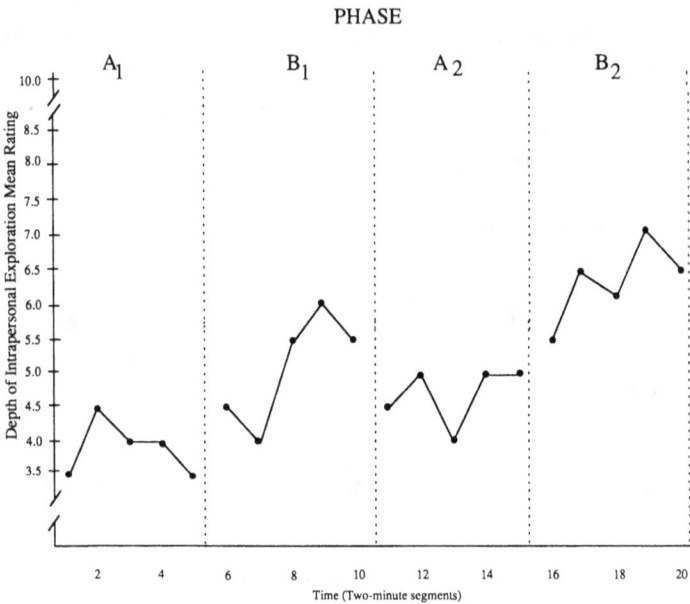

FIG. 5.5. Hypothetical data for the effects of counselor reflections on client depth of intrapersonal exploration as revealed by an ABAB withdrawal design.

Following a stable baseline in which self-exploration is at a low level, counselor reflection of feeling results in an immediate increase in depth of client self-exploration as well as in a generally accelerating trend. The third phase reveals a drop in client self-exploration and a change in trend. However, there is not a return to the initial baseline level, perhaps indicating some carryover effects and the fact that once a client begins to self-explore the process may not be easily reversible. When reflection of feeling (B_2) is reinstituted, depth of exploration immediately increases and to levels which are higher than in the initial B phase. Taken together, the data would seem to suggest that counselor reflections lead to deeper levels of client self-exploration than baseline counselor responding. If the study had actually been conducted, replications with additional clients would lend strength to the conclusion. Of course, the data are still open to other explanations. For example, it might be hypothesized that depth of self-exploration tends to fluctuate during the initial interview in a predictable pattern, and what is being reflected is that typical cyclical pattern rather than the effects of counselor reflections of feeling. To test such a hypothesis, a B–A–B–A design could be employed. If data from that design showed the opposite pattern, then such a hypothesis would not be tenable.

Although the A–B–A–B design is powerful, it does have limitations when applied to practice. Ethically, one can question the appropriateness of withdrawing treatment even though subsequent baselines phases may be short. Of course, there are counterarguments such as withdrawing treatments of unknown effectiveness is not unethical; missed client appointments or vacations allow for natural withdrawal phases; withdrawal of treatment allows for assessment of maintenance effects, etc. (see Barlow et al., 1984). Nevertheless, given that clinical change is often difficult to effect, withdrawing treatment can be difficult to justify. Finally, aside from ethical concerns, it is sometimes impossible to "reverse" some changes. For example, a client may acquire a particular concept or master a particular skill that cannot be unlearned or when learned is maintained by environmental consequences.

Multiple Baseline Designs

The multiple baseline design (Baer et al., 1968) is nothing more than a series of A–B designs (or B–C designs, etc.) in which the *same* intervention is introduced to different baselines (or initial B phases as the case may be) at different points in time in a sequential, controlled fashion. If change is observed in a baseline (or initial phase), only when the intervention is introduced to it, then the intervention can be assumed to have produced the change. Unlike the A–B design, the multiple baseline offers strong controls for instrumentation and maturation effects. Moreover, it has the advantage over A–B–A–B designs of not requiring withdrawal of treatment, but it permits strong causal inferences. Because of these factors as well as its simplicity, it is a good design for practitioners (Barlow et al., 1984).

Figure 5.6 illustrates a multiple baseline design with a multiphobic female who was treated with desensitization (Liberman & Smith, 1972). Fear of being alone was treated first. Desensitization produced a decrease in this self-reported fear as compared to baseline (a within-behavior comparison). Now, it could be hypothesized that this reduction simply reflects changes in the self-report instrument, the effects of repeated testing, or maturation effects. If any of those uncontrolled variables are operating, the three remaining behaviors, fear of menstruation, chewing hard foods, and dental work, which are untreated at this point in time, should show corresponding reductions. However, these three across-behavior comparisons remain stable thus supporting the effects of the intervention. Once the intervention effects changes in the first behavior, it is then introduced to the second behavior assuming its baseline is stable. The process is repeated, in turn, for the third and fourth behaviors, respectively. For Fig. 5.6, all within- and across-behavior comparisons depict change only when desensitization is introduced to a behavior. Moreover, change is maintained in follow-up assessment. Follow-up is a useful addition to the standard multiple baseline design.

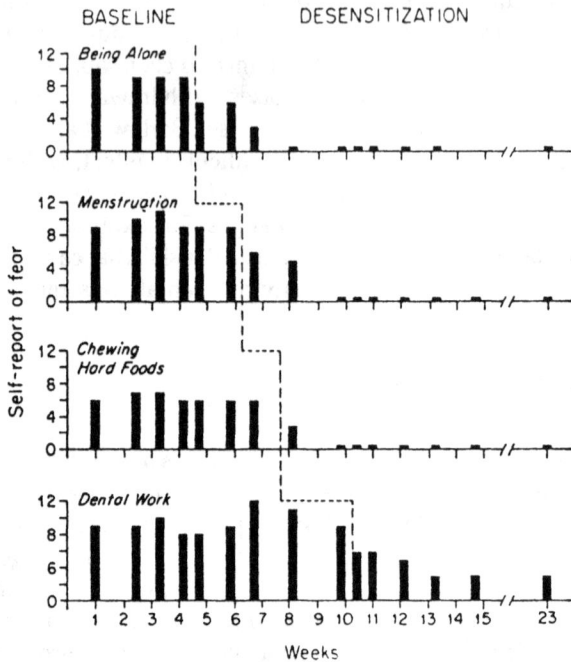

FIG. 5.6. Multiple baseline evaluation of desensitization in a single case with four phobias. (*Source*: Figure 1, p. 600 from Liberman & Smith, 1972. Copyright © 1972 by the Association for Advancement of Behavior Therapy. Reproduced by permission.)

Figure 5.7 depicts a multiple baseline example from the supervision literature (Holahan & Galassi, 1986). A supervisor applied a brief intervention to modify the percentage of questions asked by a beginning counselor in order to change client participation in the interview. Based on 4-minute behavior samples, it is evident from Fig. 5.7 that the counselor initially used questions far more than any other behavior (*M* = 61% in baseline). The intervention consisted of the supervisor and counselor listening to a randomly selected 4-minute segment of the interview and comparing notes on the target behavior (initially counselor questions) identified. In addition, the supervisor praised the counselor for using the behavior appropriately. As can be seen, each counselor target behavior changed when the supervisory intervention was applied to it. Moreover, these changes were accompanied by concomitant increases in total number of client statements and feeling statements as counselor questions and reflections, respectively, were modified. All changes were maintained in a follow-up period.

This last example can be used to illustrate a number of important points about this design. First, if effects are clear, a minimum of two baselines are needed, although four have been recommended (Barlow & Hersen, 1984). There are several reasons for this. First, baselines are assumed to be independent in this design. If an intervention is applied to one baseline and change is also observed in a nontargeted baseline, or if the intervention fails to produce change when it is applied, then it is difficult to attribute change to the intervention. With four baselines, if change is observed in one of the baselines before the intervention was applied to it or if little change is observed when the intervention is applied, it still is possible to attribute effects to the intervention if the other behaviors behave as expected. In general, the more baselines (replications) that consistently show the anticipated effects, the stronger the basis for causal inference.

As is true for other single-case designs, the decision to shift phases should

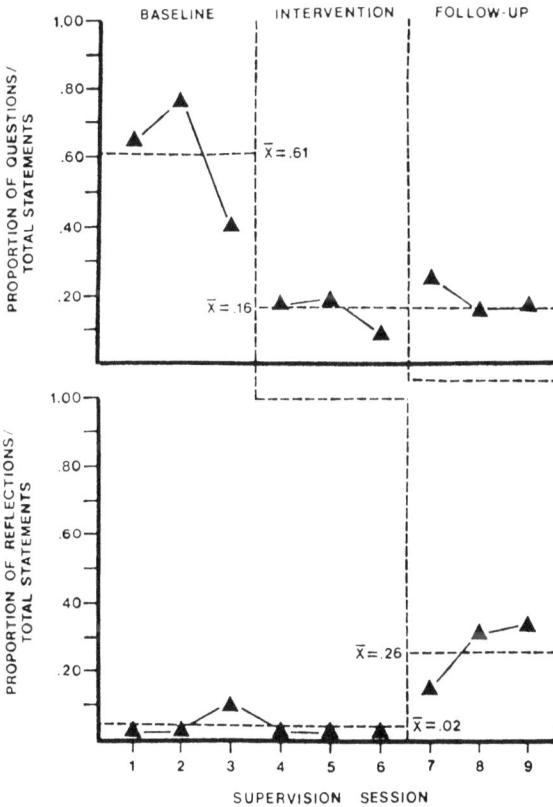

FIG. 5.7. Proportion of counselor questions and reflections of feelings to total statements. (*Source*: Figure 1, p. 171 from Holahan & Galassi, 1986. American Association for Counseling and Development copyright holder and publisher. Reproduced by permission.)

be based in large part on stability of data in the previous phase. As can be seen for counselor questions in Fig. 5.7, the decision to implement the intervention was not based on counselor performance as this baseline was not stable, a factor that weakens the causal inferences that can be drawn from the example. In this instance, the decision was based on artificial time constraints—the number of weeks available in the semester that the study was conducted.

There are a number of different ways in which multiple baseline designs can be applied. The multiple baseline across behaviors involves sequentially applying the same treatment across successive behaviors while holding other factors (e.g., setting, client, etc.) constant. The Liberman and Smith example we discussed exemplifies such an application. The design can also be applied across subjects. Whang, Fletcher, and Fawcett (1982) used this design in teaching counseling skills (opening and closing sessions, reflections, and problem-solving behaviors) to two paraprofessional staff in a community service center. For example, baseline data were taken for both staff on reflections, and then an intervention to increase reflections was applied to one of the staff while baseline was continued for the other. The design can also be applied across settings, situations, time, and so forth. Using a combination of physiological and self-report measures of anxiety, Fairbank and Keane (1982) investigated the effects of imaginal flooding with Vietnam war veterans suffering from posttraumatic stress disorder by applying the intervention successively across four traumatic memories. Thus, the design was a multiple baseline across scenes or situations.

It is also possible to apply a multiple baseline design to situations in which more than one factor varies at a time. For instance, a multiple baseline design across behaviors involves applying a treatment successively to behaviors A, B, and C while holding setting and other variables constant. However, as noted by Barlow et al. (1984), a multiple baseline design could also be implemented across Behavior A in Setting X, Behavior B in Setting Y, and Behavior C in Setting Z. Analogously, in the Holahan and Galassi example, the counselor data actually represent averaged values across several clients, thus representing a multiple baseline design across behaviors, but one in which subjects also vary.

Finally, the baselines do not always have to be taken at exactly the same time. A counselor could apply an intervention to a client in an A–B design one month and then not encounter a similar client with a similar problem for some time. When a similar client is encountered, that same intervention could be applied to the second client, but using an initial baseline of slightly different length than that of the first client. By retaining the A–B data for the two clients, the counselor would be able to turn two somewhat weaker A–B designs into one stronger multiple baseline design across subjects (Barlow et al., 1984).

The design does have some limitations. As noted earlier, if the behaviors are not independent, and some change occurs before treatment has been applied to them, then interpretation of the results is difficult.[4] Similarly, if some behaviors respond when treatment is implemented and others fail to respond, then interpretation is also difficult. Finally, if some of the baselines are of prolonged duration, ethical issues with regard to withholding treatment may come into play.

Changing Different Designs

This design (Hall, 1971; Hartmann & Hall, 1976) is a variation of the multiple baseline design. It is appropriate when gradual, stepwise client changes are expected. Unlike the multiple baseline design, only one target behavior is involved. In contrast to the A–B–A–B design, no treatment withdrawal is required, although a "mini" reversal (Kazdin, 1982) or reversion to an earlier criterion level is sometimes used to strengthen the inferences that can be drawn from the design. The design has a somewhat limited range of applicability and is useful where motivational or compliance problems are responsible for failure to meet a specified criterion (Tawney & Gast, 1984).

Experimental control in a changing criterion design is demonstrated by showing that with each criterion shift (either upward or downward), client performance closely matches the new criterion. In essence, each criterion level forms a baseline for the next phase or criterion level. As such, performance in each level should be stable in order to serve as a baseline for the next level. Moreover, client change should be immediate following each criterion shift and closely match the new criterion. In essence, each criterion shift represents a replication of the experimental effect, and a minimum of four shifts is recommended (Barlow et al., 1984).

Fig. 5.8 presents a portion of the data from a smoking reduction program reported by Hartmann and Hall (1976) to illustrate a changing criterion design. As can be seen, the baseline[5] (A) indicates a high and stable level[6] of self-reported cigarette smoking (except for the last data point). Treatment involved imposing a daily criterion level for cigarettes smoked and consequences for over- and under-indulgence. The criterion in the first phase (B) was set at 95% of baseline (46 cigarettes). Smoking more than that resulted in a $1 escalating fine ($1 for cigarette 47, $2 for 48, etc.). Smoking less than

---

[4]In such instances, inclusion of a brief reversal phase to the baseline of concern followed by a reintroduction of treatment may help to demonstrate experimental control.

[5]This design may be used when no baseline phase is possible (Barlow et al., 1984).

[6]Criteria and criterion shifts could relate to variability or trend rather than level (Barlow et al., 1984).

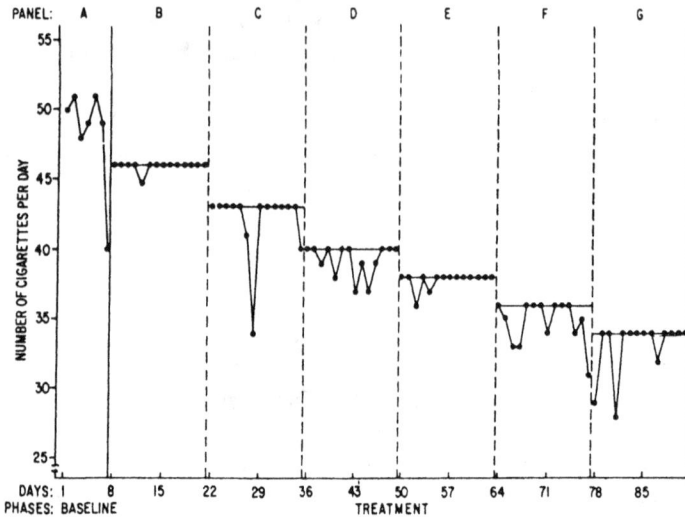

FIG. 5.8. Data from a smoking-reduction program used to illustrate the step-wise criterion change design. Solid horizontal line segments indicate criterion for each treatment phase. (*Source*: Figure 2, p. 529 from Hartmann & Hall, 1976. Copyright © 1976 by the *Journal of Applied Behavior Analysis*. Reproduced by permission.)

46 per day resulted in a 10¢ per cigarette escalating bonus. For the remaining panels presented by the authors, the criterion was set at 94% of the previous phase, and the treatment was identical to what has been described. By and large, cigarette smoking tracked criterion shifts[7] fairly closely that strongly suggests that the behavior was responsive to treatment.

Of course, a plausible rival hypothesis in changing criterion designs is that the data are mimicking naturally occurring patterns rather than reflecting the effects of treatment. A number of procedural strategies can be employed to minimize the likelihood of this hypothesis being true. These include: (a) varying the magnitude of criterion shifts, (b) varying the length of criterion phases, and (c) temporarily changing the direction (a "mini" reversal) of the criterion shift (e.g., raise rather than lower the number of cigarettes to be smoked in one or more of the phases). Client change that closely tracks these variations is unlikely to be the result of extraneous factors or naturally occurring phenomena.

The advantages of the changing criterion design to the counselor are that it does not require withholding or withdrawing treatment and that it fits with

---

[7]Hartmann and Hall (1976) also plot the data in terms of the percent of days each criterion was met. This representation allows the reader to see more clearly the multiple baseline nature of the design.

the gradual nature of many types of client change. The design has several disadvantages. First, there are no agreed upon standards for determining whether client change "closely" matches criterion levels, and too much change threatens the logic of the design just as does too little change. Second, there are no clear guidelines for determining the size of criterion shifts. The shifts must be large enough to demonstrate change; small enough to be achievable by the client; but not so small as to be regularly exceeded by the client (see Barlow et al., 1984, Kazdin, 1982; Tawney & Gast, 1984, for a further discussion of these issues).

Alternating Treatment Designs

When research is concerned with the differential effectiveness of treatments (or conditions) with a single subject (or group of subjects), an alternating treatments design (ATD) may well be the design of choice. Several names have been used to refer to ATDs (e.g., multiple schedule, multi-element, randomization, and simultaneous treatment design). This lack of consistency in terminology has produced confusion regarding the basic logic and application of the design.

In ATDs, treatment refers to condition and does not necessarily imply therapy. Multiple applications of the same treatment or condition constitute a series. To evaluate differential effectiveness, the data points for each series are compared to each other. For this reason, alternating treatment designs have been described as a type of between-series, single-case design.

A key characteristic of ATDs is that the treatments are alternated rapidly. They are also alternated randomly, although Barlow et al. (1984) recommend using no more than three of the same treatments in a row in order to avoid lengthy intervals of that treatment. How often a treatment is alternated is also influenced by what constitutes a meaningful unit of measurement (Barlow et al., 1984). The investigator will therefore need to determine the time element best suited for measuring change in the behavior under observation. Although a minimum of two alternations has been recommended (Barlow et al., 1984), the greater the frequency of alternations, the greater the precision of analysis. As the frequency of alternations increases so do the opportunities for different treatment series to diverge, thus allowing greater accuracy when comparing them. With regard to the number of treatments, Kazdin (1982) recommends two to three as optimal "for avoiding the complexities of balancing the interventions across the conditions of administration" (p. 194). In addition, discriminative stimuli that enable a client to determine which treatment is in effect at a given time are sometimes used. The most common way to facilitate such discrimination is through verbal instruction.

As an example of an ATD, Fig. 5.9 presents hypothetical data from the Rogerian counseling interaction presented earlier. Treatment A (counselor paraphrasing) is alternated with B (counselor reflections) to determine the

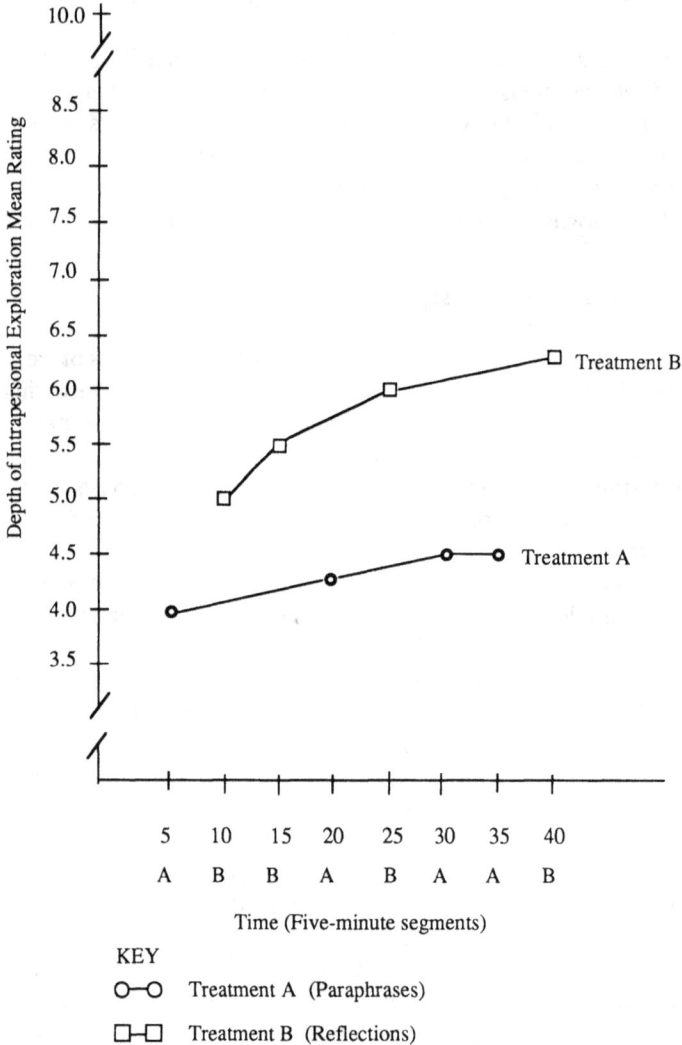

FIG. 5.9. Hypothetical example of an ATD comparing two treatments.

effects on depth of client self-exploration. From the results, it appears that treatment B (counselor reflections) leads to more in depth self-exploration than treatment A (counselor paraphrases).

Because treatments change rapidly in the ATD, data points are not usually recorded according to phase but rather in a continuous series over time for each treatment. Although phase-change elements can be added to the alternating treatments designs, they are not necessary because the stability, level, and trend of the data are arranged sequentially by treatment, rather than by time alone. Differences among treatment are inferred when there is a clear and distinct separation between series. Although the logic of the design does not require it, a baseline may be employed and even continued when the interventions are administered. Moreover, not all conditions need to be treatments (Kazdin, 1982). Rather, a baseline could be used as one of the "treatment" alternatives, thus providing greater assurance that the intervention is responsible for change. In most cases, visual analysis should be sufficient to determine differential effects, although statistical procedures are available (Barlow & Hersen, 1984). In evaluating results from ATDs, "most investigators have been relatively conservative, in that very clear divergence among the treatments has been required" (Barlow & Hersen, 1984, p. 282). In many cases, the series will not overlap. When overlap does occur, the question becomes how much is too much. Obviously, the smaller the overlap the clearer the effects.

Alternating treatments designs have been used to compare the effects of treatment with no treatment (baseline) and two or more treatments with each other. Treatments are compared alone in an ATD when their individual effectiveness is known and when differential effectiveness is the primary issue (Barlow et al., 1984). An ATD is said to be internally valid when one treatment is more "consistently associated with a different level of responding than other interventions" (Tawney & Gast, 1984, p. 313). The ATD usually has good internal validity because the rapid alternation of conditions controls for threats such as maturation and history common to multitreatments. The alternating treatments design strategy "provides one of the most elegant controls . . . for ruling out rival hypotheses in accounting for the difference between the two treatments" (Barlow & Hersen, 1984, p. 252).

Tawney and Gast (1984) have suggested three ways in which the ATD may be implemented, two of which have application in counseling and are briefly presented here. The first includes a baseline phase, an intervention phase with two treatments, and a final phase containing only the more effective of the two treatments. Drawing on our previous example, Fig. 5.10 illustrates Treatment A (paraphrasing) being alternated in 2-minute segments with Treatment B (reflection) after a stable baseline has been obtained. Because counselor reflections are associated with more depth of intrapersonal exploration than paraphrases during the second phase, counselor reflections are extended into the final phase. This final phase is also useful in determining treatment effectiveness of counselor reflections in isolation.

A second ATD application suggested by Tawney and Gast (1984) is illustrated in Fig. 5.11. Here baseline (counselor minimal encouragers) is extended into the second phase and alternated with the two previous treatments. Once again, counselor reflection is the superior treatment and is extended into the final phase.

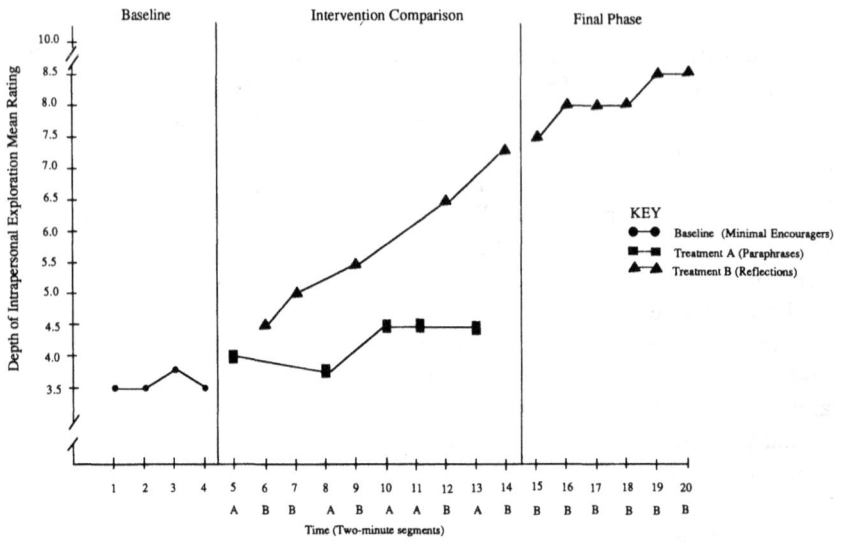

FIG. 5.10. Hypothetical example of and ATD comparing two treatments but including an initial baseline phase and a final phase.

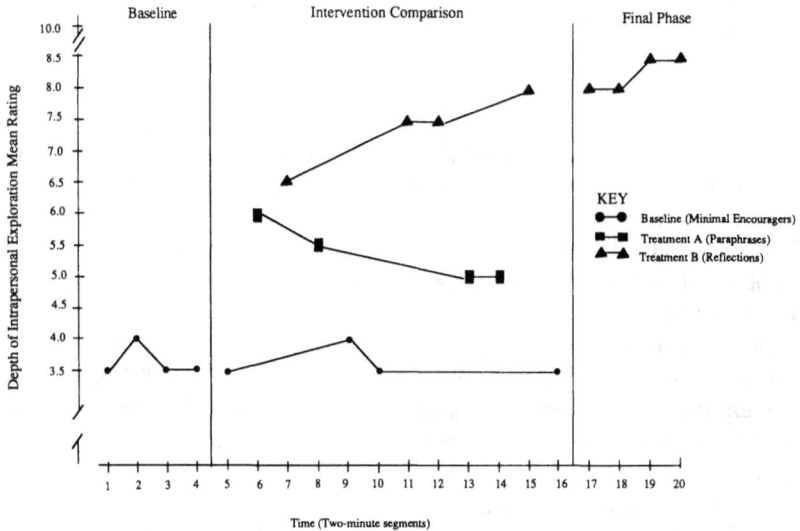

FIG. 5.11. Hypothetical example of at ATD comparing two treatments and a baseline during the intervention phase.

In addition to the issues discussed earlier, several others deserve consideration. First, potentially confounding variables will need to be determined a priori so that a schedule for counterbalancing can be implemented (Tawney & Gast, 1984). For example, times of treatment, and in some cases therapists, may have to be counterbalanced in order for the treatment effect to be clear (Barlow & Hersen, 1984).

Another consideration is multiple-treatment interference. Multiple-treatment interference is concerned with whether the results of one treatment, when alternated with another treatment, will be the same as when the treatment is applied alone. Barlow et al. (1984) describe several multiple-treatment problems specific to ATDs. First, a treatment's impact may be confounded by the order (sequence) in which it occurs. If Treatment B *always* follows Treatment A, then the effects of Treatment A are confounded by the fact that it is always the second one in the sequence. However, this problem can be addressed through the random or semi-random sequencing of treatments. A second issue, carry-over or contextual effects, refers to the effects of one treatment on another, regardless of their sequencing. Thus, the fact that the two treatments are adjacent can either retard or enhance effects as compared to when they occur alone. Once again, random sequencing perhaps coupled with short treatments may help with this problem (Barlow et al., 1984). Third, too rapid treatment alternation can actually heighten carry-over effects, and this issue also needs to be recognized in designing and interpreting results from ATDs.

In summary, ATDs offer several positive features to the investigator. First, they do not require either treatment withdrawal or a formal baseline and thus eliminate some of the practical and ethical problems encountered with withdrawal designs. Second, much more rapid treatment comparisons can be made than with withdrawal designs because technically only two data points are required in each ATD series in order for variability to be assessed (Barlow et al., 1984). Third, ATDs have the ability to minimize sequencing problems through rapid alternation of interventions (Tawney & Gast, 1984). A final advantage is insensitivity to background trends (Barlow et al., 1984) as differential treatment effects will be evident over and above such trends.

The design also has a number of limitations. Some of the most salient of these are the following: (a) rapid alternation of treatments and other design requirements make it impractical or artificial in many applied situations; (b) the effects of multiple treatment interference are not easy to determine; (c) the ATD may adversely affect behavior change if differential effects do not occur early in the sequence; and (d) the design may not be sensitive to weak treatments that are effective over a long period of time (Tawney & Gast, 1984).

CUSTOMIZING SINGLE-CASE DESIGNS

To this point, we have discussed the most common single-case designs and have ignored others such as the crossover, multiple probe, multitreatment, and simultaneous treatment designs that provide the counselor-researcher with additional design options. In addition, we have often discussed these designs as though they were fixed options that must be elected in advance of data collection. The astute reader, however, will recall that one advantage of single-case designs is their flexibility and that client data is one criterion used to select the design alternative. More importantly, the designs we have discussed can also be viewed as being composed of a smaller set of design building blocks (Barlow et al., 1984; Hayes, 1981). If the researcher understands the logic of these fundamental elements, then a variety of customized designs can be generated.

Flexible Design Elements

Single-case designs tend to use one of three strategies—within-series, between-series, or combined-series comparisons (Hayes, 1981). The most popular of these is the within-series strategy. In a within-series comparison, data for a single client (or group) is collected over time. Time is divided into several phases. In a given phase, the experimental conditions are constant for the client (or group). Changes in stability, level, and trend within the entire data series are examined in relation to the different experimental conditions (phases). To the extent that there are systematic changes within the data series as a function of an experimental condition, then change is attributed to that condition. A–B, withdrawal, and changing criterion designs all make use of within-series comparisons. The logic of within-series designs is the same regardless of whether a simple (e.g., A–B–A–B) or a complex phase change is involved. A complex phase change might be used to study the separate and interactive effects of Treatments B (the behavioral technique—emotional flooding) and C (the Gestalt technique—empty chair) in resolving strong negative emotional reactions. Thus, a within-series comparison (B/B+C/B or C/C+B/C or B+C/C/B+C or B+C/B/B+C) involving a complex phase change would be used to assess these effects.[8] In certain phases of treatment, both techniques would be used; whereas, in other phases, only one would be used. The logic for interpreting the results, however, is the same as in a simple-phase change within-series comparison.

---

[8]Because of potential sequence and carry-over effects, assessing the separate and interactive effects of Treatments B and C would actually involve implementing and replicating each of the treatment orders noted here with different clients. However, each order would be a within-series comparison.

A between-series strategy compares two or more series of data points across time. The ATD is an example of a between-series comparison. In that design, the series represent data points for two or more treatments (conditions) collected and compared for the same time period (phase). If trend is present, it is assumed to affect each of the series equally because of the random and rapid alternation of treatments. Any differences between the series represent differential treatment effects.

Combined-series strategies results when within- and between-series elements are combined into a single design. In interpreting results, the logic of a co-ordinated series of within- and between-series comparisons can be brought to bear on the data. As we discussed earlier, the multiple baseline is just such a design and results from combining together several simpler and weaker A–B designs (the individual A–B designs differ in length of the initial baseline). However, the resulting design is much stronger than its individual A–B elements because it combines both within- and between series comparisons to rule out threats to internal validity that are present in the individual A–B designs. Other combined series designs can result from adding a baseline-only, a treatment-only, or a crossover (B–C for one subject and C–B for another) element to individual within-, between-, or combined-series designs. The purpose of these additions is to control for specific threats to validity and to strengthen the simpler designs in particular ways.

Toward Even Greater Single-Case Design Flexibility

McCullough (1984a, 1984b; McCullough & Carr, 1987) viewed these designs as having only limited applicability by the average counselor, even though the recommendations of Hayes (1981) and Barlow et al. (1984) extend the utility of single-case research. One major limitation is the emphasis on internal validity rather than interfacing and modifying design structure to fit clinical goals and concerns. McCullough said that the emphasis in the individual case should be shifted to external validity and replication across matched clients that, in turn, would indirectly confirm the internal validity of therapeutic procedures.

Further, McCullough asserted that current designs are inadequate for investigating cognitive or nonoperant phenomena because they are premised on four major operant assumptions. First, the independent and dependent variable must be observable stimulus events that occur contiguously. Second, treatment effects must be demonstrated by fairly rapid rate, intensity, or duration changes in the dependent variable soon after treatment has been introduced. Third, the dependent variable must be demonstrably influenced by the presence or absence of the independent variable, and finally, the dependent variable must be stable before treatment is introduced.

The effect of these designs has been to discourage the use of self-report and psychological test measures because they are not overt and may not reflect the moment-to-moment changes required in operant research. For example, modification of a client's therapeutic attitudes or cognitive strategies might represent fundamental clinical goals in cognitive therapy, but attitude and other cognitive changes often occur less rapidly than behavioral changes and might be overlooked by current designs. In addition, these designs fail to distinguish learning from performance; fail to measure learning of clinical concepts; and do not take into account that close contiguity of independent and dependent variables is not necessary in conceptual learning (e.g., observational learning and problem solving). Moreover, many cognitive changes not only occur slowly but are irreversible once they have occurred, thereby precluding the use of withdrawal and multiple baseline designs. Finally, many cognitive phenomena may be inherently unstable prior to treatment with the goal of treatment being to reduce that variability. As such, comparison to a stable pretreatment baseline might not be realistic.

In an attempt to make cognitive phenomena more accessible to single-case research, McCullough (1984b) advanced the Stage Process Design (SPD) as a method of *predictive confirmation*. Predictive confirmation builds upon Shapiro's (1966) notion of the predictive experiment. Predictive confirmation is achieved to the extent that a learning-based program results in modification of pathological processes in predicted directions once the program has been mastered (McCullough & Carr, 1987). Predictive confirmation is more powerful than single-case research in which changes in the dependent variables are simply reported as a result of controlled introduction of the independent variable. Validating predictions strengthens the credibility of experimental control in that particular case. If the predictions made prior to the intervention match the actual outcomes, then control has been demonstrated.

The Stage Process Design is intended to be structurally isomorphic to clinical practice and assumes that psychotherapy involves teaching clients how to self-resolve a pathological dilemma. The design has several requirements in addition to the usual ones of continuous measurement, replication, and so on. First, counselor (e.g., gender, years of clinical experience) and client (e.g., DSM-III diagnoses, age, etc.) variables must be operationalized in order to facilitate subsequent replication efforts. Second, the design must include operationalized learning tasks (derived from a theoretical perspective) for the client and measurable acquisition-performance indices of that learning. Thus, what the client must learn to self-resolve problems and the extent to which he or she has learned and can perform it must be measured. For example, the client may be taught to perform a specific covert strategy such as situational analyses to a preset performance criterion. The extent to which the client has successfully mastered this strategy would be assessed, and the client would not progress to the next stage until those skills had been mastered.

Third, the needed learning strategies need to be operationalized into a stage structure. Each stage is characterized by a set of client performance task criteria and a set of therapist-stage rules. The latter represent a type of lesson plan for counselor functioning in that stage. In addition, the stages must be ordered in sequential fashion such that successive ones presuppose skills acquired in earlier stages.

Fourth, the design must contain dependent variables that reflect generalization effects (anticipated effects of mastering the learning tasks) of treatment. The generalized measures would include indices of cognitive, emotional, and/or behavioral symptoms suggested by the DSM-III-R diagnoses and enable the counselor to test the preexperimental predictions for the program. Both proximal and distal predictions are made for the generalized treatment effect measures. Proximal predictions are changes in the generalization measures expected at the end of each stage; whereas distal predictions are the results expected upon successful completion of the program. Thus, if the client has successfully mastered the program's learning tasks and mastery has been followed by the predicted changes in pathological processes at each stage and at the end of therapy, then predictive confirmation has been achieved.

McCullough and Carr (1987) illustrated the use of the SPD with a 32-year-old White female treated for dysthymic disorder and passive–aggressive personality disorder. The SPD involved three stages, baseline followed by a cognitive intervention stage and a behavioral intervention stage, respectively. Although the case appeared to be successfully treated, proximal and distal "predictions" were made retrospectively. Thus, an actual SPD was never fully implemented, and results are only suggestive.

Baseline involved collection of data on the generalized treatment measures which included three standardized measures, the Beck Depression Inventory, the Rotter I-E scale, and the Symptom-Checklist–90 as well as two additional measures, the Personal Questionnaire (PQ; Shapiro, 1961, 1964) and the Impact Message Inventory-II (IMI; Kiesler, 1986). The PQ is a versatile self-report measure that was constructed to reflect four levels of client functioning (4: most severe; 3: slight improvement; 2: great improvement 1: recovery) with respect to assertive behavior in three contexts. The IMI is a therapist measure of client in-session interpersonal impact with respect to dominance, submission, friendliness, and hostility. Therapist-stage rules prohibited leading questions about situational events and required nondirective responding. There were no specific client-learning tasks or acquisition-performance indices in this stage.

Stage 2 involved cognitive learning. The client's task was to develop a cognitive set of *perceived functionality*—to learn that her situational behavior was directly related to the negative consequences she reported. She was taught a six-step situational analysis procedure for evaluating events outside of therapy and linking her behavior to the consequences. Therapist-stage rules consisted of operationalized procedures for teaching the client situational analysis. The acquisition-performance criterion was two successful completions of the procedure in a row where the analysis was done correctly or done while self-correcting mistakes. Acquisition of this covert strategy was assessed in Stage 2 (Fig. 5.12), and criterion was achieved by Session 24.

Stage 3 was premised on the assumption that the client's mood was related to her passive–aggressive behavior and lack of assertion skills. Change in mood should follow after a set of perceived functionality and the development of assertion skills have been achieved. The acquisition-performance criterion for Stage 3 was recovery level status for two out of the three interpersonal targets for 2 consecutive weeks. This criterion was reached by Session 16 of Stage 3 (Fig. 5.13).

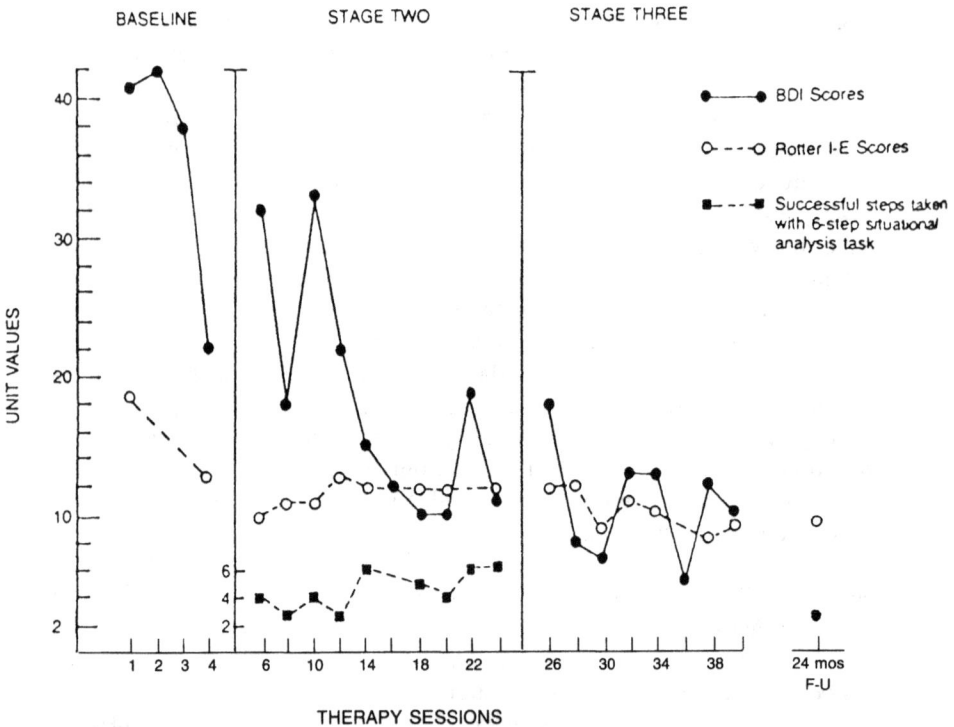

FIG. 5.12. Symptom target scores obtained by client during therapy and the situational analysis performance "hits" rated by therapist during Stage 2. (*Source*: Figure 1, p. 764 from McCullough & Carr, 1987. Reproduced by permission).

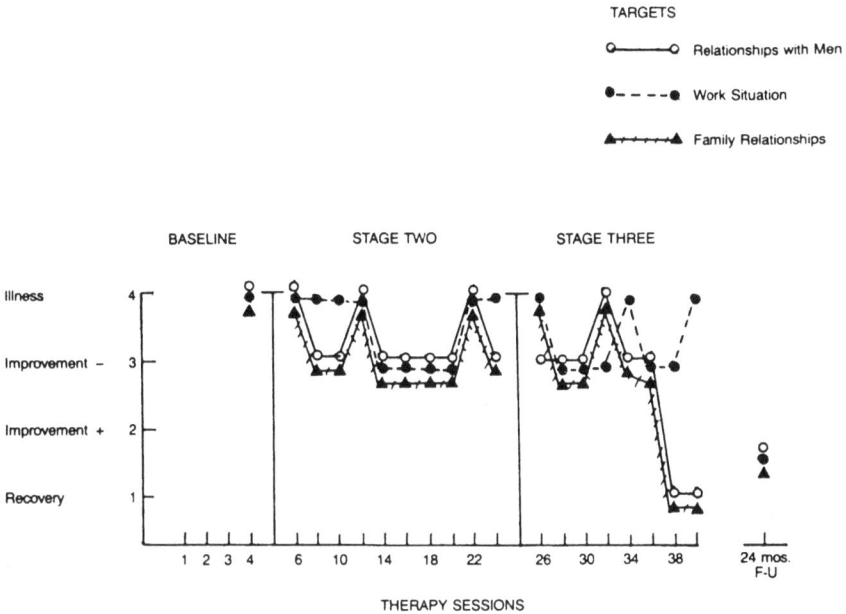

FIG. 5.13. Three personal questionnaire target ratings turned in weekly by the client. (*Source*: Figure 2, p. 765 from McCullough & Carr, 1987. Reproduced by permission.)

Proximal predictions for the Stage 2 generalized-effect measures included BDI scores in the mild depression range (11–15) and internal I-E scores (10 or less). Stage 3 distal predictions were scores of 10 or less on the BDI and I-E scales (no depression and internality); scores less than 50 on the SCL-90, high friendly and low hostility IMI scores coupled with a higher dominance than submission scores; and rescinding the dysthymic and passive–aggressive personality disorder diagnoses by the therapist and an independent rater. These predictions were largely confirmed.

The Stage Process Design appears to be a potentially useful way to extend single-case research to nonoperant varieties of counseling and psychotherapy. To the extent that preexperimental predictions are confirmed and replicated in such research, our knowledge of counseling process and outcome will be enhanced. However, until the design is routinely used in counseling, its actual strengths and limitations remain unknown.

ADDITIONAL ISSUES IN SINGLE-CASE RESEARCH

Bandura (1969) distinguished three basic change processes: *induction, generalization*, and *maintenance*. For the most part, the experimental single-case designs in this chapter have illustrated induction of therapeutic change.

However, clinicians and researchers are also interested in whether changes generalize (transfer of training) across situations, response systems, to different types of clients, and so forth, and whether these changes are maintained over time. There are a variety of procedures and issues related to generalization and/or maintenance in single-case research, and they are briefly introduced here.

One of the most important is replication. Building on work by Sidman (1960), Barlow and Hersen (1984) have distinguished three types of replication—direct, systematic, and clinical. Direct replication is concerned with the reliability of findings (internal validity) from single-case research and involves replication of the same procedure(s) by the same investigator either with the same or similar (matched) clients. Demonstration of results with a single client coupled with a direct replication with two or three additional clients typically provides strong evidence of internal validity.

In contrast, systematic and clinical replication are concerned with generalization (external validity) issues. Systematic replication is "any attempt to replicate findings from a direct replication series, varying settings, behavior change agents, behavior disorders, or any combination thereof" (Barlow & Hersen, 1984, p. 347). For example, the same experimental procedure (treatment) is employed as in the original investigation but with a different behavioral disorder. To the extent that results are similar to those in the original investigation, then generalizability of treatment effects across behavior disorders has been demonstrated. Of course, as the number of dimensions (e.g., therapists, behavior disorders, situations, etc.) that are changed from the original study is increased, the risk that results may not generalize is also increased.

Unlike direct and systematic replication in which the treatment typically consists of a single component administered in a research setting, clinical replication is concerned with a treatment package containing two or more distinct components as applied in a clinical setting to a succession of clients with multiple behaviors or emotional problems that cluster together. Clinical replication involves the "field testing" of a treatment package. The work by Masters and Johnson on the treatment of sexual dysfunction and by Wolpe with phobias represent clinical replications. By carefully analyzing successes, limited successes, and failures and linking these to co-varying client and therapist characteristics as well as procedural variations, a great deal can be learned about the generalizability of the treatment package.

Another key issue with individual single-case designs is how to assess generalization without contraindicating therapeutic control (Kendall, 1981). When the initial baseline level of responding is not recovered in a withdrawal design, it is unclear whether there has been a generalization of treatment effects or a failure to demonstrate that treatment rather than some threat to validity was responsible for the results. Similarly, in a multiple baseline design, effects on untreated baselines (generalization) contraindicate therapeutic control.

Barrios and Hartmann (1986) argued that a persuasive demonstration of generalization involves a six-step process:

1. repeated measurement of the target behavior,
2. covariation of the behavior with sequential application and removal of treatment,
3. isolating the untrained response from treatment,
4. isolating the untrained response from factors that might plausibly be invoked to account for changes produced in the target behavior,
5. continuous measurement of the untrained response, and
6. covariation of this response with the trained response.

Probe assessment is required in order to document this process. A probe is "the assessment of behavior on selected occasions when no contingencies are in effect for that behavior" (Kazdin, 1982, p. 209.) Probes can be used to assess whether a behavior or problem area that has not been treated directly changes (generalization). For example, a counselor might be concerned with helping a client increase the ability to refuse unreasonable requests using social skills training. Repeated observations of this behavior over time would be collected in role-playing situations using a multiple baseline design across different response components (e.g., eye contact, loudness, quality of verbal content, etc.). These components are then treated successively and successfully. At the same time, the client may also have difficulty expressing opinions. Although the counselor does not intervene with that behavior, he or she may be interested in determining whether generalization occurs from the refusal training. In order to do this, the counselor could employ probe assessments on untrained role-play situations involving expressing personal opinions. A variety of probe assessment designs (i.e., single-generalization probe following treatment, multiple-generalization following treatment, and continuous-generalization probes) are available. However, Barrios and Hartmann (1988) argued that only a continuous-generalization probe design in which data are repeatedly collected throughout on the trained and the untrained responses and in which the successive treatment and baseline phases are of unequal lengths allows for an unequivocal separation of both treatment and generalization effects.[9]

Probes could also be used to assess maintenance of treatment effects. Assuming that treatment effects have occurred, several follow-up probes at, for

---

[9]The reader should consult Barrios and Hartmann (1988) for an extended discussion of this topic.

example, 3 and 6 months after the conclusion of treatment could be taken. However, Barrios and Hartmann cautioned against concluding that, if current responding is comparable to end of treatment responding, maintenance of treatment effects have been demonstrated. Such an inference is unwarranted because exactly the opposite logic (effects only when treatment was present or only for treated baselines) was previously used to argue in favor of the treatment's initial controlling effects over the behavior. Thus, follow-up probes provide information only about changes in the target behavior since the termination of treatment.

In order to evaluate maintenance, Rusch and Kazdin (1981) proposed a series of withdrawal strategies (sequential-withdrawal, partial-withdrawal, or combined sequential and partial-withdrawal). These strategies should not be confused with A–B–A–B withdrawal designs, however. All of these strategies involve an initial demonstration of therapeutic control via the more common A–B–A–B or multiple baseline procedures followed by the partial or complete withdrawal of treatment. Continuous assessment is conducted throughout to document maintenance (or its absence) as withdrawal occurs. Sequential-withdrawal involves gradually withdrawing different components of a treatment package; whereas partial-withdrawal consists of withdrawing the intervention gradually across different persons or baselines. The final withdrawal strategy combines the sequential and partial strategies. Unfortunately, Barrios and Hartmann believe that this approach is susceptible to the same logical error interpretation problems as the follow-up probe procedure.

As a potential solution, they suggested differentiating acquisition from maintenance, as was suggested by Bandura, and using a simultaneous or alternating treatment design in a three-step process to evaluate response maintenance. First, comparable baseline rates for a response are obtained in two or more stimulus settings. Then, a response acquisition technique of known effectiveness is applied to each setting until comparable rates are observed. Finally, the acquisition technique is withdrawn and two or more maintenance procedures are repeatedly implemented in counterbalanced fashion across the settings. This design provides a demonstration of the relative persistence of treatment effects and permits attributing differences in persistence to the maintenance procedures compared. As such, it avoids the interpretive problem previously discussed.

Finally, meta-analytic procedures (Smith & Glass, 1977) have recently been extended to single-case research (see White, Rusch, Kazdin, & Hartmann, 1989). Meta-analysis refers to a set of statistical methods for aggregating and integrating the results of previously conducted studies. Meta-analysis is an approach to assessing the generalizability across studies as a function of any number of variables of interest as long as information about them is provided in the original studies. A variety of methodological and conceptual debates surround the use of meta-analysis in general and with single-case research in particular. (The interested reader is referred to White et al., 1989, for a further discussion of these issues.)

CONCLUSIONS

Single-case designs are a valuable tool for counseling investigators and practitioners. They can be used to address questions related to process and outcome in counseling and supervision as well as questions related to accountability of individual counselors and supervisors. The questions that can be investigated with them include: Does a treatment work? Does one treatment work better than another? Are there elements within a successful treatment that make it work? What level of treatment is optimal? In addition, their focus on the distinctiveness of the single case often makes them philosophically and practically more compatible with much of what occurs in everyday counseling and psychotherapy than the more commonly used between-groups designs.

As with any methodology, single-case designs do have their limitations. As noted by Barlow and Hersen (1984), questions about whether a treated group of clients performs significantly better than an untreated group following treatment and the percentage of clinically improved individuals in a treated group versus an untreated group require between-group designs. Moreover, in attempting to answer questions that involve interactions (e.g., determining the separate and combined effects of two or more treatment components), the investigator invariably must come to grips with the issues of multiple treatment interference and sequence effects.

Overall, however, single-case research methods represent extremely flexible procedures for counseling and psychotherapy research and practice. As such, they merit a position of greater prominence and influence in the counseling literature than they have previously been accorded.

REFERENCES

Baer, D. M., Wolf, M. M., & Risley, T. R. (1968). Some current dimensions of applied behavior analysis. *Journal of Applied Behavior Analysis, 1,* 91–97.

Bandura, A. (1969). *Principles of behavior modification.* New York: Holt, Rinehart & Winston.

Barlow, D. H., Hayes, S. C., & Nelson, R. O. (1984). *The scientist practitioner: Research and accountability in clinical and educational settings.* New York: Pergamon.

Barlow, D. H., & Hersen, M. (1984). *Single case experimental designs: Strategies for studying behavior change* (2nd ed.). New York: Pergamon.

Barrios, B. A., & Hartmann, D. P. (1988). Recent developments in single-subject methodology: Methods for analyzing generalization, maintenance, and multicomponent treatments. In M. Hersen, R. M. Eisler, & P. M. Miller (Eds.), *Progress in behavior modification* (Vol. 22, pp. 11–47). New York: Academic Press.

Campbell, D. T., & Stanley, J. C. (1963). *Experimental and quasi-experimental designs for research.* Chicago: Rand McNally.

Cook, T. D., & Campbell, D. T. (1979). *Quasi-experimentation: Design & analysis issues for field settings.* Chicago: Rand McNally.

Edgington, E. S. (1966). Statistical inference and nonrandom samples. *Psychological Bulletin, 66,* 485–487.

Edgington, E. S. (1984). Statistics and single case analysis. In M. Hersen, R. M. Eisler, P. M. Miller (Eds.), *Progress in behavior modification* (Vol. 16, pp. 83–119). New York: Academic.

Edgington, E. S. (1987). Randomized single-subject experiments and statistical tests. *Journal of Counseling Psychology, 34,* 437–442.

Fairbank, J. A., & Keane, T. M. (1982). Flooding for combat-related stress disorders: Assessment of anxiety reduction across traumatic memories. *Behavior Therapy, 13,* 499–510.

Freud, S. (1933). *New introductory lectures in psychoanalysis.* New York: Norton.

Frey, D. (1978). Science and the single case in counseling research. *Personnel and Guidance Journal, 56,* 263–268.

Gelso, C. J. (1979). Research in counseling: Methodological and professional issues. *The Counseling Psychologist, 8(3),* 7–35.

Gelso, C. J. (1982). Editorial. *Journal of Counseling Psychology, 29,* 3–7.

Gelso, C. J. (1985). Subjects, designs and generalizations in the *Journal of Counseling Psychology:* A comment on Scherman and Doan. *Journal of Counseling Psychology, 32,* 277–278.

Hall, R. V. (1971). *Managing behavior: Behavior modification, the measurement of behavior.* Lawrence, KS: H & H Enterprises.

Harmon, L. W. (1988). Editorial. *Journal of Counseling Psychology, 35,* 219–221.

Hartmann, D. P., & Hall, R. V. (1976). The changing criterion design. *Journal of Applied Behavior Analysis, 9,* 527–537.

Hayes, S. C. (1981). Single-case experimental design and empirical clinical practice. *Journal of Consulting and Clinical Psychology, 49,* 193–211.

Hill, C. E., Carter, J. A., & O'Farrell, M. K. (1983). A case study of process and outcome of time-limited counseling. *Journal of Counseling Psychology, 30,* 3–18.

Holahan, W., & Galassi, J. P. (1986). Toward accountability in supervision: A single-case illustration. *Counselor Education and Supervision, 25,* 166–174.

Howard, G. S. (1984). A modest proposal for a revision of strategies for counseling research. *Journal of Counseling Psychology, 31,* 430–441.

Kazdin, A. E. (1980). *Research design in clinical psychology.* New York: Harper & Row.

Kazdin, A. E. (1981). Drawing valid inferences from case studies. *Journal of Consulting and Clinical Psychology, 49,* 183–192.

Kazdin, A. E. (1982). *Single-case research designs: Methods for clinical and applied settings.* New York: Oxford University Press.

Kazdin, A. E. (1984). Statistical analyses for single-case experimental designs. In D. H. Barlow & M. Hersen (Eds.), *Single case experimental designs: Strategies for studying behavior* (2nd ed., pp. 285–324). New York: Pergamon.

Kendall, P. C. (1981). Assessing generalization and the single-subject strategies. *Behavior Modification, 5,* 307–319.

Kiesler, D. J. (1986). *Research manual for the Impact Message Inventory.* Palo Alto, CA: Consulting Psychologists Press.

Kratochwill, T. R. (1978). Foundation of time-series research. In T. R. Kratochwill (Ed.), *Single subject research: Strategies for evaluating change* (pp. 1–100). New York: Academic Press.

Leitenberg, H. (1973). The use of single-case methodology in psychotherapy research. *Journal of Abnormal Psychology, 82,* 87–101.

Liberman, R. P., & Smith, V. (1972). A multiple baseline study of systematic desensitization in a patient with multiple phobias. *Behavior Therapy, 3,* 597–603.

Lichtenberg, J. W., & Heck, E. J. (1986). Analysis of sequence and pattern in process research. *Journal of Counseling Psychology, 33*, 170–181.

McCullough, J. P. (1984a). Single-case investigative research and its relevance for the nonoperant clinician. *Psychotherapy, 21*, 382–388.

McCullough, J. P. (1984b). The need for new single case design structure in applied cognitive psychology. *Psychotherapy, 21*, 389–400.

McCullough, J. P., & Carr, K. F. (1987). Stage process design: A predictive confirmation structure for the single case. *Psychotherapy, 24*, 759–768.

McSweeney, A. J. (1978). Effects of response cost on the behavior of a million persons: Charging for directory assistance in Cincinnati. *Journal of Applied Behavior Analysis, 11*, 47–51.

Mueser, K. T., Foy, D. W., & Carter, M. J. (1986). Social skills training for job maintenance in a psychiatric patient. *Journal of Counseling Psychology, 33*, 360–362.

Parsonson, B. S., & Baer, D. M. (1978). The analysis and presentation of graphic data. In T. R. Kratochwill (Ed.), *Single subject research: Strategies for evaluating change* (pp. 101–165). New York: Academic Press.

Patton, M. J. (1984). Managing social interaction in counseling: A contribution from the philosophy of science. *Journal of Counseling Psychology, 31*, 442–456.

Polkinghorne, D. E. (1984). Further extensions of methodological diversity for counseling psychology. *Journal of Counseling Psychology, 31*, 416–429.

Rusch, F. R., & Kazdin, A. E. (1981). Toward a methodology of withdrawal designs for the assessment of response maintenance. *Journal of Applied Behavior Analysis, 14*, 131–140.

Scherman, A., & Doan, R. E., Jr. (1985). Subjects, designs, and generalizations in volumes 25–29 of the *Journal of Counseling Psychology*. *Journal of Counseling Psychology, 32*, 272–276.

Shapiro, M. B. (1961). A method of measuring psychological changes specific to the individual psychiatric patient. *British Journal of Medical Psychology, 34*, 151–155.

Shapiro, M. B. (1964). The measurement of clinically relevant variables. *Journal of Psychosomatic Research, 8*, 245–254.

Shapiro, M. B. (1966). The single case in clinical-psychological research. *Journal of General Psychology, 74*, 3–23.

Shostrom, E. L. (Producer). (1966). *Three approaches to psychotherapy* [Film]. Santa Ana, CA: Psychological Films.

Sidman, M. (1960). *Tactics of scientific research: Evaluating experimental data in psychology.* New York: Basic Books.

Smith, M. L., & Glass, G. V. (1977). Meta-analysis of psychotherapy outcome studies. *American Psychologist, 32*, 752–760.

Tawney, J. W., & Gast, D. L. (1984). *Single subject research in special education.* Columbus, OH: Charles E. Merrill.

Tracey, T. J. (1983). Single case research: An added tool for counselors and supervisors. *Counselor Education and Supervision, 22*, 185–196.

Truax, C. B., & Carkhuff, R. R. (1965). Experimental manipulation of therapeutic conditions. *Journal of Consulting Psychology, 29*, 119–124.

Wampold, B. E. (1984). Tests of dominance in sequential categorical data. *Psychological Bulletin, 96*, 424–429.

Wampold, B. E., & Margolin, G. (1982). Nonparametric strategies to test the independence of behavioral states in sequential data. *Psychological Bulletin, 92*, 755–765.

Watson, J. B., & Rayner, R. (1920). Conditioned emotional reactions. *Journal of Experimental Psychology, 3*, 1–14.

Whang, P. L., Fletcher, R. K., & Fawcett, S. B. (1982). Training counseling skill: An experimental analysis and social validation. *Journal of Applied Behavior Analysis, 15*, 325–334.

White, D. M., Rusch, F. R., Kazdin, A. E., & Hartmann, D. P. (1989). Applications of meta analysis in individual-subject research. *Behavioral Assessment, 11*, 281–296.

6

QUALITATIVE PROCEDURES FOR COUNSELING RESEARCH

Donald E. Polkinghorne
University of Southern California

The body of knowledge of many of the human sciences includes conclusions generated by research using qualitative procedures. Qualitative procedures use processes based on the operations of conceptual thought to analyze data that consist of statements presented in ordinary language. Qualitative procedures can be contrasted with quantitative procedures, which use data that consist of statements presented in numeric language and analytic processes based on mathematical operations.

WHAT IS QUALITATIVE RESEARCH?

Human science disciplines have referred to their research using qualitative procedures by various names. Anthropology calls it *ethnography,* sociology uses the expression *participant observation,* and nursing terms it *qualitative.* In this chapter, I use the phrase *qualitative procedures* in a general sense to refer to the characteristics common to research across disciplines that employ qualitative techniques. Qualitative procedures are employed to some degree by most all of the disciplines concerned with the human realm. Some research programs, for example, ecological psychology, holistic anthropology, ethnography of communication, cognitive anthropology, and symbolic interactionism, use qualitative procedures as their primary research tools (Jacob, 1987).

The purpose of research using qualitative procedures is to produce full and integrated descriptions of an experience or situation under study. Data are typically produced by noting observations of a situation and its participants or by conducting open-ended interviews. Rather than testing variables chosen in advance, qualitative designs seek to derive explanatory concepts and categories from the data. Qualitative analysis undertakes to identify concepts and relationships that disclose an order in the data and thus make the data more understandable. The analytic process is recursive in that a proposed conceptual order is tested against the data; on the basis of its fit and explanatory power, the proposed conceptual order is continually revised until the data become conceptually coherent.

A recent example of the use of qualitative procedures in counseling research is the study *Women's Ways of Knowing* by Belenky, Clinchy, Goldberger, and Tarule (1986). The purpose of the study was to investigate women's "basic assumptions about the nature of truth and reality and the origins of knowledge" (p. 3). Previously, William Perry (1970) had studied the intellectual stages of development in college students. His subjects were Harvard students, mainly male. His results indicated that, during their college careers, students' conceptions of the nature and origins of knowledge move through three stages: basic dualism, multiplicity, and relativism. Perry's results have been used by educators as one of the models for understanding the intellectual development of young adults in academic settings. Because those results were derived from a sample consisting primarily of male students, the authors of *Women's Ways of Knowing* wanted to investigate the various epistemological positions held by women in order to find out if Perry's generalizations about intellectual development were appropriate for female students.

For their study, Belenky et al. selected 90 women enrolled in various educational institutions, ranging from an Ivy League college to an alternative urban public high school, and 45 women participating in child-rearing and other classes provided by family agencies. They conducted open-ended interviews with the women. Part of the interviews consisted of asking the women to respond to various statements about learning experiences. For example, the women were asked to respond to the statement, "When I need to learn something, I like to just listen to the people who really know about it." The interviews, from 2 to 5 hours in duration, were audiorecorded and later transcribed. The more than 5,000 pages of transcribed text constituted the basic data of the study.

The analysis of these interviews consisted of developing a set of concepts that would organize the data into epistemological stances. Perry's stages were tried, but they did not account for all the diversity of epistemological approaches present in the data. Through the recursive movement of generating ordering concepts, then fitting them to the data, and then revising the concepts, the researchers evolved five epistemological categories into which the data cohered. The analytic work involved devising codes for the order ing concepts and using them to mark the portions of the data that fit each concept. The parts of the data that were not accounted for by the codes were used as a basis for revising the ordering configuration under development. The group of epistemological approaches not accommodated by the researchers' initial ordering concepts included an extreme denial of self and dependence on external authority for direction. To describe this group, they developed a new category termed *silence*.

Belenky et al. concluded that, although there is some overlap with Perry's developmental scheme, women approach knowledge in ways significantly different from men. The researchers found that they could accommodate their data with five patterns of women's knowledge assumptions or interpretive frameworks: silence, received knowledge, subjective knowledge, procedural knowledge, and constructed knowledge. The results are of particular importance for education and raise the question of whether the "strategies of teaching and methods of evaluation . . . are compatible with women's preferred styles of learning" (p. 5).

Although the *Women's Ways of Knowing* study demonstrates the power and utility of research using qualitative procedures, the counseling field underutilizes qualitative research. I believe one of the reasons for the limited use of qualitative designs in counseling research is that, in general, they are not fully understood. This chapter provides a greater understanding of qualitative research by describing its theory and practice. The first section focuses on the issue of methodological diversity and the inclusion of qualitative methods in counseling. Included is a review of the slow progress of implementing methodological diversity in counseling compared to other human science disciplines and an examination of the recent changes in the philosophy of science that provide support for the utilization of multiple research methods. The second section provides an overview of type of knowledge generated by qualitative research procedures. The final section describes the three aspects of qualitative research—data production, data analysis, and communication of results.

MOVING TOWARD METHODOLOGICAL DIVERSITY

Slow Progress in Counseling

Unlike research designs described in other chapters in this book, research efforts using qualitative procedures are not currently emphasized in counseling's body of research knowledge. Counseling research has traditionally featured quantitative designs. In recent years, however, voices calling for more extensive use of qualitative procedures in counseling research have become more numerous. Hill and Gronsky's (1984) statement, in their chapter in *The Coming Decade in Counseling Psychology,* is representative of the calls for the use of qualitative methods:

> We would . . . suggest that the helping professions need to adopt new models for research which more closely fit human behavior than do the models of the physical sciences. Our new models may well be similar to those used in anthropology and sociology which have long dealt with complex issues of human behavior. (p. 154)

Two of the major research journals for counseling—the *Journal of Counseling Psychology* and *The Counseling Psychologist*—have published articles advocating that the counseling profession admit research using qualitative methods into its body of knowledge (Fretz, 1989; Gelso, 1984; Goldman, 1976; Neimeyer & Resnikoff, 1982; Polkinghorne, 1984). Several research articles using qualitative designs have been published in the *Journal of Counseling and Development* since 1987 (e.g., Gordon & Shontz, 1990). Brown (1989), in an editorial in *Counselor Education and Supervision,* wrote that "editors and editorial board members . . . must accord the same status to research that chronicles the human experience using qualitative methodology that we do to the empirical research we have grown accustomed to seeing published in our journals" (p. 6).

In April 1987 the Third National Conference for Counseling Psychology was held in Atlanta to plan for the future of counseling psychology. One of the five major areas of discussion was research in counseling psychology. Speaking of methodological diversity, one research group (Gelso et al., 1988) acknowledged the increasing dissatisfaction with the exclusive use of traditional (quantitative) methodologies. Included in its recommendations were the following points:

> The trend toward "alternative methodologies" is largely a healthy one, and is supported by the Research Group. . . . Although the trend toward "alternative methodologies" will continue, the Research Group's most basic viewpoint is that all methodologies and investigative styles ought to be encouraged. Thus our strongest recommendation is for methodological diversity, such that all approaches are given a fair hearing, for example, by editorial boards. The particular research question, more than anything else, should determine the methodological approach. (p. 395)

Notwithstanding these calls, counseling lags behind other human science disciplines in the acceptance and utilization of qualitative research procedures. Currently, counseling's body of knowledge, as displayed in its major research journals, lacks methodological diversity. The task facing the counseling profession is the move past its traditional resistance to qualitative methods to a practiced methodological diversity by incorporating alternative research methods into its literature and training programs.

Resistance in Counseling

The reason counseling has not yet adequately incorporated qualitative designs may be related more to pragmatic factors than to epistemological concerns. The present generation of counselors and counseling psychologists was trained almost exclusively in quantitative research methods. In general, our present researchers, journal editors, and university professors are not experienced in using qualitative research procedures nor expert in training others in their use. The addition of qualitative procedures into counseling's research repertoire would require current researchers as well as students to learn them. Few productive researchers skilled in the use of one set of techniques are strongly motivated to restructure their methodologies. Adding instruction in qualitative procedures to the graduate programs will require adding courses to an already crowded curriculum and finding faculty with skills in qualitative procedures to teach the courses.

Counseling's historical roots are in the career-counseling and guidance functions of education and the psychotherapy functions of psychology (Stone, 1986). Its identity is linked to the disciplines of both education and psychology, some of its programs being housed in schools of education and some in psychology departments. Of these two disciplines, education has been more open to the use of qualitative procedures than psychology. Goetz and LeCompte (1984) reported: "The adaptation by educational researchers of ethnographic research design to the study of educational settings and problems has created a vast collection of studies during the past 20 years" (p. 1). Texts on educational research usually include chapters on qualitative research (e.g., Borg & Gall, 1989; Fraenkel & Wallen, 1990; Hopkins & Antes, 1990). The *Handbook of Research on Teaching*, a project of the American Educational Research Association, includes a chapter called "Qualitative Methods in Research on Teaching" (Erickson, 1986), and a recent volume of the *American Educational Research Journal* featured a special section on qualitative methodology, including criteria the journal uses to judge the scholarly adequacy of articles using qualitative procedures (Richardson-Koehler, 1987).

Counseling's second disciplinary root, academic psychology, is the most resistant of the human science disciplines to the inclusion of qualitative procedures as a research tool. In its reluctance to use qualitative procedures, counseling appears to have been influenced more by its identity with psychology than by its identity with education. Academic psychology has conceived of itself as a discipline that is the "scientific equal" of the natural sciences. To support this posture it has limited itself only to what it has established as the "most rigorous" of research approaches: those that use numerical data and statistical analysis and base their designs on the experimental model. Research programs using qualitative procedures, such as phenomenological psychology developed at Duquesne University (Giorgi, Fischer, & Von Eckartsberg, 1971; Polkinghorne, 1989b) and ecological psychology (Barker, 1968), have not been admitted into the mainstream of academic psychology.

Researchers in areas closely related to counseling—organizational consultation and curriculum and program evaluation—have shown interest in the use of qualitative procedures. Organizational consultation has benefited from research using qualitative procedures for the study of organizational culture and management styles (e.g., Schein, 1987; Van Maanen, 1983) and those engaged in classroom (Goetz & LeCompte, 1984) and program evaluation (Patton, 1990) have employed qualitative strategies. Counseling research, however, has more closely followed the lead of academic psychology in resisting the utilization of qualitative procedures in its primary research literature. This resistance has fostered a secondary literature among practitioners of counseling—a literature that incorporates aspects of qualitative procedures and draws on the clinical tradition of the case study, using as its exemplars the case studies of Freud.

The differing needs and values of academic researchers and counseling practitioners have tended to bifurcate the discipline of counseling. One aspect of the split is the existence of the two somewhat separate bodies of knowledge. One, contained in the discipline's research journals, conforms to the "most rigorous" criterion. Its research is modeled on psychology's successful early studies of perception and learning. The second body is preserved in the books about counseling practice and in the oral tradition passed on in internships and other field training (Schon, 1983). This body draws its inferences from case studies and practitioner experience rather than from academic research. For suggestions regarding their practice, counselors most often consult this second body (Morrow-Bradley & Elliott, 1986).

Diversity in Other Disciplines

Qualitative designs have been used by most human science disciplines. Historically, qualitative designs have been most closely identified with anthropology and its ethnographic field studies of "foreign" cultures (see Stocking, 1983). Malinowski's (1922) study of the Trobriand Islanders is often recognized as the beginning of the systematic use of qualitative research procedures (Easthope, 1974). Another early application of qualitative procedures was made by sociologists of the symbolic interactionist tradition at the University of Chicago in the 1920s and 1930s (Meltzer, Petras, & Reynolds, 1975). They used qualitative community-based field studies to investigate life in local settings (e.g., Wirth's, 1928, study of an urban ghetto).

In spite of the emphasis after World War II on research designs using numerical data and statistical analysis, most human science disciplines continue to accept qualitative procedures as part of their stock of research designs.

The early 1970s produced an extensive methodological literature on qualitative designs that clarified and systematized the use of qualitative procedures. Examples of this literature include Pelto's (1970) *Anthropological Research,* Filstead's (1970) edited collection *Qualitative Methodology,* Lofton's (1971) *Analyzing Social Settings,* Lazarsfeld's (1972) *Qualitative Analysis,* and Bogdan and Taylor's (1975) *Introduction to Qualitative Research Methods.* These texts continue to exert an influence on the implementation of qualitative procedures and form the backdrop to a more recent effusion of literature about qualitative designs. Sage Publications is producing the bulk of this new literature. Its series of monographs, begun in 1986 and edited by John Van Maanen, is titled *Qualitative Research Methods*; to date it includes 17 volumes. As part of its *Applied Social Research* series, Sage has also published books on qualitative methodology (Denzin, 1989; Fetterman, 1989; Jorgensen, 1989; Marshall & Rossman, 1989; Yin, 1984). Examples of other important texts in the recent surge of literature on qualitative methods are Miles and Huberman's (1984) *Qualitative Data Analysis,* Goetz and LeCompte's (1984) *Ethnography and Qualitative Design in Educational Research,* and Strauss' (1987) *Qualitative Analysis for Social Scientists.* Not only book-length texts but journal articles on qualitative procedures are currently appearing in greater numbers than ever before.

Effect on Scientist-Practitioner Model

The training design adopted by the counseling profession includes instruction in research and practice. Many students experience this is training as representing two separate disciplines—that of the scientist and the practitioner and not as training in one integrated discipline (Hoshmand & Polkinghorne, 1990). The scientist side of the model consists of instruction in mathematical thinking skills quite unlike the conceptual competence belonging to the practitioner side of the model. One of the advantages of including instruction in qualitative procedures as part of scientific training is that the conceptual skills required to carry out these procedures are closely related to those required to work successfully with clients.

Implementation of the scientist and practitioner model does not require that every counselor be engaged in both producing research articles and practicing professionally, nor does it necessarily require that practitioners directly apply the results reported in journals in their work with clients (Schon, 1983). Cohen, Sargent, and Sechrest (1984) distinguish between the instrumental and conceptual utilization of psychotherapy research. Instrumental utilization entails the direct influence of a research report on a clinician's practice; for example, the adoption of a particular technique because a research article reported it to be effective. Conceptual utilization refers to the general effect of research training on professional practice; for example, thinking more critically, sharpening observational skills, and taking empirical data more seriously. Research training that includes instruction in qualitative procedures can facilitate conceptual utilization of scientific principles in professional practice. That result should be one of the goals of an integrated scientist-practitioner model.

Philosophical Support for Diversity

Little attention is given to the philosophy of science in counseling. Galassi (1984) surveyed training directors of APA-approved counseling psychology programs, asking them to rate 11 components in training skilled researchers in counseling psychology. Philosophy of science was ranked last, significantly lower than the other 10 components. Howard's (1985) similar survey of then current and past editors and associate editors of psychology journals found philosophy of science rated second to last. Nevertheless, the philosophical assumptions underlying counseling research practices are important in assessing the role qualitative procedures might have in counseling research.

The fundamental change that has taken place in the philosophical assessment of human knowledge (Polkinghorne, 1983; Rorty, 1979; Suppe, 1977) has significant implications for counseling research. The current changes in the philosophy of science ("constructivism") have raised questions about the manner in which criteria are applied to knowledge propositions. For example, when judged according to criteria that reflect the earlier philosophy of science (often termed *positivism*), qualitative procedures appear lacking in generalizability, precision, and reliability. Given the contentions of the new philosophy of science, qualitative procedures generate useful and creditable knowledge and are a necessary addition to the present quantitative research techniques.

Traditional and Contemporary Philosophies of Science

The traditional epistemological position of Western philosophy had been that human beings could, with proper procedures, produce knowledge that was an exact description of reality. The contemporary understanding is that human knowledge is not a mirrored reflection of reality. Rather than reproducing clear pictures of the real, human knowledge is a changing collection of cognitive maps. The various maps draw from experience the elements and regularities that are useful in achieving human purposes. Cognitive maps are like road maps in that they depict only those aspects of the total environment that are necessary to accomplish a task, such as moving from one location to another. They differ in that the order and consistencies recognized by human cognitive structures and conceptual systems are not necessarily the same as the actual regularities and connections of the real. Knowledge consists of abstracting from experience the degree of consistency that is significant for human performances.

The test for knowledge is not whether it exactly corresponds to the real. In the current view, we have no way to ascertain whether there is such a correspondence. Instead, the test for knowledge is whether it functions successfully in guiding human action to attain goals. Rather than asking if a knowledge claim is an accurate depiction of the real—that is, is it true?—one asks "Does acting on this knowledge claim result in successful action?" The test for knowledge is pragmatic; thus, the new philosophy of science is sometimes called the *new pragmatism* (Margolis, 1986). Although knowledge is not an exact description of the order and relationships that exist in the real, in most cases it must, if it is to guide human action effectively, bear some resemblance to the real. One would expect that the more the knowledge description helps one anticipate the actual response to one's actions, the greater value it would have.

Knowledge is a human construction consisting of a cognitive mapping of categories and relationships on experience. The same set of experiences can be mapped in different ways. Various human communities have developed different conceptual maps and have ordered their experience according to different category systems. Mapping systems do not remain static but change through trial and error. If acting on a new understanding produces better results than the old, then over time, the new replaces the old. For both individuals and cultures, understanding evolves, with more effective knowledge succeeding the less effective (Campbell, 1974; Toulmin, 1972).

A comparison of the reconstructed view of knowledge developed by contemporary philosophers with the view that it replaced will help in appreciating how the tenets of quantitative procedures came to prevail in counseling research. It will also provide an understanding of the criticisms directed against qualitative procedures by adherents to that view.

Mathematical and Linguistic Positivism

Contemporary critics have employed various terms to designate the previous conception of how knowledge is generated. Among them are the *modern viewpoint* (as distinguished from the "postmodern" or contemporary view), the *Enlightenment view*, the *philosophic view* (as distinguished from the present "after philosophy" period), *objectivism* and *positivism* (Polkinghorne, 1990). Terms used to denote the new philosophy of knowledge are *postmodern*, the *new pragmatism, experientialism*, and *constructivism*. In this chapter I use the terms *positivism* and *constructivism* to refer to the two views.

The essential feature of positivism is that humans can positively gain true knowledge of reality. There are two types of positivism: mathematical positivism and linguistic positivism. They differ in their idea of the nature of reality and the reasoning tools required to describe it. The traditional and commonplace understanding of positivism is mathematical. This view holds that the regularities in reality are mathematical in form. Linguistic positivists, although accepting the idea that the natural realm is organized mathematically, hold that the human realm is organized according to linguistic principles. They propose that two types of reason are required: mathematical for the natural realm and linguistic for the human realm (Dilthey, 1927/1977). A brief discussion of these two types of positivism may clarify the historical arguments between quantitative and qualitative proponents.

Mathematical Positivism.   From the view of mathematical positivism, reality is made up of entities that are divided into natural kinds according to their essential properties. It includes the belief that humans can identify these divisions in reality and create words to point to them. Mathematical positivists hold that all the members of a natural kind (the members of a set) move according to specific rules, which exist independent of human minds. These rules conform to the principles of formal logic and mathematics. They maintain that among the capacities of human beings is the special capacity to reason in a manner that corresponds to the logical and mathematical structures that actually exist in the world outside of human thought. Structural understanding gained through the use of the special capacity to think logically and mathematically actually mirrors the structures of reality. When humans use this special capacity, they are able to overcome the limitations of the situated subjectivity of human existence and to achieve a "God's eye" perspective on reality. Any person who reasons using formal logic and mathematics will reach the same conclusion as and be understandable to any other who uses that capacity.

According to mathematical positivists, new knowledge is gained by devising hypothetical logical relations among the categories of reality and then testing the hypotheses by observation to see if the proposed relations hold. If they do, one can be positively assured that the hypothesized mathematical statement is a description of the actual mathematical relations that obtain among those objects in reality.

From the perspective of this position, the development of knowledge can occur only through the use of the special capacity to think logically and mathematically. Other kinds of thinking do not match the structure of reality. Normal human language is too vague and ambiguous to be suitable to describe the natural categories. Thus, knowledge generation requires the use of a special language in which observations define all terms.

Mathematical positivism was first used to study the natural realm. When the human science disciplines originated in the 19th century, they adopted the mathematical positivism of the natural sciences (Giorgi, 1986). Their pioneers took the view that all reality—both the natural and human realms—

was organized mathematically. Accordingly, the methods developed in the study of nature could be used to study humans. The human and natural sciences were thus methodologically unified, and a single mathematical method was applicable to the study of all reality (Hempel, 1942).

Qualitative procedures obviously cannot produce quantified descriptions of mathematical regularities. If one holds the mathematical positivistic view that all reality, including the human realm, is structured according to mathematical laws, and that we can know these laws through the exercise of mathematical reasoning, then it follows that qualitative procedures are flawed and deficient and cannot produce accurate descriptions of reality. Qualitative researchers use the ambiguity of ordinary language as an intrinsic element in their analysis of data. They do not filter the vagueness of experience through predefined, operationally precise variables. They use a variety of analytic logics that incorporate the prototype notions of similarity and dissimilarity. We have not yet been able to duplicate these logics electronically; they require extensive use of human judgment. Qualitative analysis does not share the character of algorithmic computation performed by computers (Dreyfus & Dreyfus, 1986). In addition, the generalizability of results from qualitative procedures is based on a theoretically informed selection of data sources. The generalization in quantitative designs is derived from probability logic. From standards applicable to probability logic, qualitative designs do not produce generalizable knowledge.

Although it is true that qualitative procedures do not produce reliable and valid knowledge of reality *according to the standards of mathematical positivism,* imposing mathematical criteria on qualitative designs is a category mistake. Qualitative designs are based on a different logic of knowledge generation and need to be judged on the standards of that logic. Those standards are discussed later in this chapter.

Linguistic Positivism. Since the founding of the human science disciplines, there have been those who have held that the use of the quantitative procedures developed to study the natural realm are inappropriate for inquiries concerned with human realities (Polkinghorne, 1983). They have contended that the human realm is organized differently from the natural realm. Its regularities are reflected in linguistic structures, not mathematical structures. Thus, what is required is a different set of methods designed to identify those linguistic structures. These methods use qualitative or natural-language data and linguistically based analytic procedures.

Many who have proposed the use of these methods have also held that they produce the same kind of positively valid and objective knowledge about the human realm that quantitative methods produce about the natural realm. I call this position *linguistic positivism.* Linguistic positivists imply that, as one can generate an accurate description of the mathematical rules that govern the events in the natural realm, one can generate accurate descriptions of the linguistic rules that structure events in the human realm. They hold that the findings of qualitative methods give an equivalent objective depiction of the human realm as it exists independent of anyone's view of it; that is, any two researchers investigating the same phenomenon will ideally come to the same conclusion.

Historically, most of those who have argued for the use of qualitative procedures for studying the human realm have shared the positivistic belief that human reality could be positively known as it is in itself. Their positions differed from mathematical positivism on which methods should be used to describe human reality, not on whether it could be described accurately and positively. If one holds a linguistic positivistic view that human reality is structured according to linguistic relationships, then quantitative procedures cannot produce accurate descriptions of human reality. Linguistic positivists argue that qualitative procedures should replace quantitative procedures for the study of the human realm. Their position is that counseling should abandon quantitative research and supplant it with qualitative studies.

Unfortunately, much of the argument about the use of qualitative procedures in counseling has taken place from within the two (outdated, I believe) positivistic positions. The tone of the discussions has been contentious, with each side downgrading the other. From the perspective of a constructivist understanding of knowledge, neither position is correct. Some writers (e.g., Lincoln & Guba, 1985; Reason & Rowan, 1981), who appear to argue for a linguistic positivism and the replacement of quantitative methods with qualitative procedures, hold that their position represents the "new paradigm" or new philosophy of science. But I believe that identifying a call for the exclusive or predominant use of one research approach with the recent changes in the philosophy of science misrepresents the "new" philosophy (Polkinghorne, 1991).

Constructivism

The current philosophy of science implies the use of multiple organizing schemes and research methods. From its perspective, neither quantitative nor qualitative procedures produce descriptions of human reality as it exists independent of human knowing. Both are conceptual systems used to fit organizing structures over the complex and flux of experience. The structures that knowledge recognizes are abstractions from the compound and multifarious interactions of reality. These abstractions serve to cull out from the real sufficient understanding to enable humans to function adequately with one another and with the world. The role of knowledge is to assist humans in achieving their purposes by allowing us to anticipate the consequences of our actions. In order to serve us, it need not perfectly and positively reflect a full description of the actual structures of reality (Segal, 1986).

The current view of knowledge denies that there is a special human capacity that allows us access to a reality independent of our experience. Reasoning with mathematical and formal logical structures is but one way humans attempt to give a meaningful order to their encounter with the world. Humans reason about their experience by the use of a variety of cognitive structures, many of them organized according to gestalt part–whole relations. Knowledge is a human creation whereby consistencies and regularities of experience are linked together so that the response to our actions can be anticipated.

Doing science does not mean a different way of thinking or the use of a special cognitive skill. Science is an extension of the ordinary cognitive processes used to make experience meaningful and inform everyday human actions. What differentiates scientific knowing from ordinary knowing is its deliberate and communal dimensions. Doing science is a purposeful and self-conscious activity; science involves a methodical effort to correct and refine an initial understanding until it clearly fits experience. The results of scientific efforts are simply knowledge proposals until they have been judged by the community of scholars as worthy of inclusion in a discipline's body of knowledge.

Conceptual Organizing Systems

The current philosophy of science provides an argument for the use of multiple analytic systems. Because all analytics construe experience in a partial way, the use of a number of organizing systems provides a more extensive understanding than does any one alone. Procedures designed with the positivistic understanding that they were uncovering the actual organizing schemes of an independent reality can continue to be used within a constructivist framework. The change in understanding is that these research procedures are now seen as human organizing systems that are fit over experience. The procedures are not necessarily uncovering independent structures that govern reality. The order they create for human understanding comes from filtering experience through a conceptual system.

The human disciplines have thus far developed research procedures for applying two basic organizing systems to experience: the logicomathematical system and the natural-language system. An organizing system is a kind of language defined by the particular categorical types and grammar it allows. Categorical types refer to the structures that define the concepts of a language. Categories can be structured like a container in which something is either inside (a member of the category) or outside (not a member of the category), for example, a feeling is either depression or not depression. The logicomathematical system is limited to categories of the container type. Natural-language systems allow, in addition to categories structured like containers, types of categories that define membership in terms of similarity or family resemblance (see the later section on cognitive models). Grammar is the system of rules used to generate all the acceptable sentences in a language. Grammar defines the kind of connections that can be made among a language's conceptual categories. The grammar of the English natural-language system allows categories expressed as nouns to serve as subjects and objects of categories of action (e.g., "The dog chased the ball"). The grammar of the logicomathematical system limits the expression of category connections to mathematical and logical terms (e.g., "The mean of the scores in Group A is greater than the mean of the scores in Group B").

Logicomathematical Conceptual System. Although arithmetic operations may fit naturally into the everyday ordering of human experience—counting, for example, is a universally practiced numeric manipulation—not all mathematics has a natural basis. The logicomathematical conceptual system used in science is a purposely developed artificial system (Whitehead & Russell, 1910–1913) created by human imagination to link the grammar of mathematics and relational logic. It limits its categories to the propositional type with closed boundaries. Particulars can be clearly identified as members or nonmembers of a category set (e.g., a particular is either A or non-A). In practice, the categories of the scientific logicomathematical conceptual system are defined by measurement operations. Within this system, relationships among members of category sets can be established by mathematical procedures. The present quantitative methods of knowledge generation are grounded in this conceptual system.

Recall that when the logicomathematical system was developed, it was thought that reality was written in this language and that statements in this language provided accurate pictures of an independent reality. The current philosophy of science understands the logicomathematical language as one of several possible organizing systems used to interpret and give meaning to experience.

Those supporters of qualitative procedures who maintain a linguistic positivism and call for counseling to discard knowledge produced by the logicomathematical system confuse the historical origins of quantitative methods with their current practice. Historically, quantitative research practices were developed during the heyday of positivism and were consistent with its foundationalist understanding of science. The logicomathematical conceptual system, however, and the research designs and enhancements to statistical procedures derived from it retain their usefulness and importance within the current understanding of science. As research tools, *quantitative procedures are neutral* with respect to a particular philosophy of science. They can serve as valued and useful instruments for increasing our comprehension of the human world independent of the mathematical positivist view that human mathematical reasoning replicates the transcendent logic of the universe. One can also establish the mathematical probabilities of relations among variables without being committed to the idea that the variables represent natural categories that make up the universe. Current quantitative research texts reflect little concern with philosophical justifications for their practices. Those that do express such concerns appear to have adapted without difficulty to the postmodern constructivist position. For example, Stanovich (1989) suggests that psychological research does not assume that its variables represent categories that actually exist in reality; rather, they are hypothetical constructs tenuously linked to observables that are assumed to denote the extent of their presence. Psychological research does not posit that a construct is the same as the variable or variables used to measure it (e.g., intelligence is not the same as the score on the WAIS-R).

Ordinary-Language Conceptual System. The ordinary-language conceptual system, as distinct from the artificially and purposefully constructed logicomathematical system, is a culturally evolved system. It encompasses a variety of category structures, including those organized by narrative, taxonomic, and "family" relations. Its categories are most often defined in terms of similarity to a prototype. The grammar it uses to connect categories allows relationships of subjects to their actions. The ordinary-language conceptual system is used by humans to structure and give meaning to everyday life events. There is no single ordinary-language conceptual system, but different systems that have been developed by diverse language communities. Despite some commonalities among the communal language systems, categories and metaphorical constructions often differ. Thus, two qualitative studies of a phenomenon may not produce equivalent results if one is conducted in English and the other in Chinese.

Qualitative research methods are conducted within an ordinary-language conceptual system. Qualitative data retain the categorical organization employed by subjects in their everyday understanding. Analysis of these data involves the use of three kinds of possible organizing categories: (a) categories used by the subjects; (b) technical categories previously developed by the discipline; and (c) researcher-created categories. Often qualitative analysis will move beyond this level of description by categories to theoretical explanations (Glaser & Strauss, 1967). Theoretical explanations in qualitative research consist of the discovery of linkages among the categories. The kinds of linkages used in the explanations are those carried by the grammatical constructions employed in ordinary language.

The current philosophy of science does not provide an argument for discarding the logicomathematical system as a tool for understanding; rather, it supports the use of a variety of analytical conceptual systems. Because all analytics construe phenomena in a partial way, the use of a variety of research systems provides a more extensive understanding than does any one alone. There is no research system that has direct access to reality; all are human abstractions designed to organize our experience in meaningfully productive ways.

THE QUALITATIVE GESTALT

Thus far I have argued that both quantitative and qualitative research procedures further understanding by positing a semblance of order on the complex flow of human experience. Quantitative designs use mathematical structures and qualitative designs use linguistic structures to gather together the diverse elements of experience. The structures used by both sets of designs are human creations and neither has cognitive privilege as descriptive of human reality. Within each system, actual research practice involves compromise and trade-offs. Both approaches to research are based on logics and rules intrinsic to their own processes, and it is a mistake to use the logic of one approach to judge the procedures and results of the other. The theory and practice of quantitative designs are addressed in other chapters of this book. The remainder of this chapter describes the theory and practice of qualitative designs.

Generation of Knowledge

For researchers trained in quantitative methods, perhaps the most difficult problem in comprehending qualitative research is its affinity with ordinary knowledge generation. Qualitative designs mimic the constructive processes that humans ordinarily use to understand their experience. Humans have a natural propensity to search for patterns of consistency in their experience (Margolis, 1987). These patterns provide the interpretive schemes through which events are understood and actions undertaken (Combs & Syngg, 1959). Ordinary knowledge is grounded in a gestalt logic in which elements are understood in relation to the whole of which they are a part. This logic differs essentially from the formal-mathematical logic in which quantitative procedures are grounded. Identification of entities in gestalt logic is relational and given in terms of links to other entities. Identification in formal-mathematical logic is given in terms of an entity's properties; that is, each entity either has or lacks a given property (the law of the excluded middle). The principles of qualitative research are based on the operations of the gestalt logic of ordinary understanding, which involve a recursive process through hypothetical approximations and revisions. It is the recursive movement between data and hypotheses that gives qualitative designs a very different character from that of quantitative designs. In research using quantitative designs, the re-

searcher makes a single linear move through the phases of research: proposing a hypothesis and then collecting and analyzing data to test the hypothesis.

The principles of gestalt logic have been variously described by different
research programs. Piaget (1954) portrayed the operation of ordinary understanding as involving two processes of meaning construction—assimilation
and accommodation. Experiential events are made understandable by assimilation into previously acquired patterns, or schemata. When an event does
not fit these patterns, the patterns are revised or new patterns conceived to
accommodate the apparent inconsistency. Studies in the hermeneutic tradition (Gadamer, 1975) describe the process of understanding as a circle (the
hermeneutic circle). This concept refers to the notion that understanding is
grasped in a reciprocal interaction of the whole schema and its parts. The
whole receives its definition from the parts, and, reciprocally, the parts can
be understood only in reference to the whole. That is, the meaning of a particular experiential event, such as your car's failure to start, can be understood only in its relation to a whole pattern, such as a trip to the university.
Recent studies on ordinary understanding and its connection to scientific thinking have been undertaken by Kuhn, Amsel, and O'Loughlin (1988). They frame
their research in terms of the coordination between theory and evidence.
Their investigations of children and adults have addressed the process of theory revision based on incongruent evidence.

This personal example of ordinary knowing provides a demonstration of
the operations of gestalt understanding.

Recently I taught a course at the University of Southern California in down-
town Los Angeles. On the same days each week, I drove to the university on a
freeway, usually leaving home at about the same time for each trip. As I came
to within 2 miles of the university exit, the traffic would come to an abrupt
stop. It would then start up again very slowly and continue with frequent
stops up to the point where I exited the freeway. I identified this slowing
down to a crawl as a pattern in the flow of traffic and learned to anticipate it.

On several occasions I had to arrive at the campus earlier for meetings.
I noticed that the traffic on those days did not slow down until a half miler
closer to my exit. As the end of the semester neared, there were more and
more meetings, and so my times of departure from home varied even more
widely. With the greater variation, a more complex pattern emerged: The
earlier I left for the university, the farther I drove before the slowdown began. My understanding of the pattern of the slowdown was more complicated now. The traffic slowdown was shortest when I arrived early, and increased
in length in direct relation to the time of day.

I wasn't satisfied merely to discover the pattern to how long I would be
in stop-and-go traffic. I was curious about why the pattern held. My tenta-
tively devised explanation was that there was a steep hill shortly beyond the
campus exit and that the large trucks would slow down and change to a

lower gear to make it up the hill. They would create a wave effect, slowing down the cars behind them, and as the day wore on the line of slowed cars would continue to lengthen. In a sense I had gathered data (the variation in the length of the slowdown), had constructed a pattern to describe the slowdown, and had developed a theory to account for the pattern.

One day, however, when I had left early for a meeting, the slowdown unexpectedly began 2½ miles before my exit. This effect did not fit the pattern I had come to expect, by which I figured how long it would take to get to the campus. I would have to abandon my understanding of the traffic slowdown pattern unless I could account for this variation. As I moved along I noticed police cars and a tow truck, which indicated that an accident had occurred. This was an unusual event that explained the variance in the pattern I had constructed. I was able to retain the understanding I had come to about the variance in the length of the slowdown and could continue to use that understanding to inform my decisions about what time to leave home in the mornings.

Qualitative analysis consists of a process in which hypothetical structural descriptions are "tried on" the data and altered until they "fit." Fittings are interspersed with additional data-collecting forays designed to test and refine the proposed descriptions. This method of producing a result through trial and error is a fundamentally different approach to analysis from that generally used in quantitative analysis. There, a hypothesis is proposed only once and the analysis provides a yes or no answer to the proposal. That step would represent but one cycle in qualitative analysis. When the hypothetical description is found not to fit the data, it is revised to approach a closer fit. Like a tailored suit, this newly adjusted hypothesis is tried on the data, marked wherever it fails to fit, and once again is revised and retried. The expectation is that through this process of successive adaptations and accommodations a hypothesis will finally emerge that adequately describes a structure for the data. Qualitative designs are built on this to-and-fro movement from data gathering to analysis back to more data gathering based on the revisions in the hypothesis. The hypothesis is "proved" or thought to be warranted, when attempts to find data that would further alter it are fruitless.

Testing of Hypotheses

Although qualitative research uses the basic recursive logic of ordinary knowing, it differs from the ongoing, daily endeavor of pattern construction in that it is deliberative, methodical, and subject to public scrutiny. The initial pattern descriptions are tested by intentionally searching for instances that would call them into question. On the basis of the analysis of this additional information, the initial descriptions are reformed to include the newly produced instances. The movement from formulation of a description to the search for instances that do not fit the description to reformulation of the description is repeated over and over until the description is sufficient to include the variety of instances. The proposed research conclusions are tested against data that is intentionally selected to show its inadequacies. Its conclusions and the analysis used to obtain them are then submitted to the community of scholars for its critique and judgment.

Hans Reichenbach (1938) introduced the phrases "context of discovery" and "context of justification" to mark the difference between the processes of developing hypotheses and of testing (or justifying) them. He held that these two phases of research should be separated and that epistemology was concerned only with the context of justification. The methods of science were applicable only to the testing of hypotheses. Once a hypothesis had been proposed, scientific procedures could determine if the hypothesis were false (Popper, 1972). The process of the creation of hypotheses was to be left to the logicians or psychologists.

Qualitative designs combine the context of discovery and the context of justification. Whereas quantitative research is designed to test a predetermined hypothesis (in actuality, a predetermined null-hypothesis), qualitative research is designed to create and refine hypotheses as they interact with the data. The process of hypothesis formation is termed *abduction* (see Williams, 1985). Initial efforts to develop a hypothesis that fits the data are revised by attempts to confirm it as the most careful and complete description of the patterns in the data. There is a recursive movement from partial discovery to partial confirmation until a hypothesized pattern configures all the data.

The function of research in counseling is to develop clear descriptions of categories that organize human experience and action into meaningful and useful patterns. Quantitative designs accomplish this task by proposing a mathematical pattern of relationship among predefined categories and analyzing the comparative instances within those categories. Qualitative designs accomplish the same function by examining the variety of instances in which the category is manifest, continuously adjusting the description of the pattern until it matches the data.

USING QUALITATIVE PROCEDURES

The following sections describe in more detail the procedures used in qualitative designs. These procedures need to be understood as activities that cannot be separated from the context of a particular research project. Their description as discrete parts of qualitative research is an abstraction from their use in practice. The three primary activities involved in doing qualitative research are data producing, analyzing, and communicating results.

Counseling has not yet developed an extensive literature depicting the specific adaptations of qualitative procedures to the investigation of its research questions (see, however, Goldman, 1978). The descriptions offered here are therefore drawn primarily from other disciplines. In places I suggest how they might be adapted to the special needs of counseling. Because most readers will be familiar with the quantitative theories of data collection and data analysis, the descriptions include comparisons between the functions of these activities in qualitative and quantitative research.

Data Production

Qualitative researchers are data scavengers. They search for and develop whatever sources might contribute to answering their research question. They typically use several types of data: observations, interviews, documents, and their own experiences. No single source of information can be trusted to provide a comprehensive view of the phenomenon under investigation. Goetz and LeCompte (1984) wrote: "A distinguishing characteristic of ethnographic research is the fluid, developmental process through which [the] means of collecting data are chosen and constructed" (p. 107).

Qualitative Versus Quantitative Designs

Data production in qualitative designs differs from the process in quantitative designs in the following five significant ways.

Ongoing Data Gathering. The choice of data sources is ongoing throughout the research process. Which sources of data are needed is determined anew at each iterative reformulation of the tentative hypotheses. Thus, it is the initial mass of data itself that points the researcher to further sources of data. Data selection is not completed prior to the beginning of analysis; rather, new sources are chosen on the basis of their contribution to testing the fit of the emerging description.

Purpose of Design. The choice of data sources is guided by the contribution the source might make to the formation of the emerging descriptive pattern. The purpose of qualitative designs is to clarify and describe the kinds of variance the occurs within a phenomenon, rather than their distributions. Qualitative designs study qualities or kinds; for example, in a study of the phenomenon "depression," qualitative studies would yield a description of the various kinds of depression people experience and the relations among these kinds. Qualitative research would not yield statements about the percentages of incidents of each kind of depression that are present in a population.

In the initial phases of research projects using qualitative methods, the researchers choose data sources that they consider to be exemplars of the phenomenon under study. After a preliminary descriptive pattern of the phenomenon is produced from analyzing these data, the researcher selects sources that are somewhat removed from the exemplar or prototypal instances of the category. In selecting these further ranging sources the researcher's criterion is their potential to enhance and extend the description.

As the descriptive pattern evolves from the accumulating data, specific aspects of the description will lack clear definition. The researcher selects further sources of data that address these particular parts of the developing description. As newly collected data tend to maintain, rather than amplify, the tentative description, the researcher purposely searches for unique or unusual instances of the category (the outliers in quantitative distributions). These are used as a further check on the adequacy of the proposed pattern. When new sources of data continue to reinforce the emerged description rather than adding new dimensions to it, the researcher brings the data collection to an end.

Application of Judgment. Data selection in qualitative designs is a process driven by the developing description. Data selection is not a sampling procedure based on the requirements of probability theory. Selection of data sources is guided by the researcher's judgment on the basis of their potential influence on the description of the phenomenon under study. Judgment about which data sources to use cannot be predetermined by the application of specific rules, such as random selection. Researchers are required to draw on their background knowledge and imagination to determine which sources are required in order to gather ample evidence from which to evolve a full and useful description of the phenomenon. Judgment that enough data have been collected is based on a "good-enough" principle (Serlin, 1987). That is, the data sources included in the study are "good enough" to warrant the conclusion. Data selection is inadequate when reviewers can point to instances of the phenomenon that could not be generated by the descriptive pattern developed by the researcher.

Judging the selection of data sources on the criterion of their sufficiency to produce a full structural description of the phenomenon is critically different from judging the selection of data sources in quantitative designs. Quantitative designs determine statements about categories by randomly sampling instances of the category. By the use of the logic of probability built into the tests of statistical significance, quantitative researchers are able to produce mathematical statements about the likelihood that what was disclosed about the phenomenon in the sample of data sources is present in the population. The selection of data sources in qualitative designs is made on theoretical grounds rather than on the grounds of probability theory. In practice, however, because of the difficulties in obtaining random samples, both qualitative and quantitative research use theoretical considerations in selecting its data sources (Serlin, 1987).

Character of the Data. Data collected in qualitative designs are "thick" in comparison with the "thin" data collected in quantitative designs (Geertz, 1973). In quantitative designs the description of the categories (variables) under study and the indicators (measuring instruments) of their presence and/or extensiveness are predetermined. Data gathering consists of selectively attending only to the presence and magnitude of instances of these categories. The focal problems in for data gathering in quantitative designs are the validity and reliability of the measuring instruments. Qualitative designs call for obtaining vivid and rich descriptions of instances of the category. The researcher is the instrument of data collection and the validity of the data is dependent on the skill, competence, and rigor of the person collecting the data. Guba and Lincoln (1981) commented:

> [Because] the inquirer is himself the instrument, changes resulting from fatigue, shifts in knowledge, and cooptation, as well as variations resulting from differences in training, skill, and experience among different "instruments," easily occur. But this loss in rigor is more than offset by the flexibility, insight, and ability to build on tacit knowledge that is the peculiar province of the human instrument. (p. 113)

The study of anxiety provides an example of the difference this makes in data collection. Qualitative designs would use data sources to collect extensive descriptions of the experience of anxiety. Thick descriptions would include information from people about how they experience their body when they are anxious, the situations in which they become anxious, how they behave when anxious, and any other aspects of their experience of anxiety that would contribute to the developing structural description. These data might be produced during an interview lasting an hour or more and make up a transcribed text of more than 20 pages. The bulk of data gathered in qualitative designs can easily consist of 1,000 pages of information. Quantitative designs may produce a single numerical index of the subject's anxiety level reflecting the score on a paper-and-pencil test or a reading of a galvanic skin meter. The analytic tools of the two types of designs require these different kinds of data. Quantitative analytic procedures determine the relationships among groups of numbers; qualitative analytic procedures develop descriptions of structures that connect the various aspects of a phenomenon.

Less Stress on Formal Controls. The underlying assumption of data production differs in quantitative and qualitative designs. Quantitative data production theory derives from the idea of stimulus–response. The data-generating instruments (e.g., paper-and-pencil tests or questionnaires) are the stimuli and the answers given by the subject are the responses. The goal in data gathering is to hold the stimuli constant in order that the variance in the subjects' responses reflects only differences in subjects and not variance in the stimuli. In quantitative studies using questionnaires it is therefore important that the stimuli—the wording and order of the questions—remain constant.

Qualitative data-production theory does not lay the same stress on formal controls. In qualitative designs the instrument of data generation is the data gatherer. Although qualitative designs sometimes incorporate data generated by test instruments, their primary data consist of observations by researchers and subject statements produced in interviews conducted by researchers. The procedures of qualitative analysis require data of sufficient complexity to display inner diversity and connections. Obtaining data of this intensity entails a different model of data generation from the stimulus–response model of quantitative design. Qualitative data collection is based on a "discourse" model (Mishler, 1986) in which data emanate from the involved interaction of researchers with their data sources. Researchers engage with their sources in enough depth to be allowed access to more than surface responses. The aim is to move from collecting disconnected bits of information to gathering more interconnected and related information. This movement is accomplished in qualitative data gathering by a somewhat personal and open exchange with data sources.

Because qualitative researchers interact closely with their data sources, they are required to retain an awareness of how their own biases and preconceptions can affect the information they are generating. They adopt a stance of "empathic neutrality" (Patton, 1990), that is, an empathic engagement with their data sources, but a neutral position regarding the content of the information generated. Qualitative designs do not normally use formal techniques (e.g., double-blind designs) to assure researcher neutrality. Instead, they call for the use of multiple sources of data and searches for data that disconfirm hypotheses. Producing qualitative data lacking in researcher bias is a result of training and awareness and, in the end, the researcher's commitment to producing credible data.

Sources of Qualitative Data

The purpose of data production in qualitative designs is to accumulate sufficient depictions of instances of the phenomenon under study to permit construction of a pattern that fully describes the diverse qualities of the phenomenon. A study using a qualitative design usually assembles data from a variety of sources. A typical qualitative study in counseling might include interviews of informants, written descriptions from observations of videotapes of counseling sessions, reports from the research literature, and process memos from the researchers. In general, these data must be put into written form to be analyzed. Interviews, which are originally spoken, are transcribed; what is observed through seeing or hearing must be translated into written descriptions; and researchers' ideas and hunches must be written down. Data from widely varied sources must all be reduced to written form for analysis and public review of research conclusions.

The data sources used in qualitative designs can be divided into four primary types: (a) written descriptions of researchers' observations, (b) transcriptions of interviews, (c) previously written materials, including personal and public documents, reports of previous research and scholarly studies, and literary descriptions of the phenomenon, and (d) memos generated by researchers relating their own experiences and reflections.

Observational Data. Observational data consist of written descriptions (sometimes supplemented with photographs) of situations observed by researchers. Researchers can record observations of the actions of individuals or groups in artificial or laboratory settings—for example, Zimbardo's mock prison study (Haney, Banks, & Zimbardo, 1973). Observational data, however, are usually collected in natural or field settings and are historically associated with anthropological field studies and the participant-observation studies of the Chicago school of sociology. Observational data gathering is now a method used to produce data for studies of classrooms, families, child behavior, and organizations (Sanday, 1983).

An extensive literature exists on observational data collection; for example, Ellen's (1984) edited volume on anthropological field work, McCall and Simmons' (1969) classic collection on participant observation, and Spradley's (1980) text. Recent monographs addressing the collection of observational data are Fetterman's (1989) *Ethnography Step by Step* and Jorgensen's (1989) *Participant Observation: A Methodology for Human Studies,* which offer a detailed treatment of the use of observational methods of data collection.

The literature focuses on two primary problem areas in developing observational data in the field: (a) access and maintenance of the researcher's relationship with the group under study, and (b) the production and management of field notes.

The kind of involvement observers have in the settings they are studying can vary considerably. At one end of the continuum they are full participants; at the other, they have no participation (at their most detached, observing through a one-way mirror). Observers need to determine whether they will identify themselves as researchers (or evaluators) or will disguise their role to some extent. At issue is the effect their presence and identification will have on the subjects' behavior.

Observers need to develop workable and unobtrusive methods for recording their observations. Historically, field observers jotted notes during their daily interactions with group members and spent the evenings writing out full field observations from their notes. The invention of portable computers makes the recording of observations easier, although often it is not appropriate to use them in a setting. Videorecorders make it possible to have a permanent visual and audio record of actions in a small and immobile setting, such as an individual and group counseling room. Many counseling settings are equipped with unobtrusively located video cameras. The profession has already collected a vast number of videotaped counseling sessions and will continue, on a regular basis, to collect more. These taped sessions offer an immense source of observational data for qualitative research on group and individual counseling processes.

Researcher observation differs from ordinary human observation in that it requires preparation and training. Research observers organize an agenda for their observations before entering the field. At times they are most interested in actions of the subjects that support or call into question a structural hypothesis they have been developing in their analysis. Yet they need to be open to the unusual and serendipitous finding that would rearrange the relational pattern they have been bringing into focus. Counselors trained in clinical observation have some awareness of the difference between ordinary and highly trained observation. Patton (1990) described the skills to be developed in the training of research observers: "Training includes learning how to write descriptively; practicing the disciplined recording of field notes; knowing how to separate detail from trivia in order to achieve the former without being overwhelmed by the latter; and using rigorous methods to validate observations" (p. 201).

In field studies, observational data are usually supplemented with data from interviews of group members. Observational data—the researcher's descriptions of what takes place—depends in part on the researcher's awareness. Interviews can provide information about the reasons for actions. They can explore the motives and purposes of actors as well as disclosing what interpretations they gave to others' actions.

Interview Data. Although research topics in counseling range widely, they have tended historically to cluster around two areas: career development and counseling process (Gelso et al., 1988). Most often, qualitative research in these clusters will not involve traditional field studies as the method of data collection. They will, instead, generate data from the observation of individual or group counseling sessions and/or interviews with clients or counselors about their therapeutic or training experiences or with people in general about career or life experiences. For example, a study of negative counseling experiences would collect data by interviewing clients who have had such experiences; a study of a stutterer's experience of social interactions would interview stutterers.

The qualitative interview is conceived of as a discourse or conversation.

It involves an interpersonal engagement in which subjects are encouraged to share with the researcher nuanced and detailed elaborations of their experiences. In the interview, subjects are asked to describe instances of their experience with respect to the topic being investigated. Although interviewers prepare a list of open-ended questions, the actual phrasing and content of the questions change in response to the unfolding description and narrative given by the interviewee (Mishler, 1986). Interviewers take care to remain open to the presence of new and unexpected elements in the description and do not shape the questions as tests of ready-made categories or schemes of interpretation. Interviewers need to explore aspects of interviewees' descriptions that are disconfirming of the hypothesis that is emerging in their analysis.

Subjects are encouraged and given time to elaborate and relate the details of their experience. The interview seeks descriptions of the experience itself, not abstract or speculative discussions of what subjects believe the experience should have been. Rather than soliciting general opinions, the interview focuses on specific situations and action sequences that are instances of the phenomenon under investigation so that the pattern or structure of the topic will be included in the description. When the statements of an interviewee are ambiguous, it is the task of the interviewer to seek clarification. The interview is a temporal process, and descriptions may become richer and clearer in the later portions of the interview.

The quality of the data developed in an interview is dependent on the skill of the interviewer, the reflective and recollecting capacities of the interviewee, and the relationship that is developed. The interviewer has an effect on subjects and the level of description they produce. Positive interviewer effects are those that encourage subjects to overcome the propensity to give guarded and socially desired descriptions. Negative interviewer effects are those that lead or bias the descriptions by causing interviewees to withhold or distort accounts of their experience.

Qualitative interviews require enough time to develop an interviewer–interviewee relationship and to explore the topic in depth. They usually run from 30 to 60 minutes; sometimes they take several hours. In some studies, subjects are interviewed more than once. The length of the interview depends on the initial comfort of the subject, the ease with which the subject can recollect and reflect on the topic, and the information emerging in the interview.

Some studies require extensive interviewing with only a few people; others need a greater variety of descriptions, and so a large number of people are interviewed. The selection of interview subjects is guided primarily by the need to produce a data base with diverse perspectives on the phenomenon being investigated. Subjects are sought out who might provide descriptions that challenge and extend the present development of the research description. Because the purpose of qualitative designs is to produce descriptions of the possible elements and structures that make up a phenomenon, rather than descriptions of the distribution of the phenomenon, randomness and representativeness are secondary considerations in selection of interview subjects.

The use of interviews to gather data involves qualitative researchers in one of the perennial problems of psychological research—the validity of self-reports (Danzinger, 1980). The untrustworthiness of introspective reports was a contributing factor to the rise of behaviorism (Lyons, 1986). Direct access to information about a person's motivation, cognitions, and emotional experience is not available to researchers, who therefore must either infer people's subjective experience from their behavior, or rely on people's reports about it. Self-reports are problematic for two reasons: (a) reflection and recollection involve reconstruction of experience rather than direct observation, and (b) not all mental activity is accessible to awareness (Dreyfus & Dreyfus, 1986). The role of self-report data in psychological research is an issue that qualitative data gatherers share with quantitative researchers who use survey questionnaires, career inventories, personality inventories, and other instruments of subject report. Qualitative researchers are not as concerned as others about how faithfully the report mirrors an experience. The description need not duplicate the subject's original understanding of the experience; it is enough that it reflects the person's understanding at the time of the interview. The descriptions are useful as examples of how it is possible to relate the elements of the experience into a meaningful whole.

Several worthwhile texts are available on qualitative research interviewing: McCracken's (1988) monograph *The Long Interview,* Spradley's (1979) *The Ethnographic Interview,* Mishler's (1986) *Research Interviewing,* and Kvale's (1983) "The Qualitative Research Interview." Morgan (1988) discussed group interviews in his *Focus Group as Qualitative Research.* In addition to discussing the qualitative research interview process in detail, these texts also address issues such as the recording of interviewer observations during the interview, the effects of the interview setting, the problems in recording and transcribing interview-generated data, and methods for increasing the validity of interview data.

Existing Literature. One of the characteristics that differentiate qualitative research from ordinary knowing is what happens to it within the context of a community of scholars. Not only are the results of a study submitted to the community for their critique and judgment but the study itself is informed by and linked to other community members' efforts to understand the phenomenon.

Qualitative studies incorporate and build on the body of knowledge developed by the human disciplines. As in quantitative studies, researchers review the scholarly literature to situate and focus the study and to learn how others have approached the topic. But qualitative studies extend the use of the literature in two ways. First, the results of qualitative research are understood as unfinished, so findings of previous studies are not taken as conclusive. Findings are the patterns that fit the data available to the study. Their "validity lasts until other cases are presented which can be proved to be cases of . . . [the experience], and which do not correspond to the necessary and sufficient constituents contained in the formula" (van Kaam, 1969, pp. 327–328). The descriptions of the structural relationships among the elements offered by qualitative researchers are always tentative and invite additional study.

Second, qualitative studies include previous studies—both qualitative and quantitative—in their database. The descriptions of the phenomenon generated in the scholarly literature become part of the data that are subjected to qualitative analysis. When viewed as data, the literature displays descriptions of the phenomenon in its definitions of variables and construct definitions underlying its measuring instruments.

Besides using the scholarly literature as data, qualitative designs search other literatures for descriptions of the object of study. In scavenging for diverse descriptions, qualitative researchers may include in their data accounts given in the clinical literature, autobiographies, and historical writings. Useful descriptions may also come from literary and popular fiction, poetry, motion pictures, television, and magazine articles. The function of qualitative designs is to produce clarifying and integrating descriptions of patterns that make experience understandable and meaningful. Any description, whatever its source, that contributes to the clarification of the structures of experience can usefully be included as data.

Researchers' Experiences. Qualitative researchers often include their own experiences of the phenomenon under study as part of the database (Colaizzi, 1978). They may begin the data collection with a self-interview in which they commit to writing their initial understanding of the structure that relates the parts of the experience. Even if they have not directly experienced the phenomenon under study, the self-interview can identify their assumptions and expectations. A self-interview not only serves as data but alerts researchers to possible biases and premises that might interfere with their adopting a neutral stance toward the content of the data.

During the research process, qualitative designs call for researchers to write down their thoughts and internal monologue about the project. "Memos are an essential part of those [internal] dialogues, a running record of insights, hunches, hypotheses, discussions about the implications of codes, additional thoughts, whatnot" (Strauss, 1987, p. 110). Writing memos prevents the loss of the fleeting ideas that come into awareness from the integrative thinking that often operates below the conscious level.

Qualitative research requires keeping a detailed record of the entire process. Researchers must record not only what and when they did something but why they did it. Because qualitative procedures draw so heavily on the researcher's judgment and discernment, a chronicle of the processes that led to the research result allows supervisors and reviewers to evaluate a dimension not apparent in the findings themselves.

Data Management

In a mid-sized qualitative research project, it is not unusual for data collection to yield from several hundred to 1,000 pages of data. Managing this amount of material requires attention and skill. Prior to the advent of the computer, researchers needed several copies of all these data; one was kept intact as a backup, and the others were cut into sections in order to gather together the sentences and paragraphs that dealt with the same themes (Lofton, 1971). The computer now stores the data electronically, with word processing programs to perform searches and cut-and-paste operations (Pfaffenberger, 1988; Tesch, 1990). The computer adds great efficiency to the management and manipulation of qualitative data; it cannot, however, eliminate the need for personal judgments throughout the qualitative research process.

Analytic Procedures

The purpose of qualitative analysis is to develop a statement delineating a structure or pattern of relationships that organizes the phenomenon under investigation into a unified whole. In their *Women's Ways of Knowing* study, for example, Belenky et al. (1986) were investigating the epistemological assumptions of women. Their analysis produced a typological structure that organized the data into five types of assumptions. During their analytic work they also attempted to use a stage structure to organize the data. In a stage structure the types are developmentally arranged so that the more advanced types emerge from less advanced ones. They found that their data did not conform to the more complex stage structure, and, thus their analysis concluded that a typological structure more accurately accounted for their data about women's epistemological assumptions.

Qualitative analysis produces a type of understanding that comes from "knowing" how a part is related to other parts and to the whole. To see the stool as related to my project of reaching a book on top of the bookcase is to understand something important about the stool. In this regard, Patton (1990) wrote: "It is important to understand that the interpretive explanation of qualitative analysis does not yield knowledge in the same sense as quantitative explanation. The emphasis is on illumination, understanding, and extrapolation rather than causal determination, prediction, and generalization" (p. 424). The kind of understanding developed in qualitative analysis is particularly useful for the practice of counseling psychology. For example, a child's fear of going to school may be understood as an instance of the developmental stage in which children have a general fear of being apart from their mothers.

Pattern Recognition

Researchers doing qualitative analysis are required to be highly skilled in pattern recognition of the sort examined by *Miller's Analogy Test*. Although training and experience can increase one's effectiveness in recognizing consistencies and connections, it may be that a basic capacity for pattern recognition is inherent. The patterns do not appear directly in the data; they are the templates that give meaning to the particulars of experience. For example, the template of the letter *a* yields the production or recognition of various markings as an *a* whether they are the near scribbled writing of a first grader, a typeset serif or sans serif form or a handwritten cursive character. The search for the patterns of connection in experience involves asking what kind of structure needs to exist to produce these data. Coding the data can serve as a tool in the analytic process, yet coding itself requires the capacity to see connections. Although the analytic process is methodical and moves through various stages, it cannot be reduced to the application of a set of formal rules. The principal qualifications for doing qualitative analysis are imagination, judgment, and decision-making ability.

As used in research in the human disciplines, the term *qualitative analysis* has some overlap in meaning with the term as it is used in chemistry. In chemistry, qualitative analysis deals with the identification of elements or grouping of elements present in a sample. The procedure followed in chemistry is to separate out groups of elements and then to further divide those groups into subgroups, until the elements themselves are left. Quantitative analysis is then used to determine the amount of the element present in the sample. Qualitative analysis proceeds in a similar manner in the human disciplines. First the larger patterns are identified, and then the constituent subpatterns. The analysis continues until it reaches the level of structural organization implied by the research question. For example, if the research question asked about the experience of test anxiety, the analysis would work from the structure of emotional responses to the structure of anxiety in general, and thence to the structure of test anxiety. Part of the analysis would be concerned with identifying how test anxiety is similar to and different from other emotional responses and other anxious responses. Given the level of this research question, the investigator would not go on to analyze the differences between anxieties related to exams in coursework and those attending comprehensive tests like the Graduate Record Examination.

Relational Structures

Researchers carrying out a qualitative analysis can benefit from recent developments in cognitive science (see Gardner, 1985). Cognitive science has addressed issues that are central to carrying out qualitative analysis; for example, how do humans make sense of their experience, what is a conceptual system and how is it organized, and what is reason? Lakoff (1987) and Johnson (1987) have offered a view of conceptual structural relations that is, I believe, of particular importance for qualitative researchers in their search for patterns.

Conceptual Categorization. Humans order their experience through conceptual categorization. Every time we "see" something as a *kind* of thing— as a chair, for example—we are categorizing. A large proportion of our categories do not group things, but categories of abstract entities, such as friendship or justice. The essential work of qualitative analysis is to make explicit the elements and structural patterns of the categories humans use to organize and provide meaning to their experience. The traditional notion of categories assumed that they were abstract containers, with things either inside or outside the category. In that view, categories are defined by common properties, and things are categorized together on the basis of what they have in common. The structure of categories within this traditional understanding is described by set-theoretical models of entities and sets. In classical set theory everything either is in the set (has a membership value of 1) or is outside the set (has a membership value of 0). The procedures of quantitative research are based on classical set theory (Kerlinger, 1973). The conceptual structure of quantitative variables and the statistical protocols used in quantitative analysis assume a traditional understanding of category structure.

In her research program on prototype effects, Rosch (e.g., 1978) challenged the traditional understanding of the entities-set structure of categories. She noted that categories have best examples ("prototypes"); for instance, in our culture, a robin, as opposed to an ostrich, serves as a prototype for the category "bird." If categories are defined only by properties, as the traditional view holds, then no member should be a better example of the category than any other member. Using Rosch's research as a starting point, Lakoff (1987) and Johnson (1987) have developed an account of conceptual categorization that yields a rich array of conceptual structures. Included within this array are part–whole structure, link structure, center–periphery structure, front–

back structure, and linear-order structure, as well as the container structure of the traditional understanding (Lakoff, 1987). Their list of conceptual structures provides qualitative analysts with a variety of organizational patterns with which to understand and describe relationships that hold among the aspects of a phenomenon. Analysts need not be limited to searching for relationships consisting of shared properties.

Lakoff and Johnson hold that our abstract conceptual structures are extensions of the primary structures that organize our bodily encounter with the world. These primary structures are of two kinds—body-image schemata and basic-level concepts.

Body-Image Schematic Structures.   Body-image schematic structures are generated by our perceptual interactions and bodily movements within our environment (Johnson, 1987). To illustrate, Johnson described the development of the containment structure:

> Let us consider briefly an ordinary instance of image-schematic structure emerging from our experience of physical containment. Our encounter with containment and boundedness is one of the most pervasive features of our bodily experience. We are intuitively aware of our bodies as three-dimensional containers into which we put certain things (food, water, air) and out of which other things emerge (food and water wastes, air, blood, etc.) . . . We move in and out of rooms, clothes, vehicles, and numerous other kinds of bounded spaces. (p. 21)

Through these bodily involvements we experience the structure of *in–out* schemata.

Johnson described a number of other body-image schemata, including common force structures such as compulsion, blockage, counterforce, diversion, removal of restraint, enablement, and attraction. He also examined the path, cycle, scale, links, and center–periphery schemata. His chief point is "to show that these image schemata are pervasive, well-defined, and full of sufficient internal structure to constrain our understanding and reasoning" (p. 126). He argued that patterns such as these exist preconceptually in our experience and are a principal means by which we generate coherence and unity within experience. The prepositions in our language (e.g., *in* and *out*, *up* and *down*, *to* and *from*) often reflect body-image schematic structures.

Basic-Level Concepts.   The second primary structures that order experience are the basic-level concepts. The study of basic-level categories is usually traced to Brown's classic paper, "How Shall a Thing be Called?" (Brown, 1958). Basic-level concepts are more richly structured than the body-image schemas, which have only the outlines of structure. Basic-level conceptual categorization is related to the level of direct human interaction with the world. They are differentiated from superordinate and subordinate level categories. For example, "dog" is a basic-level concept, whereas "animal" is superordinate and "retriever" is subordinate; "chair" is basic level, whereas "furniture" is superordinate and "rocker" is subordinate. A basic-level category is "human-sized," that is, it has the following properties: (a) category members have similarly perceived overall shapes (e.g., *ball* is a basic-level category and includes all objects that are perceived as having a spherical shape, but the category *toys* is a higher level category that includes objects with many different shapes), (b) a single mental image can reflect the entire category (the basic-level category *dog* can be reflected in one prototypic image, perhaps a cocker spaniel, but the higher order categories *pet* or *mammal* require many images), and (c) a person uses similar motor actions for interacting with category members ("flowers are marked by sniffing actions, but there are no actions that distinguish one species of flower from another," Brown, 1965, p. 318). The basic-level categories, in addition to objects and things, include actions, such as *running, walking,* and *speaking.* Basic-level concepts have an integrity of their own and are our earliest and most natural forms of categorization.

In his discussion of basic-level categorization, Lakoff (1987) wrote:

> The studies of basic-level categorization suggest that our experience is preconceptually structured at that level. We have general capacities for dealing with part-whole structure in real world objects via gestalt perception, motor movement, and the formation of rich mental images. These impose a preconceptual structure on our experience. . . . Although one can identify internal structure in them, the wholes seem to be psychologically more basic than the parts. In short, the idea that all internal structure is of a building-block sort, with primitives and principles of combination, does not seem to work at the basic level of human experience. (pp. 269–270)

Human experience congeals into structured wholes at the level at which we bodily interact with the objects of the world.

According to Lakoff (1987) and Johnson (1987), our original bodily involvement with the world (through body-image schemata and basic-level categories) is of organized wholes or gestalts. The gestalts are made up of an assortment of internal structures through which their parts are organized. This assortment of internal structures provides the conceptual repertoire humans use to organize the rest of experience. Although Lakoff and Johnson do not claim that the bodily experience is more basic than other kinds of experience— emotional, mental, or cultural—they suggest that we do conceptualize the nonbodily in terms of the bodily (Lakoff & Johnson, 1980).

Cognitive Models

The bodily repertoire of experiential structures is employed to develop the cognitive models we use to organize thought. Qualitative analysts use these cognitive models to fashion patterns that organize their data. Lakoff (1987) identified four types of cognitive models.

Image-Schematic Models. These are visual models that depict organization through graphic images. For example, oppositional vector arrows can show the pattern that links events through their opposition to one another. Organizational charts can visually model the relations among workers, and matrixes can be used to picture the relations between various processes and types of outcome (Miles & Huberman, 1984; Strauss, 1987). A person "sees" the structural relations among elements of an experience through an iconic pattern. We have an inventory of schematic models that we draw upon to bring out the structural consistencies of experience. Shapiro (1985) provided an excellent presentation of the use of image-schematic models in qualitative analysis. The researcher can use schematic models as a means of ordering the data and employ diagrammatic illustrations in the presentation of the results.

Propositional Models. The perceptual base of image-schematic patterns produces a direct conceptual understanding of the inner structure of a unified, gestalt experience. Propositional models retain their structure in the form of statements without the use of imaginative devices (see discussion of metaphorica and metonymic models). These models include a set of elements with their properties and the relations that hold among the elements; for example, a structure organized by linking agents to their actions, or a structure (such as a week) with parts organized in a linear sequence (days). Lakoff (1987, pp. 284–288) identified five of the possible structural models held in propositional form:

1. The *simple proposition.* Grammatical subjects are related to grammatical objects. For example, physicians treating patients may be understood by applying the model of agents affecting recipients.
2. The *scenario* model. There is an initial state, a sequence of events, and a final state. One use of this model is organizing events into a temporal gestalt, where they are understood as parts of a process or plot (Polkinghorne, 1988). Other applications of the scenario conceptual model are developmental stage structures and steps within a research method.
3. *Feature-bundle* structures. Used in the traditional understanding of categories, this structure consists of relationships defined by common properties. For example, all creatures with wings and feathers are birds.
4. *Taxonomic* structures. Structures are arranged hierarchically, with each higher order category being a whole and the immediate lower categories being its parts. The taxonomic pattern is one of the most important structuring devices we have for making sense of what we experience and is used often by qualitative researchers to order their data.
5. *Radial* models. In the center–periphery structure, the whole consists

of one subcategory serving as the center and other subcategories connected to it radiating from it by various links.

The patterns held in image-schematic and propositional form provide the basic structural models used for ordering the domains in which there is a discernible match with consistencies of experience. In domains where there is no clearly apparent preconceptual structure to our experience, we import such structure via metaphor and metonymy.

Metaphoric Models. Metaphoric models extend the image-schematic and propositional structures by mapping one of those structures onto a new domain. Metaphorical mapping involves a source domain and a target domain. The source domain is assumed to be structured by an image-schematic or propositional model. The mapping is typically partial; it maps the structure of the model in the source domain onto a corresponding structure in the target domain. For example, the "source–path–goal" image-schematic structure is mapped onto the experience of purpose. Purposes are understood as destinations, and achieving a purpose is understood as passing along a path from a starting point to an end point. The "link" structure has been mapped on the domain of social and interpersonal relations. We make "connections" and "break social ties." Slavery is understood as bondage, and freedom as the absence of anything tying us down. Binswanger (1958), in his well-known interpretation of the case of Ellen West, used the "up–down" structure of verticality to understand her anorexic drive to lighten herself so that her ethereal body would float upward to God.

Metonymic Models. Metonymy is a type of mapping in which the structure of one well-understood or easy-to-perceive aspect of something is used to stand for the thing as a whole or for some other aspect of it. In metonymy the whole is modeled on the structural properties of a part (Manning, 1983). For example, a place may stand for an institution located at that place: "The White House was quiet."

Goal of Clarity

The structures of the domains that qualitative researchers investigate are usually unclear. In fact, that lack of clarity is usually the very reason for the investigation. The purpose of the research is to uncover the structure that has not until now been discerned. The qualitative analytic process often produces understanding by mapping the more directly understood image-schematic and propositional structures onto the more complex and less clear phenomenon that is the object of investigation (Lofton, 1984; Patton, 1990).

The process of qualitative analysis involves fitting mental structural models to the consistencies of the data. Because the process takes place in the realm of creative thought, it has appeared to some as mysterious and without form. The work of Lakoff (1987) and Johnson (1987) helps in understanding the thinking procedures used in qualitative analysis. Their descriptions account for the source and variety of structural patterns that connect entities into meaningful wholes. They also offer an explanation of the mental operations that produce order in experience. These are the same operations, used reflectively and methodically, that researchers use in doing qualitative analysis.

Stages in Analysis

The process of qualitative analysis is like a downward helix. The analysis begins at the surface, where the data appear as a loose and disconnected assemblage of disparate bits of information. As the analysis moves below the surface, the data begin to coalesce around categories and themes. Further turns find the data becoming organized into patterned relations. Finally, the helix reaches an endpoint when the data amalgamate into a whole united by a comprehensive and illuminating structure.

Each turn in the helix can be broken down into a series of steps. First, the researcher reviews and re-reads the data. Second, units of the data (usually sentences or paragraphs) that express a single theme are identified by terms that designate the category or theme into which they fit. Usually an abbreviation or shorthand code is assigned to the theme to facilitate the marking (hence, the term *coding*). The marks identifying the themes are most often placed in the left margins of the data pages; some computer programs, for example, *Textbase Alpha* (Sommerlund & Kristensen, 1986), allow this marking to be done with the electronic text. Third, units with the same theme are collected together and analyzed to ascertain their common elements. In later stages of the analysis, the researcher looks for relations that might hold among the themes. Both of these procedures use the back-and-forth technique of noticing a possible commonality or relation, checking to see if it holds with the data, revising the description in light of that check, and then going back to the data until a "best fit" description is reached. Fourth, the researcher searches for contradictory data that could break up the unity that the descriptions are beginning to uncover. (Tesch's, 1990, qualitative study of analytic steps described by various qualitative researchers produced 10 practices that overlap with the 5 outlined earlier.)

These steps are repeated until the data from new sources continue to fit the emerged structural description. At this point the research comes to a close but only a provisional close. It now awaits further revision by other researchers who find examples of the phenomenon being studied that call the proposed description into question.

Communication of Results

Research is not finished when the data have been collected and analyzed. The results of the research need to be communicated to others. The format chosen for the communication varies depending of the purpose of the research. Patton (1990) delineated five research purposes—basic research, applied research, summative evaluation, formative evaluation, and action research—and suggested the type of report and presentation appropriate for each purpose. I limit the discussion of communicating results to the first purpose, basic research.

The purpose of basic research is to make a contribution to the body of knowledge of a discipline. Entry into a body of knowledge occurs when a research report is made public as a publication in a discipline's research literature. Judgment of the acceptability of a research report is the work of the discipline's community of scholars as represented by its editors, reviewers, and dissertation committees. The basic research report requires, in addition to a statement of the finding, inclusion of sufficient description of the research process that scholars can make judgments about its value as a contribution to knowledge (Polkinghorne, 1989a).

The tradition has developed a format for quantitative research reports that is designed to permit informed judgment of the scientific merit of the reported finding. The quantitative report format includes sections on the review of literature, the method, the results, and discussion. Because of the recursive process of qualitative research, this traditional format is not always appropriate for reporting the findings and processes of qualitative research. The format of the qualitative report is guided by the researcher's need to provide the reviewer with clear evidence for the findings. The qualitative report makes the argument for the acceptance of its findings explicit. The report not only describes what was done in the research project but also explains why it was done.

The traditional format used for quantitative reports makes use of conventions of expression and argumentation that are based on the assumptions inherent in the logic of the mathematical conceptual system. Because qualitative designs make use of the range of human thinking processes, researchers are required to spell out the reasoning by which the data lead to the finding. Qualitative designs are fluid and require researcher choices throughout the process. The report needs to include explanations of these choices. For example, descriptions of why data sources were chosen and why the data gained from these sources are trustworthy. The analytic procedures need to be fully documented and explained. Using the memos written during the project, the researcher describes how the initial patterns were corrected by later data. The findings are supplemented by selections from the data that demonstrate how the proposed structural description provides a deepened understanding of the phenomenon under study.

In order to provide the full documentation, explanations, and argumentation for the findings, qualitative reports usually need to be of monograph length. The economics of most research journals require reports of six to eight pages. I suggest that qualitative researchers produce two reports: (a) a full report of monograph length that provides reviewers with sufficient information to judge the worthiness of the finding, and (b) a six- to eight-page summary report that would accompany the monograph for publication in journals.

The purpose of the research report is to provide reviewers with suitable description of the process in order that they can judge its appropriateness for admission into counseling's body of literature. Although the report should also discuss the implications the findings have for practice, the format of the report is not designed to present the research in a form that demonstrates its relevance for practice (Cohen et al., 1984). The results of both qualitative studies and quantitative studies will need to be reformatted and translated into the language of practitioners (Harmon, 1989) if they are to be useful to them. It may be necessary to write an additional report addressed directly to practitioners if the research is to be utilized in clinical settings.

In qualitative designs, the writing of the report is an integral part of the research process itself. It is not the mere reporting of a completely finished process, but an extension of the analytic process. In recounting and reviewing the data and their analysis, new insights and patterns emerge. Strauss (1987) related that while doing the write up "researchers always find themselves discovering something that tightens up or extends the total analysis" (p. 212). At times, further data collecting or re-coding may be found to be necessary.

Doing a qualitative project provides the researcher with rich personal experiences—the struggle to clarify the topic of the investigation, interpersonal engagement with those who serve as sources of data, and the effort to find patterns and make sense of the immense amount of data. The transformation of these experiences into a written document that justifies the findings is a creative and complex task. Until recently it was one that received little attention in the literature; recently, however, authors (e.g., Geertz, 1988; Van Maanen, 1988) have begun to attend to this crucial aspect of qualitative research.

Qualitative research procedures are based on the processes of ordinary knowing. They elevate these processes through deliberation and reflection. Other human science disciplines have found them to be a worthwhile and useful adjunct to methods based on quantitative procedures. The current philosophy of science holds that viable knowledge can be generated through a variety of methodological approaches. The use of qualitative research procedures requires considerable intellectual effort and is time consuming. Yet, if counseling is to become methodologically diverse, training in and research using qualitative procedures will need to added to our present repertoire.

REFERENCES

Barker, R. G. (1968). *Ecological psychology: Concepts and methods for studying the environment of human behavior.* San Francisco: Jossey-Bass.

Belenky, M. F., Clinchy, B. M., Goldberger, N. R., & Tarule, J. M. (1986). *Women's ways of knowing: The development of self, voice, and mind.* New York: Basic Books.

Binswanger, L. (1958). The case of Ellen West. In R. May, E. Angel, & H. F. Ellenberger (Eds.), *Existence: A new dimension in psychiatry and psychology* (pp. 237–364). New York: Harper Torchbooks.

Bogdan, R., & Taylor, S. J. (1975). *Introduction to qualitative research methods: A phenomenological approach to the social sciences.* New York: Wiley.

Borg, W. R., & Gall, M. D. (1989). *Educational research: An introduction* (5th ed.). New York: Longman.

Brown, D. (1989). Editorial: Logical positivism and/or phenomenology. *Counselor Education and Supervision, 29,* 5–6.

Brown, R. (1958). How shall a thing be called? *Psychological Review, 65,* 14–21.

Brown, R. (1965). *Social psychology.* New York: The Free Press.

Campbell, D. T. (1974). Evolutionary epistemology. In P. A. Schilpp (Ed.), *The philosophy of Karl Popper* (pp. 413–463). La Salle, IL: Open Court.

Cohen, L. H., Sargent, M. M., & Sechrest, L. B. (1984). Use of psychotherapy research by professional psychologists. *American Psychologist, 41,* 198–206.

Colaizzi, P. F. (1978). Psychological research as the phenomenologist views it. In R. S. Valle & M. King (Eds.), *Existential-phenomenological alternatives for psychology* (pp. 48–71). New York: Oxford University Press.

Combs, A. W., & Syngg, D. (1959). *Individual behavior: A perceptual approach to behavior* (rev. ed.). New York: Harper & Brothers.

Danzinger, K. (1980). The history of introspection reconsidered. *Journal of the History of the Behavioral Sciences, 16,* 241–262.

Denzin, N. K. (1989). *Interpretive interactionism.* Newbury Park, CA: Sage.

Dilthey, W. (1977). The understanding of other persons and their expressions of life. In W. Dilthey (Ed.), *Descriptive psychology and historical understanding* (R. M. Zaner & K. L. Heiges, Trans., 121–144). The Hague: Martinus Hijhoff. (Original work published 1927)

Dreyfus, H. L., & Dreyfus, S. E. (1986). *Mind over machine: The power of human intuition and expertise in the era of the computer.* New York: The Free Press.

Easthope, G. (1974). *A history of social research methods.* London: Longman.

Ellen, R. F. (Ed.). (1984). *Ethnographic research: A guide to general conduct.* London: Academic Press.

Erickson, F. (1986). Qualitative methods in research on teaching. In M. C. Wittrock (Ed.), *Handbook of research on teaching* (3rd ed., pp. 119–161). New York: Macmillan.

Fetterman, D. M. (1989). *Ethnography step by step.* Newbury Park, CA: Sage.

Filstead, W. J. (Ed.). (1970). *Qualitative methodology: Firsthand involvement with the social world.* Chicago: Markham.

Fraenkel, J. R., & Wallen, N. E. (1990). *How to design and evaluate research in education.* New York: McGraw-Hill.

Fretz, B. R. (Ed.). (1989). Alternative research paradigms [Special issue]. *The Counseling Psychologist, 17.*

Gadamer, H.-G. (1975). *Truth and method.* (G. Barden & J. Cumming, Trans.). New York: Seabury.

Galassi, J. P. (1984). *A survey of research training.* Paper presented at the convention of the American Psychological Association, Toronto.

Gardner, H. (1985). *The mind's new science.* New York: Basic Books.

Geertz, C. (1973). *The interpretation of cultures.* New York: Basic Books.

Geertz, C. (1988). *Works and lives: The anthropologist as author.* Stanford, CA: Stanford University Press.

Gelso, C. J. (Ed.). (1984). Philosophy of science and counseling research [Special section]. *Journal of Counseling Psychology, 31,* 415–476.

Gelso, C. J., Betz, N. E., Friedlander, M. L., Helms, J. E., Hill, C. E., Patton, M. J., Super, D. E., & Wampold, B. E. (1988). Research in counseling psychology: Prospects and recommendations. *The Counseling Psychologist, 16,* 385–406.

Giorgi, A. (1986). Status of qualitative research in the human sciences: A limited interdisciplinary and international perspective. *Methods, 1*(1), 29–62.

Giorgi, A., Fischer, W. F., & Von Eckartsberg, R. (1971). Preface. In A. Giorgi, W. F. Fischer, & R. Von Eckartsberg (Eds.), *Duquesne studies in phenomenological psychology* (Vol. 1, pp. v–vii). Pittsburgh: Duquesne University Press.

Glaser, B., & Strauss, A. L. (1967). *The discovery of grounded theory: Strategies for qualitative research.* Chicago: Aldine.

Goetz, J. P., & LeCompte, M. D. (1984). *Ethnography and qualitative design in educational research.* Orlando, FL: Academic Press.

Goldman, L. (1976). A revolution in counseling psychology. *Journal of Counseling Psychology, 23,* 543–552.

Goldman, L. (Ed.). (1978). *Research methods for counselors: Practical approaches in field settings.* New York: Wiley.

Gordon, J., & Shontz, F. C. (1990). Living with the AIDS virus: A representative case. *Journal of Counseling and Development, 68,* 287–292.

Guba, E. G., & Lincoln, Y. S. (1981). *Effective evaluation: Improving the usefulness of evaluation results through responsive and naturalistic approaches.* San Francisco: Jossey-Bass.

Haney, C., Banks, C., & Zimbardo, P. (1973). Interpersonal dynamics in simulated prison. *International Journal of Crime and Penology, 1,* 69–97.

Harmon, L. W. (1989). The scientist/practitioner model and choice of research paradigm. *The Counseling Psychologist, 17,* 86–89.

Hempel, C. G. (1942). The function of general laws in history. *Journal of Philosophy, 39,* 35–48.

Hill, C. E., & Gronsky, B. R. (1984). Research: Why and how? In J. M. Whitely, N. Kagan, L. W. Harmon, B. R. Fretz, & F. Tanney (Eds.), *The coming decade in counseling psychology* (pp. 149–159). Schenectady, NY: Character Research.

Hopkins, C. D., & Antes, R. L. (1990). *Educational research: A structure for inquiry* (3rd ed.). Itasca, IL: F. E. Peacock.

Hoshmand, L. L. S., & Polkinghorne, D. E. (1990). *Redefining the science-practice relationship and professional training.* Manuscript submitted for publication.

Howard, G. S. (1985). *The queen is dead! Long live the queen!* Unpublished manuscript.

Jacob, E. (1987). Qualitative research traditions: A review. *Review of Educational Research, 57*(1), 1–50.

Johnson, M. (1987). *The body in the mind: The bodily basis of meaning, imagination, and reason.* Chicago: University of Chicago Press.

Jorgensen, D. L. (1989). *Participant observation: A methodology for human studies.* Newbury Park, CA: Sage.

Kerlinger, F. N. (1973). *Foundations of behavioral research* (2nd ed.). New York: Holt, Rinehart & Winston.

Kuhn, D., Amsel, E., & O'Loughlin, M. (1988). *The development of scientific thinking skills.* San Diego: Academic Press.

Kvale, S. (1983). The qualitative research interview. *Journal of Phenomenological Psychology, 14,* 171–196.

Lakoff, G. (1987). *Women, fire, and dangerous things: What categories reveal about the mind.* Chicago: University of Chicago Press.

Lakoff, G., & Johnson, M. (1980). *Metaphors we live by.* Chicago: University of Chicago Press.

Lazarsfeld, P. F. (1972). *Qualitative analysis: Historical and critical essays.* Boston: Allyn & Bacon.

Lincoln, Y. S., & Guba, E. G. (1985). *Naturalistic inquiry.* Beverly Hills, CA: Sage.

Lofton, J. (1971). *Analyzing social settings: A guide to qualitative observation and analysis.* Belmont, CA: Wadsworth.

Lofton, J. (1984). *Analyzing social settings: A guide to qualitative observation and analysis* (2nd ed.). Belmont, CA: Wadsworth.

Lyons, W. (1986). *The disappearance of introspection.* Cambridge, MA: MIT Press.

Malinowski, B. (1922). *Argonauts of the Western Pacific: An account of native enterprise and adventure in the archipelagoes of Melanesian New Guinea.* New York: Dutton.

Manning, P. K. (1983). Metaphors of the field: Varieties of organizational discourse. In J. Van Maanen (Ed.), *Qualitative methodology* (pp. 225–245). Newbury Park, CA: Sage.

Margolis, H. (1987). *Patterns, thinking, and cognition.* Chicago: University of Chicago Press.

Margolis, J. (1986). *Pragmatism without foundations: Reconciling realism and relativism.* New York: Basil Blackwell.

Marshall, C., & Rossman, G. B. (1989). *Designing qualitative research.* Newbury Park, CA: Sage.

McCall, G. J., & Simmons, J. L. (Eds.). (1969). *Issues in participant observation: A text and reader.* Reading, MA: Addison-Wesley.

McCracken, G. D. (1988). *The long interview.* Newbury Park, CA: Sage.

Meltzer, B. N., Petras, J. W., & Reynolds, L. T. (1975). *Symbolic interactionism: Genesis, varieties, and criticism.* London: Routledge & Kegan Paul.

Miles, M. B., & Huberman, A. M. (1984). *Qualitative data analysis: A sourcebook of new methods.* Newbury Park, CA: Sage.

Mishler, E. G. (1986). *Research interviewing: Context and narrative.* Cambridge, MA: Harvard University Press.

Morgan, S. L. (1988). *Focus groups as qualitative research.* Newbury Park, CA: Sage.

Morrow-Bradley, C., & Elliott, R. (1986). Utilization of psychotherapy research by practicing psychotherapists. *American Psychologist, 41,* 188–206.

Neimeyer, G., & Resnikoff, A. (1982). Qualitative strategies in counseling research. *The Counseling Psychologist, 10*(4), 75–85.

Patton, M. Q. (1990). *Qualitative evaluation and research methods* (2nd ed.). Newbury Park, CA: Sage.

Pelto, P. J. (1970). *Anthropological research: The structure of inquiry.* New York: Harper & Row.

Perry, W. G. (1970). *Forms of intellectual and ethical development in the college years.* New York: Holt, Rinehart & Winston.

Pfaffenberger, B. (1988). *Microcomputer applications in qualitative research.* Newbury Park, CA: Sage.

Piaget, J. (1954). *The construction of reality in the child* (M. Cook, Trans.). New York: Basic Books.

Piaget, J. (1968). *Structuralism* (C. Maschler, Trans.). New York: Harper & Row.

Polkinghorne, D. E. (1983). *Methodology for the human sciences: Systems of inquiry.* Albany: State University of New York Press.

Polkinghorne, D. E. (1984). Further extensions of methodological diversity for counseling psychology. *The Journal of Counseling Psychology, 31,* 416–429.

Polkinghorne, D. E. (1988). *Narrative knowing and the human sciences.* Albany: State University of New York Press.

Polkinghorne, D. E. (1989a). Communicating results: The qualitative research report. *Methods, 3,* 63–85.

Polkinghorne, D. E. (1989b). Phenomenological research methods. In R. S. Valle & S. Halling (Eds.), *Existential-phenomenological perspectives in psychology* (pp. 41–60). New York: Plenum.

Polkinghorne, D. E. (1990). Psychology after philosophy. In R. N. Williams & J. E. Faulconer (Eds.), *Reconsidering psychology: Perspectives from Continental philosophy* (pp. 92–115). Pittsburgh: Duquesne University Press.

Polkinghorne, D. E. (1991). Two conflicting calls for methodological reform. *The Counseling Psychologist, 19,* 103–114.

Popper, K. R. (1972). *Objective knowledge.* Oxford: Clarendon.

Reason, P., & Rowan, J. (Eds.). (1981). *Human inquiry: A sourcebook of new paradigm research.* New York: Wiley.

Reichenbach, H. (1938). *Experience and prediction.* Chicago: University of Chicago Press.

Richardson-Koehler, V. (Ed.). (1987). Qualitative methodology [Special section]. *American Educational Research Journal, 24,* 171–218.

Rorty, R. (1979). *Philosophy and the mirrow of nature.* Princeton, NJ: Princeton University Press.

Rosch, E. (1978). Principles of categorization. In E. Rosch & B. B. Lloyd (Eds.), *Cognition and categorization* (pp. 27–48). Hillsdale, NJ: Lawrence Erlbaum Associates.

Sanday, P. R. (1983). The ethnographic paradigm(s). In J. Van Maanen (Ed.), *Qualitative methodology* (pp. 19–36). Newbury Park, CA: Sage.

Schein, E. H. (1987). *The clinical perspective in fieldwork.* Newbury Park, CA: Sage.

Schon, D. (1983). *The reflective practitioner: How professionals think in action.* New York: Basic Books.

Segal, L. (1986). *The dream of reality: Heinz von Foerster's constructivism.* New York: Norton.

Serlin, R. C. (1987). Hypothesis testing, theory building, and the philosophy of science. *Journal of Counseling Psychology, 34,* 365–371.

Shapiro, K. J. (1985). *Bodily reflective modes: A phenomenological method for psychology.* Durham, NC: Duke University Press.

Sommerlund, B., & Kristensen, O. L. (1986). *Textbase alpha* [computer program]. Aarhus, Denmark: Center for Qualitative Research.

Spradley, J. P. (1979). *The ethnographic interview.* New York: Holt, Rinehart & Winston.

Spradley, J. P. (1980). *Participant observation.* New York: Holt, Rinehart & Winston.

Stanovich, K. E. (1989). *How to think straight about psychology* (2nd ed.). Glenview, IL: Scott, Foresman.

Stocking, G. W. (Ed.). (1983). *Observers observed: Essays on ethnographic fieldwork.* Madison, WI: The University of Wisconsin Press.

Stone, G. L. (1986). *Counseling psychology: Perspectives and functions.* Pacific Grove, CA: Brooks/Cole.

Strauss, A. L. (1987). *Qualitative analysis for social scientists.* Cambridge: Cambridge University Press.

Suppe, F. (Ed.). (1977). *The structure of scientific theories* (2nd ed.). Urbana, IL: University of Illinois Press.

Tesch, R. (1990). *Qualitative research: Analysis types and software tools.* New York: Falmer.

Toulmin, S. (1972). *Human understanding: The collective use and evolution of concepts.* Princeton, NJ: Princeton University Press.

van Kaam, A. (1969). *Existential foundations of psychology.* New York: Image Books.

Van Maanen, J. (Ed.). (1983). *Qualitative methodology.* Newbury Park, CA: Sage.

Van Maanen, J. (1988). *Tales of the field: On writing ethnography.* Chicago: University of Chicago Press.

Whitehead, A. N., & Russell, B. (1910–1913). *Principia mathematica.* Cambridge: Cambridge University Press.

Williams, W. J. (1985). *The miracle of abduction: Applied epistemology as a method of inquiry.* Los Angeles: Epistemics Institute Press.

Yin, R. K. (1984). *Case study research: Design and methods.* Newbury Park, CA: Sage.

CAREER COUNSELING
RESEARCH

Samuel H. Osipow
Nancy E. Betz
Ohio State University

Career counseling has a long and mostly distinguished history. As readers are no doubt aware, the formal enterprise that has become what is now called *career counseling* began with the work of Frank Parsons (1909), who reasoned that the modern approach to the systematic analysis of individuals and work environments coupled with appropriate feedback to the individual would enhance the quality of career decisions with respect to variables such as performance and satisfaction.

Since then, many counselors and psychologists have proposed variations on ways to conduct the systematic analysis and feedback that Parsons suggested. Many writers have asserted that career development and career counseling represents the most vigorous subspecialty of counseling psychology (e.g., Borgen, 1984; Gelso & Fassinger, 1990; Osipow, 1987).

What Parsons and others writing after him often failed to do, however, was to take the step of carefully documenting the procedures used in the analysis and counseling of career counseling. Although some notable exceptions exist (e.g., Campbell, 1965) for many years the database upon which to conduct career counseling was thinner than many might prefer. However, in the late 1940s and after, a stream of writing and research began that went considerably beyond the psychometric bases of individual qualities important in career decision making. These writings included speculation about theoretical concepts potentially important to career deciders and empirical data evaluating these concepts. Gradually, studies moved increasingly to examine the techniques to use in accomplishing effective career counseling, and research involving estimates of the outcomes. A number of papers examined issues related to the problem of career counseling outcomes (e.g., Fretz, 1981; Oliver, 1979; Osipow, 1982). In 1983, a seminal meta-analysis of career counseling outcomes was published by Spokane and Oliver (1983) which, overall, indicated positive results of career counseling interventions.

Consequent to these efforts, a considerable body of literature has been accumulated that can guide career counseling efforts. This chapter is designed to accomplish a number of objectives with respect to this body of knowledge:

1. To review the bases of career counseling.
2. To briefly review the major theories of career development and adjustment that underlie much of career counseling and its research.
3. To review the process of career counseling.
4. To review the context of career counseling research.
5. To identify issues yet to be resolved.
6. To examine the general research design of outcome studies in career counseling research.
7. To discuss issues in selecting the interventions to examine in our research.
8. To measure outcomes of career counseling.
9. To make recommendations for further research.

BASES OF CAREER COUNSELING

A number of variables underlie all attempts to understand career choice and development and the career counseling that results to help people with career decisions and their adjustment to work. These variables may be subdivided into two categories: individual differences and environmental variables.

Individual Differences

These are variables that differentiate each individual from each other individual. These are the variables that counselors and psychologists focus on in studying human behavior. Counselors and psychologists, especially those involved in counseling or clinical interventions, need to know how their clients differ from each other, and furthermore, how these client differences contributed to individual problems, assets, and response to various interventions. Ideally, counseling consists of pinpointing differential methods that work with varying effectiveness on different clients who have different problems. Career counseling research should attempt to further our understanding of what works with whom under what conditions. Therefore, it is important to know what the individual variables are that must be considered in our research.

Abilities underlie all assumptions about career choice and adjustment. Sufficient data exist to convince us that people differ significantly in their inherent ability to learn and perform different kinds of tasks. Although much ability testing has been called into question because of concern with the ways that tests of ability have inappropriately discriminated on the basis of race, ethnicity, and gender, we must, first, recognize that some individual differences are inherent or at least appear very early in life, and second, that it is possible to use these data and methods in career counseling in the interest of clients without resort to prejudicial procedures and data. Without getting into discussions of genetic versus environmental influences on performance, we do know that performance differences exist among people, that these differences significantly influence people and the choices they make, and, thus, must be taken into account one way or another in career counseling. Similar reasoning would apply to how skills operate in career decision making and adjustment, and the impact of skills differences in the way that a career counselor would approach a client problem.

Interests have also been a long-standing variable of importance to counselors concerned with career decision making. Interest measurement has a long and effective history, and has traditionally been one of the major products attracting clients to career counselors. The sources of interests remain somewhat murky, although there are data on the one hand to suggest a strong biological basis for interests (see, e.g., Grotevant, Scarr, & Weinberg, 1977) and, on the other hand, that interests may be the product of learning and reinforcement (see, e.g., Osipow & Scheid, 1971). Hansen (1984) has reviewed much of the literature examining the relationship between interests and abilities, interests and career success, and interests and career satisfaction, and found relatively disappointing results. Interests and abilities do not appear to be related; interests and success are at best, only modestly related; and interests and satisfaction are also related to only a very modest degree.

Experienced career counselors may not be surprised at the nonexistent relationship between interests and abilities or interests and success (indeed, that is the presenting problem of all too many clients) but they may be surprised about the low relationship between interests and satisfaction. Hansen (1984) suggested that the research designs may be at least partly at fault in producing the modest relationship between satisfaction and interests in that most workers studied in the research on job satisfaction and interests were satisfied with their work, thus, restricting the range significantly and reducing the resulting correlations.

Values and attitudes are also important individual differences with respect to career counseling. Although much research on values and career choices has been reported (see Osipow, 1983), the relationships between values and choices are generally relatively low. Attitudes, on the other hand, are coming in for more attention because a number of social psychological approaches have been applied to counseling. Dorn (1990) has reviewed career counseling from a social influence process perspective. This point of view sees counseling to reflect counselor attempts to influence client behavior as a function of counselor attributes related to persuasibility. Thus, client attitudes toward power, trustworthiness, or expertness would need to be assessed in order to display the counselor to the client in a manner that enhances the counselor's ability to influence the client suitably.

Life stage is also an important individual difference variable in attempts to provide career counseling. Building in general on the career work of Donald Super (reviewed later), life stage and careers has been reviewed by Jepsen (1984, 1990). Two important issues emerge from these analyses. The first is that career-related variables emerge developmentally. That is to say, the skills and attitudes needed to choose and implement careers grow developmentally, mainly through early adulthood, but to some extent throughout the work lifespan. The second is that the contextual demands of career choices are a function of one's life stage: The early context focuses on broad-based educational and training issues as they relate to careers, mid-life issues focus on advancement and adjustment, and later-life issues focus on reducing work involvement and the shape of retirement. Career counseling for people at different life stages will obviously need to vary according to the client career decision skill levels as well as the context of decisions to be made.

General personality variables, such as traits measured by instruments such as the California Psychological Inventory, or adjustment, such as measured by diagnostic instruments like the Minnesota Multiphasic Personality Inventory, have a long history of relevance to career counseling. Many studies have been conducted on the relationship between career interests and personality adjustment (see Brandt & Hood, 1968), which have generally shown that maladjusted individuals do not have interest patterns that predict their career entry as well as better adjusted people. In addition, many professions have studied the adjustment of aspirants to their field in terms of potential psychopathology (see Osipow, 1973). Few of these latter studies have found reliable differences of interest to career counselors in pathology by occupational field. Overall, it is reasonable, however, to observe that personality variables are important in understanding how people choose their careers and how they adjust to them as well. Such understanding is of obvious importance to career counselors.

Physical variables, such as attractiveness, height and weight, and motor dexterity have not been widely studied by career counselors but deserve attention. Appearance variables may operate in two important ways: when young and developing, the rate of maturation will affect size and coordination. Such differences may well be important in determining self-concepts in young people because of the feedback received as a function of others' expectations of them based on their appearance. Such self-concepts, positive and negative, may persist beyond the time when they have any validity. The second way physical appearance variables may be important is in determining the individual's capacity for certain occupational activities. Thus, size and shape may be important to success in careers in athletics, theater, and some arts.

Last, variables involving gender, race, and ethnicity should be considered. Although some aspects of these variables do represent individual differences (see Betz & Fitzgerald, 1987, for a thorough review of these as they effect women), they seem more appropriately discussed in the section on environmental variables that follows because social beliefs about gender, race, and ethnicity perpetuate stereotypes that have had, and continue to have, major effects on occupational aspirations and access.

Environmental Variables

Less often considered by career counselors are the important environmental variables reflected by the cultural context of the chooser, the economy in which the choice occurs, its geographical setting, and the political beliefs and policies that influence important social institutions, such as schools.

A debt is owed to the career social learning theorists (e.g., Mitchell, Jones, & Krumboltz, 1979) who have highlighted the environmental variables just noted. However, other writers have stressed the environment as important in career choice and adjustment, notably Holland (1985) whose person–environment theory gives equal weight to environmental and personal variables. An entire special issue of the *Journal of Vocational Behavior* (edited by Arnold Spokane, 1987) was recently devoted to work and environmental issues.

The gender and racial variables mentioned earlier have been important in determining occupational access and aspiration. Despite major gains in social openness for women and racial minorities, many occupations are more difficult for women and minorities to enter simply because of prejudice and/or special barriers placed before them. Sometimes the discrimination is more subtle and takes the form of long-term social conditioning in which women and/or minorities accept the social judgment made of their group, and do not develop the skills and interests needed to pursue certain careers.

A word about the economy is needed. In times of economic growth the nature of career choice and implementation is different from that in times of economic hardship. In the former, people seem more likely to have problems selecting from an array of good alternatives than in the latter time, when few alternatives exist. Thus, career counselors should expect to see different kinds of problems in their clients as a function of the state of the economy. Little, if any attention has been paid to this in general, and in particular in the research enterprise dealing with career counseling.

Finally, the social policies promulgated by the political climate affect career life issues significantly, including schooling issues, degree of support for retraining adults and retirement age to name a few. Demographic bulges such as produced by the "baby boom" are important determinants of social policy and job competition. Again, these are too infrequently seen as important determinants of the problems clients bring to career counselors, and a research base needs to be developed to help counselors proceed more rationally.

MAJOR THEORIES OF CAREER DEVELOPMENT

Career counseling research has been guided by theory about how careers are chosen and develop, thus, some brief review of those theories is needed for our analysis of career counseling research. Many career theories or theory fragments have been developed and all cannot be reviewed here. For more extensive reviews of the major theories about careers, the interested reader should see Brown and Brooks (1984) or Osipow (1983, 1990).

Four of the most influential theories are summarized: Holland's Person-Environment Theory; The Work Adjustment Theory of Dawis and Lofquist; Life Span Career Development Theory, largely influenced by Donald Super; and the Social Learning Theory applied to careers, promulgated primarily by John Krumboltz and his colleagues.

Holland's theory is one of the most well known and widely used by career counselors. Its attractiveness lies in several sources. First, it has been made easily operational by Holland's development of instrumentation, such as the Self-Directed Search and the Vocational Preference Inventory. Second, it possesses substantial face validity in that clients can easily see that the questions posed on the measures, and the interpretations made by their counselors, clearly relate to their career concerns. Third, because it is so operational, outcomes in terms of congruence of person and choice are easily assessed. Fourth, Holland has developed a vocational classification system that is extremely useful both in counseling and in research on careers. Last, and not least, it has a large body of research that, overall, suggests that the main tenets are sufficiently valid to use in applied settings (see, e.g., the Spokane, 1985, congruence review).

Holland's theory simply assesses the person in terms of two or three personal types, and the environments in similar terms (Holland, 1985). The goal is to match the individual types as closely as possible with the environmental aspects of potential careers. A modern trait-factor approach, it predicts that the better the match, the better the outcome in terms of variables such as congruence, satisfaction, persistence, and, possibly performance.

The Work Adjustment Theory, most recently revised extensively by Dawis and Lofquist (1984) is another modern day, sophisticated trait-factor model of career choice and adjustment. This approach shares some of the attributes of Holland's theory: it is operational and a number of instruments have been developed in connection to its use in counseling and in criterion assessment; a taxonomy of careers has been developed (Dawis, Dohm, Lofquist, Chartrand, & Due, 1987) which is also of use in counseling and research.

In the Work Adjustment Theory, the main variable of interest is correspondence, which is seen to be the fit between the individual's attributes and those required by an occupation. As for Holland, matches between person and occupation can be appraised (an atlas has been developed by Dawis and Lofquist, 1984, for just such a purpose) so a prediction about the correspondence for an individual with a variety of occupations can be made. High correspondence should theoretically lead to greater tenure, persistence, satisfaction, and performance than would low correspondence.

For a current review of the status of trait-factor theory and research, the interested reader should see Betz, Fitzgerald, and Hill (1989) and Rounds and Tracey (1990).

The life-span development theories are best represented by the work of Donald Super (reviewed in Osipow, 1983). Jepsen (1984, 1990) has reviewed not only Super's work but life-span career theories in general. This view takes the perspective that careers reflect individual maturation, and thus, career-related tasks occur at all ages. The adequacy with which one masters these tasks is presumably an indicator of the ease and adequacy with which one's career life will unfold.

Herein lies the special value for the career counselor: life stage, and relevant task mastery should provide diagnostic cues for career counseling, help identify methods to be used, and lead to appropriate criteria for career counseling outcome. In this manner, then, the life-span approaches have much potential to offer the career counseling researcher.

Last to be discussed is the Social Learning Theory application to careers. This approach has applied many of the concepts of Albert Bandura (1977) to the study of how people respond to career problems. The main proponents have been John Krumboltz and several associates (A. Mitchell, Jones, & Krumboltz, 1979; L. Mitchell & Krumboltz, 1984).

The Social Learning Theory application to careers emphasizes several variables and processes. Learning, self-observation, and task-approach skills and social–cultural–political–economic–educational contexts interact to shape a set of propositions describing how career interests and aspirations develop, along with the relevant skills needed to make and implement decisions.

The particular relevance of Social Learning Theory to careers lies in its focus on developing decision-making skills. Clearly, one major role of career counseling is aiding clients to learn how to make decisions. In a recent paper,

Mitchell and Krumboltz (1984) listed the steps involved in making good decisions. These steps, when applied to counseling, are designed to improve client decision making, a major goal of career counseling.

CAREER COUNSELING

Counseling Process. A major feature of interest to career counseling investigators lies in whether to focus on outcomes such as career choice or on outcomes such as career adjustment. Of course, it is better to rephrase the problem to state that the issue is not whether one or the other is important, but rather when and under what circumstances one should take precedence over the other.

Often, the issue is resolved in a simple fashion. For the young client, perhaps making preliminary or early career decisions, issues associated with choice come to the fore. Thus, the content tends to lie with self-exploration. Counselors help their clients ask such questions as: What are my interests, talents, values? Tests and inventories are used. Outcome criteria tend to be process oriented, that is, client level of comfort with the status of decision following counseling and level of self- and environmental knowledge. Some outcomes may reflect criteria such as those associated with the Social Learning Theory, that is, knowledge of how decisions are best made. For many clients, the outcome will include a tentative career (or educational) decision, perhaps occupationally specific, or perhaps in terms of careers located in a particular Holland code area.

These approaches are not always restricted to youthful, naive, first-time choosers. Some experienced workers, dissatisfied with their careers, or forced by layoffs or disability, may choose to review their career options or perhaps consider them systematically for the first time.

However, older workers, who seek career counseling more often, need help in their adjustment to work. In this effort, the Taxonomy of Adult Career Development Problems developed by Campbell and Cellini (1981) should be of considerable use. This taxonomy classifies a number of adult problems in specific categories, which include deciding about work, implementing career plans, problems in performance, and problems in adaptation. Location of the client's problem in one or more of the specific problem areas should help in focusing counseling and in determining methods and criteria that are most suitable.

Other diagnostic approaches may also be useful to the career counselor. These include analysis of decision-making styles (e.g., Buck & Daniels, 1985), levels of career decision and indecision (Holland & Holland, 1977; Osipow, Carney, Winer, Yanico, & Koschler, 1976), career maturity (Crites, 1978; Super, Thompson, Lindeman, Jordaan, & Myers, 1979), and finally, environmental assessment as represented by the approaches suggested by the Work Adjustment Theory or Holland's environmental categories.

CONTEXTUAL ISSUES IN CAREER COUNSELING RESEARCH

Finally, we turn our attention to the questions of settings for career counseling. Most career counseling is conducted in educational settings, although it is becoming somewhat more common for private centers to provide such counseling. One problem with this situation is that educational settings tend to serve relatively younger than older clients, and relatively more well-educated, affluent clients in cases where older clients are served.

This skews the nature of service provided, as well as the perspective of professional counselors on the kinds of career problems people have. Because young clients are more concerned with choosing their career direction than with adjusting to it, one result is that issues related to career choice have been considerably overestimated in counseling research as contrasted with problems of career adjustment. Consequently, the research conducted along with the conclusions drawn from its results may have more limited generality than we think.

Implications for career counseling research are clear. We need to define client populations, and work to broaden those represented in our research base. We need to describe in detail what counseling procedures are used, and the settings in which they are used, in order to detail the outcomes that are sought and the effectiveness of the methods to achieve them.

ISSUES IN CAREER COUNSELING RESEARCH

A number of authors (e.g., Fretz, 1981; Gottfredson, 1978; Myers, 1971; Oliver, 1979; Rounds & Tinsley, 1984) have suggested the need for more and better quality studies of the effectiveness of career counseling. Although design problems are not unique to career counseling research and are, in fact, shared by counseling outcome research in general, there are some specific as well as some general issues that should be considered in designing a high quality outcome study of career counseling. These issues are discussed in the next sections of general design issues, selecting and measuring outcomes, and recommendations for further research.

General Design of Outcome Studies

Consistent with the definition of Spokane and Oliver (1983; Oliver & Spokane, 1988), a career counseling outcome study for present purposes is a study using a vocational intervention or vocational outcome variable. Vocational interventions can include individual or group vocational counseling, test interpretation (e.g., the Strong Interest Inventory), classes or workshops focusing on career exploration, selection, and/or choice implementation, self-help materials, and computer-based career guidance systems (see Lunneborg, 1983, for a review of career counseling techniques and Taylor, 1988, for a recent review of computer-based guidance systems). Outcome measures discussed in detail in a later section, can include measures of attitudes, competencies, and behaviors related to career decision making.

Experimental Design. The general design of an outcome study in career counseling is similar to that of any counseling outcome study in that it involves the examination of the effectiveness of one or more treatment groups (often called *experimental groups*) and, ideally, one or more control groups. Control groups can be no-treatment groups or placebo control groups (where an inert "treatment" is provided), but studies lacking such groups are extremely difficult to interpret (e.g., Cook & Campbell, 1976; Gottfredson, 1978).

In some cases, positive change can occur simply through the passage of time, particularly when relevant intervening experiences (e.g., college coursework) are occurring. Thus, if effects are to be attributed to the treatment per se, passage of time as a cause of the change must be ruled out—use of a control group allows this to be done, as subjects in the control group experienced only the passage of time, whereas the treatment group experienced both the treatment and the passage of time. Rounds and Tinsley (1984) noted that the control group provides the base rate of improvement for nontreated clients.

Control groups are also necessary because of "nonspecific factors" (e.g., see Rounds & Tinsley, 1984). These are variables that are not included as active ingredients in the treatment but that may, in fact, induce positive change. For example, Lambert (1976) reviewed studies that suggested that the initial assessment contact may have therapeutic benefits for some clients. Related to this is the fact that control groups often involve at least some attention being given to individuals. The Hawthorne studies, done in the 1930s in the Hawthorne plant of the Western Electric Company, were designed initially to examine the effects of variations in levels of illumination on workers' productivity. Researchers were surprised to find that productivity improved regardless of the experimental condition the worker was in—it appeared that being in an experiment improved workers' morale and motivation even if the treatment they were given had not been postulated to improve their productivity (see Roethlisberger & Dickson, 1939; also cf. Landy, 1985). Finally, in some vocational outcome studies a nonspecific factor is used that may in fact be defined as an active ingredient in another vocational outcome study—an interest inventory used as an outcome measure would be a good example, because in other studies a self-interpreted interest inventory might be the treatment itself (e.g., Hoffman, Spokane, & Magoon, 1981; Zytowski, 1977).

Thus, to attribute changes in behavior to the treatment itself, the passage of time and nonspecific effects must be controlled for through the use of a control group. More fundamentally, in order for positive (or negative) effects to be attributed to the treatment, all other things must remain equal between treated and non-treated subjects. For these reasons, control groups are essential to interpretable outcome research. As discussed in depth by Gottfredson (1978), it is unfortunate that so many outcome studies, including those on career counseling, have neglected to use control groups. For example, of the 140 vocational outcome studies identified by Oliver and Spokane (1988), 40 (or 29%) were not usable in their meta-analysis because they failed to use a no-treatment control group.

Assignment of Subjects to Groups. In addition to control groups, careful selection and assignment of subjects is advisable. Subjects may be obtained from several sources (e.g., Oliver & Spokane, 1988): vocational clients, solicited clients, (i.e., subjects responding to a posted or published advertisement of the services offered), nonclient volunteers, no-choice subjects, and convenience samples. Generally speaking, the more relevant the treatment to the real, current concerns of the subjects, the more the findings are interpretable. Many studies use convenience samples, but the results of such research may be less generalizable to the treatment of people with "real" vocational concerns.

There are a number of ways to assign subjects to treatment and control groups. These include random assignment, assignment to alternative groups as the subjects appear for treatment, and matching subjects across treatment groups or variables that could influence the outcome of the research. Such variables could include gender, ethnic/minority group, year in school, and/or the degree to which the individual is troubled about career issues. The most desirable method of assignment is random (e.g., Cook & Campbell, 1976; Gottfredson, 1978), and blocking variables can be used to incorporate demographic or individual differences variables of possible relevance to the outcome of treatments. Thus, a possible design might include two treatments (Factor 1) and a second factor consisting of subjects' gender, and a third of high versus low decidedness (as measured by a scale such as the Career Decision Scale of Osipow et al., 1976). Such a design would then be analyzed using a three-way analysis of variance.

Gottfredson (1978) decried the large number of outcome studies that involve the provision of treatment to subjects seeking help and the assignment to a no-treatment control group of subjects who did not seek help—it should be obvious to the readers that the level of motivation of people seeking help is vastly different from that of people who did not seek it, so that the effects of treatment cannot be separated from the effects of initial motivation for help and for personal change. Fretz (1981), for example, reported in his review article that in studies of demographic, intellective, and psychological predictor variables of 296 clients undergoing vocational counseling and rehabilitation, the best overall predictor of improvement was level of client motivation. Clearly, if motivation is not controlled for, attributions of change to the treatment itself are probably unjustified.

Often, such designs are justified on the basis of ethical concerns about the necessity of providing treatment to people who request it, but Gottfredson (1978) made two convincing arguments against this excuse for poor design features. First of all, worries about denying treatment assume that the treatment is effective. This is an empirical question—precisely the one the study is designed to test. Second, the use of a wait-list control group for people who did seek treatment allows the comparison of treated versus nontreated subjects equivalent in initial motivation, and the nontreated subjects receive the treatment once the experiment has been completed. Suffice it to say, the importance of control groups and randomization to a high quality outcome study cannot be overestimated.

Timing of Posttest and Follow-Up Assessments. A final aspect of the design of outcome studies on career counseling involves the selection of outcome measures and a determination of how often and when to administer them. The variety of possible outcome measures and criteria for selecting them is covered in detail in a subsequent section, but some common outcome measures include indices of career maturity, career decidedness/undecidedness, and the number and nature of career exploration activities. Outcome measures can be administered pretest, posttest, and in follow-up assessments. The former would be administered prior to treatment, posttests are administered immediately following treatment, and follow-up data are collected at some later point in order to assess the durability of treatment effects.

Although the collection of follow-up data is important, it can be difficult due to problems of subject attrition (Gonyea, 1962), for example, drop-out from college or leaving the workplace where the study was initially done. Also, because follow-up is usually done by mail or phone call, changes of address can reduce the number of subjects who can be followed up. Thus, although such data could be collected weeks, months, or years after the treatment was administered, longer intervals will probably be accompanied by lower response rates. Also, the longer the interval, the more likely it is that other intervening experiences have influenced change in career related attitudes, competencies, and behaviors (e.g., Oliver, 1979). Thus, ideal follow-up periods probably include those ranging from 1 to 6 months (Fretz, 1981).

In addition to methodological problems in the collection of follow-up data there is disagreement as to how much long-term change we should actually expect. Myers (1971) argued that because most of our treatments are short term, expectations of long-term changes are probably unrealistic. According to Myers (1971), career development is a series of choice points, where each choice made strongly influences the next one to be made—thus we may be able to influence one choice point, but after that the choice that has been made may be a stronger influence of what follows. Rounds and Tinsley (1984), on the other hand, argued that longer term follow-up is essential to determine whether or not subjects are actually using the interventions provided. The answers to this question probably depend on the more fundamental question of the nature of client problems and the ways in which we postulate vocational treatments to affect those problems. This issue is dealt with in the next sections.

Issues in Selecting Interventions to Study

The most important issue in selecting interventions is that they be based on a meaningful taxonomy of career problems. As stated by Osipow (1982): "A career problem taxonomy is needed to (a) identify criteria to be sought in career counseling; (b) identify and apply appropriate methods of intervention to achieve these criteria; and (c) guide efforts to develop instruments that will permit the measurement of changes counseling produces related to these criteria" (p. 30).

Although a number of issues are discussed in the next sections, the importance of a basic problem taxonomy should not be forgotten.

Nature and Number of Interventions. As previously mentioned, vocational interventions can range from individual and group counseling to classes and workshops to self-help materials and computer-assisted guidance systems (see Lunneborg, 1983). Fretz (1981) provided a helpful and more specific discussion of modes or parameters of treatment. He mentioned, first, that interventions can be described according to theoretical approach, for example, the Crites (1974) categorization of psychodynamic, behavioral, developmental, trait-factor, and client-centered approaches to career counseling. He also distinguished three parameters of an intervention: content domain, interpersonal context, and degree of structure.

Content domain refers to the focus of the treatment, that is, on occupational information, self-knowledge, and/or information and decision-making processes (e.g., anxiety management, decision-making skills). Treatments also vary in their interpersonal context, that is, individual, group, and self-administered (see Brandt, 1977, for examples of each). Finally, they differ in their degree of structure, varying from high structure to semistructured to low in structure. These dimensions can, to some extent, be crossed—that is, we could design high and low structure treatment administered through individual counseling or through self-help materials. Fretz suggested that studies be designed to include at least two levels from at least two of these treatment parameters.

At least as important as the mode and the theoretical basis are the particular problem areas of interest to the researcher. For researchers in applied settings the particular concerns of their clientele would seem most appropriately targeted for treatment. Other researchers, however, may be interested in particular problem areas and would design their interventions accordingly.

Regardless of the type of treatment selected for study, the design must be of the highest quality and utilize the most recent knowledge concerning effective treatment of the problem at hand. A study using a poorly designed and implemented treatment wastes the time of both researcher and subject and is likely to yield either uninformative or misleading results concerning the potential effectiveness of similar but better designed and implemented treatments.

In some cases, psychometric quality of the treatment may be a consideration. Many interventions are based on or at least include the use of tests such as interest and values inventories (see Zytowski & Borgen, 1983; and Betz, in press, for a discussion of assessment in career counseling). It is vital that these tests be high in both reliability and validity if they are to give the client/subject accurate and usable information. Thus, evidence for the psychometric quality of tests used as interventions should be available if they are to be used in an outcome study. Questionable uses include the lack of differential validity evidence for such multiple aptitude batteries as the Differential Aptitude Tests (see Walsh & Betz, 1990) and use of tests with gender or ethnic/minority groups for whom they have not been validated (see, e.g., Carter & Swanson, 1990, for an excellent review of the validity of the Strong Interest Inventory with Black Americans). Betz (1990) and Walsh and Betz (1990) provided more complete reviews of the use of ability, interest, and other types of tests with women and with ethnic minorities—a complete understanding of these issues is essential to the counseling or research use of these tests with "special groups." (It should also be noted in this regard that research on the psychometric quality and cross-group utility of tests and assessments, particularly those used as treatments, is a much needed focus of career counseling research.)

Finally, treatments should be described in detail when reporting the study. The guideline for specificity in reporting a study is that other researchers could replicate the study given the information in the method section (or, in addition, that available from the author as indicated in a footnote to the article). Clear and concise descriptions of treatments also allow practitioners to extrapolate or generalize those treatments relatively easily to applied settings.

Nature of the Target Population. It may seem obvious to say, but the target population and, consequently, the obtained sample, should be appropriate to the treatments studied. Such determination of appropriateness involves both the problems and life/career stage of the population of interest and the relevance of the treatments of interest to the problem. Thus, understanding of career development stage theory (e.g., Super's and as summarized by Jepsen, 1984) and taxonomies of vocational issues facing people at different life stages. The overview of career development theory provided at the beginning of this chapter and the Rounds and Tinsley (1984) discussion of the need for vocational problem taxonomies as bases for the design and evaluation of vocational treatments are essential starting points for the theoretical sophistication so necessary to the design and application of effective treatments.

Thus, as strongly stated by Rounds and Tinsley (1984) and others, understanding of the problem of the client, if any, is necessary to determining which treatments would be recommended. Vocational treatments, like counseling approaches in general, do not have an existence independent of a problem or problems for which they are postulated to be effective treatments. To apply a treatment to a problem for which it was never intended and for which no theoretical justification for its application can be provided does not give a fair test of the treatment and, worse, may harm the reputation of vocational counseling for people who receive inappropriate or even harmful treatments. Oliver and Spokane (1988) gave the example of a treatment designed to expand career alternatives to a manageable number. The opposite case would be a treatment leading to actual decision making for someone too young or simply not ready to make such decisions. Oliver and Spokane (1988) were disturbed by their finding that not one of the studies reviewed in their meta-analysis used intake procedures to assess client preferences for or motivation to receive career counseling and that very few used one of the readily available descriptive classifications of problem types (e.g., Campbell & Cellini, 1981, and see Rounds & Tinsley, 1984) prior to administering treatment.

In addition to the question of appropriateness of the treatment to a problem is the fact that the same treatments may work better for some people than others. Fretz (1981) provided an excellent and extensive discussion of the dangers of the client "uniformity myth" in career counseling. The uniformity myth (Kiesler, 1971) referred, of course, to assumptions that a treatment will be equally effective for all clients. Fretz suggested that career counseling outcome researchers carefully consider the client attributes that might affect the efficacy of treatments. Fretz reviewed a number of studies that have showed Attribute-Treatment Interactions (or ATIs, as originally dubbed by Cronbach & Snow, 1977), in the context of the interaction of aptitudes with educational treatments. Fretz provided a detailed list of potentially relevant client attributes (also called *blocking variables* or *moderators,* e.g., Oliver &

Spokane, 1988) that researchers should consider. These include: (a) demographic variables such as gender, race, and age; (b) psychological variables such as intelligence, need for achievement, (Holland's, 1985, themes or the Myers-Briggs types) self-confidence, defensiveness, and personality type (e.g., Holland's themes or the Myers-Briggs types); and (c) career-related variables, such as career maturity, type of undecidedness, career decision style, and motivation for treatment (Fretz, 1981).

Thus, the appropriateness of the treatments to the group under investigation, the level of motivation or psychological pain of individual subjects, and the possibility of ATIs or blocking variables that may moderate the effectiveness of treatments are important but often overlooked concerns of the researcher in career counseling.

Measuring Outcomes

General Issues. In addition to designing a good study, it is important to make a careful selection of high quality outcome measures. The best treatments available will not appear to be effective if outcome measures are inappropriate to the goals of the treatment or to the clients themselves or are of poor psychometric quality. Problems in outcome measurement in counseling research have been addressed by many noted counseling researchers, beginning with Williamson and Bordin (1941), Gelso (1979), Goldman (1978), Oliver (1979), Rounds and Tinsley (1984), and Zytowski and E. Betz (1972). These problems, and their implications for career counseling research, are discussed here.

The first consideration in the selection of outcome measures should be the postulated nature of the treatment itself, that is, what beneficial effects is it postulated to have or, conversely, what problem(s) was it designed to address? Outcome measures, or criteria of effectiveness, should be viewed as constructs requiring both careful definition and measurement. Too often researchers select criterion measures reflexively or based on what was used in another study, rather than carefully defining the criterion construct of interest (see Mitchell, Jones, & Krumboltz, 1975, Zytowski & Betz, 1972). For example, there are several conceptual definitions of career maturity and also several instruments to measure the construct (see Betz, 1988). Similarly, career indecision can be defined and measured in different ways (see Slaney, 1988).

Once the criterion construct has been defined, one or more measures of the construct should be selected for use. More than one measure is useful, especially if one of them is self-report, and, therefore, reactive to the experiment (see the next section for a discussion of reactivity). Zytowski and Betz (1972) noted in their review of outcome measures in counseling research that two thirds of the measures were self-report. For example, a self-report measure of exploratory activity should be accompanied by an objective measure (e.g., records of visits to the career library on campus or occupational knowledge in areas reported to have been explored).

Generally the selection of instruments should be based on a thorough review of measures used in previous studies focusing on similar criterion constructs, followed by a selection of the instrument(s) for which the best evidence for psychometric quality is available. Development of new instruments should be avoided if possible for at least several reasons. First, development of a new instrument serves only to "reinvent the wheel" (e.g., as discussed by Oliver, 1979)—this wastes time and is contrary to the goal of cumulation of methods and results in science (rather than duplication). Also, it makes more sense for a researcher to continue to gather information on the reliability and validity of an existing instrument (which can usually be done easily as part of the intervention study) rather than to devote the necessary time and effort to pilot studies examining the reliability and validity of a new instrument. Third, use of existing instruments allows comparability of findings across studies.

It may be noted that good criterion measures for many important vocational constructs are simply not available and, therefore, the researcher may need to "start from scratch" in order to have the kind of criterion measure needed. In fact, Oliver and Spokane (1988) recommend that some group of career counseling researchers devote the next several years of their lives to the development of a high quality set of criterion measures, a set that would then be available to all the researchers whose preference is to study interventions rather than to develop new instruments.

Types of Outcome Measures.   Although there have been other approaches to the categorization of career counseling outcome measures, the system used by Oliver and Spokane (1988) in their meta-analysis of career counseling is offered herein. The category system is shown in Table 7.1 and contains three classes of outcome variables: career decision making, including instrumental behaviors and attitudes toward choice; effective role functioning, including both performance and adjustment variables; and counseling evaluation (the satisfaction of the client with counseling and her or his ratings of its helpfulness). The list shown in Table 7.1 is not intended to be exhaustive of the possibilities for criterion variables in career counseling research but, rather, suggestive of both general categories and specific examples within those categories.

The reader should note that for most of the criterion variables shown in the table there are a variety of resources available regarding how the construct has been previously conceptualized and measured. Some examples for specific criterion variables include career maturity (Betz, 1988) and career decision making attitudes (Slaney, 1988).

TABLE 7.1
Categories and Examples of Outcome Variables Used in
Career Counseling Intervention Studies

Category and Variables

Career decision making
    Accuracy of self-knowledge
    Appropriateness of choice (realism)
    Instrumental behaviors
        Career information seeking
        Securing job or probability of hire
        Decision-making skills
        Attendance or still in school
    Attitudes toward choice
        Certainty/decidedness
        Satisfaction
        Career salience/importance
    Other characteristics of choice
        Career choice options (number, time spent thinking)
        Traditionality of choice (gender role)
        Miscellaneous
Effective role functioning
    Performance variable
        Academic performance
        Career-related knowledge
        Skills (interview, writing, and problem solving)
    Adjustment variables
        Career maturity
        Self-concept changes (self-adjustment, congruence, in corporation, interpersonal
          competence, and self-esteem)
        Attitude change
        Locus of control
        Cognitive complexity
        Anxiety
        Need for achievement
Counseling evaluation
    Satisfaction/effectiveness/helpfulness
Miscellaneous

Adapted from Oliver and Spokane (1988, Table 9, p. 455).

Psychometric Quality of Outcome Measures. One of the most overlooked areas in psychological research is the psychometric quality of criterion variables. In industrial/organizational psychology, for example, for years much more attention was paid to the quality of predictor variables than to that of criterion variables. Similarly, in research in counseling psychology, including the prediction of educational and occupational achievement and satisfaction as well as counseling outcome research, the quality of criterion measures has received much less attention than has that of either predictors or interventions.

The reader should be familiar with the components of a good quality psychological or behavioral test or assessment, as detailed in the Joint Technical Standards for Educational and Psychological Testing (APA, AERA, NCME, 1985) and for review should see texts in the areas such as Anastasi (1988) and Walsh and Betz (1990). The chapter by Betz (1990) on social and ethical concerns in the use of tests (including the APA standards) in the Watkins and Campbell (1990) book *Testing in Counseling Practice* provides useful guides, as many other chapters in the latter volume.

The major requirements for high quality assessment are evidence of reliability, evidence of validity, complete information regarding the administration, scoring and interpretation of test scores, and concern for gender and ethnic/racial issues in the use of test scores (see Betz, 1990). Reliability evidence should include that for internal consistency reliability and test–retest stability. The most important kind of validity evidence is that pertaining to construct validity, which can include such evidence as arguments for the theoretical basis of test content, factor analyses, concurrent validity, and correlational relationships with other measures postulated to be related theoretically to the criterion construct. Discriminant validity, that is, demonstration that the construct is distinct from other constructs, is also important. For example, one of the major problems with the measurement of career maturity has been the high correlations of some measures of career maturity with measures of intelligence. Since intelligence is postulated to be a fixed trait of the individual, we would not necessarily expect a criterion based heavily on intelligence to be modified by treatment.

Sources of information about tests and assessment devices are detailed in the same sources mentioned above, but also include the *Mental Measurements Yearbook*, test manuals (if available), and published research using those measures.

In summary, Zytowski and Betz (1972) concluded, in agreement with Oliver (1979), the present authors, and many other authors, that counseling outcome research should not be published without some "indications of the reliability of the instrument on which the research is based" (p. 78).

Reactivity of Outcome Measures. Measures used in career counseling research have tended to be *reactive* measures (e.g., Webb, Campbell, Schwartz, & Sechrest, 1966). A reactive measure is one in which subjects' responses may be influenced by the fact that they were being studied, for example, by the administration of a pretest that then alerted them to the desired changes or familiarized them with the domain of interest. Thus, reactivity must be a concern to career counseling researchers.

One way of addressing the problems of pretesting is through the use of a Solomon four-group design. For those rusty in their knowledge of experimental design, a Solomon four group involves two treated groups, one with and one without pretest and two control groups, one with and one without pretest. This allows evaluation of the effects of pretesting as well as the effects of the treatment (e.g., Campbell & Stanley, 1966). Another alternative is to use a posttest only control group. In addition to modifications in experimental design, Oliver (1979) suggested the development of nonreactive outcome measures. One strategy for reducing reactivity is to increase the unobtrusiveness of the measure, that is, the client's awareness that a measurement has been taken. More directly, objective measures can be used, that is, objective measures of the congruence between interests and field chosen, decisional status as indicated by college major choice (or lack of choice), and performance in school.

In summary, much more attention to criterion conceptualization and measurement is needed. It is essential that criterion constructs be carefully conceptualized and then measured using one or more high quality constructs. It is desirable that at least some of the measures utilized be objective or unobtrusive. The range of potential criterion constructs has only begun to be explored (e.g., see Blustein, Ellis, & DeVenis, 1989; Serling & Betz, 1990, for recent developments in the conceptualization and measurement of problems in committing to a career choice, problems clearly amenable to vocational intervention), and readers are encouraged to expand our thinking in these areas as well as to design better evaluations of interventions.

RECOMMENDATIONS FOR FURTHER RESEARCH

The Current State of Knowledge

The state of knowledge concerning the effectiveness of vocational interventions has been summarized both in review articles and in meta-analyses of the outcome literature.

Although not a review article, an important early article related to the methodology of career counseling outcome studies was the Williamson and Bordin (1941) paper on the evaluation of educational and career counseling. They asked for more research to help us determine "what counseling techniques and conditions will produce what types of results with what types of students?" (p. 8). Their question has still not been adequately answered, nor really addressed systematically.

Probably the first review of the literature in this area was that of Roger Myers (1971) in the first *Handbook of Psychotherapy and Behavior Change* (Bergin & Garfield, 1971). Although Myers did not include many outcome studies in his review, he did conclude that an array of potentially useful vocational treatments was available for use by interested researchers and practitioners.

Subsequent reviews have appeared in the *Annual Review of Psychology* series and in the annual reviews published each October in the *Journal of*

Vocational Behavior (JVB). In the former series, the article by Krumboltz, Becker-Haven, and Burnett (1979) reviewed intervention studies appearing in the years 1976–1978. The authors concluded that there was evidence for the salutary effects of vocational interventions on career decision-making skills and career maturity, but little evidence for effects on job success and satisfaction. Holland, Magoon, and Spokane (1981) also concluded, based on studies done in 1978 and 1979, that a variety of vocational interventions can have beneficial effects. Osipow (1987) and Gelso and Fassinger (1990) also addressed career counseling outcome studies in their review articles. Reviews published in JVB have included those of Slaney and Russell (1987); Phillips, Cairo, Blustein, and Myers (1988); and Fitzgerald and Rounds (1989).

A review in 1981 by Fretz, in the *Journal of Counseling Psychology,* resulted in the strong recommendation for more research using at least two levels of at least two treatment parameters and at least one subject blocking variable, in other words, ATI studies in the tradition of Cronbach and Snow (1977).

Rounds and Tinsley (1984), in the first *Handbook of Counseling Psychology* (Brown & Lent, 1984), criticized vocational intervention researchers for their failure to base their designs and interventions on a systematic classification of vocational problems. As was mentioned in an earlier section, evaluating treatments should be based on a specification of target vocational behaviors to be changed, which itself depends on a classification of vocational problem areas. Rounds and Tinsley also noted, in a related vein, that studying ATIs requires two classification systems, one for client characteristics and one for types of treatments—thus, even the desirable ATI studies may be premature and relatively useless if based on sloppy systems of diagnosis and classification (see also Tobias, 1981, for a more extensive discussion of conceptual and methodological hazards in ATI research).

Myers (1986) again concluded that various vocational treatments do have beneficial effects and made a number of suggestions designed to make outcome studies more relevant to actual counseling practice.

Meta-Analyses. In contrast to literature reviews, the method of meta-analysis (Glass, 1976; Glass, McGraw, & Smith, 1981; Smith & Glass, 1977) is a quantitative method of combining results from many studies to determine an overall effect. For example, meta-analyses of the research on gender differences in intellective and personality traits (Hyde & Linn, 1986) and of the research on gender bias in psychotherapy, as well as on the effectiveness of therapeutic treatments (Smith, Glass, & Miller, 1980), have now appeared in the literature.

The statistical methods used in meta-analysis summarize the results of each study in terms of a standard score that is directly comparable to the effect standard scores obtained from the other studies in the review. The "effect size" is a standard score that usually represents the size of the difference on the dependent variable between treated subjects and control group subjects.

Because the unit of measurement is standard deviation units, like standard deviations, an effect size is most often within the range of +3 to −3 and usually within +1 to −1 (and few effect sizes are actually negative, because that would mean that the treated group was "worse off" on the variable of interest than was the control group). Because effect sizes are, in essence, z scores, they can be interpreted with reference to their percentile equivalents in the standard normal distribution. For example, a z score of +1 corresponds to the 84th percentile on a normal distribution—an effect size of +1 would mean that the average score of the treated group on the outcome variable was at the 84th percentile in comparison to the control group subjects.

The first meta-analysis including vocational studies was that of Smith et al. (1980), which covered outcome studies done between 1900 and 1977. For studies of vocational–personal development interventions, the effect size was .65, whereas the average for all the studies reviewed was .85. Because a z score of .85 corresponds to the 80th percentile, the average person receiving therapy of all kinds was better off the 80% of nontreated controls.

The first meta-analysis focusing specifically on vocational studies was that of Spokane and Oliver (1983) in the *Handbook of Vocational Psychology* (Walsh & Osipow, 1983). These authors reviewed 52 studies using vocational interventions done between 1950 and 1979. They found an overall effect size of .85 for treated subjects versus controls. The effect size for group or class treatments was 1.11 versus that of .87 for individual treatments, but this may have been due to one extreme effect size, that is, 8.23 for the study done by Bartsch and Hackett (1979). If this one study had been excluded, the effect size for groups would be .85, comparable to that found for individual treatments. Related to the issue of outliers, two other points should be noted. First, effect sizes tend to be positively skewed, that is, they lump in the region of .25 to 1.0 and then tail off in the extremes. This skewness is important because, as is well known, skewed distributions provide misleading means—the median may be a better index of the average level of improvement than the mean in such cases. The median effect size in the Spokane and Oliver review was .51. Also, group versus individual treatments vary in many ways other than the mode of delivery, for example, the amount of time a client actually gets treated (usually group treatments give more time to the participants because they are less costly on an individual basis). They may also involve differences in when posttests are administered, and may involve essentially different treatments.

Baker and Popowicz (1983) reviewed career education intervention studies and found an effect size of .50.

Oliver and Spokane (1988) updated their earlier review by including an additional six studies done in the years 1980–1982. Overall their analysis covered 58 studies involving 240 comparisons of treated with no-treatment groups and 7,311 subjects. The average number of treatments was 1.81, covering a range of from 1 to 30 sessions (M = 3.74) and .25 to 30 hours (M = 7.87), and using outcome measures.

The overall results indicated a positive effect for vocational treatments, an average effect size of .82 across all comparisons. However, the distribution of effect sizes was badly skewed in the positive direction—while most effect sizes clustered in the range of .40 to .60, they ranged from −.14 to 8.234. When the two largest outliers were deleted from the analysis (effects sizes of 3.06 and 8.23), the resulting average effect size was .65. Average effect sizes also varied somewhat depending on whether or not they were weighted by sample size but, overall, Oliver and Spokane (1988) concluded that the average treated client/subject was better off on the outcome measures than were 66%–75% of the control group subjects. As stated by Fitzgerald and Rounds (1989), "Any type of career counseling intervention has a moderate to strong effect on any type of client measured by any type of outcome (p. 122).

Oliver and Spokane (1988) also analyzed their data according to characteristics of the study. Probably the most important variable influencing effectiveness was "treatment intensity," defined as the number of hours and sessions the subjects received treatment. When a multiple regression using effect size as the dependent variable was performed, the only significant contributor to effect size differences was the intensity variable. The most effective treatment, as indicated by effect size *(ES)* alone, was class treatments *(ES* = 2.05), with workshops *(ES* = .75), individual counseling *(ES* = .74), and group counseling *(ES* = .62) in the range more typical of effect sizes. However, class treatments also involved more time than did the other treatments, so it may be treatment intensity that leads class treatments to have their large effects.

When Oliver and Spokane examined effect size as a function of the amount of time actually expended in treatment, it was found that individual counseling was most effective in terms of counseling gains per unit of time expended. In terms of cost effectiveness, however, workshops, followed by classes, were most effective per amount of counselor time expended to achieve given gains across individuals. (Because individual counseling, by definition, helps only one person at a time, it is less cost effective than treatment modalities that deliver services to several or many people simultaneously.) Overall, individual counseling and classes and workshops came out well in the analysis, with groups and no-counselor treatments (e.g., self-administration of the Strong Interest Inventory or Self-Directed Search) showing less effectiveness.

Other findings may prove useful to researchers, but they should be interpreted in light of the fact that no variable other than intensity of treatment contributed significantly to the prediction of effect size—thus additional findings are more suggestive than conclusive. Given this caveat, it was also found that effects were largest for no-choice subjects *(ES* = 1.34), but these tended to be the same subjects in classes and workshops, shown to be effective at least in part because they offered more time in treatment than did other modes. The mean effect size for vocational clients was .86, while that for solicited clients was .74. Half the studies used college-age students (ES = .85), and 25% used high school-age subjects (ES = 1.02); the remaining 25% were too heterogeneous to characterize. Studies using random assignment (57% of the total) had an effect size (ES = .80) similar to that of studies using non-equivalent groups (18.6% with an ES of .89). The largest effect sizes were found for studies with mid-range sample sizes (Ns of 50 to 100, ES = 1.16), with smaller effect sizes for small Ns (below 50, with an ES = .77) and large Ns (over 100, with an ES = .57). Ironically, the largest study, involving 2,245 subjects, had an effect size of zero.

Fewer than half the studies reported level of counselor experience, with trained counselors (ES = .72) doing somewhat less well than counselors in training (ES = .83). One variable that could not be analyzed because it was so infrequently reported by researchers was the dropout rate from either the experimental or control groups. This is a serious omission that should be rectified by authors of subsequent outcome research.

Based on their findings, Oliver and Spokane (1988) made a number of recommendations for both researchers and practitioners in the field. These include more attention to design and analysis issues, including more use of blocking variables, systematic attention to the development of a complete set of outcome measures, and complete reporting of the details of outcome studies for purposes of replication, meta-analysis, and actual use in practice. In terms of practice, the necessity for diagnosis cannot be overemphasized, and longer term treatments seem preferable to short-term treatments.

In interpreting findings such as these, it should be noted that there are a number of criticisms of the methodology of meta-analysis (just as there are criticisms of every known method of statistical and logical analysis available to scientists). For example, Fitzgerald and Rounds (1989) noted that the Oliver–Spokane meta-analysis is based on nonindependent sample sizes and that tests of homogeneity were not conducted.

Recommendations for Subsequent Research

Recommendations for subsequent research include the many implications for methodological improvements that have been mentioned throughout this chapter. As suggested by Osipow (1982), the most helpful improvements would involve developments in the area of a taxonomy of career problems, from which interventions could be designed and outcomes selected. Second, development of a psychometrically sound set of outcome measures based on a career taxonomy would help to increase both the quality and utility of outcome research. Design issues like using random assignment of people expressing the problem of interest to treatment and wait-control groups, along with the careful consideration of individual difference variables that moderate the effects of treatments, must be more carefully considered and implemented. Fitzgerald and Rounds (1989) noted that, with all the conceptual and methodological flaws in career counseling research, Oliver and Spokane's (1988) failure to find different effects for different treatments is not particularly surprising (even though it is quite disturbing in its implications for the efficacy of our treatments). Thus, there is much to be done in terms of improved designs and assessment of outcomes.

In addition, our knowledge is quite limited in terms of the applicability of treatments to special populations (e.g., women, ethnic/minorities, the disabled) and, in fact, special populations have special needs that should be incorporated into a career problem taxonomy. For example, we know that both women and such ethnic minorities as Blacks, Hispanics, and Native Americans tend to avoid careers in the mathematics and the sciences even when they have the ability to pursue those careers—rather they tend to pursue socially oriented but, unfortunately, less well paid career fields in disproportionate numbers. Thus, one target for interventions in those groups might be increasing range of perceived career options to include scientific and engineering fields. Other ethnic groups may perceive other familial or social barriers to their career development and need special assistance to have truly free choices (see Betz', 1989, concept of the null educational environment for a full discussion of passive discrimination, of discrimination through failure to actively support and encourage people whose options have been restricted by society).

Also needed is more attention to a range of underserved and understudied groups (Osipow, 1982). Osipow strongly recommended more attention to career interventions with adults in the workplace and to older people facing issues of retirement, stagnation, and so on. Our research has been focused too much on high school and college-age students, and the particular developmental issues they face, while spending too little time on interventions that could facilitate job satisfaction and success, as well as successful management of occupations stress.

Vocational psychology and career development have provided us with a rich knowledge base of theory and an array of individual difference and outcome measures and intervention techniques. It is time that we more systematically and actively put this knowledge to work in the design and evaluation of interventions capable of assisting people at all stages of the lifelong career development process.

REFERENCES

American Educational Research Association, American Psychological Association, and National Council on Measurement in Education. (1985). *Standards for educational and psychological testing.* Washington, DC: American Psychological Association.

Anastasi, A. (1988). *Psychological testing* (6th ed.). New York: Macmillan.

Baker, S. B., & Popowicz, C. L. (1983). Meta-analysis as a strategy for evaluating effects of career education interventions. *Vocational Guidance Quarterly, 31,* 178–186.

Bandura, A. (1977). Self-efficacy: Toward a unifying theory of behavior change. *Psychological Review, 84,* 191–215.

Bartsch, K., & Hackett, G. (1979). Effect of a decision-making course on locus of control, conceptualization, and career planning. *Journal of College Student Personnel, 20,* 230–235.

Bergin, A. E., & Garfield, S. L. (Eds.). (1971). *Handbook of psychotherapy and behavior change.* New York: Wiley.

Betz, N. E. (1988). The assessment of career development and maturity. In W. B. Walsh & S. H. Osipow (Eds.), *Career decision making* (pp. 77–136). Hillsdale, NJ: Lawrence Erlbaum Associates.

Betz, N. E. (1989). The null environment and women's career development. *The Counseling Psychologist, 17,* 136–144.

Betz, N. E. (1990). Contemporary issues in the use of tests in counseling. In C. E. Watkins, Jr. & V. Campbell (Eds.), *Testing in counseling practice* (pp. 419–450). Hillsdale, NJ: Lawrence Erlbaum Associates.

Betz, N. E. (in press). Career assessment. In S. Brown & R. Lent (Eds.), *Handbook of counseling psychology* (2nd ed.). New York: Wiley.

Betz, N. E., & Fitzgerald, L. F. (1987). *The career psychology of women.* New York: Academic Press.

Betz, N. E., Fitzgerald, L. F., & Hill, R. E. (1989). Trait-factor theories: Traditional cornerstone of career theory. In M. B. Arthur, D. T. Hall, & B. S. Lawrence (Eds.), *Handbook of career theory* (pp. 26–40). Cambridge: Cambridge University Press.

Blustein, D. L., Ellis, M. V., & DeVenis, L. E. (1989). The development and validation of a two-dimensional model of the commitment to career choices process. *Journal of Vocational Behavior, 35,* 342–378.

Borgen, F. H. (1984). Counseling psychology. *Annual Review of Psychology, 35,* Palo Alto, CA: Annual Reviews.

Brandt, J. D. (1977). Model for the delivery of career development programs by the college counseling center. *Journal of Counseling Psychology, 24,* 494–502.

Brandt, J. E., & Hood, A. B. (1968). Effect of personality adjustment on the predictive validity of the Strong Vocational Interest Blank. *Journal of Counseling Psychology, 15,* 547–551.

Brown, D., & Brooks, L. (Eds.). (1984). *Career choice and development.* San Francisco: Jossey-Bass.

Brown, S. D., & Lent, R. W. (Eds.). (1984). *Handbook of counseling psychology.* New York: Wiley.

Buck, J. N., & Daniels, M. H. (1985). *Assessment of career decision making manual.* Los Angeles: Western Psychological Service.

Campbell, D. P. (1965). *The results of counseling: Twenty-five years later.* Philadelphia: Saunders.

Campbell, D. T., & Stanley, J. C. (1966). *Experimental and quasi-experimental designs for research.* Chicago: Rand McNally.

Campbell, R. E., & Cellini, J. V. (1981). A diagnostic taxonomy of adult career development problems. *Journal of Vocational Behavior, 19,* 175–190.

Carter, R., & Swanson, J. (1990). The validity of the Strong Interest Inventory with Black Americans: A review of the literature. *Journal of Vocational Behavior, 36,* 195–209.

Cook, T. D., & Campbell, D. T. (1976). The design and conduct of quasi-experimental and true experiments in field settings. In M. D. Dunnette (Ed.), *Handbook of industrial and organizational psychology* (pp. 223–326). Chicago: Rand McNally.

Crites, J. O. (1974). Career counseling. *The Counseling Psychologist, 43,* 3–23.

Crites, J. O. (1978). *Theory and research handbook for the Career Maturity Inventory.* Monterey, CA: CTB/McGraw-Hill.

Cronbach, L. J., & Snow, R. E. (1977). *Aptitudes and instructional materials.* New York: Wiley.

Dawis, R. V., Dohm, T. E., Lofquist, L. H., Chartrand, J. M., & Due, A. M. (1987). *Minnesota Occupational Classification System III.* Minneapolis: Department of Psychology, University of Minnesota.

Dawis, R. V., & Lofquist, L. L. (1984). *A psychological theory of work adjustment.* Minneapolis: University of Minnesota Press.

Dorn, F. J. (1990). Career counseling—a social psychological perspective. In W. B. Walsh & S. H. Osipow (Eds.), *Career Counseling: Contemporary topics in vocational psychology* (pp. 193–223). Hillsdale, NJ: Lawrence Erlbaum Associates.

Fitzgerald, L. F., & Rounds, J. B. (1989). Vocational behavior, 1988: A critical review. *Journal of Vocational Behavior, 35,* 105–163.

Fretz, B. R. (1981). Evaluating the effectiveness of career interventions [Monograph]. *Journal of Counseling Psychology, 28,* 77–90.

Gelso, C. J. (1979). Research in counseling: Methodological and professional issues. *The Counseling Psychologist, 8,* 7–36.

Gelso, C. J., & Fassinger, R. F. (1990). Counseling psychology: Theory and research on interventions. *Annual Review of Psychology, 41,* 355–386.

Glass, G. V. (1976). Primary, secondary, and meta-analysis of research. *Educational Researcher, 5,* 3–8.

Glass, G. V., McGraw, B., & Smith, M. L. (1981). *Meta-analysis in social research.* Beverly Hills, CA: Sage.

Goldman, L. (1978). *Research methods for counselors.* New York: Wiley.

Gonyea, G. (1962). Appropriateness of vocational choice as a criterion of counseling outcome. *Journal of Counseling Psychology, 9,* 213–219.

Gottfredson, G. D. (1978). Evaluating vocational interventions. *Journal of Vocational Behavior, 13,* 252–254.

Grotevant, H. D., Scarr, S., & Weinberg, R. A. (1977). Patterns of interest similarity in adoptive and biological parents. *Journal of Personality and Social Psychology, 35,* 667–676.

Hansen, J. C. (1984). The measurement of vocational interests. In S. D. Brown & R. W. Lent (Eds.), *Handbook of counseling psychology* (pp. 99–136). New York: Wiley.

Hoffman, M. A., Spokane, A. R., & Magoon, T. M. (1981). Effects of feedback mode on counseling outcomes using the Strong-Campbell Interest Inventory: Does the counselor really matter? *Journal of Counseling Psychology, 28,* 119–125.

Holland, J. L. (1985). *Making vocational choices.* Englewood Cliffs, NJ: Prentice-Hall.

Holland, J. L., & Holland, J. E. (1977). Vocational indecision: More evidence and speculation. *Journal of Counseling Psychology, 24,* 404–414.

Holland, J. L., Magoon, T. M., & Spokane, A. R. (1981). Counseling psychology: Career interventions, research and theory. *Annual Review of Psychology, 32,* 279–305.

Hyde, J. S., & Linn, M. C. (1986). *The psychology of gender: Advances through meta-analysis.* Baltimore: Johns Hopkins University Press.

Jepsen, D. A. (1984). The developmental perspective on vocational behavior: A review of theory and research. In S. D. Brown & R. W. Lent (Eds.), *Handbook of counseling psychology* (pp. 178–215). New York: Wiley.

Jepsen, D. A. (1990). Developmental career counseling. In W. J. Walsh & S. H. Osipow (Eds.), *Career counseling: Contemporary topics in vocational psychology* (pp. 117–157). Hillsdale, NJ: Lawrence Erlbaum Associates.

Kiesler, D. J. (1971). Experimental designs in psychotherapy research. In A. E. Bergin & S. L. Garfield (Eds.), *Handbook of psychotherapy and behavior change* (pp. 36–74). New York: Wiley.

Krumboltz, J. D., Becker-Haven, J. F., & Burnett, K. F. (1979). Counseling psychology. *Annual Review of Psychology, 30,* 555–602.

Lambert, M. (1976). Spontaneous remission in adult neurotic disorders: A revision and summary. *Psychological Bulletin, 83,* 107–119.

Landy, F. J. (1985). *Psychology of work behavior*. Homewood, IL: Dorsey Press.

Lunneborg, P. W. (1983). Career counseling techniques. In W. B. Walsh & S. H. Osipow (Eds.), *Handbook of vocational psychology* (Vol. 2, pp. 41–76). Hillsdale, NJ: Lawrence Erlbaum Associates.

Mitchell, A. M., Jones, G. B., & Krumboltz, J. D. (Eds.). (1975). *A social learning theory of career decision-making* (AIR-47600-6/3FR). Palo Alto, CA: American Institutes for Research.

Mitchell, A. M., Jones, G. B., & Krumboltz, J. D. (Eds.). (1979). *Social learning and career decision making*. Cranston, RI: Carroll.

Mitchell, L. K., & Krumboltz, J. D. (1984). Research on human decision making: Implications for career decision making and counseling. In S. D. Brown & R. W. Lent (Eds.), *Handbook of counseling psychology* (pp. 238–280). New York: Wiley.

Myers, R. A. (1971). Research on educational and vocational counseling. In A. E. Bergin & S. L. Garfield (Eds.), *Handbook of psychotherapy and behavior change: An empirical analysis* (pp. 863–891). New York: Wiley.

Myers, R. A. (1986). Research on educational and vocational counseling. In S. Garfield & A. Bergin (Eds.), *Handbook of psychotherapy and behavior change* (3rd ed., pp. 715–738). New York: Wiley.

Oliver, L. W. (1979). Outcome measurement in career counseling research. *Journal of Counseling Psychology, 26,* 217–226.

Oliver, L. W., & Spokane, A. R. (1988). Career-intervention outcome: What contributes to client gain? *Journal of Counseling Psychology, 35,* 447–462.

Osipow, S. H. (1973). *Theories of career development* (2nd ed.). Englewood Cliffs, NJ: Prentice-Hall.

Osipow, S. H. (1982). Research in career counseling. *The Counseling Psychologist, 10*(4), 27–34.

Osipow, S. H. (1983). *Theories of career development* (3rd ed.). Englewood Cliffs, NJ: Prentice-Hall.

Osipow, S. H. (1987). Counseling psychology: Theory, research and practice in career counseling. *Annual Review of Psychology, 38,* Palo Alto, CA: Annual Reviews.

Osipow, S. H. (1990). Convergence in theories of career choice and development: Review and prospect. *Journal of Vocational Behavior, 36,* 122–131.

Osipow, S. H., Carney, C. G., Winer, J., Yanico, B., & Koschier, M. (1976). *The career decision scale*. Odessa, FL: PAR.

Osipow, S. H., & Scheid, A. B. (1971). The effects of manipulated success ratios on task preferences. *Journal of Vocational Behavior, 1,* 93–98.

Parsons, F. (1990). *Choosing a vocation*. Boston: Houghton-Mifflin.

Phillips, S. D., Cairo, P. C., Blustein, D. C., & Myers, R. A. (1988). Career development and vocational behavior, 1987: A review. *Journal of Vocational Behavior, 33,* 119–184.

Roethlisberger, F. J., & Dickson, W. J. (1939). *Management and the worker*. Cambridge, MA: Harvard University Press.

Rounds, J. B., Jr., & Tinsley, H. E. A. (1984). Diagnosis and treatment of vocational problems. In S. D. Brown & R. W. Lent (Eds.), *Handbook of counseling psychology* (pp. 137–177). New York: Wiley.

Rounds, J. B., & Tracey, T. J. (1990). From trait-and-factor to person-environment fit counseling: Theory and process. In W. B. Walsh & S. H. Osipow (Eds.), *Career counseling: Contemporary topics in vocational psychology* (pp. 1–44). Hillsdale, NJ: Lawrence Erlbaum Associates.

Serling, D., & Betz, N. E. (1990). Development and evaluation of a measure of fear of commitment. *Journal of Counseling Psychology, 37,* 91–97.

Slaney, R. B. (1988). The assessment of career decision making. In W. B. Walsh & S. H. Osipow (Eds.), *Career decision making* (pp. 33–76). Hillsdale, NJ: Lawrence Erlbaum Associates.

Slaney, R. B., & Russell, J. E. A. (1987). Perspectives on vocational behavior, 1986: A review. *Journal of Vocational Behavior, 31,* 111–173.

Smith, M. L., & Glass, G. V. (1977). Meta-analysis of psychotherapy outcome studies. *American Psychologist, 32,* 752–760.

Smith, M. L., Glass, G. V., & Miller, T. I. (1980). *The benefits of psychotherapy.* Baltimore, MD: Johns Hopkins University Press.

Spokane, A. R. (1985). A review of research on person-environment congruence in Holland's theory. *Journal of Vocational Behavior, 26,* 306–343.

Spokane, A. R. (Ed.). (1987). Special issue on environmental psychology. *Journal of Vocational Behavior, 31,* 217–361.

Spokane, A. R., & Oliver, L. W. (1983). Outcomes of vocational intervention. In W. B. Walsh & S. H. Osipow (Eds.), *Handbook of vocational psychology, Vol. II: Applications* (pp. 99–136). Hillsdale, NJ: Lawrence Erlbaum Associates.

Super, D. E., Thompson, A. E., Lindeman, R. H., Jordaan, J. P., & Myers, R. A. (1979). *Career development inventory.* Palo Alto, CA: Consulting Psychologists Press.

Taylor, K. M. (1988). Advances in career planning systems. In W. B. Walsh & S. H. Osipow (Eds.), *Career decision making* (pp. 137–212). Hillsdale, NJ: Lawrence Erlbaum Associates.

Tobias, S. (1981). Adapting instruction to individual differences among students. *Educational Psychologist, 16,* 111–120.

Walsh, W. B., & Betz, N. E. (1990). *Tests and assessment* (2nd ed.). Englewood Cliffs, NJ: Prentice-Hall.

Walsh, W. B., & Osipow, S. H. (Eds.). (1983). *Handbook of vocational psychology, Vol. II: Applications.* Hillsdale, NJ: Lawrence Erlbaum Associates.

Watkins, C. E., Jr., & Campbell, V. (Eds.). (1990). *Testing in counseling practice.* Hillsdale, NJ: Lawrence Erlbaum Associates.

Webb, E. J., Campbell, D. T., Schwartz, R. D., & Sechrest, L. (1966). *Unobtrusive measures: Nonreactive research in the social sciences.* Chicago: Rand McNally.

Williamson, E. C., & Bordin, E. S. (1941). The evaluation of vocational educational counseling: A critique of methodology of experiments. *Educational and Psychological Measurement, 1,* 5–24.

Zytowski, D. G. (1977). The effects of being interest-inventoried. *Journal of Vocational Behavior, 11,* 153–157.

Zytowski, D. G., & Betz, E. L. (1972). Measurement in counseling research: A review. *The Counseling Psychologist, 3,* 72–86.

Zytowski, D. G., & Borgen, F. H. (1983). Assessment. In W. B. Walsh & S. H. Osipow (Eds.), *Handbook of vocational psychology: Vol. II: Applications* (pp. 5–40). Hillsdale, NJ: Lawrence Erlbaum Associates.

III

ISSUES AND INNOVATIONS IN COUNSELING RESEARCH

THE ETHICS OF RESEARCHING
COUNSELING/THERAPY PROCESSES

Naomi M. Meara
University of Notre Dame

Lyle D. Schmidt
Ohio State University

Conducting research and practicing counseling can be viewed as the expression of two interacting cultures that have differing mores, customs, and routines. Yet ethical behavior is integral to, and a high priority for professionals in both areas. Indeed each culture has clear statements of ethical principles and guidelines (cf. APA, 1981a, 1981b, 1982, 1990) that can help us to picture the differences and similarities in these cultures and to understand the theoretical, methodological, practical, and ethical difficulties for investigators and counselors in conducting research on therapeutic events.

As ethics is the area of difficulty considered in this chapter, we begin by describing the range of the questions to be addressed. First, our focus is on the issues where research, counseling process, and ethics coverage rather than on issues where there is little or no overlap. For example, there are many ethical issues related to research with human subjects whatever the setting and to the counseling of clients who are not research participants. Second, we assume the ethics of the research and practice cultures are operative and binding in counseling research on counseling processes. For instance, failure of an investigator to obtain informed consent from research participants or the violation of confidentiality by a therapist is considered unethical (APA, 1981, 1990), and does not depend on understanding the complexities of clients as research participants. Third, we do not consider analogue studies, or other research arrangements with counseling implications in which the research participants are not clients or counselors. Although issues of consent and welfare of human participants are serious ethical ones that do pertain to research with clients, the general issue of human welfare is not unique to clients who are research participants. Fourth, we do not discuss generic issues of experimental design because we consider them to be primarily issues of research competence that are not unique to research on counseling processes. Finally, as our title implies, the ethics of researching the processes of counseling and therapy focuses on situations where members of the interaction (i.e., clients, counselors, supervisors) are research participants, the research is about the counseling, and the participants were solicited by virtue of their participation in counseling.

Our chapter is divided into several sections. We begin with discussion of the nature of research and counseling to provide background for how the processes, goals, and other differences in these two activities can present special ethical questions. We then discuss the nature of ethics, with particular attention to principle ethics. We argue that there are several ethical principles that can serve as guidelines for professionals who are making ethical decisions in regard to counseling research.

The next section of the chapter presents examples of ethical issues in conducting research where clients and/or other members of the interaction are the research participants. When considered in the context of researching the counseling process, issues have distinctive aspects that may not exist apart from this special setting (e.g., see Stricker, 1982). The issues are not exhaustive but rather were chosen to serve as exemplars of the ethical reasoning that is required when conducting research about counseling. They include such topics as (a) the counseling relationships, (b) informed consent, (c) participant selection (e.g., treatment groups, control groups, placebo), (d) risk–benefit ratios, and (e) special populations.

Because no clear answers exist to many of the issues we raise, we offer guidelines to assist in understanding and coping with ethical dilemmas. The guidelines relate to (a) consultation and review, (b) evaluation of the effects of ethical decisions on the counseling research context and its participants, and (c) the relevance of knowledge in science, practice, and ethics in conducting this research. We close with a summary of the themes we present and a few thoughts about future directions.

SOME CONTRASTS BETWEEN THE CULTURES OF COUNSELING AND RESEARCH

There are some major differences in the goals, processes, and routines (i.e., accepted conventions or procedures) of counseling and of research and in the values and priorities of those who are therapists and those who are investigators. The goal of research is to produce knowledge, whereas the goal of counseling is to help someone; consequently, research is a public activity and therapy is a private one. A major activity of researchers is publishing or in other ways "announcing" and disseminating what they are doing. A major concern of counselors is the opposite, maintaining confidentiality, assuring clients that their participation will not be made public; that the conversations and the progress are indeed private. This difference makes consultation and collegial activity qualitatively different practices for researchers and therapists. Typically, the standard for sound science is the ability to replicate, to demonstrate that a phenomenon is reliable. A cornerstone of therapy is its individual nature, its uniqueness. Reliable patterns in certain types of clients might be expected, but the direct or systematic replication of a specific therapy experience is unlikely. While in their broadest applications, both serve the community and its members; science is more focused on people in general, and counseling, on a person or persons in particular.

Many professionals who are primarily researchers or primarily practitioners understand these differences and work with and accommodate the needs of those professionals who are primarily in the other culture. Sometimes, and this is not without its unique problems, the investigator and the therapist are the same person and thus very attuned to these pragmatic and value differences. Nonetheless, there are differing mores, customs, and routines that characterize the cultures of research and practice that need be acknowledged.

THE NATURE OF ETHICS

From childhood most of us begin to acquire intuitive understandings of fair play, appropriate treatment of others, and our rights as an independent individual. These intuitive understandings of mores, morals, or accepted behaviors of a community (e.g., our family) reflect interpretations of values in our milieu. The values that we retain, along with others that we acquire, become for each of us an implicit, if not explicit, set of guidelines for personal conduct that often are referred to as morals, ethics, or ethical responsibilities. Typically, when we speak of ethics or morals of daily life, we are referring to phenomena separate from, but not totally unrelated to, the laws of a community or the legal rights and responsibilities of its citizens. In addition, those who become professionals (e.g., psychologists, teachers, physicians, clergy, or lawyers) often are trained in ethical rules or codes that apply specifically to the responsibilities of a professional role in the special circumstance of that particular profession.

Because in both the everyday and the professional worlds the term *ethics* is often used to convey different ideas (e.g., ranging from personal morals to written codes of professional conduct), it seems appropriate to present a definition. Dictionaries offer several, ranging from "moral principles" to "rules of conduct for a particular group"; but the following from *The Random House*

Dictionary of the English Language (Flexner, 1987) seems helpful in establishing some common background for considering the material presented in this chapter. Ethics is defined as: "that branch of philosophy dealing with values relating to human conduct, with respect to the rightness and wrongness of certain actions and to the goodness and badness of the motives and ends of such actions" (p. 665). This definition helps to clarify how the term, even when correctly used, presents many subtleties and variations in meaning. The definition also serves to introduce the complexity of ethical decision making. Even a cursory reading indicates that for an individual to translate this definition into ethical actions and decisions requires judgments from multiple perspectives, which encompass various levels of reasoning, and that have variable magnitudes (e.g., individual, local community, larger society) of effect.

Our focus here is limited to normative ethics as applied to the counseling research context. Normative ethics means the examination of what is ethically or morally acceptable and why (Beauchamp & Childress, 1989). Normative ethics can be contrasted with nonnormative ethics. Examples of such contrasts would be descriptive ethics (i.e., what are the ethical practices of certain individuals or groups) or metaethics (i.e., analyzing the language and logic of moral reasoning). Our goal here is not to describe or analyze what is, but to provide guidelines for assisting professionals in deciding the ethicality (i.e., "the what ought to be") of policies, procedures, and behaviors in researching the counseling/therapy process.

As Western culture has become more professionalized, more emphasis has been placed on professionals' application of ethics to their work. Increasingly, professionals with particular expertise and special relationships with their clientele are entrusted with making or guiding decisions that involve the welfare of others. In the process, professionals become privy to some of the most intimate details in the lives of others. From the ministry, law, and medicine the professions have expanded and with this expansion professional responsibility for ethical practice has increased. More aspects of individuals' lives are being put in the hands of others. Technology has made more things possible in both research and practice; hence, created a need for more ethical decisions. Family mobility, longevity, single parents, and dual-career couples have made the care of dependent family members increasingly more professional, or professionally assisted, than personal. The declining influence of religious codes and the attendant need to seek expertise elsewhere places greater burdens on professionals to provide standards for their behavior and guidelines for others. This confluence of events makes ethical self-awareness and reflection a more distinctive part of the responsibilities of professionals and stipulates the development of applied professional ethics. Collegial dialogue and explicit codes of conduct are needed to guide the exercise of one's professional responsibilities and in particular the relationships with clients, patients or research participants. The American Psychological Association (APA) was a leader in recognizing the need for such guidelines in applied professional ethics. Members of the APA began to formally discuss these issues in 1938 and adopted their first formal code in 1953 (Schmidt & Meara, 1984). Other organizations concerned with research and counseling have followed suit.

Applied ethical issues, which are now commonplace in newspapers and other media, first gained public attention in the area of biomedical ethics. Technological advances presented difficult decisions in health care (e.g., how to allocate scarce resources to persons of different ages or whether to prolong the lives of the dying with assistance of such devices as respirators or feeding tubes). The combined impact of increasing pluralism in values, the realities of modern medicine, and a growing litigious climate in Western society have generated a level of ethical debate that seems to indicate that professionals need explicit and continuing education in matters of ethical judgment and professional behavior.

There is a need to supplement both the intuitive level of ethical decision making in everyday life and comprehensive philosophical theories that may implicitly guide such decisions. Usually, study of ethical theory is not a major part of professional education. But even if professionals understood ethical theories as well as philosophers and ethicists who study and interpret moral discourse, they still would need collegial dialogue, professional codes and other guides in applying ethical theory to daily activities of scientific and professional life. Such assistance has been provided in the recent literature of applied professional ethics.

Much of the literature on applied professional ethics has been guided by "principle ethics" (cf. e.g., Beauchamp & Childress, 1979, 1983, 1989; Jordan & Meara, 1990). Principle ethics focuses on certain universal or *prima facie* rules, which appear to be important and binding responsibilities for professionals. Jordan and Meara (1990) characterized principle ethics as "approaches that emphasize the use of rational, objective, universal and impartial principles in the ethical analysis of dilemmas" (p. 107).

The teaching of principle ethics examines strategies of reasoning to be used in instances where these principles or rules are in conflict. Often these conflicts are presented through a case study example that poses a dilemma or quandary for which various "solutions" and forms of reasoning for arriving at these "solutions" are discussed.

A useful conceptualization of principle ethics and one that guides our discussion in this chapter has been presented and refined over the years by Beauchamp and Childress (1979, 1983, 1989). Although originally applied to decision making in the field of biomedical ethics, principle ethics, as developed by Beauchamp and Childress and others is applicable to the science and practice of psychology (see especially, Drane, 1982; Kitchener, 1984).

The Beauchamp and Childress approach seems especially appropriate for examining the ethical issues we have selected. The principles they propose, which are discussed here, seem at the heart of several of the ethical conflicts that arise in planning research with clients and others involved in the counseling process.

To place this work in context we briefly review their model for moral justification (Beauchamp & Childress, 1979, 1983, 1989), which has been adapted for ethical decision making in psychology and related fields by Kitchener (1984). The model proposes two levels of ethical reasoning: the intuitive level and the critical-evaluative level. The intuitive level refers to the common sense of daily life and depends on the ordinary moral sense of individuals. The critical-evaluative level is divided into three hierarchical subcategories that are (from low to high) rules, principles, and theories. *Rules* refer to specific laws and codes of professional conduct that are adopted by various professional organizations. As Drane (1982) noted, *principles* are "ethical values in verbal or propositional form which either have or presume to have universal applicability" (p. 31). A rule loses its salience if it can be demonstrated that it violates a higher level principle. For example, after attempts by civil rights groups to change the rule that Blacks must sit in the rear of a bus, Rosa Parks brought national attention to this rule by refusing to obey it (Williams, 1987). In the events that followed it was clear to most that this rule violated the principle of justice. Typically, it is easier to argue about or dispute a rule than a principle, and conceptually at least the assumption is that rules are based on higher principles.

The highest of the critical-evaluative levels is that of *theory* or what one might call a "philosophy of life." This level encompasses the critical "why" questions of human existence and meaning. At this level, one confronts such questions as why is justice important? or freedom? or is there value in being ethical? The way one poses these questions and answers them is often a manifestation of religious conviction or philosophical beliefs. Beauchamp and Childress (1989) said that "a well developed ethical theory provides a framework of principles within which an agent can determine morally appropriate actions" (p. 25). In the view of Beauchamp and Childress (1989) there is no completely satisfactory ethical theory, and individuals can arrive at the same ethical decision starting from different theoretical bases. The two theories they use most extensively in the development of their principles are rule utilitarianism, which is a specific form of consequentialist theory, and deontological theory. Utilitarian theorists generally judge actions as right and/or good with respect to the consequences they produce. Rule utilitarians do not judge each act in isolation but rather in a context with an integrated system of rules or principles where the standard of rightness or goodness is ultimate or cumulative effects of the action performed by many persons. They allow exceptions to or the disregarding of a rule only when another moral rule is more binding. Rule utilitarians do not consider the consequences of breaking a specific rule in isolation from the effect the exception would have on the other rules or principles in the integrated system. In contrast, deontological theorists "hold that some features of acts other than, or in addition to, their consequences make them right or wrong and that the grounds of right or obligation are not wholly dependent on the production of good consequences" (p. 36). There are basic differences between these theoretical approaches; for example, utilitarians hold that the most fundamental moral relationship between individuals is that of benefactor–beneficiary; whereas deontologists claim we are related to individuals in a number of ways through our previous interactions with them and these relationships confer duties and obligations that are binding "no matter what." Differences such as these imply that one's theoretical orientation and the firmness with which one holds it influence what rules and principles are more salient. Full appraisal of such influences is clearly beyond the scope of this chapter. (For a more thorough discussion of ethical theory, various versions of these theories and a comparison of theoretical strengths and weaknesses the reader is referred to Beauchamp & Childress, 1989.)

These three subcategories of the critical evaluative level of ethical reasoning—rules, principles and theory—are considered hierarchical and related. As noted earlier they are considered to be hierarchical because if one is unable to resolve an ethical question at one level, there is more opportunity for possible resolution at the next level. The next higher level is more encompassing, more abstract, and less particular. The levels are related to each other and to the intuitive level because, depending on the circumstances, one can focus on certain kinds of information by moving among the levels in deliberating a decision or course of action. And, implicitly at least, decisions at any level affect or are affected by considerations at another level. For example, in daily life one might renounce violence of any kind (e.g., verbal abuse, pushing, hitting, using a gun); and justify that decision at every level (e.g., by recourse to intuition, the rules of a religious group, the principle of respect for autonomy and/or a philosophical position regarding the sanctity of human life).

Although psychologists may not be expert in ethical theory, it seems they need to understand the critical evaluative levels of rules, principles, and theory to make ethical decisions regarding the conduct of counseling research and other aspects of their professional life. If such understanding is important, an immediate question is deciding what theoretical perspective one should take in learning more about critically evaluating these problems and in formulating solutions to a specific event or series of events. It is unlikely psychologists would agree on one theoretical perspective even if from an explanatory perspective there were a completely satisfactory theory of ethics. Psychologists are too diverse in training and personal and professional lives to arrive at substantial theoretical consensus. Even our documents of consensus (cf. Blackstone's, 1975, discussion of the APA research guidelines) carry few explicit proscriptions (Jordan & Meara, 1990). Because there is often no satisfactory objective standard to which either the researchers or the practitioners of our profession can appeal, we need decision-making guidelines for our own professional development and for the welfare of those we serve. And we need experience and vigilance in the exercise, application, and revision of such guidelines.

PRINCIPLES OF ETHICAL REASONING

Beauchamp and Childress (1989) offered a partial solution to the problem of choosing a perspective by defending what they called a "composite theory" that permits basic principles to have weight, without giving any principle per se weight over any other. They propose universal principles that they conceive as *prima facie* binding; "on the face of it" these principles are binding unless in the circumstances in question there is a conflicting, overriding *prima facie* obligation. The principles are conceptualized as more than rules of thumb or guides that can be abandoned because some good might result, but they are not absolutely binding in all circumstances. Codes and rules of professional organizations can also be viewed as *prima facie* binding. Like some codes or rules adopted by professional organizations, the principles Beauchamp and Childress proposed represent a compromise or partial reconciliation of theoretical perspectives. Although such an approach allows appropriate ethical and professional decision making to evolve over time and to be applied differentially in special circumstances, it places more responsibility on professionals for making decisions and learning about the principles and how to evaluate their applicability in specific situations. It is the principle approach of Beauchamp and Childress we adopt for evaluating the issues we discuss later.

At the principle level of moral or ethical justification Beauchamp and Childress (1989) developed "four moral principles applicable to scientific research, medicine and health care" (p. 307). These *prima facie* principles, which are defined as they are discussed, are (a) respect for autonomy, (b) nonmaleficence, (c) beneficence, and (d) justice. From these principles are derived ethical rules such as veracity, privacy, confidentiality, and fidelity. These principles and rules serve as guidelines for appropriate behavior in professional relationships (i.e., relationships between researcher–participant or counselor–client) and for rational analysis of dilemmas that arise in such relationships when principles or rules are in conflict. When applied to professional relationships in contrast to the relationships of everyday life, these principles and rules acquire additional meaning; because in such relationships, there are certain fiduciary responsibilities that are not necessarily a part of, or are in addition to, the responsibilities or obligations of nonprofessional relationships.

Kitchener (1984), building on the work of Beauchamp and Childress (1979, 1983, 1989) and Hare (1981), presented the four principles and the derived concept of fidelity as pivotal in the ethical decision-making processes for those in the helping professions, particularly counseling psychologists. Here, we present a brief definition of each of the principles (for a more comprehensive discussion the reader is referred to Beauchamp & Childress, 1989, and Kitchener, 1984).

Respect for Autonomy. This principle refers to allowing other individuals the right to choose and to determine personal destiny. It is a particularly important value in the United States; one that requires care in both research and counseling and extreme sensitivity in the counseling research context. For example, vulnerability of clients to the influence of the therapist makes resolving issues related to autonomy of clients as research participants even more problematic than resolving such issues in other research contexts. As Beauchamp and Childress (1989) noted this principle involves both an attitude and actions on the part of professionals and ordinary citizens that enable others to act autonomously. Respect for autonomy is based on belief that the each individual is a person of intrinsic worth. Questions of autonomy can present complicated choices for professionals working with such individuals as minors, terminally ill patients, or others thought to have diminished judgmental capacity. Informed consent is one of the major issues rooted in the principle of autonomy.

Nonmaleficence. Reduced to its most elementary definition, *nonmaleficence* means "do no harm." Although few professionals would intentionally harm a client or a research participant, it is not always obvious what procedures may cause harm to others, now or later. For example, certain types of research could interfere with the therapeutic relationship in unknown ways. Professionals often have actual or perceived obligations to clients of diminished judgment; these obligations can take precedence over or at least be in conflict with respect for autonomy. When that happens the injunction of nonmaleficence is particularly important, as it is easy to assume less competency that is actually the case.

Beneficence. The principle of *beneficence* demands more of an individual than refraining from doing harm; this principle enjoins professionals and others to benefit (i.e., "do good for") others. For example, it might be far easier to establish that particular research projects or therapeutic procedures do no harm, than to establish that they are beneficial. Some scholars (e.g., Frankena, 1973) combine the notions of beneficence and nonmaleficence into a concept with several parts; but the Beauchamp and Childress (1989) distinction between the two seems important and meaningful for the counseling research context. Most psychologists would agree that counseling that the professional believes is not beneficial to the client should be terminated; it is not enough that we do no harm. Psychologists may have different ideas with respect to research; if the research participant is in no way harmed, it does not seem as crucial that he or she is benefitted. In the counseling research context decisions regarding the priority that should be given to beneficence and nonmaleficence often can be in conflict.

Justice.   This principle refers to the equitable distributions of burdens and benefits. The concept is easy to state but difficult to realize. Intuitive and professional judgments as well as legal constraints all are components of justice. Concerns of justice are inherent in each of the selected issues we review later. For example, when weighing the cost–benefit ratios of research, it often is difficult to weigh the burdens for a client of being an individual research participant against the potential benefits for future clients if something significant is learned from the research.

Fidelity.   This is a principle (as are veracity, confidentiality, and privacy) that is derived from the other four and its particular focus is on relationships. Kitchener (1984) said that for persons in therapeutic relationships the principle of fidelity is as important as the principles of respect for autonomy, nonmaleficence, beneficence, and justice. For professionals, the concern with fidelity seems especially appropriate because professional relationships are fiduciary relationships. The role of the professional (e.g., teacher, researcher, or counselor) in such a relationship requires certain responsibilities that are not necessarily encountered in everyday life. Although one may argue that all relationships have ethical responsibilities, counselors and researchers need to be particularly attentive to their power, the potential for abusing that power, and the danger of creating dual relationships. For instance, a researcher whose career is dependent on recruiting people to participate may consider incentives (e.g., free or reduced-fee therapy) as a means of obtaining research participants. Although this could be acceptable, the ethics of specific incentives in specific situations with specific individuals need to be carefully considered. Fidelity means fulfilling one's responsibilities of trust in a relationship. When counselors ask clients to participate in research, this can raise concern related to the appropriateness of the request and its effect on the trust level of the counseling relationship.

This brief discussion of principles indicates their overlap and possible conflict with one another. For example, how should one decide between the principles of preventing harm or doing good when contrasted with infringing upon a person's autonomy? If, as sometimes happens, clients do not decide matters in their own best interest, when, if ever, does a therapist intervene? These principles just discussed are not exhaustive, but they can serve as a guide to decision making. Codes of ethics provide some help; but often they are written as much to protect the profession as to assist in individual decision making. Even the principles on which professional associations have based their codes of conduct may not be made explicit. The codes may say little about specific decision making when conflict occurs. Here, we hope to demonstrate how principles are more encompassing than rules; yet less abstract than theories and can be applied to the problems of making ethical decisions in the counseling research context.

SELECTED ISSUES

Therapeutic Relationship

The relationship between counselor and client is special, a frequent topic of research and discussion in the literature, and a pivotal concern of most practitioners. When interacting with their counselors, clients often reenact significant relationships from their lives and demonstrate their ways of relating with others. As this occurs, there is great potential for distorting the purposes of the relationship or for misinterpreting the meaning of certain participant actions. Usually, clients who come for help are psychologically vulnerable, experience loss of control, perceive an inability to manage their own lives, and are in search of some kind of solution for their discomfort. These relationship and participant characteristics make a therapeutic alliance, which many believe to be a central factor in successful therapy, different from most other relationships.

A therapeutic alliance is a professional relationship in which certain actions that are appropriate in other relationships or are appropriate for the client in a counseling relationship are inappropriate for the professional. These actions are considered to be inappropriate because they violate the principle of fidelity. For example, it is considered appropriate for friends to share their personal troubles, but not appropriate for a counselor to do so with a client. Both the counseling process and the therapeutic alliance that develops can be considered contractual arrangements with implicit and often explicit promises between counselor and client. Each party trusts the other to be faithful to his or her obligations and promises contained within that contract. In the counseling contract the professional is obligated to act in the best interests of the client, to preserve confidentiality and privacy for the client and to maintain proper professional or relational boundaries. Therapy or counseling is an intimate relationship where the expectation that clients be candid and self-disclosing renders them dependent on the ethical behavior of the therapist to maintain the therapeutic contract and not to exploit the vulnerability that accompanies candidness and self-disclosure. One form of exploitation is a dual relationship (i.e., influencing the client to relate with the therapist in some way other than as a client). Such dual relationships can range from the seemingly innocuous, such as asking a client to "baby sit" one's children, to the very serious; for example, borrowing large sums of money from clients or asking them for dates. Any request that induces the client to change the nature of the relationship defined by the counseling contract, and thus creating a dual relationship, can be seen as a potential violation of the principle of fidelity or fulfilling one's promise of trust.

According to Beauchamp and Childress (1989), fidelity derives from other principles, in particular, that of respect for autonomy. One can see how the nature of therapy increases the importance of this principle and why Kitchener (1984) considered it a significant one for professionals in helping relationships. For our purposes here, the issues explored with respect to counseling research also must take into consideration the therapeutic relationship and the principle of fidelity. A significant question with respect to all research in the counseling context is the effect of the research or the effect of asking clients and therapists to participate in the research on the therapeutic alliance and the contractual obligations of counseling. It can be helpful to professionals in weighing the pros and cons of research to start by analyzing questions related to the principle of fidelity.

The research relationship between investigator and participant also raises questions of fidelity; but these questions become much more complex when entangled with the therapeutic relationship. The contract of the research relationship, particularly in psychological research differs markedly from the counseling or therapy relationship. Usually, the research relationship is more transient and much less personal. The participant often engages in the research to assist the researcher, make a contribution to science, or to achieve some other unrelated goal such as course credit or money. As contrasted with certain research endeavors in medicine, the psychology research participant typically is not seeking an experimental treatment for some disorder for which there is no known effective treatment or cure. A major difference between the counseling relationship and the research relationship has to do with who is the beneficiary; there is little question that in counseling it is the client, but that is less clear in psychological research. Typically, participants in such research accrue no major benefits. Some would argue, however, that each of us has an obligation to society to participate in some research that will benefit the common good but is of no specific benefit to the participants. A researcher or therapist who stands to gain by the research must be careful in advancing such an argument to potential participants.

The nature of the contract and thus the understandings of what it means for the professional (i.e., either researcher or counselor) to be faithful to the nonprofessional (i.e., either participant or client) provide us with a primary example of the differences in the accepted values of the two cultures. Each culture answers questions of fidelity differently, which means careful consideration is needed to reconcile the views before research is begun within the counseling context. It is not surprising that often there are difficulties between those who are primarily researchers and those who are primarily therapists regarding the appropriateness of certain kinds of research with clients. These groups have different views and obligations with respect to issues of fidelity which influence all the decisions regarding research in the counseling context. From the therapist's point of view, the researcher must demonstrate why the proposed research may qualify for overriding the *prima facie* binding requirements of fidelity to the therapeutic contract. Because all such research potentially poses a dual relationship, the burden of proof that the benefits of the research outweigh its negative effects is more stringent. Determining such an issue is the responsibility of both counselors and researchers. They need to realize that either course of action (i.e., conducting or not conducting the research) could contain negative consequences for the person or for the advancement of science.

Informed Consent

One of the most difficult issues in any professional relationship and in particular in the research relationship is that of informed consent. Since the Nuremburg trials following the defeat of Nazi Germany, there has been extensive discussion about this concept and its abuse. Some scholars believe that it is not possible for persons to be fully informed about what participation in a future event, such as a research project, would mean for them. Therefore, these scholars would maintain that informed consent is not possible. Even if this were true, it seems unwise, if not impossible to halt either therapy or research in search of the unattainable goal of fully informed consent. From a practical perspective, therefore, it is necessary to have the consent of research participants and clients; to provide as much relevant information as possible; and to present that information in a supportive noncoercive manner.

The principle of greatest concern in informed consent decisions is that of autonomy. The questions become: Does an individual's participation in research about personal therapy represent free choice? Does the individual have the relevant information to make that choice? and Is the individual competent to make such choices? These questions represent the criteria of voluntariness, information, and competency. These three conditions need to be present before informed consent can be said to exist (Beauchamp & Childress, 1989). With respect to researching the counseling process, the nature of the therapeutic relationship makes questions about voluntariness especially sensitive. It is reasonable to believe that if the counselor asks a client to participate in research, it could be difficult for the client to refuse. The client is being asked to do something that is not typically part of therapy, and probably will have no direct benefit for the client. The counselor is risking a dual relationship, and using the therapeutic alliance to further a nontherapeutic purpose. On the other hand, knowledge about facilitating therapy may be helpful to the client and to future clients. One can argue that the present client/research participant is the beneficiary of past research and may have a responsibility to consider participation. On the other hand, there are clients who are extremely anxious to please their therapist. One needs to exercise even more caution with such clients than with those who are able to freely exercise their autonomous right to refuse participation.

The issues of competency and the providing of relevant information may be easier to resolve than the issue of voluntariness in the counseling research context. Apart from the influence of the therapeutic relationship, most therapists are qualified to assess if a person is competent to make a decision about participation in research. Extremely psychotic individuals, very young children, and persons suffering from severe organic brain syndromes probably are not competent to give consent. The more intrusive the procedure, the higher the level of competence required.

Although there is no indisputable test of what information is relevant and how much is sufficient, one can make judgments about the aspects of a research project (e.g., invasion of privacy, excessive time commitment) likely to be relevant to most individuals considering participation. There is no way to know what information may be idiosyncratic to a particular individual and would be considered by that person as "relevant" to the consent decision. It is important, therefore, to present as much information as possible, be sensitive, responsive, and open to all questions, and allow ample time for decision making. Time to invite and discuss participation should not be taken from the therapy hour, so additional time is required. Often, the therapist is not involved in the request to participate but may be asked for advice by the client. Even when the request comes from someone other than the counselor, it may be difficult for a counselor to balance the importance of research and the autonomy of clients. Most people in the helping professions want to encourage both values.

In the final analysis, every situation that requires informed consent needs to be decided on a case by case basis. Although the benefits and costs in some decisions seem greater than in others, each decision is critical to virtually everyone in the helping professions. Both researchers and practitioners, in effect, create policy every time they make a decision and each decision has potential for shaping some part of the public's image of science and practice. The obvious question is: Have I as a counselor or researcher respected the autonomy of clients to decide whether to participate in research related to their counseling? When a researcher has much to gain by the completion of a project, it is difficult not to use whatever influence one has to recruit participants. Clients are particularly vulnerable and the participation requested of them often is more personal than what is expected from participants in other kinds of psychological research. In counseling situations, requests for participation could be infringements upon respect for autonomy.

Research Design and Procedures

Contemporary experimental research designs favor random assignment of participants to research conditions. Such experimental designs often are at odds with the realities of everyday life. For example, it is difficult to obtain parental permission to randomly assign elementary school children to specific classrooms or teachers for research purposes. Most parents want their children to have the "best" teachers and the "best" instruction, rather than to have them assigned randomly to an instructor or a method of teaching for experimental purposes.

Clients may have similar concerns. Counseling is a difficult, personal enterprise that many clients begin with reluctance. To add the constraints of true experimental designs (Campbell & Stanley, 1966) to this situation requires careful reflection. Professionals can be guided in such reflection by the principles of nonmaleficence and beneficence. Compromises to true experimental design need to be considered in establishing the protocols for and interpreting the results of research in the counseling context. The dilemma can be conceptualized as not doing experimental research, and thus not knowing the effectiveness of therapy, but eliminating harm to clients by research procedures as contrasted with conducting many experimental studies of counseling effectiveness because it seems unethical to treat clients without a firm scientific basis. For example, it seems unreasonable to assign clients to wait lists if counselors are available; yet if one needs to know the effects of spontaneous remission, this is a method, although it is surely imperfect, to obtain such information. But we must consider the question of whether a client who may finally have decided to seek help will be harmed by having to wait; and thus would the therapist or researcher have violated the principle of nonmaleficence without compelling reason. The principle that might supercede the *prima facie* obligation to "do no harm" is the principle of beneficence. From a beneficence perspective one could question whether we are meeting our responsibilities to future clients if we refrain from conducting research relevant to counseling effectiveness.

In research on counseling/therapy process, it would seem that the quality of the research design and the importance of the information it could provide must be even more highly scrutinized than in more typical, noncounseling psychological research situations. In the latter, the dangers of violating the principle of nonmaleficence may not be as great because the participants are less vulnerable. Typically these participants are students in psychology courses who are not seeking therapy, have a variety of projects from which to choose, and have alternatives for credit to participation in research activities.

Related to the issue of research design are those of informed consent that become even more complex with experimental research in the counseling context than with naturalistic descriptive research. For instance, telling participants their group assignment (e.g., experimental, control, other treatment control) could result in threats to the integrity of the design such as specific group "mortality" or "subject demoralization." Such threats negatively affect the validity of the inferences one can make from the data. If participants perceive one group as being preferred (e.g., not having to be on a waiting list) the results could be confounded by influences of being "preferentially treated" as contrasted with a less biased test of the variables of interest. For researchers not to explain about the research in detail runs the risk of violating participants' autonomy as they may not have sufficient information to make an informed judgment. Either course of action has consequences for the integrity of both the research and counseling enterprises. One could argue that with the exceptions that must be made to random assignment (e.g., in emergencies) and the problems with informed consent, true experimental research is not possible in the counseling context.

Naturalistic observations or other nonexperimental studies that do not require assignment to research conditions, are less problematic but not free from ethical considerations. If the appropriate consents are obtained, the threats to the relationship minimized or eliminated, and there is no exploitation or dual relationship problems, one still has to contend with the ethical issue of justice. Psychological research participants often are rewarded, however minimally, for their assistance. They receive such things as small sums of money, course credit, or coupons that can be redeemed for food or other goods. In some funded research, where it may be difficult to obtain participants who meet specific sample requirements, larger incentives may be provided. Typically, in counseling research there are few incentives or satisfactory ways to offer them. If reduced fees for therapy are offered, the counselor or the agency, who may or may not be conducting the research, bears the cost. If the researcher compensates the agency in money or service, the client does not benefit. In many instances a just solution may be to provide small monetary rewards to clients, but for the relationship reasons discussed here the counselor should not provide them. If the incentives are very small, the reward matter may not be important, but we may question whether those research participants from whom we ask the most, (i.e., those who are vulnerable and seeking help) may receive the least in return. Clients, therapists, and others may wish to participate for altruistic reasons, but the issue of justice with respect to personal benefit could be an important one. Even when significant incentives, such as substantial fee reductions, can be provided, then justice issues arise as to which clients should be offered the opportunity to participate, and how those decisions should be made.

Risk–Benefit Ratios

In professional life, resolving ethical dilemmas often hinges on deciding whether to risk an exception to a *prima facie* principle in hopes of obtaining a benefit great enough to justify the risk or the exception. A therapist might restrict the autonomy of clients whom the therapist believes are not acting or might not act in their own best interest and whose actions could result in greater harm than could be done by violating the principle of respect for autonomy. The threat of suicide is an example. Or with appropriate consultations and review board approvals, a researcher might deceive research participants and thus limit their ability to make an informed judgment with respect to participation in the project. If such deception is essential to conducting the research, the risk of harm is minimal, and if the potential benefits to science and by inference other persons is substantial, there may be few if any, ethical problems.

Although there are no formulae to apply to this process, professionals making decisions about research in the counseling context, can inform those decisions and the process of making them by weighing the importance of each of the relevant principles in a cost–benefit manner from several perspectives. However, with no established method for evaluating the applicability of the principles (i.e., respect for autonomy, nonmaleficence, beneficence, justice, and fidelity) to a specific dilemma presented in the counseling research context, underlying conflicts arise. In part, there is conflict between the perspective of the researcher whose priority is the pursuit of knowledge and the perspective of the counselor whose priority is the welfare of the client. Equally important are the perspectives and values of the community, the client/participant, and others who may be asked to participate, such as therapists and supervisors.

It does not take much imagination to envision the sophisticated ethical judgments required to resolve these problems. The rights and obligations of individuals and the societies that sustain them are often in conflict. It is not necessarily valid to assume that what is good for a specific individual is good for a society, nor is it necessarily valid to assume the opposite. Even if there was agreement on what constitutes the common good, it would be difficult to establish the obligations, if any, of individual citizens in contributing to that good. The counseling research context is a case in point: what might be best for the client might not be helpful to science; what science needs most, knowledge, could often be detrimental to clients if they help provide that knowledge. Even after a cost–benefit decision is made (e.g., pursue the research in question or not pursue it), in many instances it is hard to judge if the decision has been correct. And in some cases it is difficult to reach any decision without making an exception to some *prima facie* principle, or favoring one perspective (e.g., the client's or the researcher's) over another. Instruction and practice in weighing cost–benefit ratios of all the principles from multiple perspectives would seem helpful to professionals in developing sophisticated skills in ethical decision making.

Special Populations

Since the mid-1960s, the helping professions have focused increasing attention on the needs and rights of special populations. Such focus is appropriate from an ethical perspective as well as from the perspective of developing sound science and practice (Meara, 1990). Special populations have special needs and researchers and practitioners have responsibilities to be aware of those needs and their abilities to fulfill them.

Special populations may be divided into two groups for purposes of our discussion here: those with reduced competency, and those who are distinctive in ways other than reduced competency. Minors, some mentally retarded individuals, persons with severe psychotic conditions, and others with diminished mental capacities are included in the first category. The second category consists of persons who feel or who have been treated by society as distinctive by virtue of such characteristics as gender, race, cultural heritage, religious orientation, age, associational preference, or physical disabilities. For example, men who come for counseling may feel self-conscious and distinctive as seeking professional help is a less common occurrence for men than for women. Psychological researchers and practitioners are ethically bound to understand those who are distinctive; and to be aware that assumptions they may make about clients and research participants (e.g., with regard to such things as informed consent, the implicit agreements of the therapeutic alliance, the values of research and other matters) who are much like themselves may not apply as well to members of groups who are less like them.

Minors ordinarily cannot give consent, and although it is generally legal for parents to consent for their children, there is debate among ethicists about this. Is it ethical for parents to consent to experimental procedures that have little chance of benefitting their children, or run the risk of causing pain, discomfort, or other harm to them? For minors and others in this first category who are not fully competent even greater caution is required in soliciting their participation in research. It also is important not to underestimate their competence. Although a guardian may have the legal right to consent, it is important from an ethical perspective to provide the less competent with information and choices appropriate to their abilities and where possible respect their autonomy by providing them opportunities to assent (cf. Code of Federal Regulation, 1983). Children who are quite young and others in this category can grasp the meaning of fairly complicated procedures and have coherent opinions about their willingness to participate.

For individuals in the distinctive category the issue is not so much competency, but providing a climate to facilitate voluntary choices and the information needed to make those choices. Often members of these groups are in or perceive themselves to be in an inferior or disadvantaged position with respect to the professional and to the policies of research or counseling. It is possible to exploit such individuals as a "captive audience" for research. For example, persons on welfare who receive psychological services may not understand that they have choices with respect to research participation, but may believe that they are obligated to participate as a means of paying for the service.

Another special population that deserves mention consists of those clients who are participating in group counseling. As the group literature has shown (cf. e.g., Davis, 1980) confidentiality can never be assured by a group leader. Although the leader or the research directors may keep the confidences of group members, they cannot guarantee that the other research participants will. This point needs to be emphasized when asking group members to participate in research about their counseling experiences where that being investigated is public to other group members. Researchers and group leaders can foster policies about appropriate behavior outside the group, but cannot guarantee that these policies will be honored.

GUIDELINES FOR DECISION MAKING

The discussion presented here is not meant to imply that research cannot be conducted in the counseling context without violating some ethical principle. Most of the research conducted in this context is ethical beyond question. In addition, one must not confuse an ethical violation with making an exception to a *prima facie* principle when it seems that a conflicting principle takes precedence. It is apparent that in many instances there are no clearcut answers to ethical dilemmas. Often researchers and practitioners are compelled to deliberate and exercise their best judgment, using principles such as those of Beauchamp and Childress (1989) discussed earlier.

How is good judgment on ethical issues developed? Psychology and other helping professions attempt to recruit students of good judgment and good will and expose them to instruction, experiences, and consultations in ethical decision making. Although this provides a beginning, increasing ethical decision-making skills are part of career-long professional development. The following are offered as guidelines that might prove useful in this development.

1. One of the professional's best resources in resolving dilemmas is collegial consultation. This can be particularly helpful when a professional is confronting decisions related to a dual relationship. For instance, if the therapist is the researcher, his or her judgment about the appropriateness of asking a client to participate in a research project could be influenced by the desire to complete the work. Or this same therapist could err in the opposite direction by refraining from asking clients whose participation would be appropriate and who in fact might welcome the opportunity. Trusted, knowledgeable colleagues who do not have the same investment in the project as the therapist/researcher are better able to make such judgments or advise about them.

Collegial consultation may concern hypothetical issues that could arise in counseling research and ways to avoid or resolve them. Such discussions not only serve as practice in decision making, they also provide opportunities to develop designs that may accomplish the purposes of the research without raising ethical problems. Being available to colleagues for such consultation is an intellectually stimulating and enjoyable way to learn about other perspectives and strategies.

2. Another guideline to decision making relates to interactions with institutional review boards (IRBs). IRBs were created to prevent re-occurrences of past abuses, especially in the biomedical, social, and behavioral sciences. In recent decades, more emphasis has been placed on the responsibilities of institutions to respect the rights of citizens. IRBs are one means of fulfilling those responsibilities. The complaints made at professional meetings by researchers about some action of their IRBs suggest that an adversarial relationship develops between the IRB and the scientist. At times this may be necessary, but as a general strategy, a more collegial approach is recommended in which researchers and IRB members attempt to view themselves as collaborative partners in developing significant and ethical research projects. If no one on the IRB is in the researcher's discipline or shares his or her philosophy of science, conflicts may arise. If so, these may create opportunities to inform the IRB members about one's point of view. The same collaborative approach is recommended when one is a member of an IRB, and in particular, when confronted with an adversarial-minded scientist.

3. Another guideline is to learn from ethical decisions by evaluating their consequences. Psychologists characteristically examine research results carefully; and many are experts at program evaluation. But there seems to be little systematic evaluation of the consequences of a sequence of ethical de-

cisions, particularly ethical decisions made in the counseling research context. For example, we do not typically ask participants after they have completed their participation how a deception affected them, or how free they felt to refuse to participate or how likely they would be to withdraw their data later if they began to feel uncomfortable about having it on record. Researchers and practitioners in the counseling context do not routinely ask clients their views with respect to how their research participation may have affected the therapeutic relationship, or how being in therapy may have influenced their feelings of freedom to refuse to participate in the research. Even if some of these topics are discussed informally with clients who are research participants, there seems to be little systematic investigation of these issues. Although, as noted earlier, there are many ways to judge the ethical acceptability of a course of action, one important criterion for judging is to evaluate its consequences. Data with respect to consequences could provide important directions for future ethical decision making.

A SUMMING UP AND A LOOK AHEAD

This chapter has reviewed some ideas related to ethical decision making in the counseling research context. A major premise of the discussion has been that the values, goals, and mores of the counseling and research cultures are different, thus complicating the resolution of ethical dilemmas. We have presented some ethical principles developed by Beauchamp and Childress (1989) to anchor the discussion of ethical issues and to be applied to situations where a decision is in doubt or "accomplishing one good is in conflict with accomplishing another good." We acknowledge that these principles are not exhaustive, can overlap with one another, and are often in conflict. We have presented examples of how these principles relate to the counseling research context; and we have presented some guidelines for assisting professionals to learn more about the principles and their application to ethical decisions. We close with some thoughts about the future in that special arena of professional life where science, practice and ethics intersect.

The future bodes to hold more complexity for those who must make ethical decisions in daily life, professional life, and in the counseling research context. Principles (e.g., justice) will acquire additional meaning as increasing numbers of persons from diverse backgrounds enter the professions and develop and interpret ethical policy. Questions will be raised as to what the principles are and how they ought to be applied. For example, the nature of what it means to be faithful to an explicit or implied contract with a research participant/client will change in the future as it has in the past.

The increasing complexity of ethical decision making and the increasing diversity and pluralism between and within the research and practice communities may exacerbate the value differences between these two cultures. Such events could prevent further development of the scientist practitioner model. From an ethical point of view this could have a very adverse effect on research in the counseling context. In fact, for such research to flourish requires the opposite to occur. The researcher and the practitioner need common ground to promote knowledge and human welfare for particular individuals and for society in general. Doing research in the counseling context requires knowledge and skill in science, practice, and ethical decision making. At a time when it is important for professionals to learn more about both science and practice, they seem to be specializing in one or the other. Among other things that leaves them less aware of the ethical issues involved in the arena in which they are not specializing.

There are many factors in the academy and in professional life that seem to be bifurcating science and practice. Some are innocuous enough such as having enough time to learn about both; but the result for the disciplines and professions and those they serve are the same. Clients who are research participants can be adversely affected if those who are conducting the research do not understand the mores, customs and routines of therapy, or if those who do therapy do not understand the mores, customs and routines of research. Ethical reflection can be a means of providing some common ground for science and practice. Such reflection also can provide a foundation for ethical decision making. For those interested in counseling and research, few topics are more critical than conducting research in the counseling context. Applying ethical principles to this context in deciding how the research should be conducted is critically important from the point of view of the client/ participant.

The future development of counseling psychology and like specialties can be enhanced by a more knowledgeable integration of science and practice, more knowledge about nuances of applied ethics, and more highly developed skills in ethical decision making. This is especially true for persons who choose to work in the counseling research context. Both the pursuit of knowledge and the protection of individual client/participants demand such integration, knowledge, and skills. All client/participants deserve no less.

ACKNOWLEDGMENT

The authors would like to thank Professor Jeanne D. Day of the University of Notre Dame for her expert comments on earlier drafts of this chapter.

REFERENCES

American Psychological Association. (1981a). *Ethical principles of psychologists.* Washington, DC: Author.

American Psychological Association. (1981b). Specialty guidelines for the delivery of services by counseling psychologists. *American Psychologist, 36,* 652–663.

American Psychological Association. (1982). *Ethical principles in the conduct of research with human participants* (rev. ed.). Washington, DC: Author.

American Psychological Association. (1990). Ethical principles of psychologists (Amended June 2, 1989). *American Psychologist,* 390–395.

Beauchamp, T. L., & Childress, J. F. (1979). *Principles of biomedical ethics.* New York: Oxford University Press.

Beauchamp, T. L., & Childress, J. F. (1983). *Principles of biomedical ethics* (2nd ed.). New York: Oxford University Press.

Beauchamp. T. L., & Childress, J. F. (1989). *Principles of biomedical ethics* (3rd ed.). New York: Oxford University Press.

Blackstone, W. T. (1975). The American Psychological Association code of ethics for research involving human participants: An appraisal. *The Southern Journal of Philosophy, 13,* 407–418.

Campbell, D. T., & Stanley, J. C. (1966). *Experimental and quasi experimental designs for research.* Chicago: Rand McNally.

Code of Federal Regulation, Title 45 Public Welfare. (1983, March 8). Washington, DC: Department of Health and Human Services, National Institutes of Health, Office of Protection from Research Risks.

Davis, K. L. (1980). Is confidentiality in group counseling realistic? *Personnel and Guidance Journal, 59,* 197–201.

Drane, J. F. (1982). Ethics and psychotherapy: A philosophical perspective. In M. Rosenbaum (Ed.), *Ethics and values in psychotherapy: A guidebook* (pp. 15–50). New York: The Free Press.

Flexner, S. B. (1987). *The random house dictionary of the English language, unabridged* (2nd ed.). New York: Random House.

Frankena, W. (1973). *Ethics* (2nd ed.). Englewood Cliffs, NJ: Prentice-Hall.

Hare, R. (1981). The philosophical basis of psychiatric ethics. In S. Block & P. Chodoff (Eds.), *Psychiatric ethics* (pp. 31–45). Oxford: Oxford University Press.

Jordan, A. E., & Meara, N. M. (1990). Ethics and the professional practice of psychologists. *Professional Psychology, 21,* 101–112.

Kitchener, K. S. (1984). Intuition, critical evaluation and ethical principles. *The Counseling Psychologist, 21*(3), 43–55.

Meara, N. M. (1990). Science, practice and politics. *The Counseling Psychologist, 18,* 144–167.

Schmidt, L. D., & Meara, N. M. (1984). Ethical, professional and legal issues in counseling psychology. In S. D. Brown & R. W. Lent (Eds.), *Handbook of counseling psychology* (pp. 56–96). New York: Wiley.

Stricker, G. (1982). Ethical issues in psychotherapy research. In M. Rosenbaum (Ed.), *Ethics and values in psychotherapy: A guidebook* (pp. 403–426). New York: The Free Press.

Williams, J. (1987). *Eyes on the prize: American civil rights years, 1954–1965.* New York: Viking.

9

THE PLACE
OF THE COMPUTER IN
COUNSELING RESEARCH

James P. Sampson, Jr.
Florida State University

The computer has been associated with counseling research for some time. Since the 1950s, the computer has become an increasingly valuable tool in the statistical analysis of data. At first computers were used to improve the speed at which traditional hand calculations were completed. Today computers are being used to complete calculations that far exceed the practical capacity of human beings. As a result, new and more powerful options for statistical analysis are evolving. It is difficult to imagine completing a major counseling research project today without the assistance of a computer.

The potential of the computer to facilitate research is, however, only being partially realized. The most dominant use of the computer in counseling research occurs in statistical analysis of data and in the preparation of manuscripts via word processing. Many other potential uses of the computer in research exist. In order to more fully use the capabilities of the computer in support of the research process, researchers need to become more fully informed of the potential benefits and limitations of this technological resource. This chapter is intended to explore potential uses of the computer in support of counseling research, both as a tool and a topic of research (Sampson, 1990a). The chapter begins with an examination of the computer as a *tool* for research in terms of research planning, presentation of treatment conditions, data collection, data analysis, and dissemination of results. The computer is then examined as a *topic* for research in terms of impact on individuals and impact on service delivery. *Ethical issues* related to the use of computers in counseling research are explored, as are *implications* for the use of this technology. The chapter concludes with a reminder of the importance of maintaining a balanced perspective with regard to the *role* of the computer in counseling research.

THE COMPUTER AS A TOOL FOR RESEARCH

The computer has the potential to influence, either directly or indirectly, almost every aspect of the research process in counseling. In the following section, current and potential contributions of computer technology are explored in relation to research planning, presentation of treatment conditions, data collection, data analysis, and dissemination of results.

Research Planning

Effective planning is critical to the conduct of valid and generalizable research. The majority of research problems emanate from this stage of the research process. Computer technology can be used to facilitate literature reviews, reference management, research design, and collaboration among researchers.

Literature Reviews. A comprehensive review of the literature is an essential initial step in research planning. A traditional manual search of bibliographic indexes, however, is a tedious and time-consuming process. CD-ROM systems and modems can improve the efficiency and effectiveness of literature reviews. Using a CD-ROM, which is a small laser disk mass storage device connected to a microcomputer, multiple key word searches of a large bibliographic database (e.g., PsycLIT, ERIC, Dissertation Abstracts International) can be completed. Using a modem, which allows the transfer of data between computers via telephone lines, remote catalogs, and databases can be searched from the home or office (Dickel, 1988). Research planning is potentially enhanced due to the greater comprehensiveness of the review of the literature that in turn provides the foundation for research.

A word of caution, however, is needed in relation to computer-assisted bibliographic searches. A search is only as effective as the key terms used in the search process. Individuals who create key word descriptors for a manuscript (typically the author or an indexer) may use widely divergent schemas for identifying the relevant content of a paper. For example, the key term *computer* may be selected by one person, whereas the term *information technology* may be selected by a second person, both referring to the same concept in a document. The failure to search by all relevant key terms can result in the failure to locate important references. A brief traditional manual search to identify the range of typical key terms related to a particular topic, or consulting with a reference librarian skilled in the bibliographic search process, can minimize this problem. Problems may also occur when key citations of historical value are omitted from a search because the database is limited to relatively recent research.

Reference Management. Research is generally enhanced by adopting a programmatic approach. By investigating numerous aspects of a single or related topics in a sequential manner, the knowledge gained from one research effort informs and extends subsequent research. The literature accumulated by a researcher becomes the cornerstone of programmatic research. As the literature base grows, however, problems in managing the literature grow as well. The database management capability of present microcomputers offers at least a partial solution. Dickel (1988) stated, "Having a database management system working for you will enable the cataloguing of what has been read as well as the accessing of specific material by author, title, subject, journal, date, location, keyword(s), etc." (pp. 8–9). In this manner, researchers can create efficient customized databases that combine citations from multiple sources (e.g., PsycLIT, ERIC, Dissertation Abstracts International, technical reports, and unpublished manuscripts). Hutton and Hutton (1981) provide an example of a reference management system organized by type of document, subject area, topic(s), and summary/findings. Reference management software is now commercially available.

As with literature reviews, a word of caution is relevant. Although reference management systems have the potential to improve efficiency, the software invariably takes longer to learn how to use than initially anticipated. Most computer software has a fairly steep initial learning curve, taking longer to complete tasks at first, with efficiency improvements accruing gradually. In order to obtain the ultimate time savings, more time needs to be spent initially in learning how to complete tasks.

Research Design Planning. Following a comprehensive review of the literature, research questions are formulated (hypotheses may also be created), and a research methodology is planned. Many practitioners,[1] however, are reluctant to initiate research projects due to the complexity of the process discussed here. In particular, statistical analyses are often perceived as a formidable barrier to conducting research. Even when practitioners are willing to conduct research, decisions about statistical analyses tend to inappropriately dominate research planning.

Decision support systems (DSSs) have an important potential role to play in facilitating research planning. Although the term *DSS* has tended to be

---

[1]The term *practitioner* in this chapter refers to counselors, psychologists, and other mental health professionals who are qualified by virtue of their training and experience to engage in the delivery of counseling services.

used in a vague and imprecise manner (Ballantine, 1986), an explicit description of the characteristics of a decision support system has been provided by Vogel (1985, p. 68):

1. DSS are intended to be *supportive* to decision-makers, not to replace them;
2. DSS are aimed at *less well structured* problems which tend to lack complete specification;
3. DSS seek to *combine the use of models and analytic techniques* with more customary data access and retrieval functions;
4. DSS are *interactive and "friendly"* to the decision-maker, and thus seek to be supportive to users who are not "computer people;"
5. DSS are intentionally *flexible* in order to adapt to changes in the organization's environment and to the needs of the decision-maker;
6. DSS often involve the use of *large data bases* whose structure and content may be overwhelming to the decision-maker in absence of supportive tools.

The nature of the research-planning process and the resources typically used are congruent with the DSS characteristics just described. A DSS for research planning for an empirical study could function in the following manner. The researcher or student would begin by formulating a research question. The DSS would clarify the research question, identifying the implicit independent and dependent variables, as well as the relationships among variables. Potential problems in terms of omissions and inconsistencies could be noted by the DSS, with necessary changes being made by the researcher. If hypotheses are appropriate, they could be formulated by the researcher with prompting from the DSS. Potential problems with the hypotheses could then be noted by the DSS and revised by the researcher. The DSS could then assist the researcher in identifying appropriate measures for the dependent and independent variables, checking for the existence of appropriate reliability and validity. The DSS could then suggest alternative research designs, with the researcher making the appropriate selection. The necessary sample size could then be calculated and procedures for sample selection in relation to the research questions could be clarified by the DSS. The researcher could then list potential procedures to be used in applying the treatment and control conditions, with clarification provided by the DSS in terms of inconsistencies or omissions. A sample research participation release form could be generated by the DSS. The DSS could then suggest alternative statistical analyses based on the research questions and related hypotheses, number and nature of independent and dependent variables, research design, and sample characteristics. The availability of DSSs to facilitate research planning also would provide an important instructional resource for graduate courses in counseling research.

Computer-Assisted Research Collaboration.   Many research efforts, especially empirical studies, are completed by multiple authors. It is not uncommon for individuals who are collaborating on a research project to reside in different geographic locations. Various forms of telecommunication allow researchers in remote locations to contribute to research planning by sharing ideas (via *electronic mail* on a one-to-one basis or via *computer conferencing* on a group basis), and by exchanging text and numerical data (via *electronic file transfer* or *facsimile transfer*). A microcomputer with a modem and communications software or a FAX machine is required. The ability to send and receive messages at any time as well as to transmit text and numerical data, represent important advantages over the traditional telephone call. However, the previous caveat about the time investment required to learn the new technology before realizing the benefits of improved efficiency also applies to telecommunication.

Presentation of Treatment Conditions

When a computer is used in the presentation of treatment conditions, a standardized presentation of the stimulus is possible (Jepsen, 1990; Katz & Shatkin, 1987; Meier, 1989). For example, a computer-assisted instruction program on a specific topic, such as study skills, presents a standardized treatment for each subject. Katz (1990) stated:

> it is often difficult to define actual counseling treatments, and therefore to ascribe outcomes to specified treatments and to compare the effects of one treatment with another. The treatment represented by a computerized [career guidance] system, on the other hand, is perfectly consistent. It may be responsive to individual differences, but the distinctive responses emerge from a consistent content and structure. "System" itself implies coherent structures and functions, an orderly attempt to accomplish certain specified purposes. These purposes, structures, functions, and all their components can be made accessible to scrutiny. Thus, effects of different treatments can be observed with the treatments explicitly defined. (p. 49)

Some computer applications, such as a large and diverse computer-assisted career guidance system, do allow considerable variability in the type and amount of assessment and instructional options that can be accessed by an individual user. By recording how each individual uses the available options provided by the system (this capability is described in the following section), objective verification of the treatment (Jepsen, 1990) is possible even for large and diverse computer applications.

Hummel, Lichtenberg, and Shaffer (1975) described CLIENT 1, a computer program that simulates the behavior of a client during an initial counseling interview. The simulation was designed for use in counselor education to help counselor trainees in facilitating client problem identification. The system was also designed to facilitate research on the theoretical aspects of the cognitive functioning of clients during counseling. By using a simulated client in the research process an increased degree of control was possible. According to Hummel, Shaffer, and Lichtenberg (1973), they have "already begun collecting protocol data from experienced counselors who talk out loud as they make decisions concerning what to say next to CLIENT 1" (p. 4). Using this approach, data are available from both the computer record and counselor statements. Lichtenberg, Hummel, and Shaffer (1984) stated:

> as a research medium, CLIENT 1 provides a standardized problem-solving task environment for counselors. By permitting a slowing down of the counseling process, it becomes possible for researchers to study the ways counselors make moment to moment decisions regarding what to say to their clients, how they recognize affect, how they construct reflections, how they generate interpretations, and how they decide when to reflect and when to probe or when to interpret. (p. 165)

Lichtenberg (1984) described INTERACT, a computer program used to facilitate counselor trainees' understanding of the process of interpersonal influence in counseling. The program can also be used to facilitate research on social influence in counseling.

Data Collection

The unique data collection and storage capacities of the computer make it practical to conduct research that previously was prohibitively difficult or impossible (Space, 1981). Computer applications such as computer-assisted instruction programs or computer-assisted career guidance systems can be programmed to include unobtrusive measures of subject performance. Katz (1990) stated the following:

> There was another feature of the original SIGI [System of Interactive Guidance and Information] that I was particularly enamored of. That was the program to capture, for a random sample of every nth user, an individual record of each student's path through the system, and also to cumulate statistics across all users. The individual record was retrieved only with the informed consent of each person, and anonymity was preserved in publications. A printout of the individual record served as a powerful tool for understanding how people used the system and for related research in CDM [career decision making]: A researcher could trace consistencies across the various sections for a given user, could ex-

amine differences in CDM between defined subgroups, and could use the record as a basis for focused interviews to enrich and deepen understanding of each step of the CDM process. With interviewer and student both looking at the record the interviewer could find out why students responded as they did, what they had in mind, and what they carried away from a given set of interactions. The individual record opened a new "window" on the CDM process as it was actually taking place. (p. 48)

Norris, Katz, and Chapman (1982) examined gender differences in career decision making using the unobtrusive data-collection capability of SIGI just discussed.

Another form of unobtrusive data collection involves the collection of ancillary data during computer-assisted test administration. Ancillary data can include random rapid response patterns, testee fatigue, and changes in response latencies for items comprising a specific scale (Stout, 1981). The computer can automatically collect and analyze data on client behavior in relation to various items and computer-assisted test administration strategies (Sampson, 1990b).

Meier (1989) examined the validity of a computer-assisted instruction program on alcohol education as an unobtrusive measure of alcohol consumption. The results indicated that unobtrusive blood alcohol level measures were valid and reliable. When clients were aware the computer was recording answers to interview questions (an obtrusive measure), Lucas, Mullins, Luna, and McInroy (1977) found that clients were more honest in responding to a computer in comparison to a human interviewer.

Johnson, Hickson, Fetter, and Reichenbach (1987) used a microcomputer to provide instruction and unobtrusively collect data in a field setting. The authors stated the following advantages of this approach. First, programmatic research is enhanced. "Because the research procedure is operationalized as a computer program, research questions derived from one study can often be addressed in subsequent studies by making minor, but substantive modifications in the program or by using the program with different populations of subjects" (p. 67). Second, replication of research and extension over time to include longitudinal data are now more feasible. Third, it is possible to obtain "precise, yet unobtrusive, cognitive, and affective measures in field settings" (p. 67). Fourth, a greater degree of experimental control is possible in the presentation of treatments and randomization of subject selection and assignment to treatments. Fifth, the administration of the treatment is more economical in terms of the reduced time required of the researcher.

Data Analysis

The computational power of the computer has proven to be an invaluable aid in statistical computation. Using computers for calculation has resulted in increased speed and accuracy over more traditional methods. Also, over time the nature of computations have evolved from the automation of traditional hand calculations (e.g., analysis of variance), to the development of new analytical techniques that would not be feasible without computer technology (e.g., LISREL analysis).

Microcomputers have had an important impact on the use of computers in data analysis. As a result of the increased data-processing speed and data-handling capacity of recent microcomputers, and the availability of newer high performance software, micros now have the capability to analyze data from most counseling research and evaluation efforts. Exceptionally large, complex, or unusual research and evaluation projects still require the extended capacity mainframe computers and software.

Several types of statistical analysis software are available for microcomputers. Relatively expensive versions of popular mainframe statistical software are available in microcomputer versions (although micro versions tend to have fewer capabilities in comparison with mainframe versions). Less expensive software designed expressly for micros is available ranging from fully featured integrated systems to software designed to run one particular statistic. Many of the systems discussed here can use standard ASCII numerical data files created by popular word-processing software. This capability allows the researcher or student to begin the analysis process (data entry) with familiar software. Dickel (1988) and Yager and Wilson (1986) noted that electronic spread sheets can also be used to analyze data. Although this type of software is typically limited in the range of statistical procedures available, the capacity for data input prompting, viewing cause-and-effect relationships as data changes, and developing graphic presentations of the data, represent useful features for the researcher.

Many practitioners and students, however, express little apparent interest in conducting research and evaluation studies. In my opinion, a factor contributing to this problem involves the perceptions that successful use of statistical software requires substantial mathematical aptitude and experience in computer programming. Many mainframe computers do in fact have relatively cumbersome operating systems (e.g., obscure error messages, complicated screen editors, obtuse program submission commands, inadequate input prompting, and confusing print routing procedures). This is not necessarily the case with microcomputers. The origins of the ease-of-use differences between mainframes and microcomputers lies in the typical intended user for each type of hardware. Large mainframe computers were designed for computer specialists and other professionals with substantial mathematical backgrounds. Highly technical operating systems posed relatively few problems for highly trained individuals who used the computer on a regular basis. Microcomputers, however, were designed for a large diverse group of users with varied mathematical aptitudes and varied experience with computers. Computer hardware and software that is difficult to operate simply does not sell. For the most part, microcomputer operating systems are easier to use in comparison to mainframe systems. This is particularly true for microcomputer operating systems that are more intuitive and use icons that represent various computer functions. In spite of these improvements, many practitioners and students have outmoded mainframe-based perceptions that are incongruent with current microcomputer characteristics. Effective training and experience can help to change these misconceptions.

Another issue related to the microcomputer involves the user's perceived degree of control over the computer. Microcomputers tend to operate as dedicated systems with one user in control at a time. Micros do not disconnect if too much time elapses between inputs, as is the case with many mainframe computers. Data can be "held" and transported in the form of floppy disks. The printer is usually directly connected to the microcomputer, providing immediate feedback in the form of data output. No other operator is required to make the system function, such as loading tape drives on mainframes. The microcomputer also can be seen and touched as opposed to the computer being in a secure remote location. In my opinion, this higher degree of individual control over computer hardware has the potential to help practitioners and students perceive themselves as more capable of successful use of statistical software.

Whether or not practitioners and students actually make effective use of available microcomputer statistical software depends on several factors. First, attitudes about computers and research, especially misconceptions related to mainframes and microcomputers, will need to be clarified. Second, realistic expectations need to be created about the time and effort required to become proficient with statistical software. Although microcomputer software is often easier to use in comparison with mainframe software, considerable time is still required initially to understand and effectively use the microcomputer operating system and statistical software. Third, a human support system is needed in the form of: (a) a network of practitioners and students using the same hardware and software who are willing to share their expertise; and (b) hardware and software specialists who are trained to provide expert consultation for problem situations.

Dissemination of Results

If the research goal of advancing theory and practice in counseling is to be realized, then the results of research studies need to be quickly and broadly disseminated. The traditional publishing time-lag of several months to several years for journal articles, monographs, and books, however, is a major barrier to rapid dissemination. Computer technology can be used to improve research dissemination via document preparation and telecommunication.

An issue related to referencing computer applications in research documents is also examined in this section.

Computer-Assisted Document Preparation. The preparation speed, accuracy, and presentation quality of documents can be improved with the use of several computer applications. Most manuscripts are currently prepared using word-processing software, with either the authors directly inputting text and data, or by having support staff input text and data from written rough drafts. Dickel (1988) stated, "With increased sophistication, word processing can incorporate software that checks spelling and grammar as well as that which provides a thesaurus for the writer" (p. 5). Software is also available that checks a document for congruence with APA style. By integrating graphics and word-processing software, additional options become available for creating camera-ready figures depicting theoretical constructs or data relationships. Desktop publishing can be used to eliminate the need for typesetting prior to publication (Dickel, 1988). By reducing publishing costs, this option provides researchers with the capability of publishing their own research in the form of research reports and monographs. In addition to the improved quality of presentation, more detailed reporting of research can be provided in comparison with typically shorter length journal articles. Research can also be disseminated without the time-lag associated with journal publication. Even after a shorter version is published as a journal article, research reports can then be disseminated to other researchers who need more detailed data tables, copies of instruments and forms, that are not typically included in journal articles.

Several advantages exist for authors to make direct use of word-processing software as opposed to delegating this function to support staff. First, it is possible to write and edit concurrently, thus saving time. Second, time is saved by not waiting for drafts to be keyed in by support staff. Third, accuracy is improved because no translation of text or data takes place. Fourth, portable computers can be used in libraries and other remote locations for note taking. With the outlining features of some word-processing software, these notes can be relatively easily edited and directly incorporated into the text of a document. Also references that accompany library notes can be directly imported into a final document, further saving time and reducing the chances of translation errors.

The improved preparation speed, accuracy, and presentation quality of documents made possible by computer technology is, however, not without cost. Far more significant than the cost of the hardware and software is the time necessary for the researcher to become a competent user of word-processing software and all of the attendant checking systems. Desktop publishing in particular requires many hours of training and use before anything beyond minimal proficiency is reached. Like many other activities, substantial investment in learning is a prerequisite to substantial gain in productivity.

Research Dissemination Via Telecommunication.   The technology used to support research collaboration, described earlier, can also be used to support dissemination functions. Completed research documents, data sets in numerical form, and annotated bibliographies can be transmitted almost anywhere in the world in a matter of minutes via electronic file transfer or facsimile transfer. Presentation of research abstracts and instruction for direct access of files can be included in electronic bulletin boards and electronic newsletters. Following initial dissemination, research methods, results, and conclusions can be discussed via electronic mail on a one-to-one basis or via computer conferencing on a group basis. With a microcomputer, modem, and communication software (or FAX machine), researchers can rapidly disseminate and receive feedback on research efforts. As before, an investment of time is required to make this possibility a reality.

Referencing Computer Applications.   When describing research that includes a computer application as part of the treatment, it is important for authors to provide a full APA style reference for the computer application. Reardon, Sampson, Ryan-Jones, Peterson, and Shahnasarian (1988) noted that computer applications change and evolve more quickly than traditional counseling and guidance resources due to the relatively low cost of disseminating new versions. This makes it difficult to generalize across versions of a particular system when major additions, deletions, or modifications have occurred in system content. Thus, it is important to clearly identify in research reports the exact version of the system that was used.

In general, the computer has an important role to play as a tool in counseling research. This role includes research planning, presentation of treatment conditions, data collection, data analysis, and dissemination of results. Continued improvements in computer hardware and software are likely to further increase the use of computers in counseling research. This type of increasing technological impact is not limited, however, to research functions. Almost every area of human endeavor is influenced to some extent by computers. The following section explores how the computer is an important topic for research in counseling.

THE COMPUTER AS A TOPIC FOR RESEARCH

The computer now influences, either directly or indirectly, almost every aspect of daily living. Because counseling deals with resolving problems of daily living, counseling research needs to examine the broad impact of the computer on individuals. Computer technology is also having an impact on the delivery of counseling services, especially in the areas of testing and career counseling and guidance. It is important to understand how this technology supports and/or limits the delivery of counseling services.

Examining the Impact of the Computer on Individuals

Skill in using computer applications is becoming increasingly important in education and work. Beginning as students, and later as employees, growing numbers of individuals are required to be proficient in various text and numerical processing functions such as word processing, database management, and electronic spread sheet analysis. Although many individuals are proficient and have little aversion to computer use, some individuals exhibit considerable reluctance in using computers. Meier (1985) noted that terms such as *computer phobia, computer anxiety,* and *computer resistance* have been used to describe aversive reactions to computer use. Meier broadly classified this phenomena as *computer aversion,* which he defined as "a negative affective reaction with concomitant behaviors and cognitions" (p. 171). Jay (1981) noted that computer phobia involved resistance to talking or thinking about computers, anxiety related to computers, and hostile or aggressive cognitions about computers. Weinberg and Fuerst (1984) estimated that 25% of college students and business people suffer from mild computer phobia, with 5% experiencing negative psychological symptoms such as high blood pressure, nausea, and dizziness.

Given that counseling is typically directed toward resolving problems of daily living, examining computer aversion and the related educational and work issues is a relevant topic for counseling research. Efforts toward establishing and validating a conceptual basis for this phenomena (e.g., computer aversion, Meier, 1985; computer phobia, Rosen, Sears, & Weil, 1987; and computer anxiety, Glass & Night, 1988) need to be continued. Additional effort is also needed toward developing instrumentation to measure computer anxiety (e.g., the Computer Aversion Scale, Meier, 1988; and the Computer Anxiety Rating Scale, Heinssen, Glass, & Knight, 1987), as well as the development and validation of treatment interventions (e.g., computerphobia reduction program, Weil, Rosen, & Sears, 1987). A better understanding of the factors associated with computer aversion can lead to improved counseling interventions directed toward helping individuals more adequately adapt to inevitable technological changes in education and the workplace.

Counselors are also facing inevitable technological change in the workplace in the form of computer applications. Computer-assisted client record keeping, testing, and career guidance systems are now widely used in counseling. The attitude of counselors toward computer applications ranges along a continuum from uninformed rejection to uncritical acceptance (Herr & Best, 1984; Walz, 1970). In a study on perceived barriers to practitioners' use of computers, Levitan and Willis (1985) found:

> that what is perceived to be a barrier varies somewhat with the kind of application. Business applications, including word processing were of greatest interest, and the reported barriers were primarily time, money and finding appropriate systems. Clinical applications such as on-line testing, on-line patient interviews, patient education, games, etc., elicited a much greater [negative] response. (p. 32)

As with the previous discussion related to individuals, efforts need to be continued toward establishing and validating a conceptual basis for this phenomenon (e.g., structural and process resistance variables, Hammer & Hile, 1985), and developing valid instrumentation (e.g., Practitioners' Attitudes Toward Computer Applications Scale, Farrell, Cuseo-Ott, & Fenerty, 1988).

Advanced technology is also having a further, more generic impact on the nature of work and the work environment. Herr (1989) noted that as a result of advanced technology, new job skills are required resulting in workers needing more education and training on a more frequent basis. A shift in dominance from manufacturing to service industries, with automation and computer technology reducing the number of jobs in manufacturing, has substantially reduced the number of some jobs while creating new employment options. These developments have introduced an increasing amount of uncertainty into the work environment, thus complicating the career and educational planning process.

In order to help adolescents and adults cope with the developments just discussed, practitioners need to understand more completely how uncertainty and rapid change impact career behavior. For example, how does the career decidedness of an individual interact with a rapidly changing advanced technology work environment? Do individuals identified as "indecisive" (Peterson, Sampson, & Reardon, 1991) experience more or less difficulty in lateral job change in rapidly changing technological environments, in comparison with individuals who are identified as "undecided?" The impact of advanced technology also needs to be integrated into additional theory development and subsequent validation. The evolution of Gelatt's original concepts of the decision-making process (Gelatt, 1962) into the construct of "positive uncertainty" (Gelatt, 1989) reflect the integration of advanced technology impact.

Advanced technology, particularly computer technology, has influenced the social psychology of work in terms of the degree of autonomy available, the nature of work supervision, altered relationships among workers, and changes in the organizational exchange of information (Herr, 1989).

> Depending how computers are designed and implemented in a particular work setting, they can either "deskill" the worker or enhance the worker's role, or

they can change a worker's role from one of high task involvement to one of monitoring and troubleshooting what the computer does. Such shifts in workers' roles and self-perceptions in relation to computer technology may be positive or negative, enhancing or demeaning. (Herr, 1989, p. 42)

In order to help individuals effectively deal with this situation, practitioners need to understand more completely how changes in the social psychology of work impact job satisfaction. What personality variables differentiate effective versus ineffective coping behaviors of individuals who are employed in deskilled work situations? Also, given the interrelatedness of work and family roles, what impact do these changes have on marriage and family issues? In terms of theory development and validation, how can Super's (1980) concept of the life-career rainbow be used to help workers make broader role adjustments when job change is not feasible?

Herr (1989) further stated the following:

The effects of advanced technology are not isolated or confined to the content of work. They affect where the work is done, when, by whom, and for what purposes as well as the levels of stress and anxiety that accompany rapid and wide-ranging change. Thus, in the last analysis, the implementation of advanced technology in society is not a technical matter; it is rather a matter of human perceptions, skills, and flexibility; a matter of social technologies designed to accommodate the psychological, physical, and educational demands of different groups of youths and adults attempting to explore, choose, prepare, retrain, or adjust to work in a condition of dynamic flux. (p. 82)

Research can help practitioners and the general public to understand the complex interaction of human and technological variables identified by Herr. These understandings, however partial, integrate with theory to form the basis of counseling interventions that are delivered to millions of adolescents and adults.

Examining the Impact of the Computer on Service Delivery

Computer technology is used, to varying degrees, in all major aspects of counseling service delivery, including client record keeping and information systems, testing and assessment, diagnosis, and intervention, for example, computer-assisted career guidance and computer-assisted instruction (Sampson, 1983, 1986). Both the literature and practice have been dominated by computer-assisted testing and assessment and computer-assisted career guidance.

Initial research on the use of computers in counseling was concerned with establishing the general validity (credibility) of this type of technology. The question was as follows: Should computers be used as part of the counseling process? In testing, numerous studies were completed comparing the results obtained from traditional and computer-assisted test administrations (Sampson, 1990b). In career guidance, studies compared the effectiveness of information disseminated by counselors and computer systems (Sampson, 1984). After this initial period of demonstrating the general efficacy of computer applications, research has tended to focus on:

1. Establishing the validity of a particular computer application (e.g., the initial validation of the SIGI PLUS computer-assisted career guidance system by Norris, Shatkin, Schott, & Bennett, 1986);
2. Comparing two or more computer applications to isolate differences in impact and usage patterns between systems (e.g., the comparisons of DISCOVER and SIGI by Kapes, Borman, & Frazier, 1989, and Sampson, Shahnasarian, & Reardon, 1988); and
3. Examining the differential effectiveness of computer applications in terms of the influence of user characteristics (e.g., the examination of the impact of SIGI PLUS on vocational identity and career decidedness for users with different Holland codes by Lenz, 1990).

Future research efforts will likely focus on the first and third trends just described. There will always be a need to validate new computer applications. Ideally, this should be completed both by system developers as part of the software development process (pilot studies and field-test efforts), and by independent researchers who replicate and extend earlier investigations. Hinkle (1989) and Peterson and Burck (1989) have advocated strongly for more practitioners to conduct evaluation studies to provide data to improve services and to establish accountability.

Examining the differential effectiveness of computer applications with clients having varying needs is congruent with two general goals in counseling. The first goal involves paying particular attention to the needs of various special populations, especially multicultural groups (Sampson, 1990a). The second goal involves improving the congruence between client needs and the type of services provided (Peterson et al., 1991). Achieving this congruence is dependent on theorists and researchers explicating the relationships between user characteristics and system effectiveness, and practitioners utilizing this information when recommending tailored approaches to clients who use computer applications.

The ultimate aim of conducting research on the impact of computer applications is to improve the quality and availability of computer-assisted counseling services for clients. A common theme of all research on computer system impact is to establish the value-added benefit of using this technology— to tease out the unique contribution of the computer. What does the computer add to the interaction between the counselor and the client? What is the most cost-effective way of integrating the computer into the counseling process, while still attending to the needs of the individual? In what situation and with what type of client is the use of the computer inappropriate? Similarly, in what situation and with what type of client is "stand-alone" use of the computer appropriate (and counseling unnecessary)?

In any research examining the impact of computer applications in counseling, three major variables need to be taken into account: (a) the *individual,* (b) the *computer* system, and (c) the *context* for system use. First, research reports need to fully describe the nature of the clients (subjects) who are using the computer application, not only in terms of demographic variables, but also in relation to constructs being examined. For example, it would be important to describe the career decidedness (or some similar construct) of clients in a study examining the impact of a computer-assisted career guidance system.

Second, research reports need to describe the specific nature of computer application use (part of the treatment condition). This is particularly important for interactive computer systems that respond to client requests for information. For example, two clients may both use a computer-assisted instruction system on alcohol education for an hour as a homework assignment for a drug abuse counseling group. Due to the flexible nature of the program, however, the two clients may have used very different aspects of the program, thus receiving very different treatments. Tracking of data input and output for individual clients (described previously) is an effective approach to dealing with this problem. In this way the unique treatment applied to each client can be observed.

Third, research reports need to describe the context for client use of a particular computer application. Context includes the nature of human intervention before, during, and after system use, as well as the nature of other support materials available to the client. For example, when a computer-assisted instruction program on parenting techniques is used in conjunction with family therapy, how is the software integrated into the counseling process? How are clients prepared to use the software? Are concepts covered in the software reinforced in counseling? What handouts or worksheets are provided to support the software? Are other concepts discussed or materials presented that are at variance with the content of the software? It is difficult, if not impossible, to isolate the impact of computer applications without fully understanding the characteristics of those who use the system, the specific nature of system use by individuals, and the broader context in which system use occurs.

ETHICAL ISSUES

The use of computer applications in counseling research poses some unique ethical issues. The enhanced data collection and storage capabilities of the computer can be harmful as well as beneficial. Specific ethical issues involve unauthorized data collection and the subsequent confidentiality of computer-maintained records.

Unauthorized Data Collection

An important distinction needs to be made between "unobtrusive" and "unauthorized" data collection. Just because data are collected unobtrusively does not mean that existing ethical statements regarding unauthorized data collection can be ignored. In other words, it is inappropriate to conclude that "What the research subject doesn't know can't hurt them." The 1988 *Ethical Standards* of the American Association for Counseling and Development (Section D: Research and Publication) state that:

> 5. All research subjects must be informed of the purpose of the study except when withholding information or providing misinformation to them is essential to the investigation. In such research the member must be responsible for corrective action as soon as possible following the completion of the research.

> 6. Participation in research must be voluntary. Involuntary participation is appropriate only when it can be demonstrated that participation will have no harmful effects on subjects and is essential to the investigation. (p. 6)

Jacob and Brantley (1987) surveyed practicing school psychologists to examine current and potential ethical problems related to the use of computer applications. In response to the statement, "Psychologists may use computerized pupil records for research purposes without obtaining informed consent," 4% of the respondents reported that this had already occurred, whereas 40% of the respondents reported that this was a potential problem. It appears that the unauthorized collection of research data is indeed an issue.

Obtaining prior informed consent to participate in a research study does not necessarily eliminate the possibility of obtaining unobtrusive measures of subject performance. For example, if unobtrusive measures are taken during a subject's use of a computer-assisted career guidance system, then the use of a general research participation release statement should not nullify the validity of unobtrusive data collection. The research participation release statement should inform the subject that research data will be collected, indicate that the subject's responses will not be identified by name in any research report, and state that a follow-up session can be scheduled to answer any questions the subject may have.

In an attempt to deal with the problem of unauthorized data collection via computers, Sampson and Pyle (1983) suggested the following standard of practice for counselors:

> 6. Ensure that research participation release forms are completed by any individual who has automatically collected individually identifiable data as a

result of using a computer-assisted counseling, testing or guidance system. (p. 285)

In a similar manner, Jacob and Brantley (1987) stated:

> E. School psychologists using computerized school records in research comply with all laws, regulations, and policies pertaining to requirements for informed parent consent for such research. (p. 75)

Confidentiality of Computer-Maintained Records

Potential problems in the collection of unauthorized data are compounded when the confidentiality of computer-maintained records is violated. The capacity of the computer to maintain large amounts of data for extended periods of time and to allow easy access to data via local area computer networks or telecommunication, increases the likelihood that inappropriate individuals can gain access to confidential client data. The 1988 *Ethical Standards* of the American Association for Counseling and Development (Section B: Counseling Relationship) state that:

> 6. In view of the extensive data storage and processing capabilities of the computer, the member must ensure that data maintained on a computer is: (a) limited to information that is appropriate and necessary for the services being provided; (b) destroyed after it is determined that the information is no longer of any value in providing services; and (c) restricted in terms of access to appropriate staff members involved in the provision of services by using the best computer security methods available. (p. 5)

In my opinion, the collection of research and evaluation data can be considered an "appropriate and necessary" activity in relation to the provision of counseling services as described in the ethical standard just stated.

Jacob and Brantley (1987) noted that, in response to the statement, "Computerized record-keeping increases the risk of unauthorized access to psychological records and violations of confidentiality of pupil records" 3% of the respondents reported that this had already occurred, whereas 35% of the respondents reported that this was a potential problem. It appears that the security of computer-maintained data as part of students' psychological records is also an issue.

In an attempt to further deal with this problem, Sampson and Pyle (1983) suggested the following standard of practice for counselors:

> 6. Ensure that it is not possible to identify, with any particular individual, confidential data maintained by a computerized data bank that is accessible through a computer network. (p. 285)

Jacob and Brantley (1987) stated:

> A. School psychologists establish procedures to assure that only authorized persons have access to computerized client information. Recommended procedures to safeguard confidentiality of computerized records include requiring passwords to gain access to files or substituting client codes for names in record-keeping.
>
> B. The school psychologist makes every effort to avoid undue invasion of privacy in the gathering of student/client information. Confidential information is purged from computer storage when it is no longer needed. The school psychologist complies with all laws, regulations, and policies pertaining to the storage and disposal of records. (p. 75)

Practitioners and researchers need to resolve potential ethical issues related to unauthorized data collection and the subsequent confidentiality of computer-maintained records. The ultimate acceptability of using unobtrusive measures in research will likely depend on the refinement of professional standards that both protect client interests and facilitate research.

IMPLICATIONS

Improved Preservice and Inservice Counselor Training in Research

Successful use of computer capabilities in support of the research process are dependent on researchers receiving training on the use of research software and telecommunications software. Lowe (1987) suggested that computer literacy for counselors needs to include training in the use of the computer as a research tool. Dickel (1988) provided the following specific suggestions for infusing computer competence within preservice counselor training:
The student will be required to:

1. Use a word processor to write a research proposal.
2. Incorporate an electronic spreadsheet into the data collection portion of a research proposal.
3. Use a database management program to assemble a bibliographic database of material related to the research proposal.
4. Use a desktop publishing program to construct an instrument to be used in a program of professional quality control.
5. Use telecommunication or data communication to access a major bibliographic database to provide citations relevant to the research proposal.

Yager and Wilson (1986) suggested that computer simulations and games can be used to demonstrate research concepts in counseling research classes. Although less time is typically available for inservice training, basic familiarization with research and telecommunication software is still needed. The ethical issues discussed previously need to be addressed in both preservice and inservice training efforts.

Continued Support for Maintaining Bibliographic Databases

The availability of high quality bibliographic databases is an essential element of effective research planning. As the number of journals, books, monographs, and electronic media expands, bibliographic databases such as Psyc-LIT, ERIC, and Dissertation Abstracts International, will require additional resources to keep pace with the available information. The governmental agencies, professional associations, and private companies that maintain these databases need to provide adequate funding (or capital investment) to allow the expansion of these systems in relation to the increased information available. Also, as these systems expand, continued effort is needed to validate the efficacy of key word indexing and search procedures.

Continued Development of Research Software

The quality of research in counseling can be improved with the development of additional research software. The use of decision support systems in research planning is a prime example. Although such systems are currently feasible in terms of hardware capability and software design expertise, considerable costs would be involved in developing a valid system. Establishing specific costs and benefits of such software would be an important first step in securing public or private funding for development. A second example involves the availability of unobtrusive data-collection elements of computer systems used in the delivery of counseling services. Again the establishment of specific costs and benefits of this feature would assist software developers in deciding whether or not to fund this effort.

Continued Support for Maintaining Telecommunication Networks

Computer-assisted research collaboration is heavily dependent on the availability of low cost telecommunication networks such as the BITNet system. BITNet allows researchers at most universities, research centers, and laboratories to use electronic mail and electronic file transfer as well as to gain access to electronic newsletters and bulletin boards on a worldwide basis. Financial and political support needs to be continued in order to make this resource available to interested researchers in the future.

Continued Research on Computer Applications

Computer applications are having an increasing impact on the workplace in general and on the delivery of counseling services in particular. Research has the potential to clarify the positive and negative impact of this technological resource. However, as public funds available for research remain constant (or decline), researchers will need to more clearly stipulate how their proposed research relates to current and future organizational and governmental priorities. System developers and public policymakers need to then commit the funds necessary to allow researchers to study the most important aspects of system impact. Finally, practitioners, system developers, and public policymakers need to be effective consumers of research results, modifying the use of computer technology in light of new knowledge.

CONCLUSION

From this discussion, it would seem that the computer has an important role to play in counseling research. First, beginning with a strong historical role in data analysis, the computer has become a valuable tool in research planning, presentation of treatment conditions, data collection, and dissemination of results. However, as with other uses of the computer in counseling, the current potential of this technological resource is not being realized, especially with regard to the integration of decision-support systems. Second, as computers are used more often in our society in general, and in the delivery of counseling services in particular, it will be increasingly important to examine the impact of the computer as a topic of research. Third, in addition to developing improved software, attending to ethical and training issues is essential if we are to make better use of the computer in counseling research.

Irrespective of how powerful a tool the computer becomes in the research process, it still remains a tool. The use of a computer in counseling research is analogous to the use of a camera in photography. The camera, although certainly interesting as an object in and of itself, achieves its potential only in the hands of a skilled photographer who seeks to record an image of beauty or a significant event. The computer, although a relevant topic for research as discussed previously, achieves its potential as a *tool* only in the hands of a skilled researcher who asks socially relevant research questions that are firmly grounded in theory and practice and examined in a rigorous and ethical manner.

ACKNOWLEDGMENTS

Appreciation is expressed to Byeongseok Kim and Stephen J. Leierer for their assistance with the literature review and to Carol A. Chenoweth, Gary W. Peterson, Robert C. Reardon, and Sandra M. Sampson for their review of an initial draft of this chapter.

REFERENCES

American Association for Counseling and Development. (1988). *Ethical standards.* Alexandria, VA: Author.

Ballantine, M. (1986). Computer-assisted careers guidance systems as decision support systems. *British Journal of Guidance and Counselling, 14,* 21–32.

Dickel, C. T. (1988, October). *Counselor computer competence: Future agenda for counselor educators.* Paper presented at the National Conference of the Association for Counselor Education and Supervision, St. Louis, MO. (ERIC Document Reproduction Service No. ED 304 619)

Farrell, A. D., Cuseo-Ott, L., & Fenerty, M. (1988). Development and evaluation of a scale for measuring practitioners' attitudes toward computer applications. *Computers in Human Behavior, 4,* 207–220.

Gelatt, H. B. (1962). Decision-making: A conceptual frame of reference for counseling. *Journal of Counseling Psychology, 3,* 240–245.

Gelatt, H. B. (1989). Positive uncertainty: A new decision making framework for counseling. *Journal of Counseling Psychology, 36,* 154–158.

Glass, D. H., & Knight, L. A. (1988). Cognitive factors in computer anxiety. *Cognitive Therapy and Research, 12,* 351–366.

Hammer, A. L., & Hile, M. G. (1985). Factors in clinicians' resistance to automation in mental health. *Computers in Human Services, 1*(3), 1–25.

Heinssen, R. K., Glass, C. R., & Knight, L. A. (1987). Assessing computer anxiety: Development and validation of the computer anxiety rating scale. *Computers in Human Behavior, 3,* 49–59.

Herr, E. L. (1989). *Counseling in a dynamic society: Opportunities and challenges.* Alexandria, VA: American Association for Counseling and Development.

Herr, E. L., & Best, P. (1984). Computer technology and counseling: The role of the profession. *Journal of Counseling and Development, 63,* 192–195.

Hinkle, J. S. (1989). *Single-subject research and computer-assisted career guidance: A scientist-practitioner approach to accountability.* Unpublished manuscript, University of North Carolina at Greensboro, NC.

Hummel, T. J., Lichtenberg, J. W., & Shaffer, W. F. (1975). CLIENT 1: A computer program which simulates client behavior in an initial interview. *Journal of Counseling Psychology, 22,* 164–169.

Hummel, T. J., Shaffer, W. F., & Lichtenberg, J. W. (1973, April). *CLIENT 1: A computer program which simulates client behavior in an initial interview.* Paper presented at the Annual Convention of the American Educational Research Association, New Orleans, LA.

Hutton, S. S., & Hutton, S. R. (1981). Microcomputer data base management of bibliographic information. *Sociological Methods & Research, 9,* 461–472.

Jacob, S., & Brantley, J. C. (1987). Ethical-legal problems with computer use and suggestions for best practices: A national survey. *School Psychology Review, 16,* 69–77.

Jay, T. (1981). Computerphobia: What to do about it. *Educational Technology, 21,* 47–48.

Jepsen, D. A. (1990). A useful but limited consumer's guide. *Journal of Career Development, 17,* 129–132.

Johnson, C. W., Hickson, J. F., Fetter, W. J., & Reichenbach, D. R. (1987). Microcomputer as teacher/researcher in a nontraditional setting. *Computers in Human Behavior, 3,* 61–70.

Kapes, J. T., Borman, C. A., & Frazier, N. (1989). An evaluation of the SIGI and Discover microcomputer-based career guidance systems. *Measurement and Evaluation in Counseling and Development, 22,* 126–136.

Katz, M. R. (1990). Yesterday, today, and tomorrow. In J. P. Sampson, Jr. & R. C. Reardon (Eds.), *Enhancing the design and use of computer-assisted career guidance systems: Proceedings of an international teleconference on technology and career development* (pp. 41–50). Alexandria, VA: National Career Development Association.

Katz, M. R., & Shatkin, L. (1987). The need for research. *Career Planning and Adult Development Journal, 3*(2), 63–70.

Lenz, J. G. (1990). *John Holland's theory and the effective use of computer-assisted career guidance systems.* Unpublished doctoral dissertation, Florida State University, Tallahassee, FL.

Levitan, K. B., & Willis, E. A. (1985). Barriers to practitioners' use of information technology utilization: A discussion and results of a study. *Journal of Psychotherapy & the Family, 1,* 21–35.

Lichtenberg, J. W. (1984, April). *A computer program to assist counseling trainees in understanding interpersonal influence processes in their counseling.* Paper presented at the annual meeting of the American Educational Research Association, New Orleans, LA. (ERIC Document Reproduction Service No. ED 248 426)

Lichtenberg, J. W., Hummel, T. J., & Shaffer, W. F. (1984). CLIENT 1: A computer simulation for use in counselor education and research. *Counselor Education and Supervision, 23,* 155–167.

Lowe, D. W. (1987). Designing and implementing a computer literacy course in a graduate clinical/counseling psychology program. *Teaching of Psychology, 14,* 26–29.

Lucas, R. W., Mullins, P. J., Luna, C. B. X., & McInroy, D. C. (1977). Psychiatrists and a computer as interrogators of patients with alcohol-related diseases: A comparison. *British Journal of Psychiatry, 131,* 160–167.

Meier, S. T. (1985). Computer aversion. *Computers in Human Behavior, 1,* 171–179.

Meier, S. T. (1988). Predicting individual differences in performance on computer-administered tests and tasks: Development of the computer aversion scale. *Computers in Human Behavior, 4,* 175–187.

Meier, S. T. (1989). *Use of a computer-assisted instruction program as an unobtrusive measure of alcohol consumption.* Unpublished manuscript, State University of New York at Buffalo, NY.

Norris, L., Katz, M. R., & Chapman, W. (1982). *Sex differences in the career decision-making process.* Princeton, NJ: Educational Testing Service.

Norris, L., Shatkin, L., Schott, P. S., & Bennett, M. F. (1986). *The field test of SIGI PLUS, the computer-based System of Interactive Guidance and Information . . . PLUS MORE.* Unpublished manuscript, Educational Testing Service, Princeton, NJ.

Peterson, G. W., & Burck, H. D. (1989, June). *An accountability model for computer-assisted career guidance systems.* Paper presented at an International Teleconference on Technology and Career Development, Florida State University, Tallahassee, FL.

Peterson, G. W., Sampson, J. P., Jr., & Reardon, R. C. (1991). *Career development and services: A cognitive approach.* Pacific Grove, CA: Brooks/Cole.

Reardon, R. C., Sampson, J. P., Jr., Ryan-Jones, R. E., Peterson, G. W., & Shahnasarian, M. (1988). *A comparative analysis of the impact of two generations of a computer-assisted career guidance system—SIGI and SIGI PLUS* (Tech. Rep. No. 7). Tallahassee, FL: Florida State University, Center for the Study of Technology in Counseling and Career Development, Tallahassee.

Rosen, L. D., Sears, D. C., & Weil, M. M. (1987). Computerphobia. *Behavior Research Methods, Instruments, & Computers, 19*(2), 167–179.

Sampson, J. P., Jr. (1983). An integrated approach to computer applications in counseling psychology. *The Counseling Psychologist, 11*(4), 65–74.

Sampson, J. P., Jr. (1984). Maximizing the effectiveness of computer applications in counseling and human development: The role of research and implementation strategies. *Journal of Counseling and Development, 63,* 187–191.

Sampson, J. P., Jr. (1986). The use of computer-assisted instruction in support of psychotherapeutic processes. *Computers in Human Behavior, 2,* 1–19.

Sampson, J. P., Jr. (1990a). Computer-assisted testing and the goals of counseling psychology. *The Counseling Psychologist, 18,* 227–239.

Sampson, J. P., Jr. (1990b). Computer applications and issues in using tests in counseling. In C. E. Watkins, Jr., & V. L. Campbell (Eds.), *Testing in counseling practice* (pp. 451–474). Hillsdale, NJ: Lawrence Erlbaum Associates.

Sampson, J. P., Jr., & Pyle, K. R. (1983). Ethical issues involved with the use of computer-assisted counseling, testing and guidance systems. *Personnel and Guidance Journal, 61,* 283–287.

Sampson, J. P., Jr., Shahnasarian, M., & Reardon, R. C. (1988). Factors influencing the use of DISCOVER and SIGI. *Journal of Career Development, 15,* 75–86.

Space, L. G. (1981). The computer as psychometrician. *Behavior Research Methods & Instrumentation, 13,* 595–606.

Stout, R. L. (1981). New approaches to the design of computerized interviewing and testing systems. *Behavior Research Methods & Instrumentation, 13,* 436–442.

Super, D. E. (1980). A life-span, life-space, approach to career development. *Journal of Vocational Behavior, 16,* 282–298.

Vogel, L. H. (1985). Decision support systems in the human services: Discovering limits of a promising technology. *Computers in Human Services, 1,* 67–80.

Walz, G. R. (1970). Technology in guidance: A conceptual overview. *Personnel and Guidance Journal, 49,* 175–182.

Weil, M. M., Rosen, L. D., & Sears, D. C. (1987). The computerphobia reduction program: Year 1. Program development and preliminary results. *Behavior Research Methods, Instruments, & Computers, 19*(2), 180–184.

Weinberg, S. B., & Fuerst, M. (1984). *Computer phobias.* Effingham, IL: Banbury.

Yager, G. G., & Wilson, F. R. (1986, October). *Ten suggestions on teaching research to counseling students.* Paper presented at the annual meeting of the North Central Association for Counselor Education and Supervision, Kansas City, MO. (ERIC Document Reproduction Service No. ED 274 890)

EPILOGUE

10

RESEARCH IN COUNSELING: SOME CONCLUDING THOUGHTS AND IDEAS

C. Edward Watkins, Jr.
Lawrence J. Schneider
University of North Texas

In this chapter, we conclude by presenting and considering some integrative, summative postulates about research in counseling. We present 16 postulates that derive either directly or indirectly from our readings of and reflections on the foregoing chapters. More postulates could certainly be derived from the rich material of the various chapter contributors, but we discuss those that seemed most salient and important to us.

1. *At its most elemental level, counseling research has one simple goal: To help us better understand the counseling phenomenon or some aspect of it.* Whatever the method used or form of research in which one engages, counseling research is first and foremost designed to help us gain a better understanding about counseling. Counseling research can explore many and varied topics, ranging from counselor sensitivity to client motivation to process and outcome aspects of the counseling relationship itself, among others. But all such research has increased understanding as its goal. And of course, as we become better able to understand counseling from a research perspective, we have more information at our disposal that can positively affect future theorizing about counseling, our practice of counseling, and our thinking about further counseling research efforts.

2. *If considered with a proper perspective in mind, counseling research can indeed inform counseling practice and ultimately be useful to counseling practitioners.* The relevance of counseling research to practice has long been an issue of concern in the counseling literature (Anderson & Heppner, 1986; Gelso, 1985; Heppner, Gelso, & Dolliver, 1987), and we doubt that it will dimin-

ish to any significant degree in the near future. Numerous observers (e.g., Howard, 1986b; Magoon & Holland, 1984), in one way or another, have addressed this issue, and its importance remains preeminent. Is counseling research relevant to counseling practice? If not, can it be made more relevant? These questions surface repeatedly when the research–practice issue is raised. Some (e.g., Howard, 1986a) believe our concept or vision of science needs to change; others (e.g., Goldman, 1976, 1989) have strongly advocated alternative research strategies as one possible solution; and still others (e.g., Gelso, 1979) have spoken in favor of methodological diversity as yet another possible solution. All this can surely make one's head spin, but are there any real answers to be had on this issue?

In chapter 1, Tracey provides a good discussion about the relevance–rigor debate and concludes that counseling research cannot ever *directly* affect counseling practice. As he points out, however, counseling research can *indirectly* affect counseling practice through its tests of models to which counselors adhere. Such tests can affect our thinking about how counseling is done and guide our counseling behavior as a result. His points are well taken and are certainly worth consideration and reflection.

Gelso (1979) has proposed that counseling research be considered from the perspectives of both direct and indirect relevance. Other noted counseling researchers have also supported one or both sides of the relevance issue (Krumboltz, 1968; Stone, 1984). Although these arguments may be a little different from Tracey's arguments (chapter 1), they are all worth taking into account. Counseling research, either directly or indirectly, seemingly can give us reasons to pause, think differently about, and even behave differently in counseling. All of the chapters in this book attest to that. But it seems most important that both direct and indirect relevance be considered. If the relevance of research to counseling is to be most viably taken into account, the avenues of potential research utility vis-à-vis counseling must remain open rather than closed.

3. *Core tenets of the scientific research process parallel and are appropriate for practice.* Perhaps Galassi and Gersh (chapter 5) make this point most clearly. The single-case design seems to approximate closely individual counseling—perhaps the most common type of a counselor's endeavors. Conscientious counselors observe their client's behavior in the context of the client's social environment, formulate hypotheses based on behavior inside the interview as well as the client's reports of outside activities, and intervene on the basis of these hypotheses and observations. The validity of the counselor's hypotheses about the client are evaluated in terms of the client's behavior in response to the counseling intervention. The interventions are appraised as facilitating or hindering the movement toward the desired goal. Hypotheses are then retained or modified in accordance with the direction of client change. All of this calls for an attitude of repeated observation, con-

ceptualization, intervention, assessment, replication, and re-formulation. These steps comprise the heart of empirical, scientific research efforts.

Although these parallels seem most evident in individual counseling in an operant mode, their extension to group counseling, preventive work, program evaluation, and other forms of intervention is relevant. The application of this scientific perspective to the counselor's work allows for the tentativeness and modification of procedures that are essential to provide counseling services.

4. *The scientific base of counseling is built through sustained and systematic research inquiry, which is cumulative in its nature and effects.* Calls for more and better counseling research are not new (see Osipow, 1979; Reed, 1986; Whiteley, 1984). Without question, the best counseling research is high quality in execution and programmatic in nature. Through sustained, systematic inquiry, we are able to build a broader, more informed knowledge base about counseling. Each effort builds upon the other and ultimately stretches and extends our conceptions and understandings about the topic under study. These efforts, then, are cumulative, and bit by bit, piece by piece, they add to the scientific base of what counseling is and what we understand it to be.

Sustained, systematic counseling research efforts are nicely in evidence in the literature today as Gelso and Fassinger (1990) pointed out. Hill's (1984, chapter 4, this volume) ongoing work is a good example. Tracey's (1985; Tracey & Hays, 1989) work on complementarity and symmetry in the counseling interaction is yet another. And further still, the efforts of Elliott (1985; Elliott et al., 1987), Martin (1984; Martin, Martin, & Slemon, 1989), and Stiles (1980; Stiles, Shapiro, & Firth-Cozens, 1988) also deserve mention. Research endeavors such as these provide the counseling enterprise with an ever-growing, increasingly sound scientific base; they help us to truly see the value of sustained, systematic inquiry and the cumulative benefits that can be reaped from it.

5. *Establishing a scientific base for counseling is typically slow, demanding, and arduous work.* To provide such a base one must proceed with thoughtful carefulness. Seligman (1971) noted that a sense of purpose is necessary for scientific discovery. Anything creative and worth doing requires an ability to tolerate failure, frustration, and boredom. If a particular creative achievement was easy, exciting, and stimulating someone else would have already done it. Any emotionally felt gratification or joy coming from a research endeavor typically comes at the conclusion of the effort, if at all. Seligman noted that only through holding one's abilities to a standard that is matched or overcome does a sense of one's own worth develop. It seems to us that this sense of self-worth, mastery, and esteem are central to establishing competence as a researcher or a consumer of counseling research. These personal characteristics cannot be given away or bestowed and, if they were, we believe (as Seligman) counselors in training would perceive them as not having much value.

Hill (chapter 4) alerts us to the time commitment, attention to detail, energy expended, patience, and financial commitments consumed by research endeavors. She aptly calls attention to the importance of the investigator's attitude while engaged in the research process. This attitude is vital and related to heuristic productivity.

Freud (1914) claimed that only by experience does meaningful learning take place. For the practitioner, this implies that there is no magical or easy way either to effect real therapeutic benefit from counseling or to learn to conduct counseling in a masterful way. Freud's observation is also informative for counselor trainers and counseling graduate trainees as well in thinking about research. There is no simple or quick way to dispense research skill and foresight. One learns to do, evaluate, and appreciate research from practice at it. For any research-related project we embark upon, there is no assurance what the final level of accomplishment will be. Establishing, strengthening, evaluating, or integrating a scientific-research base takes time and inevitably turns down some blind alleys.

Progress in establishing the scientific base most often proceeds in slow increments. At times, major or serendipitous discoveries occur. Although we welcome these and value them noless, it is important to understand that advances of this type are likely to be of the less common variety. Fledgling counseling researchers will probably be wise not to expect these kinds of results from their own efforts.

6. *Counseling research efforts should be built upon, grounded in, and guided by a solid and informed sense of professional ethics and standards.* As Meara and Schmidt's chapter illustrates, this is a critical point of which we need to be ever mindful. Counseling research has not and never will operate in a vacuum. It is most fundamentally a human effort (Howard, 1984) that involves clients, potential clients, or pseudoclients (e.g., nonclient college students). These people must be treated with a special respect and sensitivity. Without them, our research would not be possible, and the time and effort they invest in helping us should not be overlooked or underestimated.

As researchers, we must also work to protect the rights of research participants and to render the research process as meaningful as possible to them. Maintaining confidentiality of data and ensuring client anonymity are always *sine qua nons* of ethical research (unless some alternate arrangements have been presented to and agreed on by the research participants beforehand; Schmidt & Meara, 1984). Helping participants "get something" from their research participation, although not always possible, is also a useful goal toward which to strive. At a minimum, a debriefing seems in order (see chapter 8), and if we can do more than that, then that would be even better still. Whatever the case, our approach to research participants and research work cannot and should not ever be conducted in isolation from our ethical and professional standards (cf. Bersoff, 1978). To do so would be a grievous error that would violate even the most basic assumptions and goals (e.g., to be of assistance to clients) that underlie the counseling profession itself.

7. *At some level, irresolvable polarities probably exist between counseling research and practice as basic enterprises.* This point may be more obvious and less contentious in respect to analogue research. Research using *in vivo* strategies may require greater attention. Rychlak (1965, 1981) claimed multiple reasons determine why counselors engage in providing (and clients enter into) treatment services. Some counselors have abiding interest in building a theoretical and empirical knowledge of the nature of client problems and counseling procedures. For them, the provision of counseling services comprises a vehicle for scientifically verifying and honing hunches. Other counselors have sustaining interest in applying methods whose validity has been empirically tested and validated.

Difficult ethical and practical dilemmas may arise between clients motivated to enter counseling in order to change their lives (or for a "cure") and researchers who harbor enduring interest in verifying theoretical constructs or evaluating the efficacy of counseling interventions. Meara and Schmidt's chapter points out potential conflicts between motives of researchers and clients when they interface with each other in counseling. (In chapter 1, Tracey points out sensitivities researchers must broach in gathering information from agencies and counselors as well.) The researcher's interest in discovering, replicating, generalizing, and announcing effective counseling methods is frequently juxtaposed to clients' wishes for privacy, unique situations, pain of self-disclosure, and disinterest in research participation. Researchers try to discover ways to make counseling more effective, whereas clients generally are concerned with obtaining relief from their own current stress. At times, research about and practice of counseling may proceed to the mutual benefit of both these polarities. We believe, however, that it would be a grave error for those wishing to engage in counseling research to presume their efforts would be minimally intrusive on or interfering with client motives for counseling.

8. *The adoption and utilization of a methodologically diverse stance is important if counseling research is to most fruitfully advance.* Methodological diversity can be defined as follows: being open to, believing in, and using (when appropriate) diverse research methods to answer the different questions that present themselves to us in our research endeavors. All of the chapters in Part II introduced us to diverse research methods and approaches, and they all can be quite useful in studying some different aspects of the counseling experience. However, to judge what methods best answer which research questions, it stands to reason that counselors should be trained in a methodologically diverse fashion (Wampold, 1986). Counseling research training, then, should be more multimethod than monomethod in its emphasis.

Such multimethod training, by helping us to know how to best answer

and research experimental questions, ultimately enriches the scientific base
of counseling and contributes to its advancement. That the counseling experience is a multifaceted process that demands a multifaceted approach to
its study would seem a logical conclusion to draw. Howard (1983), in discussing his views about counseling research, also seems to communicate this belief.

> a complete understanding of humans needs to consider a range of ontological
> perspectives, a variety of views of the nature of humans, and consequently it
> must employ a multiplicity of empirical research methods. I believe that a
> thorough understanding of humans will be facilitated by "methodological plural-
> ism." (p. 20)

Perhaps Howard's quote says it best. If we are to truly allow the science of
counseling to most fruitfully advance, we need to be open to and to use different research methodologies as our research questions warrant (cf. Hoshmand,
1989; Watkins, 1989). Only by doing this can we begin to most fully explore
the many and varied facets of the counseling endeavor and what it is all about.

   9. *There are multiple conceptual organizing systems from which to consider counseling research and each contributes to our understanding of counseling.* The chapters in this volume touch on a range of research fields and
methodologies. Admittedly, the areas covered are limited. Remaining open
to diverse epistemological assumptions and methodologies is most likely to
push the frontiers of counseling research beyond their current boundaries.

   In chapter 6, Polkinghorne argues that to some degree what gets accepted as valid research-based knowledge (and published in counseling's flagship
journals) is related to the predominant conceptual organizing systems in effect at the time when the contemporary generation of established counseling researchers received its training. For the most part, hybrid conceptual
organizing schemas from which to view counseling research are likely to grow
slowly. It seems unwise to train students in or wed counseling research itself
to a single conceptual scheme at this point. No one organizing conceptual
system has a direct and complete correspondence to reality. We simply do
not yet sufficiently understand how counseling works or how closely our current level of understanding fits human reality.

   10. *There are multiple paths of entry to the counseling research enterprise.*
Hill (chapter 4) recounts the experience (as can this volume's editors) of not
being thoroughly familiar with previous work related to a research project
she was working on. This generally causes delays and frustrations as well
as compounds expenditure of energies and other resources. Hill alerts new
researchers to the wisdom of apprenticing with experienced researchers and
developing realistic expectations about how one's research efforts fit into
the broader scheme of the area being studied. For the overwhelming majority of graduate students enrolled in counseling programs, we believe the

apprentice–mentor relationship provides a desirable avenue of introduction to the research enterprise.

Royalty, Gelso, Mallinckrodt, and Garrett (1986) provide more specific clues about ways to introduce research to counseling students and hint at ways a research training environment could be structured to enhance its value. This group has also shed light on how intensity of interest in research varies in some predictable ways (e.g., Mallinckrodt, Gelso, & Royalty, 1990; Royalty & Reising, 1986). Their work reminds us to avoid the pitfalls of assuming every counseling student in training has (or should have) the same interest in research. Polkinghorne (chapter 6) further cautions against presuming that all counseling researchers must be committed to the same organizing schemas as their peers or their trainers.

11. *A core battery for use in counseling research efforts, though elusive and difficult to pin down, is still a highly valid concept that we should continue to work toward making a tangible reality.* The idea behind the core battery concept is simple: A standard set of counseling evaluation measures is gathered together to compose a "core battery," and this battery is then used to evaluate counseling effectiveness across settings, counselors, clients, and situations. As Waskow and Parloff (1975) said, "a hope behind the proposal of such a battery was that, if researchers working in different settings with different treatment orientations were to use the same standard set of instruments, it would become possible to compare and integrate the results of different studies" (p. 3). The core battery concept without question represents a noble idea and hope, which unfortunately has been very difficult to realize in any tangible way.

In the late 1970s, Bergin and Lambert (1978) even said that it was not possible (at that particular point in time) to reach agreement about what such a battery should consist of. Although their statement still has a ring of truth to it today, the core battery concept has not yet been abandoned (see Lambert et al.'s chapter). Osipow and Betz (chapter 7) also bring up the idea of a core battery for use in career counseling research. In career counseling research, as in personal–social counseling, the development and utilization of a core battery does not appear to have fared much better either. But as Lambert et al.'s and Osipow and Betz's chapters suggest, this idea still seems to be well worth further reflection and consideration. If we can develop core batteries for use in career, personal–social, and other forms (e.g., academic) of counseling, then we will be in a better position to indeed "compare and integrate the results of different studies" (Waskow & Parloff, 1975, p. 3). Realizing the core battery concept will surely continue to be a formidable project to undertake, but the potential gains and ultimate benefits that could result from it seem to far outweigh and overshadow any difficulties we might encounter in the process.

12. *Over the years, counseling research has become increasingly refined*

and sophisticated in the research questions asked, methodological approaches drawn on, and methodological strategies used. This is nicely illustrated by each of the chapters in Part II and is certainly echoed in one way or another by the other chapters in our book. We are glad we can make this point here, because we would not particularly enjoy having to make it in reverse fashion. As mentioned earlier, calls for more and better counseling research have been made (again see Osipow, 1979; Reed, 1986; Whiteley, 1984). Slowly but surely, we seem to be getting there (e.g., consider the three different types of questions posed by Lambert et al., chapter 3, Table 3.1, and their progressive nature). As Gelso and Fassinger (1990) stated:

> as the progression of knowledge becomes apparent, equally evident is our pursuit of increasingly refined questions. Over a relatively long period (e.g., the 1960s and 1970s vs. the 1980s), this research progression may represent the most powerful trend in all of counseling psychology (p. 376)

We could not agree more. More refined questions better focus and guide our research efforts, and any trend in this direction is certainly welcome.

If our research questions have become more refined and sophisticated, so too have our methodological approaches (e.g., process, single-subject) and strategies (e.g., cluster analysis). Again each chapter in Part II illustrates the former; the latter has been well illustrated through recent journal issues (Wampold, 1987), interesting debates about statistical procedures (Aiken et al., 1990; Larrabee, 1982; Leary & Altmaier, 1980; Strahan, 1982), and the utilization of more advanced statistical procedures in research articles (Gelso & Fassinger, 1990). To once more repeat ourselves, we appear to be getting there. If the advances made in the last decade are any indication at all, the future of counseling research—in regard to approaches drawn on, strategies used, and questions asked—seems to hold much promise.

13. *The computer, when effectively utilized to its fullest extent, has tremendous potential to facilitate our research efforts and enhance our research knowledge about counseling.* Sampson (chapter 9) shows us how this is surely so. The potential uses of the computer seem to be almost boundless, and this appears especially true when speaking of the computer vis-à-vis counseling research. We are all familiar with the importance of the computer for data analysis and word-processing purposes. But when we then consider other potential research uses of the computer—for example, design planning, presentation of treatment conditions, and the facilitation of research collaboration—we really begin to get a feel for the lengths to which we have stretched this tool and the lengths to which it has stretched us in the process. If any tool can fully maximize and potentiate our research efforts, then the computer appears to be it.

14. *Although research has contributed to establishing the validity of counseling, much work remains to establish a substantial empirical base for the*

myriad of activities and techniques subsumed under the rubric of counseling and to account for mechanisms of change. It is generally acknowledged that evidence supports the claim that counseling and psychotherapy work (Myers, 1986; Spokane & Oliver, 1983; also see chapter 3, this volume). We have no idea of the actual number of systems and techniques of counseling that exists today. Herink (1980) briefly summarized over 250 systems and techniques. Each of these reflects a particular individual's imaginative vision and all of these have attracted the attention of numerous counselor colleagues. The growth of self-help movements and "pop psychology" increases the plethora of counseling strategies at a pace that outstrips our ability and efforts to scientifically validate (or invalidate) them. Just as we begin to feel somewhat confident in our understanding and use of a technique in counseling or as a particular counseling strategy gains stature, how often does a theoretical critique or empirical evidence challenge the position? For example, Breger and McGaugh (1965) raised thorny questions about our understanding of some behavioral techniques that were widely used in the 1960s. It is a truism, however, that the more we learn, the more we come to an appreciation of how little we know and how much we do not understand about what makes counseling effective. We do not want for research questions to ask.

15. *From a scientific perspective, counseling research remains committed to seeking out and elucidating cause–effect relationships. Even within this deterministic-sounding objective, there is freedom.* Gelso (1970) distinguished between objective–scientific–outer and subjective–ascientific–inner dimensions of experience. (Both dimensions seem essential for counselors and clients.) The former dimension is necessary to validate answers to questions about counseling and how it works. In this framework, we come to understand others' behaviors and motivations behind their actions. The latter dimension attends to one's own subjective experience or empathic experience of another individual. It focuses on the exercise of one's own choice making and ability to influence the direction of one's life. Gelso suggested that counselors may have to accept the paradoxes accompanying the possibilities of these multiple realities. He speculated that counselor–scientists may need to wear different hats at different times, relying on deterministic tenets when in the scientific realm and on the polemics of freedom in counseling encounters.

We would extend these contradictions to researchers also in their efforts to broaden our understanding of counseling. Objectivity, specificity, and replicability are cornerstones of empirical research. The decision to conduct research is thought to rest upon "considered judgment" itself (American Psychological Association, 1990). At the same time, the researcher has many choices regarding which questions to pursue, what methodology to employ, and which interpretations to assign to obtained results. Many graduate counseling students address research requirements by approaching professors and asking what they should investigate (or requesting professors to give them a research idea). How often have we advised or urged these students to choose a topic or project in which they were really interested? To some degree, then, we believe that elements of the subjective–ascientific–inner dimension lie at the heart of every successful research project that is brought to full fruition. In short, counseling research efforts cannot advance without elements of both objective and subjective realities.

16. *We should remain modest about the fruitfulness of our research findings and unpretentious regarding what we have learned. Our acquired knowledge is bounded by nondeterminate and uncontrollable factors.* What we know is limited by the adequacy of our investigative techniques, sensitivity of our measurements, and the geopolitical times in which we live. Factors that influence research and the practice of counseling in one epoch may be absent in another, for example, state of the general economy, political atmosphere. Shifts in those conditions may in a very real sense color our view of various human problems and their prevalence, thereby influencing priorities given to our research energies.

Our contemporary era varies from the social and technological realities of 50 years ago. Movement away from labor intensive manufacturing and agriculture and toward a more service-oriented economy influences the client anxieties, coping methods, and disorders that counseling researchers and practitioners are likely to encounter. Research has informed us of the wheres, hows, and whys of some contemporary counseling processes and outcomes and their applicability for segments of our catchment population. However, uncertainty remains about the permanent applicability of answers for the situations we face today or how well they generalize to other cultures (e.g., non-Western countries).

Even within our own culture and times, we must stay mindful of larger social forces (e.g., shifts in population demographics) that are beyond anyone's control but nonetheless have a bearing on our research and on placing our findings in context. Osipow (1983, chapter 7, this volume) reminds us of the existence of such influences in researching career psychology. These factors would seem no less valid considerations for our conceptualizations of other areas of counseling research (e.g., personal–social problems).

CONCLUSION

In this concluding chapter, we have presented 16 summative postulates that have derived either directly or indirectly from the previous chapters' material. In our opinion, counseling research is a primary means by which our profession will further advance. That counseling research has much to offer the counseling profession seems clear. Among many counseling professionals, we now perceive a heightened interest, energy, and enthusiasm about counseling research and its seemingly unlimited possibilities for helping us to better understand the phenomenon of counseling. In its own way, this book is a testament to that interest, energy, and enthusiasm, as well as the vitality and promise of the counseling research enterprise itself.

REFERENCES

Aiken, L. S., West, S. G., Sechrest, L., Reno, R. R., Roediger, H. L., Scarr, S., Kazdin, A. E., & Sherman, S. J. (1990). Graduate training in statistics, methodology, and measurement in psychology: A survey of PhD programs in North America. *American Psychologist, 45,* 721–734.

American Psychological Association. (1990). Ethical principles of psychologists. *American Psychologist, 45,* 390–395.

Anderson, W. P., & Heppner, P. P. (1986). Counselor applications of research findings to practice: Learning to stay current. *Journal of Counseling and Development, 62,* 152–155.

Bergin, A. E., & Lambert, M. J. (1978). The evaluation of therapeutic outcomes. In S. L. Garfield & A. E. Bergin (Eds.), *Handbook of psychotherapy and behavior change* (pp. 139–189). New York: Wiley.

Bersoff, D. N. (1978). Legal and ethical concerns in research. In L. Goldman (Ed.), *Research methods for counselors* (pp. 363–406). New York: Wiley.

Breger, L., & McGaugh, J. L. (1965). Critique and reformulation of "Learning Theory" approaches to psychotherapy and neurosis. *Psychological Bulletin, 63,* 338–358.

Elliott, R. (1985). Helpful and unhelpful events in brief counseling interviews: An empirical taxonomy. *Journal of Counseling Psychology, 32,* 307–322.

Elliott, R., Hill, C. E., Stiles, W. B., Friedlander, M. L., Mahrer, A. R., & Margison, F. R. (1987). Primary therapist response modes: Comparison of six rating systems. *Journal of Consulting and Clinical Psychology, 55,* 218–223.

Freud, S. (1963). Further recommendations in the technique of psychoanalysis: Recollection, repetition and working through. In P. Reiff (Ed.), *Freud: Therapy and technique* (pp. 157–166). New York: Collier. (Original work published 1914)

Gelso, C. J. (1970). Two different worlds: A paradox in counseling and psychotherapy. *Journal of Counseling Psychology, 17,* 271–278.

Gelso, C. J. (1979). Research in counseling: Methodological and professional issues. *The Counseling Psychologist, 8,* 7–35.

Gelso, C. J. (1985). Rigor, relevance, and counseling research: On the need to maintain our course between Scylla and Charybdis. *Journal of Counseling and Development, 63,* 551–553.

Gelso, C. J., & Fassinger, R. E. (1990). Counseling psychology: Theory and research on interventions. *Annual Review of Psychology, 41,* 355–386.

Goldman, L. (1976). A revolution in counseling research. *Journal of Counseling Psychology, 23,* 543–552.

Goldman, L. (1989). Moving research into the 21st century. *The Counseling Psychologist, 17,* 81–85.

Heppner, P. P., Gelso, C. J., & Dolliver, R. H. (1987). Three approaches to research training in counseling. *Journal of Counseling and Development, 66,* 45–49.

Herink, R. (1980). *The psychotherapy handbook.* New York: Meridian.

Hill, C. E. (19840. A personal account of the process of becoming a counseling process researcher. *The Counseling Psychologist, 12,* 99–109.

Hoshmand, L. L. S. T. (1989). Alternate research paradigms: A review and teaching proposal. *The Counseling Psychologist, 17,* 3–80.

Howard, G. S. (1984). Toward methodological pluralism. *Journal of Counseling Psychology, 30,* 19–21.

Howard, G. S. (1984). On studying humans. *The Counseling Psychologist, 12,* 101–109.

Howard, G. S. (1986a). *Dare we develop a human science?* Notre Dame, IN: Academic.

Howard, G. S. (1986b). The scientist-practitioner in counseling psychology: Toward a deeper integration of theory, research, and practice. *The Counseling Psychologist, 14,* 61–105.

Krumboltz, J. D. (1968). Future directions for counseling research. In J. M. Whiteley (Ed.), *Research in counseling: Evaluation and focus* (pp. 69–81). Columbus, OH: Merrill.

Larrabee, M. J. (1982). Reexamination of a plea for multivariate analysis. *Journal of Counseling Psychology, 29,* 180–188.

Leary, M. R., & Altmaier, E. M. (1980). Type I error in counseling research: A plea for multivariate analyses. *Journal of Counseling Psychology, 27,* 611–615.

Magoon, T. M., & Holland, J. L. (1984). Research training and supervision. In S. D. Brown & R. W. Lent (Eds.), *Handbook of counseling psychology* (pp. 682–715). New York: Wiley.

Mallinckrodt, R., Gelso, C. J., & Royalty, G. M. (1990). The impact of research training environment and counseling psychology students' Holland personality type on interest in research. *Professional Psychology: Research and Practice, 21,* 226–232.

Martin, J. (1984). The cognitive-mediational paradigm for research on counseling. *Journal of Counseling Psychology, 31,* 558–571.

Martin, J., Martin, W., & Slemon, A. G. (1989). Cognitive-mediational models of action—act sequences in counseling. *Journal of Counseling Psychology, 36,* 8–16.

Myers, R. A., (1986). Research on educational and vocational counseling. In S. Garfield & A. Bergin (Eds.), *Handbook of psychotherapy and behavior change* (3rd ed., pp. 715–738). New York: Wiley.

Osipow, S. H. (1979). Counseling researchers: Why they perish. *The Counseling Psychologist, 8,* 39–41.

Osipow, S. H. (1983). *Theories of career development* (3rd ed.). Englewood Cliffs, NJ: Prentice-Hall.

Reed, J. R. (1986). The call for more and better research: Challenges and difficulties. *The Counseling Psychologist, 14,* 133–137.

Royalty, G. M., Gelso, C. J., Mallinckrodt, B., & Garrett, K. (1986). The environment and the student in counseling psychology: Does the research training environment influence graduate students' attitudes toward research? *The Counseling Psychologist, 14,* 9–30.

Royalty, G. M., & Reising, G. N. (1986). The research training of counseling psychologists: What the professionals say. *The Counseling Psychologist, 14,* 49–60.

Rychlak, J. F. (1965). Motives to psychotherapy. *Psychotherapy: Theory, Research and Practice, 2,* 151–157.

Rychlak, J. F. (1981). *Introduction to personality and psychotherapy: A theory-construction approach* (2nd ed.). Boston: Houghton Mifflin.

Schmidt, L. D., & Meara, N. M. (1984). Ethical, professional and legal issues in counseling psychology. In S. D. Brown & R. W. Lent (Eds.), *Handbook of counseling psychology* (pp. 56–96). New York: Wiley.

Seligman, M. E. P. (1971). *Helplessness: On depression, development, and death.* San Francisco: Freeman.

Spokane, A. R., & Oliver, L. W. (1983). Outcomes of vocational intervention. In W. B. Walsh & S. H. Osipow (Eds.), *The handbook of vocational psychology, Vol. II: Applications* (pp. 99–136). Hillsdale, NJ: Lawrence Erlbaum Associates.

Stiles, W. B. (1980). Measurement of the impact of psychotherapy sessions. *Journal of Consulting and Clinical Psychology, 48,* 176–185.

Stiles, W. B., Shapiro, D. A., & Firth-Cozens, J. A. (1988). Do sessions of different treatments have different impacts? *Journal of Counseling Psychology, 35,* 391–396.

Stone, G. L. (1984). Reaction: In defense of the "artificial." *Journal of Counseling Psychology, 31,* 108–110.

Strahan, R. F. (1982). Multivariate analysis and the problem of Type I error. *Journal of Counseling Psychology, 29,* 175–179.

Tracey, T. J. (1985). Dominance and outcome: A sequential examination. *Journal of Counseling Psychology, 32,* 119–122.

Tracey, T. J., & Hays, K. (1989). Therapist complementarity as a function of experience and client stimuli. *Psychotherapy, 26,* 462–468.

Wampold, B. E. (1986). Toward quality research in counseling psychology: Curricular recommendations for design and analysis. *The Counseling Psychologist, 14,* 37–48.

Wampold, B. E. (Ed.). (1987). Special issue: Quantitative foundations of counseling psychology research. *Journal of Counseling Psychology, 34,* 363–489.

Waskow, I. E., & Parloff, M. B. (1975). *Psychotherapy change measures.* Rockville, MD: National Institute of Mental Health.

Watkins, C. E., Jr. (Chair). (1989, August). *The place of qualitative research in counseling psychology.* Symposium presented at the annual meeting of the American Psychological Association, New Orleans, LA.

Whiteley, J. M. (1984). Counseling psychology: A historical perspective. *The Counseling Psychologist, 12,* 2–109.

AUTHOR INDEX

SUBJECT INDEX

For Product Safety Concerns and Information please contact our EU
representative GPSR@taylorandfrancis.com
Taylor & Francis Verlag GmbH, Kaufingerstraße 24, 80331 München, Germany